W9-DDJ-179

Phat Beats, Dope Rhymes

Ian Maxwell Phat Beats

Dope Rhymes

Hip Hop
Down Under
Comin Upper

WESLEYAN UNIVERSITY PRESS

Middletown, Connecticut

Published by Wesleyan University Press,
Middletown CT 06459
Copyright © 2003 by Ian Maxwell. All rights reserved.

Printed in the United States of America

Designed by Rich Hendel
Set in Charter, and Indecision types
by B. Williams and Associates

Library of Congress Cataloging-in-Publication Data
appear on the last printed page of this book.

ISBN 0–8195–6637–3 cloth
ISBN 0–8195–6638–1 paper

Contents

A section of illustrations appears after page 170.

Acknowledgments

I wish to express my gratitude to a great many people for making this book possible.

First, to J. Lowell Lewis for his committed mentorship, and to my erstwhile teachers and colleagues, supporters, friends, fellow students, and my own students at the Department of Performance Studies at the University of Sydney: Gay McAuley, Tim Fitzpatrick, Terry Threadgold, Tony Day, Russell Emerson, Paul Dwyer, Kim Spinks, Marjorie Moffatt, and Kate Rossmanith, among others.

To Phil Hayward and Tony Mitchell.

To Steven Feld, Robert Walser, and Michael Jackson.

To colleagues in Music and Anthropology at the University of Sydney: Ghassan Hage, Allan Marrett, and Graham Hardie.

To the members of the writers' group ("The Group") who met through the mid-1990s to exchange words and ideas: Martin Thomas, Martin Harrison, Lesley Stern, Diane Losche, Vivienne Kondos, Ruark Lewis, Cathy Paine, Andrew Lattas, Colin Hood, Michael Taussig, and guests.

To all my informants: Blaze and Angela, Mr E, Kane, WizDM, Special Ed/J.U., and Bullwinkle.

To Def Wish Cast—Def Wish, Ser Reck, DJ Vame and Die C–Simon, Paul, Shane and Pablo (including thanks for permissions to use lyrics and photographs)—E.S.P. and Mick E, Pewbick the Hunter, Marcelo Pena, Raul, Puma, Minky, Absolute Zero, Loco, Jakl, The Chief (Cec), Felicitè and Andrew, Charlene, Goie and Pauline, Sound Unlimted (for permission to use lyrics), and all the Lounge Room freestylers.

To my parents, Brian and Maureen, and brother Charles. My wife Vanessa Liberiou.

To my friends: Patrick Nolan, Richard Byrne, Mark and Lucy, Geneviève Souillac, Lisa Stefanoff, Cameron Tonkinwise, Anna Broinowski, and Genevieve Blanchett.

To Suzanna Tamminen at Wesleyan for her patience, and to Paul Betz for the stunning editing work.

Preface
A Brief History of Race in Australia

Writing about Hip Hop in Australia with a predominantly North American readership in mind is hard work. In fact, notwithstanding the profile of media-friendly crocodile hunters and the like, writing about Australia itself (and particularly urban Australia), with a predominantly North American readership in mind, is hard work: some such readers, no doubt, would consider Sydney to be "a relatively obscure local scene."[1]

I

From where I sit, the scene I deal with is neither remote nor obscure. Nonetheless, and as uncomfortable as it might be for North American readers, from where I am writing (at the edge of cultural empire, perhaps) the center-periphery logics implicit in such an appraisal constitute a genuine barrier to communication. I need to address these barriers from the outset, head on, not least because this book is about exactly these issues: the relationship of center to periphery; "authenticity" versus "imitation"; the ways in which cultural material circulates in a media-saturated world; and the ways in which that material is taken up in local scenes — scenes in which, perhaps, anticipated topographies of authenticity might have a completely different valency.

To write about Hip Hop, however, is immediately to be imbricated in questions of race, racialism, and racism. In effect, there is an implicit demand placed upon my writing to acknowledge the practices of my informants as bearing a relationship (analogic, perhaps, rather than homologic) to a long history of white appropriations of black musics. Indeed, it would be as inappropriate for me to whitewash the issue as it was for the presenters of the opening ceremony of the Sydney Olympics to whitewash black Australian history, reducing that history to the dreaming of a (normative) Anglo-Celtic girl. The agents of whom I write are implicated in racialized structures and infrastructures, as I, as an Anglo-Celtic Australian, am. That needs to be acknowledged.

I also need to acknowledge that the appropriation of black art forms by whites has a long global history, a history in which race tends to be erased, with a normative whiteness making the claim that, somehow, the use of those artforms is simply that: an unproblematic "use" in which the forms are somehow divested of their embeddedness in lived struggles.

Indeed, it is the case that the taking up of Hip Hop by "white" teenagers in the far western suburbs of Sydney does reproduce a pattern of such appropriations over the last two centuries, and that there is a deep ambivalence at play, although perhaps, in this "remote" context, not as extreme as the "love and theft" identified in blackface minstrelsy by Eric Lott (1993). Australia is cut through with ambivalences and anxieties about place and identity. There is, indeed, a sense in which African-American blackness figures (and, it has to be acknowledged, is promoted, and promotes itself) to these Australian teenagers as an exotic, somewhat sexualized other.

The most important contribution that my work here can make is to explore the logics and practices by which the subjects I researched justified and sustained their claim to Hip Hopness. I take as my lead Keith H. Basso's observation that "the ethnographer must somehow fashion a written account that adequately conveys his or her understanding of other peoples' understandings" (1996:57). It is my limited endeavor in the pages that follow to convey such a set of understandings, with all their attendant shortcomings. Following Charles Saunders Peirce, I also want to expand the rubric of "understanding" here to include modes of embodiment, practice, and habit, so as to open up the possibility of affective states as (particularly compelling) modes of understanding.

It may well be the case that the boys in my study run the risk of erasing race from their use of these forms, making their claim to those forms on a ground of a totalizing (white) consciousness, which on one analysis might be framed in terms of a globalizing, postmodern right of access to culture; on another analysis, as I have suggested, we might understand such a claim as reproducing a long history of appropriation — in fact erasing history, or, worse, claiming participation in a history to which they have no — or, at best, a limited — access. However, it is not my intention to reveal these understandings as somehow misguided, ideological, or otherwise inauthentic; others may wish to make such claims — I am not prepared to do so. It may well be that readers in North America — particularly those close to North American Hip Hop — do not even recognize these practices of which I am writing as Hip Hop; perhaps the people of whom I am writing themselves have misrecognized Hip Hop. In their grasping for something to fill the void that they clearly perceive in their worlds, they have, perhaps, appropriated something that is not, and never can be, theirs.

x

And perhaps, in doing so, they have themselves had to erase the specificity of that something: in this case, the racial dimension of Hip Hop.

One thing is for certain, as evidenced by the extraordinary range of essays in the collection recently edited by Tony Mitchell (2001). Hip Hop is out there, in circulation in the world: not only Black Noise, but Global Noise. Hopefully, in what follows, the processes by which a group of white boys in Sydney negotiated these tensions, in order to "discover" (that is, to create) an abstract essence of Hip Hop in which they — non-African-American, and imbricated in a different logics of race, masculinity, and class — can then participate, will become clear.

II

Australia has a profoundly racist history, and, notwithstanding the happy face of cosmomulticulturalism (Hage 1997, 1998) presented, for example, at the opening ceremony of the 2000 Summer Olympics in Sydney, it is still plagued, if not defined, by unresolved racial tensions. The (quasi-official) narrative of nation played out in that event, a fantasy of normative whiteness, is instructive. Recall: a pretty, prepubescent white girl (what could be more innocent, more natural?) lays out a beach towel, massages sunscreen into her porcelain skin (what could be more Australian?), lies down, and drifts into sleep. In her sleep, she quite literally dreams Australia — a dream that not only appropriates the indigenous Australian cosmological rubric of "the Dreamtime" (itself an inadequate, appropriative translation), but also manages to dream up indigeneity itself. The history and prehistory of Australia, its European and pre-European past, are bundled together in white fantasy, in which the colonizer precedes the colonized, and the repressed returns as a domesticated, unthreatening aestheticized presence.[2]

By contrast, the closing ceremony celebrated a kitschy postmodern cosmomulticulturalism, the surface veneer of which was rippled, if not shattered, by two gestures on the part of popular music performers: the lead singer of Savage Garden wore a T-shirt emblazoned with the red, black, and gold Aboriginal flag, while Midnight Oil's black trousers and shirts were stenciled with the word "sorry," a none-too-subtle dig at Prime Minister John Howard's refusal to make an apology to the indigenous people of Australia for past government policies, including, as recently as the 1960s, the forceful removal of Aboriginal children from their families.

Both displays — the faux dreaming of the opening and the brash, irony-laden extravagance of the closing ceremony — bespeak a terrible anxiety informing contemporary Australia: a yearning to ground a being-together as nation in pseudo-mythical narratives of origin, and a(n almost embarrassing) feint toward global postmodernism: nation as celebration of integrative polyculturalism. Were I a psychoanalyst, with Australia on the couch, I would be tempted to offer all kinds of diagnosis: here is a nation in denial — of its bastard birth, of ugly primal scenes of unbridled violence and terror, of unresolved oedipal conflict — a nation characterized by a compensatory narcissistic overinvestment, a misplaced sense of its own stature. A nation that, in a 1999 referendum, voted against becoming a republic, overwhelmingly reaffirming collective obeisance to the monarch of the United Kingdom.

None of these diagnoses would actually come as a great surprise to anyone who casts more than a cursory glance over the cultural and historical landscape of Australia. Australia is a strange, unsettled, unhappy place, in which questions of identity, debated and worried over among the intelligentsia, rarely move, in the popular imagination, beyond sporting prowess or the capacity of cultural producers to shift their product in Great Britain or, better yet, in North America. A place where, beyond the "she'll be right," beach and barbeque optimism spruiked by Paul ("Crocodile Dundee") Hogan, or the colorful quirkiness of the local cinema, young men commit suicide more frequently than anywhere else in the developed world.

III

A potted history of Australia would need to remark upon a number of successive waves of immigration. The first was that of those who were to become indigenous Australians: the Aboriginal peoples, crossing from the Indonesian archipelago 50,000 to 70,000 years ago, and who, spreading across the continent, established complex cosmologies grounded in a powerful sense of place and land, patterns of itinerant land use, languages, and exchange. The second was the colonization of this same land by English jail keepers, with their cargoes of convicts, largely drawn from the urban poor and, significantly, Ireland. This transportation of convicts to the colonies of Australia, commencing in 1788, continued until the 1850s. The strange alliances forged between erstwhile jailers and emancipated prisoners, constituting an entrepreneurial, land-owning elite — the "squattocracy," named for the squatters' rights extended to those flocking to the sheep-herding and crop-bearing plains west of the Great

Dividing Range — established social fault lines in Australia that bore little relation to the bloodlines of the English class system.

As a land of opportunity, Australia Felix — the Lucky Country — traded upon the perceived failure of indigenous Australians to exploit the land. Aborigines were seen as primitive, without permanent dwellings or agriculture. Devastated by smallpox and the musket, the indigenous inhabitants of the continent were denied any place in the scheme of things — a denial entrenched in the official colonialist discourse of *terra nullius:* the land belonging to no one. The squattocracy surged inland, lured by the promise of an inland sea affording fertility and trade routes to the north. In the foiling of this promise, however — beyond the plains of the southeast, the land turned out to be largely barren — was born the white man's dreaming: mateship — the mythos of the laconic, classless, unaffected, tight-lipped, stoically suffering, self-deprecating Aussie male. Not in this land the brash exuberance of the American frontiersman; here there were no rich alluvial plains to farm or herds of buffalo to fight over. Here there was suffering, isolation, and disappointment, rewarding only those who endured. This was the crucible of the dreaming of Australian masculinity — classes leveled by the severity of the land; a man's world in which mateship came first, and no questions were asked.

Of course, it helped if you were white. In fact, prior to the gold rushes of the late 1840s, the colonists were almost exclusively white. Slavery did not extend to the Australian colonies, except in the form of convict labor: Irish nationalist/Catholic prisoners endured the classism, colonial imperialism, and racism of English jailers; in turn the Europeans were united in their appalling, unforgivable treatment of the indigenous peoples. Considered too lazy or unreliable for work, the Aboriginal people were enlisted as guides and, later, as station (ranch) hands. In fact, it is worth noting that the east coast Australian colonies became places of refuge, first, for runaway African-American slaves and, later in the nineteenth century, when Australia became part of the trans-Pacific circuit, African-American vaudevillians (see Waterhouse 1990).

Slavery did manifest, however, in the form of indentured labor. First, with the influx of Chinese workers during the gold rush years of the 1850s, and then in the cane fields of the tropical north, where Pacific Islanders — the Kanakas — were used as cheap, easily exploited labor. Urban white resentment, ostensibly generated by fears that nonwhite workers would accept lower wages and worse conditions and thereby threaten jobs, but fueled by deep racism, directed against "Asiatics" and "coloureds," culminated, contemporaneously with the Federation of the Commonwealth of Australia in 1901, when the White Australia Policy was promulgated: racism by act of Parliament. The Immigration Restriction Act of 1901 placed restrictions on immigration, including prohibitions on the insane, anyone likely to become a charge upon the public or upon any public or charitable institution, and any person suffering from an infectious or contagious disease or of a loathsome or dangerous character. It also prohibited prostitutes, criminals, and anyone under a contract or agreement to perform manual labor within the Commonwealth (with some limited exceptions). So while boastfully championing its commitment to democracy — the extension of the franchise to women, the (supposedly progressive) banning of indentured labor — the new commonwealth instituted racism as a core value. In 1919, Prime Minister William (Billy) Hughes hailed this legislation as "the greatest thing we have achieved."

Australia at Federation, then, understood itself as a bastion of English Empire, a glistening white outpost, a jewel in the colonial crown second only to the Raj, willingly sending its young men to fight colonial wars, first in South Africa and then in the First World War, most famously at the "glorious" defeat by the Turks at Gallipoli, an event that was to become the touchstone of Australian ideals of masculinity and national identity (see Carlyon 2001).[3] Declaring war against Japan in 1941, Labor prime minister John Curtin declared that "this country shall remain forever the home of the descendants of those people who came here in peace in order to establish in the South Seas an outpost of the British race."

After the Second World War, however, things began to change. In 1949, Liberal[4] minister for immigration Harold Holt's decision to allow 800 non-European refugees to stay and Japanese war brides to be admitted to Australia was the first step toward a nondiscriminatory immigration policy. It is significant that his Labor predecessor, Arthur Calwell, had vigorously opposed any such weakening of the White Australia Policy. The acceptance of an influx of refugees and, in the 1950s, workers largely drawn from Mediterranean Europe, recruited for work on major national infrastructure projects (and in particular, the Snowy Mountains hydroelectric scheme), radically altered the racial mix in Australia. Immigration was profoundly discriminatory, with the infamous language test — by the terms of the 1901 legislation, migrants could be asked, at the discretion of an immigration officer, to "write out dictation and sign in the presence of an officer, a passage of 50 words in a European language directed by the officer" — being used to actively discriminate in favor of (white) northern Europeans. Nonetheless, southern Italian and Greek immigrants flocked southward, earning the derogatory tag "New Australians," or "wogs"; their experience was largely one of Anglo-Australian racism, until a generation later, by which time a subsequent wave of Asian immigration displaced the New Australians as a preferred object of racial enmity.

Through the same years, attitudes toward indigenous Australians had not moved beyond those enshrined in the colonialist doctrine of *terra nullius*. Aboriginals, it seemed, would do best to simply disappear — in official terms, the policy was one of assimilation. Only in 1967, under the Liberal/conservative government of Harold Holt, was the vote extended to indigenous peoples, who also, for the first time, were to be included in the national census figures. (Prior to this, Aboriginal people had been counted among fauna.) Well into the 1970s, however, Aboriginal children were forcibly removed from their parents and fostered to white families in the name of a paternalistic assimilationism.

And while immigration restrictions were loosened through the 1960s in order to accommodate, in the first instance, European settlers,[5] events to Australia's north further entrenched pandemic racism directed toward a homogenized "yellow" Asia. The cold war logics of the domino theory reinforced the "yellow peril" scares of the Japanese invasion of Southeast Asia; the Vietnam War and the subsequent influx of "boat people" in the late 1970s are still having their effect, even as I write in mid-2002.

Following some twenty-six years of anglophile conservative government, however, it is Labor prime minister Gough Whitlam's short-lived government (1972–75) that is generally recognized as having sought to redress long-standing racial wrongs. Among the achievements of the government were the recognition of Aboriginal land rights, legislation to make all migrants, of whatever origin, eligible to obtain citizenship after three years of permanent residence, the issuing of policy instructions to overseas posts to totally disregard race as a factor in the selection of migrants and the ratification of all international agreements relating to immigration and race. Whitlam's progressiveness deliberately distanced his party from its shameful commitment to the White Australia Policy, and saw the genesis of state-sponsored multiculturalism in Australia, a policy position that reached its zenith during the early 1990s and the leadership of Labor prime minister Paul Keating: the time when I conducted the research on which this present text is based.

In the interim, a certain complacency around this progressiveness has been exploded by the election (and subsequent reelections) of John Howard's reactionary Liberal–National Party Coalition government and the emergence of an unreconstructedly pro-assimilationist, antiglobalization, nationalist movement. Although the initial electoral success of the One Nation Party has evaporated, this is only because its xenophobic policy agenda has been appropriated almost in its entirety by the Coalition. Promises of reconciliation and treaty with indigenous Australians (modeled, perhaps, along the lines of Aotearoa–New Zealand's Treaty of Waitangi) have been replaced with an explicitly anti-intellectual attack on apologism and what the conservatives label "the Black Arm Band" school of history. Most recently, we have seen the callous treatment of asylum-seeking refugees, including indefinite mandatory incarceration in remote desert internment camps and the outsourcing of refugee processing to offshore set-ups in Nauru and Papua New Guinea: "the Pacific Solution". The overall picture is horrendously bleak: the claim to sophisticated multiculturalism paraded in the Olympic spectacle has been thoroughly shown up as a white man's dreaming.

IV

How, then, might this racial history play out in the outer western suburbs of Sydney, when a bunch of boys respond to their sense of alienation from their (own) place and to the eroticized, exotic (but also proselytizing, heavily promoted) cool of a vibrant African-American world? What follows is offered as a partial account of an unfinished project of identity-making against the backdrop of the broader context outlined above.

Phat Beats, Dope Rhymes

Prologue

MCs should know their limitations . . .
— Souls of Mischief, "Limitations" from '93 til Infinity

Sydney, June 1994. High above the city streets, in a public broadcast radio studio, two rappers are about to battle.

A sinuous, looping bass line thumps through and around the small room, setting feet tapping and heads nodding in absent-minded, meditative unison; five bodies alive with driving sounds and rhythms, the repetitive, visceral, gut-trembling riffs of a slamming Hip Hop beat.[1]

Abruptly, a switch flicked, the room is thrown into silence: a yawning sonic void just as tangible as the suddenly missing beat. From behind the console, the producer points an outstretched index finger toward one of the rappers, indicating, "You're *on!*" The studio is live on air. The rapper, a clean-cut, T-shirted youth, about sixteen years old, moves closer to the microphone in front of him. Muscular rhythms register visibly in his body as he concentrates on the regular, tinny ticking of the beat, now only just audible to the rest of us through the padded cuffs of the headphones clasped to his ears. He nods his head, the motion building, spreading into his shoulders, until his whole body seems to quiver with a growing electric tension, stretching and reaching for the beat. Then, a sudden release: at once, the rapper *is* the beat, snapping into a rhyme, the first move in the battle.

He starts to rap:

Here we are at 2 SER
I've got J.U. on my right
I didn't want to diss him,
But I did, right!?

This rapper calls himself Mick E. In an inflammatory breach of Hip Hop etiquette, Mick and his DJ, E.S.P., had recorded a rap questioning, insulting, and disrespecting the skills of certain other crews, rappers, and local Hip Hop personalities. One of the targets of this diss had been a rival crew, the Urban Poets. And J.U., from the Poets, was seeking redress, staring daggers from a second microphone to Mick's right.

Hence the battle.

Mick E steps to the issue defiantly, without apology, confidently emphasizing the third beat of each measure, delaying the final, rhetorical syllable of the opening quatrain (*right*) so as to allow it to fall on the stressed backbeat. Having established a metrical regularity, Mick subtly alters his rhythm, happy to anticipate and fall minutely behind the strict pulse, running together some syllables, drawing others out, free within the rhythmic structure to semantically shade his delivery, moving into an explication of and a justification for his actions.

> *— because I was gettin' down*
> *With the hard core . . .*

Hard core is *the shit:* to claim to be down with the hard core is to assert your Hip Hop credentials, your *authenticity,* in the strongest possible terms. To *kick reality.* To *be true* to Hip Hop.

Using a slowly descending tonal pattern arriving at the words "hard core," Mick starts to construct an argument. These two syllables are drawn out, marked less with a strictly observed rhythmic stress than with a carefully weighted, almost sneering, inflection over almost a full measure each. Mick lets everyone savor the weight of his words and, with a confident swagger in his voice, sets up a tiny anticipatory space within the metrical field for the next line.

> *I got . . .*

Mick's attack into this line is brought up short. He appears to be momentarily nonplussed, stopping in mid-flow, his body dropping out of its rhythmic ease and into a frozen attention. A crisis registers on his face the barest split second later; he hesitates and loses momentum.

> *. . . lost the beat, for sure . . .*
> *Where's the beat gone?*
> *It's outta my headphone*
> *I wanna kick to you*
> *I was talkin' to you on the phone . . .*

The backing track has fallen out, leaving Mick stranded without a rhythmic pulse. He loses the line of argument he was developing, and turns to the crisis at hand to keep his rhyme going, gesturing frantically to Miguel, the console operator, to get the beat back.

Responsible for having initiated this battle, and having been given the first use of the microphone, Mick is under some pressure to maintain his flow. Now, drawing on the still warm body-memory of the rhythm, he kicks out a series of rapid-fire triplets: "kick to you," "talkin'-to," "on-the-phone," flattening the syllable "phone" into a nasal drone, more Los Angeles than Sydney. He has recovered well; the beat returns, and Mick regathers his momentum:

> *You said that we started*
> *some ill shit*
> *. . . The mike's gone . . .*
> *What 'm'I gonna do with it?*

Another technical crisis: the microphone arm has started to sag, leaving Mick floundering again. He is good enough to get a rhyme out, but only just, managing to squeeze the words in before getting off the hook, passing the mike to J.U.:

> *J.U. take a diss to me . . .*
> *I wanna start a battle so we can get down*
> *With the 2-SER dissin' shit*
> *. . . J.U. rip it.*

By the time that he gets to his final line, Mick is struggling. The beat is failing him; he slides and skates over and around it, but without the playfulness and confidence that allows an MC on the flow to tease and cheat the rhythm, pushing it to the point of collapse and reeling it back in. By the time he gets to "dissin' shit," Mick is just talking. Annoyed, he throws to the other rapper, surrendering the initiative after only a handful of lines.

J.U. is hyped. He is older, angular; compared to Mick's fresh-faced boyishness, J.U.'s shaven head and dark eyes make him look dangerous, rough. As Mick stumbles and steps back, J.U. moves closer to his own mike, and mutters, somewhat ambiguously, "Yeah . . . ill shit . . . ," before, screwing his shoulders up toward his ears and bringing his hands up in front of his chest, he starts to rhyme, chopping at the air with his hands as if turning the pages of a crazy book:

> *I flip skills at the kids all round the east*
> *And say well yeah the boy is like he's \ rising to the*

3

occasion Caucasian that's right \ yeah \ breaking \ graffiti \ rapping
  DJing
That's the Hip Hop mike that we sort of rock not the dissin'
bullshit because \ I've got the skills on the mike
so wanna \ flip with me?[2]

In contrast to Mick E's laid-back, measured observation of the beat, J.U.'s flow is a breathless, headlong rush; a cascading of words that ebbs and flows with each sharp intake of air, the pulse of the backing track discernible only in these momentary, fleeting pauses. Each phrase, defined by the length of breath, charts out a gradually descending tonal pattern, with extra syllables crammed in toward the end, pitching the rhyme forward toward cataclysmic crisis points as J.U. forces the last traces of wind from his lungs.

Where Mick E's verbal play derived from slight anticipations and extensions of the strict measure of the beat, J.U. plays with the energy of his own delivery, marking significant words — "breaking / rapping / Djing" — by isolating them in his flow and then tumbling full-speed into the rest of his line.

And J.U. really starts to flow. The chopping motion of his forearms and hands, as he lays out key ideas with pantomimic precision, gives way to a more relaxed, almost fluid rocking through his whole body. His hips sway, his shoulders weave through the flow:

Yeah that's it . . . sorta loose-and-limber
Then you better quiver
When you then remember
*That you shouldn'a come slanging that shit about the east and the city *
It's not that pretty
*At the Lounge with my stylee *
I get wily \ and then you know with my stylo
My pen and my bic I flick and then
My \ lips go wrapping around the syllable again
*A-verbalising, over the top of the horizon *
My friend you see this is off the top of my mind
I've got the skills I think that you can get a kick from the
high g on ya behind.

J.U. rhymes by free association, stringing words together and enjoying the not-quite-right rhymes: "then / again," "verbalising / horizon." The found words create new logics, leading him on into unknown territory and unexpected rhymes, regathered into his central theme: I'm *good* at this; better than you.

And somewhere in there, as J.U. starts to flow, the atmosphere of the room starts to change. At the end of Mick E's verse, both rappers were laughing at the drooping microphone arm, but now there is tension: J.U. has raised the stakes, shifting from a playfulness to something more like anger, suggesting that Mick E's diss was, in the first instance, not appropriate Hip Hop behavior, and, second, not particularly well advised, given his own (J.U.'s) superior skills as an MC.

And it's back to Mick E again:

I'm comin' again I'm harder than the average norm
I'm blowing the horn I've got more flavour than the butter on a corn
I'm wicked here at 2-SER
I rock it out
The mike is hard I'm comin' it to you kickin' the clout
Cos I'm hard core
Harder than . . . the city, if the city's hard
You know that's not funny
That wack cassette
Harder than the boy in blue . . . kick it to you

The swagger is back; Mick starts out full of confidence, meeting and matching J.U.'s intensity. He moves into a boasting rap, bragging about his own ability as a rapper, stressing his *hardness*.

He is let down, however, by his inability to produce an appropriate metaphor: "harder than . . ." Nothing. After what feels like an age, but is only a split second, he manages to come up with what his body and delivery betray as a lame image: ". . . the city." Mick has grabbed at the image from J.U.'s use of it seconds beforehand. The tiny, reaching pause before he lights on the word "city" is enough to throw him off his game, and even as he delivers the word, he realizes just how weak it is. His rap loses confidence as J.U. laughs (again somewhat ambiguously), and his next line is a concession; an admission that the dissing tape that has precipitated this confrontation is *wack,* before he again passes on the microphone to J.U.

J.U. does not miss a beat, literally. He launches into rhyme, throwing Mick E's pretensions to being *hard core* back in his face.

I'll kick to you a rhyme about the hard core
That's my man the Sabotage Organisation out there doin' more
For the \ Hip Hop cause than slanging all that bullshit
*That only ceases to divide *
Yeah cos then you realise
That in my mind skills hide
They come out \ on the high g in the morning
*With Miguel \ I rock it yeah I excel on 2-SER with my boyz *
*Yeah, that's it, we sorta kick it *
For you think that I'm slippin'
No because I am ripping \ the microphone
Yeah I stand alone.

Delivering his lines directly to Mick E, J.U. has worked himself into a groove, thoroughly enjoying his complete domination of the microphone, relaxing in his flow ("yeah, that's it") and then quickly moving to dispel any impression that he might be losing his flow by asserting his unique microphone technique. And then he pushes himself even further, moving in for the kill:

*You think you can fuck with this? *
*I'll fuck with you *
I'll fuck with your crew
And I'll swear on the air too . . .

J.U. is *going off,* his eyes fixing Mick E with an unsettling steeliness, punching out the words that are now, unambiguously, a threat, relishing the harsh, fricative plosions, the illicit thrill of uttering the transgressive syllable "fuck" over the air. Uncertain laughs, half-shocked, half-over-joyed, ripple around the studio, bringing J.U. back to himself. He regathers, offering a general apology to the rest of us caught in the verbal cross fire:

*Sorry about that, peace to my homeboys behind the console *
*Yeah I sort of rock it from my tonsils *
From my vocals peak up to Ben
*With the Voodoo Flavor *
Yeah they're gonna guida sign got the shit that's gonna psych us
*At ya grumba jack I'm comin' back no wack *
At the freestyle sessions at Lounge

We'll bring you sack filled of rhymes
*And then we'll see who can kick it *
Not on the air but on the floor I got more yeah!

The battle is won; the rest of J.U.'s rhyme backs down, returns to matters of procedure. He sends a *shout out* to a fellow rapper, Ben, from another crew, Voodoo Flavor, and spills out a tour de force stream of syllables bordering on nonsense, rounding off with an advertisement for "the freestyle sessions at Lounge," where, he suggests, more of this virtuoso rhyming might be heard, live, in the flesh, "on the floor," wrapping it all up with a final promise (or is it a warning?) that he is not done yet . . .

But he has done more than enough for Mick E. The studio is silent, the backing track suddenly audible to all of us, leaking into the extended pause as Mick, now deflated, no longer the swaggering Mick E, but just a rather sheepish, chastened boy, steps up to the microphone again. Now his voice is disarmingly normal – *Australian* – free of rapper attitude.

I'm not meaning to get a head-swell
Wanna say what's up to my man Miguel . . .

A brief pause, as Mick assesses his best move, delivering a final burst of rapid-fire syllables:

Kickin' it behind the turntable
Spinning the discs . . .

He decides that enough is enough, and, and offers his capitulation:

. . . enough of that diss . . .

The battle is over.

part one
introduction

What the fuck is happening?
Is Sydney turning into the home of Rodney King?
— Illegal Substance, "Drive By"

I had arranged to meet with Shane Duggan, aka DJ Vame of Def Wish Cast. We sat down early one afternoon in an inner city bar in the heart of Sydney's nightclub precinct. Over gin and orange juices, Vame and his friend Bomba (pronounced "bomma"), a writer visiting Sydney after a stint behind bars (for graffiti-related vandalism offenses) in his home city, Adelaide, brought me up to date with Vame's new project. In mid-1994 Vame was in the throes of leaving the crew to pursue his own project, Dope Runner Productions. He planned to record, produce, and distribute Hip Hop from the west of Sydney, offering young rappers studio experience and protecting them from the predatory dangers of mainstream recording companies.[1]

Vame had insisted that we meet "in the city," rather than somewhere closer to his own home in the far western suburbs. He and Bomba, he said, would enjoy a day out, visiting record shops (and, I guessed, getting up) and hanging out. Besides, there really wasn't anywhere to meet "out west," other than at home . . .

We talked for a few hours about Hip Hop, the technicalities of sampling and DJing, writing, about what I was doing. The time came to head off to our respective afternoons, and I thanked Vame for his trouble in traveling two hours into town to talk with me. "That's cool, man . . . ," Vame reassured me:

". . . anything for Hip Hop."

Theoretical Frames

This book is about Hip Hop in Sydney, Australia. More specifically, it is a study of a particular Hip Hop Scene observed in Sydney during the period from August 1992 to October 1994, a study taking as its point of departure a question not dissimilar to the one posed by Mick E in his rap "Drive By": What is happening? Rap in Sydney? Hip Hop with Australian accents? Australian boys rapping, break-dancing, writing graffiti, claiming to be a Hip Hop *Community?* A Hip Hop *Nation?* Hip Hop *Culture? White* Australian boys, staging a rapped battle in order to establish who is being the more authentic member of that Culture, who is being truer to their Hip Hop Community.

I want to be clear about one thing before going any further: I am not a fan of rap music. My interest in what I came to know as hip hop (or, subsequently, the capitalized "Hip Hop") was stirred in mid-1992, when Public Enemy was touring Australia. I liked their politics and attended a concert at Sydney's Hordern Pavilion, where P.E. was supported by Ice T and a local Hip Hop dance act, Sound Unlimited.[1]

This resulting study proceeds as an ethnography: already it is framed by a thick description of a key performative event, to which I will return shortly. The deceptive simplicity of the fundamental questions I have posed will shortly yield to a more elaborate complex of questions, which will mark out the trajectory of the analysis. In this introductory chapter, I want to lay out a range of theoretical debates and thematic concerns and to introduce several key concepts. I will be using theoretical approaches drawn from a range of disciplines – anthropology, postcolonial studies, performance studies, semiotics, phenomenology, sociology, popular musicology, subculture studies. I make no apology for this eclecticism; its justification lies in the potential of various approaches to illuminate the phenomena under investigation.

The two chapters in this introductory section will outline some theoretical issues before turning to flesh out the account of the battle, above. In Part Two, three chapters will locate this battle in historical, mediated (global) and immediate, geographical contexts. Chapter Three will examine the narratives of origin circulating within the ethnographic present of the early 1990s Sydney Hip Hop Scene, with a view to understanding how social agents in that local present furnished themselves with an authenticating history, bridging apparently insuperably radical historical, cultural, and geographical discontinuities. Chapter Four will locate those accounts within a broader analysis of the circulation of cultural material through a global mediascape. In the fifth chapter, I will examine the construction of place – specifically, the ways in which a particular Hip Hop cartography of Sydney was produced, and how that cartography was then used, once again, to sustain discourses of authenticity within, and emanating from, the Hip Hop Scene.

The third part of the book will develop a more thoroughly phenomenological analysis, locating (and understanding the power and efficacy of) these discourses of authenticity within a range of embodied practices and experiences. Chapter Six will focus on music and the articulation of meanings to musical performances and recordings; chapter Seven will, similarly, deal with dance. In the final section, a phenomenology of these performative forms will be used to understand the construction of a sense of an authentic, antipodean Hip Hop Culture. I will argue that what authenticated a claim to *being* Hip Hop was not necessarily a continuity of experience, culture, race, class, or history with an originary authentic African American Hip Hop. Rather, I will conclude that the claim to authenticity is sustained not only through the location of self within (global) narratives, but also through the processes of articulation of embodied experience to those narratives – articulations in the sense of linkages, which are effected through social practice and negotiation: the labor of interpretation and the institution of interpretation within a specific social field by a community of investigators.

The overarching conceptual frame for this book, then, is that of the phenomenological project as described by Michael Jackson (drawing on

Ricoeur's definition): phenomenology as "an investigation into the structures of experience which precede connected expression in language . . . the scientific study of experience . . . an attempt to describe human consciousness in its lived immediacy" (Jackson 1996: 2).

As I have suggested, I am also interested in the "connected expression in language" with which people "explain" their lives. The dimensions of "experience" and "explanation," insofar as they are separable, must be understood as being in a complex, forever unfolding dialectical relationship with each other, co-creating the social and the individual (insofar as they, too, are separable). This relationship – between experience and explanation – is explored by Homi Bhabha in his analysis of the production and maintenance of nationalisms.

Bhabha traces the efforts of postcolonialist and feminist theorists to "redefine the symbolic processes through which the social imaginary – nation, culture or community – becomes the subject of discourse, and the object of psychic identification" (1994: 153). Writing of the social imaginary called nationalism, Bhabha argues that "terms of cultural engagement . . . are produced performatively" (1994: 2), in a process involving a doubling of the self: cultural agents are *subjects* engaged in a "process of signification"; at the same time, however, in what Bhabha calls the "double-time" of the narrative of nationalism, cultural agents are the *objects* of a nationalist pedagogy. According to Bhabha, "In the production of the nation as narration there is a split between the continuist, accumulative temporality of the pedagogical, and the repetitious, recursive strategy of the performative" (1994: 145). The pedagogic must constantly be articulated to unfolding (and I would add, "embodied, affectively experienced") performance: the "split" must be papered over, the performative lined up with and integrated with the pedagogy. The "living people," Bhabha argues, "represent the cutting edge between the totalising powers of the 'social' as homogeneous, consensual community, and the forces that signify the more specific address to contentious unequal interests" (146).

Recasting Bhabha's argument in phenomenological terms, the process of the narration of nation involves a moment in which the phenomenological *subject* of the living, embodied human life identifies itself as the *object* of a nationalist pedagogy. Practice, or "performance," is not simply generated *by* "tradition" (pedagogy), but, in all its difference, in all its potential inequality and specificity, it is articulated *to* a body of discourse. "Tradition" becomes an explanation *for* practice: what one *does* in synchronic time is accounted for in terms of the body of discourse that precedes, diachronically, that embodied performance. It is with this model in mind that I have named Parts Two and Three of the book.

In an often (in popular music studies circles, at least) celebrated paper, Will Straw has highlighted "the long-standing preoccupation of popular-music scholars with the concept of community," associating it with a growing engagement with concepts of space and nation in cultural theory (1991: 368). I will return, below, to an extended consideration of the various Hip Hop imaginaries; it will be useful, however, at this point, to offer a brief account of Straw's analysis of "music communities," in the first instance to stress that my use of the words "Hip Hop Community" is derived from that term's ubiquity within the field, and to establish that my use of the term is to be read under erasure.

Straw cautions against "notions of cultural totality or claims asserting the expressive unity of musical practices," suggesting that notwithstanding the fact that "the articulatory force of specific musical practices has often displaced [in analysis] the cultural communities as the guarantee of music's meaningfulness," there remains a tendency to privilege the geographically local (1991: 369). Straw's endeavor is to critique attempts to array valorizing discourses of "authenticity" "rooted in geographical, historical and cultural unities" (369) against an "increasingly universal system of articulation" (Said quoted by Straw, 369) which itself is seen as a totalizing effect of political economy. Citing Paul Gilroy (1987, and, I would add, 1993), Straw advocates an attention to the processes of diaspora and the global circulation of cultural forms" that create "lines of influence and solidarity different to, but no less meaningful than, those observable within geographically circumscribed communities."

Straw advocates replacing the use of the word "community" with "scene." The former, he suggests "presumes a population group whose composition is relatively stable – according to a wide range of sociological variables – and whose involvement in music takes the form of an ongoing exploration of one or more musical idioms said to be rooted within a geographically specific historical heritage" (1991: 373). "Scene" marks a "cultural space in which a range of musical practices coexist, interacting with each other within a variety of processes of differentiation"; a terrain of negotiation and of genre-policing, productive of powerful affective links between a contemporary musical practice and heritage "seen to render this contemporary activity appropriate to a given context" (373). The point of Straw's analysis is to understand the unity of purpose constituting a musical "community" as an "ideological effect," not in order to "expose the relative status" of such communities, but to account for the production of communities that share such unities without being "organically grounded in local circumstances," resourcing themselves through "an attentiveness to change occurring elsewhere" (374).

The appropriateness of such thinking to Hip Hop in Sydney should be apparent. It is not my intention to "expose" the inauthenticity of this scene, notwithstanding the ascription within Hip Hop of authenticity to practices that are quite literally "inauthentic": sampling as both a compositional device and a trope for the adoption of practices from "elsewhere" (graffiti, break-dancing, clothing, language, and so on). However, in no way might these processes be seen as being (merely) culturally promiscuous, as celebrating a postmodern valorization of the pastiche, a privileging of the playfully eclectic for its own sake. On the contrary, the use of the term "community" precisely bespeaks a concern with "the authentic," with tradition and the fixing of values.

In her analysis of the early 1990s English club scene, Sarah Thornton identifies three "overarching distinctions" through or with which participants in youth cultures determine "what is legitimate" (1996: 3): "the authentic versus the phoney, the 'hip' versus the 'mainstream,' and the 'underground' versus 'the media'" (3–4). The "cultural logics" of these distinctions build affinities, "socializing participants into a knowledge of (and frequently a belief in) the likes and dislikes, meanings and values of the culture," generating transient "*ad hoc* communities with fluid boundaries that may come together and dissolve in a single summer or endure for a few years" (3).

For J.U., Mick E, and others like them, Hip Hop was in no way ad hoc or ephemeral. It was not a *sub*culture, but a fully proportioned *culture,* whatever that might mean. Mick E and J.U.'s battle is a way into understanding a self-conscious project of the production of culture, revealed through a complex of contested, negotiated, and disputed knowledges, practices, desires, and, as Thornton only tentatively suggests, *beliefs.* Of course, the field of Hip Hop does not exist in hermetic isolation: these knowledges, practices, beliefs, and desires are themselves enmeshed within a metafield of beliefs, knowledges, practices, and desires: that concatenation of beliefs and knowledges Appadurai calls "the ideoscape," identified with "the master-narrative of the Enlightenment" (1990: 10), to which I will return.

Andrew Goodwin, recognizing that notwithstanding the superficial "post-modernism" of late 1980s pop music "the old ideologies and aesthetics are still on the menu," asks whether, in order to understand postmodern cultural forms, we need a postmodern theory (1990: 272). Similarly, I want to suggest that it is possible to understand the cultural phenomena I am describing without subscribing either to a celebratory theory of playful cultural promiscuity, of eclectic sampling and arbitrary mixtures (see, for example, Shusterman 1991; Wark 1992; and Costello and Wallace 1990), or to a postmodern theory that predicates a yearning for lost authenticities on a nostalgic pessimism and can only understand any contemporary claims to "the real" as wistful simulacra. I do not want to mistakenly understand, for example, the use of the technology of the electronic sampler in Hip Hop compositional practice as being indicative of a liberatory *bricoleur* sensibility (see Wark 1992); the Hip Hop Scene I encountered did not consider itself to be an artistic or culturo-political avant garde, as I will show, instead espousing decidedly conservative discourses of nationalism and community. What might appear to be eclectic sampling is actually the product of carefully negotiated processes of interpretation and the making of distinctions in social practice. In the sense in which Lyotard (1986) wrote of the undoing of the sustaining metanarratives of Western ontology, this account is of the practical effort – that is in a people to co-creatively negotiate meanings from a world that is, genuinely, phenomenologically, "postmodern." In fact, I want to suggest that in this cultural milieu there was an experiential grounding for the inventory of recent theoretical "posts," including "postindustrial" and "postcolonial" (see, for example, Appadurai 1990; Rose 1994b; Castles 1993).

This is not to banish "playfulness" from analysis, but to suggest that in practice play is often framed as being *serious*. Activities such as graffiti writing, break-dancing, and rapping, for example, come to be endowed by their participants (and often by theorists) with political stakes, with antecedent, primal, causal dimensions, cast in discourses of "Culture," "Knowledge," "Truth," "Community," "Nationhood," "Freedom," "Blackness," and "Political progressiveness"; discourses that operate to consolidate, legitimate, and reify a range of adopted practices – practices that are, on other occasions, described as being, simply, great, fun things to do. This is not to deny the "serious" side of these discourses and their effects; I just want to set out with a weather eye cocked toward the eagerness of left-leaning theory to enlist youth culture, and particularly those youth cultures "derivative" (in whatever sense) from African American forms, to a revolutionary cause, which simultaneously erases the social agents themselves from the analysis.[2]

I want to approach an understanding of cultural flow, syncretism, disjunction, diaspora, mixing, and so on from the perspective of the agents involved in this moment, who can only be at the center of a profusion of discourses and practices to which they are variously and differentially exposed, and with which they are variously and differentially engaged. I am not concerned with the broad flow of History, but rather with the labor of individuals to furnish themselves with *a* history, a culture, tradition, an account of their belonging to something out of the multifarious, often regulating, disciplining, but also sometimes liberating, enabling institutions and interpretations constituting their fields of experience.

C. S. Peirce wrote that there "is but one state of mind from which you can 'set out,' namely, the very state of mind in which you find yourself at the time you do 'set out'" (Peirce [1905] 1960: 278). Taking this as a guiding axiom, I want to suggest that there is no beginning to find here, other than in the accounts of beginning that are offered in the ethnographic present, as logics of necessity, as justifications for present practices, values, knowledges, and beliefs. In unpacking J.U. and Mick E's battle, it is of little use for me to determine an "objective" truth of the past events in order to evaluate the merit of their relative claims: instead, I will focus on their accounts of "truth."

Perhaps the best way to approach this book is as an attempt to (simply) explain this single episode, to understand, in simple terms, how and why two middle-class, well-educated, fair-skinned, Anglo-Saxon youths living in Sydney in the mid-1990s would be engaging in an exchange of improvised verses, derived from Afro-Caribbean-American oral practices, in an attempt to establish who, of the two, was being more *true* to this thing that they are calling Hip Hop Culture.

In some important ways, Straw's analysis of the terrain of "alternative rock" does part company with my own needs; his concern "as someone who studies musical institutions" is less with the "substance of [the] values" that allow the coalescing of discrete populations into (musical) communities than with the "[institutional] alliances produced by their circulation" (1991: 385). My project, on the other hand, *is* concerned precisely with the values that constitute the "feelingful" possibility of a Sydney Hip Hop Community; that constitute, for the people involved, the possibility of thinking about such a culture.

In addition to using the Bourdieuan term "field" (that "set of objective, historical relations between positions anchored in certain forms of power" [Wacquant in Bourdieu and Wacquant 1992: 16]), I have adopted Straw's use of the term "scene" to refer to the context within which the attempts to establish a "Hip Hop Community" are enacted, or "performed." This has the advantage of maintaining a critical attitude toward the word "community," rather than endowing it with a strict positivity. The "scene" is that heterogeneous space within which the various practices constituting, within the discourse of "Hip Hop," "Hip Hop" itself, are enacted. By "heterogeneous," I only mean that this is a space within which agents might graffiti, listen to rap music, even rap themselves, wear Hip Hop–styled clothing, and so on, without thinking themselves to be participants in a "community" of Hip Hop. The process of articulating these practices to the discourse of Hip Hop, in order to constitute a "Hip Hop Community" is a kind of disciplining or closure of the field of articulation that operates to enroll the actors involved in such activities to that discourse. And of course, the "discourse of Hip Hop Community" itself is one of the disciplining or "suturing" (Laclau and Mouffe 1985) delimitations of the potential meanings of those activities, constructing its own "positivity" in the process of its own reproduction.

This is also an appropriate moment to consider just how to refer to these "individuals," these "cultural (or social) agents." They are not all "rappers," "rhymers," "writers," "bombers," "DJs," "selectors." "breakers," or "b-boys," and I rarely heard the term "Hip Hoppers."[3] Unlike "punks," "goths," "ravers," "hippies," "bikers" . . . the whole pantheon of subcultural identities (see Polhemus 1994), the people (almost exclusively male) whose practices, beliefs, discourses, and knowledges I came to know were not so explicitly, self-consciously concerned with constructing their own identity as with the alignment of their (already existing) selves *with* "Hip Hop." Thus, I would hear "I'm *into* Hip Hop," or "90 percent of my life is Hip Hop; the other 10 percent I'm asleep," or, better still, "I eat, breathe *and sleep* Hip Hop."

I will, then, throughout my account, fudge on this question a bit, preferring the clumsiness of Bourdieuan formulations such as "social (or cultural) agents," or even "individuals" (although not wanting to predicate, through such a usage, an unreconstructed self-present *subject*), to a more global term such as "Hip Hopper," a term that would not quite ring true ethnographically. Where possible I will follow the insider practice of referring to these various agents in terms of their particular "Hip Hop practice": "writer," "rhymer," "DJ," and so on, reflecting the notion, circulating within the scene, that Hip Hop offered a vocational variety catering to all sensibilities and physiognomies. As one rhymer describes his introduction to rapping: "I was about seven years old, eight years old my cousin sort of introduced me to it you know like full break-dancing and stuff like that I was a pretty chubby kid so I couldn't do it good you know. And graffiti . . . all my friends were into it and I wasn't very good at that either so I just strayed into the rhymes you know."

I want to note, too, that this characteristically ethnographic mode of engagement with the object of my research is intended to stand as a corrective to what I consider to be the disturbing cultural studies approaches in which "the media" (which itself will form a large part of my own text) is reified and theorized without regard to cultural agents (other than the cultural theorist doing the writing). I take as exemplary of this kind of work McKenzie Wark's *Virtual Geography* (1994), in which a discourse of "weird events" and "media vectors" displaces any possibility of engaging with any cultural agents other than the writer himself. Notwithstanding his claim to "not want to abstract weird global events too far out of time of lived experience in everyday life in which we find them" (x), the "everyday experience" to which Wark refers throughout his text is inevitably his own. This is not necessarily a problem, except insofar as the personal account ("I'm lying in bed with my lover and the cat . . ." [6]) is, throughout this text, generalized into the totalized "we" of the foregoing sentence, a "we" that can only really make sense when it is understood as *a* community of investigators, the dimensions of which extend roughly around that group which Wark, attempting to locate himself at the epicenter of a community, collects under the label "Sydney poststructuralism" (xii).

Wark writes that "[i]ncreasingly, culture . . . abstracts itself from all particularity" (xiii). Although this does not seem to trouble Wark's own attempt to construct an oxymoronically totalizing poststructuralist subject, I do not necessarily want to mount an ad hominem argument.[4] Rather, I want to set against this straw man of poststructuralist cultural studies orthodoxy an ethnographic account of the efforts of a group of social agents attempting to increasingly *engage* itself with, rather than to abstract itself from, "particularity." This present book is all about the attempts of a group of cultural agents to actively resist any such process of abstraction, by, perhaps, particularizing a mediated, globalized cultural formation (Hip Hop), and "claiming" it, as it were, for their own particular circumstances. Indeed, I would argue that, in the course of this research, I am presenting an example of an attempt on the part of particular social agents, in response to an increasingly decentered, mediated, "postmodern" cultural context, to (literally, in a geographical sense, as I shall show) ground, to center, and to fix the bases of their experience.[5]

Throughout my fieldwork, I presented myself as a researcher, as someone writing about Hip Hop in Sydney. I did not consider myself to be a "participant observer," although I did (of course) came to enjoy the performances, the graffiti, the break-dancing, the freestyling, the recordings, and the company of those with whom I spent time. I accumulated (sub-)cultural capital (Thornton 1996), the ability to pass informed aesthetic judgments about various (sub-)cultural artifacts, whether they be recordings or pieces, and was recognized as someone who "respected" the "culture" I was observing.

The fieldwork on which this book is based developed from my initial approaches, subsequent to the Public Enemy concert, to anybody I came across wearing a Public Enemy T-shirt or baseball cap. Within a couple of weeks, I had met Blaze;[6] over a longer period I met other characters in the scene. I read local magazines, listened to recordings and to specialist radio programs, attended performances, hung out with writers, and allowed myself to be talked to and educated. I do not claim that I saw *all* of the scene, or that I followed *every* lead. It is not my intention to offer either a complete history of the local scene or an exhaustive, inclusive sociology. Nor do I claim to be "up to date" with the scene: my research concludes arbitrarily, abruptly, in October 1994. I interviewed individuals formally and informally, video-recorded some performances, recorded some others. What became apparent over this period, and what now constitutes this writing, was an intense desire on the part of a number of geographically dispersed (Sydney is a very broad city) young people, once again, mostly male, from mixed ethnic and socioeconomic backgrounds, to constitute themselves as a community, to claim for that community the status of a culture, a claim accompanied and supported by claims to specific knowledges, traditions, and practices, and to locate that culture as part of a transnational movement, the Hip Hop Nation.

2

Making Culture

Because the social is made out of conflicting practically based views trying to practically shape social reality, the specificity of sociological practice cannot be to provide knowledge of a "reality" that is often still in the making, but rather knowledge of the making of this social reality.
. . . Because it perceives social reality as the result of conflicting political struggles to create it, any sociology that consciously aims to resolve disputes in order to assert what "reality" is, is merely a politics using sociological authority to try and create that reality.
—Ghassan Hage, "The Limits of 'Anti-Racist Sociology'"

The episode between J.U. and Mick E recounted above took place live on the air from the studios of public radio station 2 SER-FM in June 1994, toward the end of my research into Sydney's Hip Hop Scene. This battle is the point of departure for my account of that scene, not because it might be read as a defining ritual moment, a key event to be unpacked in order to reveal a structure, an organizing logic of differences and oppositions from which I might be able to offer an account of a cultural object, order, or essence surrounding, underlying, or generating the moment. Instead, I will set out from this brief, five-minute episode precisely because it was *not* a ritual. It was, rather, a moment that illuminates an intense desire to *have* a ritual in order to have a *culture.*

THE *DISS*

Every Tuesday afternoon throughout 1994,[1] between 2:00 P.M. and 4:00 P.M., Miguel d'Souza, a twenty-four-year-old journalist and DJ, hosted a program on 2 SER: *The Mothership Connection,* named for the George Clinton P-funk album of 1976, an LP that, in the words of one recent historian of Hip Hop, "defined a whole funk universe" (Fernando 1994: 67). By the middle of 1994, Miguel, in addition to playing the latest North American, English, and sometimes European (France's M.C. Solaar was gaining some popularity) Hip Hop releases, had embarked on a project of allowing young local rappers the opportunity to try out their skills on the air.

On this particular day in June 1994, Miguel had invited Illegal Substance, consisting of Mick E and DJ E.S.P., up to the twenty-sixth-floor studio overlooking central Sydney for a chat about their recently released, self-funded, self-distributed debut CD. I had also dropped by to see Miguel, and managed to record some of the proceedings on a small audio recorder: the battle and the conversations both preceding and following it. I had met J.U. on previous occasions and subsequently met with Mick, E.S.P., Miguel, and J.U. several times.

Miguel introduced the boys to his listeners: seventeen-year-old Mick, still a schoolboy in Sydney's well-off Eastern Suburbs, and twenty-year-old Steve (E.S.P.), who worked part time in a chicken shop, spending the bulk of his time composing hard core beats on his sampler. Both lived with their parents.

Off the air, the snaky, sensuous beat of one of Illegal Substance's recently recorded tracks wound around the room; a driving, metabolic noise that always seemed to fill the space between and around people wherever I went throughout my research. Miguel asked the boys about a rumor he had heard:

> Miguel: I've heard a lot of stories about this "diss" . . . what is
> *supposed* to be a diss. Has it been blown out of proportion?
> Mick: Yeah . . .

On a later occasion, Steve and Mick played me this *diss,* catchily titled "Ain't That a Bitch." Not included on their CD, the track consisted of four rapped verses, one making thinly veiled reference to two other local Hip Hop crews, The Fonke Knowmaads[2] and The Urban Poets, suggesting that they were, quite simply, not very good. Two other verses dissed one of Mick's old girlfriends and a couple of club DJs not involved in the Hip Hop Scene. The final verse was directed at Blaze, a central Hip Hop figure. E.S.P., looking a bit uncomfortable in the studio, tried to put a bit of perspective on it: "we don't even mention their names in the song . . ."

Miguel probed the boys for details.

> Miguel: Do you wanna talk about it?
> Steve: . . . no, uh yeah . . .
> Mick: We want to start battles . . .

BATTLES

To battle is to engage in a rapping (or break-dancing) contest.

This is not the place to rehearse historical arguments about the origins of rapping as a form of vocal delivery: scholarly and popular work on the development of various combative/playful African-American oral practices – the dozens, signifyin', toasting, boasting, vouting, talkin' shit – into the contemporary form abound.[3] As these accounts stress, there were strategic benefits to be gained by slave populations able to appropriate and to "signify on" (Gates 1988) "master" tongues; good signifiers/toasters/rappers stood to gain prestige, status, physical gratification, and fiscal reward for their skills in the social context of the male-dominated space of the street, "hanging out" (Leary 1990).

But it's not (necessarily) all serious. Lewis, writing on Brazilian *capoiera* (1992), uses Kochman's concept of "strategic ambiguity" to account for the tension characteristic of many African-derived practices: an ambivalence of intention that allows a contest to slip between play and fight through the discretionary response of the players in any given situation. The encounter between J.U. and Mick turns on precisely this ambivalence.

So, the boys from Illegal Substance wanted to start battles in Sydney.

Mick and Steve understood that competition, and specifically *battling,* was part of the historical tradition of Hip Hop Culture; this *knowledge* was an integral part of the global folklores of that culture.[4] In the inner cities and recording studios of North America, raps and rappers took the performative discussion of their own skill with words as their most privileged theme from the very outset, while the question of dissing was foregrounded on Hip Hop album releases throughout the early 1980s, particularly through the brouhaha surrounding Roxanne Shanté (see Nelson and Gonzales 1991: 199–202; Toop 1991: 167–68), a near-legendary piece of backward and forward recorded dissing that Miguel during his exchange with J.U. and Mick E. referred to as the "Shanté phase." To again anticipate Appadurai's model for the analysis of global cultural flows, all these sources of material constitute components of the "mediascape" informing the local Hip Hop Scene, contributing to the "ideoscape" within which the participants in that scene frame their knowledges, beliefs, desires, discourses, and practices.

Miguel asked Mick to "flesh out" and to explain the thinking behind the diss, warning him that "if you're gonna say it on record you might have to be prepared to back it up . . ." Mick responded: "Yeah well what we're trying to do is, um, start battles in Sydney. I mean it happened in the States what, ten, fifteen, twenty million years ago . . ." With flamboyant rapper's license, Mick charted out a historical narrative placing "the States" at the vanguard of history, with the local, antipodean scene trailing (geological) ages behind. As Mick explained to me later, the appeal of "American culture" was that "everything is so *new* there, everything happens there first."

Miguel agreed with Mick that "[battling] *is* part of the African-American Hip Hop tradition," but asked whether "it is necessarily part of the *Australian* Hip Hop tradition?" This is where Mick started to make a bit of trouble for himself. In Sydney, battling, and specifically the break-dancing contests that occurred particularly in the city's Western Suburbs in the 1980s, constituted a central part of a collective memory, recounted anecdotally or preserved as oral history in recorded raps and in locally published magazines.

However, Mick made an assertion sure to put other noses out of joint: "There *is* no Hip Hop in Australia." What they (Illegal Substance) were trying to do, he continued, was to *start* this culture; this was a potentially inflammatory assertion, implying at the least that all those who had tried to create Hip Hop or Hip Hop Culture in Australia beforehand had, well, got it wrong . . . Miguel, smoothing potentially ruffled feathers, offered a placatory qualification, suggesting that perhaps there was no "*mainstream*" Hip Hop in Australia, with Mick quickly agreeing that "it all starts underground and works its way up" (cf. Thornton 1996).

TRADITION

So, leaving aside the political problem Mick had just created for himself, here is one way to make a culture: (simply) reproduce the "original" model. If we are to have Hip Hop, Mick is saying, we need to have the battles that took place in the Bronx, in Philadelphia, L.A. We need to recapitulate, in a local context, a temporally and spatially removed series of events.

Miguel started to develop the question of the translatability of "Hip Hop Culture" from its black, North American context to Australia: "[I]n many ways you're right, it [battling] doesn't happen here, because what you're talking about is battling, battling each other and challenging and maybe that doesn't happen so often, particularly in an environment where it's so friendly." The conversation was inflected by what I came to think of as Miguel's "organic intellectualism"; he had recently graduated with a mass communications degree, and his involvement in Hip Hop was informed by his own investment in ideas of ethnic and cultural diaspora. He was a point of dissemination of academic ideas about Hip Hop and youth culture into the local scene, a scene that took questions of *knowledge* very seriously.

For Mick there was a fundamental obstacle to be overcome: "[T]he Hip Hop Community in Sydney is all too friendly . . ." When Miguel suggested that this "friendliness" of the local scene was in fact a good thing, Mick replied that "we've got to take it, you know, further, steps further, so [we must] try and get the battles. We write a song about people . . . I mean we're not saying we don't like 'em, but we just, um, pick someone who people have heard about, they'll come back with a diss against us, also get our name out on their records as well."

So here is another way to make a culture, to start to create a sense of *community*: Mick wanted to create a vigorous, dense network of cross-references. "Get[ting] our name out on their records as well" is like *shouting out* or *name-checking;* repeated invocations of names, crews, neighborhoods, creating the all-important sense of a Hip Hop *Community:* this is the oral equivalent to graffiti tagging – a night out in the city or an afternoon's random travel through the city's train system is organized around "getting up": writing one's tag in as many places as possible. As local Hip Hop acts started to release recordings, album sleeves and compact disc inserts would include extended lists of names, generically informed by recording credit lists, but in these instances labeled *shout out to,* or *props to.* When guests appeared on Miguel's weekly broadcast the shout-outs were made orally; to omit somebody from a shout-out could constitute a deliberate slight on that person's status. As a result, shout-out lists tended to be long and comprehensive and to take on an incantatory quality, as *respect* was paid to core members of the community. Additionally, Mick hoped that the layering up of cross-references provoked by his diss would yield the added benefit of furnishing the local scene with an episode, a chapter like the "Shanté Phase," that might come to constitute part of a tradition, further establishing, concretizing, reifying this fragile local Hip Hop Culture.

EXPRESS YOURSELF

Miguel suggested that a local Hip Hop Scene need not recapitulate the chronology of African-American Hip Hop exactly:

> Do you think that, I mean . . . that in Australia with Hip Hop being the way it is, and being produced by people from all sorts of different ethnic backgrounds, not necessarily . . . I mean in a sense there's an opportunity here to sort of move it into a direction that maybe it's never been before. I mean maybe in the same way that you have crews in South Africa and Japan and they're not necessarily kind of adopting all the elements of Hip Hop Culture because they're sort of creating a new one. Do you think that that's a possibility here?

Miguel understood Hip Hop as a global phenomenon, capable of transcending context to manifest itself in disparate "locals": the process that Tony Mitchell has called, after the writing of Roland Robertson, "glocalisation" (Mitchell 1999, 2002: 11). The *Hip Hop Nation* is frequently invoked in Hip Hop literature and in the accounts of individuals describing their sense of belonging to a community that transcends national and ethnic differences. Graffiti writers, in particular, claim that their practices constitute grounds for friendship and shared experience across the world.

Mick, in response, agreed that the most important obligation that a local Hip Hop Scene has is to produce its own styles. Contradicting his earlier assertion that there is "no Hip Hop here," he conceded that Def Wish Cast [5] had already started this process of marking out a distinct *Australian* Hip Hop Culture by "rapping with Aussie accents." Here we find that which will become familiar as the Hip Hop discourse of self-expression; nestled side by side with the discourse of Hip Hop as global phenomenon is the predication of "truthfulness," and therefore of (Hip Hop) authenticity, on the grounds of the (Niggaz with Attitude) injunction to *express yourself,* of *truth* to one's self, of being *true to the music,* to one's own place. A writer, a rapper, a breaker was said to *represent,* through their practice, Hip Hop itself.

And so Mick moved on to a new argument in favor of battles. He conceded that the Australian Hip Hop Community need not *necessarily* slavishly imitate the American experience *in toto,* and even that Hip Hopness might manifest differently in this new context, that it might not follow the American model. However, Hip Hop still relies on self-expression, on this truth function. Self-expression – *representing* – relies on *practice:* you must perform the correct genres, and affect the correct embodiments, but you must do so in a manner that expresses your *self* at the same time. You must develop your *style* – that which marks your difference as a rapper, a tagger, a breaker, a DJ – and your *skills* – your expertise in those practices; the best way to hone those skills, to work on your style, Mick argued, is through competition. Battles.

ENTER J.U.

As Mick offered this account, J.U. walked into the studio, having monitored the foregoing discussion.[6] He had heard about – but not actually listened to – the diss directed at him by Mick, and had been standing outside the window of the studio (Mick told me later) staring daggers through the soundproof glass. Miguel turned off the studio microphones, and the subsequent exchange between J.U. and Mick took place off the air. Once again, I recorded proceedings.

J.U. was furious at Mick.

His complaint was that the obligation to *respect* one's *brothers* in the Hip Hop Community must take precedence over the desire to compete. To commit a diss to tape constituted, he argued, lack of *respect* and, even worse, cowardice. He told Mick that "what we're pissed about man is you can battle us anytime, I'll step now, anytime, anytime, anywhere, that's cool man. But put it on record, put it on a recording, it's gonna last man, and we'd never do that. We'd *never* do that . . ." To *step* is to confront, face to face, to put one's money where one's mouth is.

Mick tried to justify his actions: "It's a way to take it [Hip Hop] further." J.U. later told me that Mick's grasp of what Hip Hop *was,* and what it *meant,* was hopelessly "childish." As he explained to Mick: "Man, the way to take it further is to come with us and freestyle with us, kick any rhymes, any time, anywhere, that's cool man. But to take it further by dissing someone, that's not taking it further to me, that's counter-productive, especially when it's so small, man, 'cause it makes us angry, and we're not angry people. At all." To rap *freestyle* is to improvise. J.U. was effectively upping the *ante* here, reminding Mick that battling, "traditionally," was extemporized rhyming, with the "test" of *skills* being the ability to think quickly, on one's feet: to *step.* And where Mick's rhyming practice was based on the careful crafting of written rhymes, J.U.'s skills were those of the improviser.

J.U. was barely keeping his cool. Afterward he revealingly explained to me that "you have to try to remember that the Hip Hop Community, it's a fucking sensitive thing, man, because you're dealing with egos, that's what rappers are, man, they're egos . . . and what you try and go and do is . . . help to split it up more . . . We're upset about it . . . I mean, this is ill, we don't need this shit." The first person plural refers in the first instance to J.U.'s crew, the Urban Poets: ". . . we're not angry people . . . we're upset . . . we don't need this shit." J.U. was positioning himself, moreover, as representative of the "Community"; the "us" that had been upset by Mick are *all* of us," the small, tight community that needed to be nurtured, that could not tolerate division.

The debate went backward and forward, with Miguel mediating, offering a historical perspective that acknowledged cultural difference. He suggested that maybe in Australia in the 1990s it might be possible to have a Hip Hop Culture in which these concerns could be negotiated; where "we" (Miguel, too, couched his contribution in the plural) would be able to abstract, from an originary African-American Hip Hop Culture, core values that might obviate the need to slavishly imitate the surface phenomena of the culture, those features that are context-derived, rather than necessary. Miguel's recapitulation of arguments he had already put to Mick met with J.U.'s complete approval; J.U. cannily aligned himself with Miguel's intellectual authority. Miguel explained:

> We live in an environment where our Hip Hop Culture that's here is actually, I mean what we're all kind of doing is create an Australian . . . I've always wondered whether dissing would come in here, because playing the dozens is part of an African-American tradition, and none, or very few of the Hip Hop people here are from an African-American background. Their ethnicity is totally different and often dissing isn't necessarily part of everybody's ethnicity, ethnic background, so maybe that's why it hasn't happened here.

The conversation was winding up; J.U., having forcefully made his complaint, was prepared to accept a retraction from Mick, and a promise that the Illegal Substance boys would "put a bar" on the diss recording itself. Things had been pretty much resolved, when a bombshell was dropped . . .

In the course of mumbling an apology, Mick explained that in dissing Blaze, J.U.'s friend and a central figure in the local scene, he had meant no offense to Blaze himself . . .

. . . J.U. heard nothing beyond the admission of the diss. "I can't believe that," he gasped (I mean it – he *actually* gasped). "You dissed *Blaze?* I can't believe that anyone could do that to someone who has done so much for the Community! Oh man, that's *it!!* We gotta step right here, right *now!*"

Mick accepted the challenge. Miguel dug around in his stack of records for a suitable instrumental track, and battle was joined.

DEFINING HIP HOP

So what do we have here? A radio studio on a winter afternoon; two teenagers, one Anglo-Australian (the rapper), one Greek-Australian (the DJ); a slightly older Anglo-Australian rapper; an Australo-Pakistani university graduate/radio announcer; and a post-grad researcher (Scottish-Australian), arguing about "Culture," "Community," "Identity," "Tradition," "Respect." What were they all doing? Simply this: they were trying to define Hip Hop.

In his freestyle, Mick claimed that he was, in dissing, "getting down with the *hard core*." To be hard core is to *respect* in one's practice the *true* values of *Hip Hop*. To be, rapped Def Wish Cast, "*true to the music*." If there is a certain circularity or tautological quality in this formulation, it is because there is an assumed self-evidence implicit in the term. Mick's claim to be hard core, repeated in a subsequent rhyme, is based on his desire to battle, to prove himself as a *hard rhymer*.

J.U., in his second reply, offered an alternative understanding of hard core:

> I'll kick to you a rhyme about the hard core;
> That's my man the Sabotage Organisation
> Out there doin' more for the Hip Hop cause

J.U. was telling Mick, "*I'll* tell you what hard core *really* means." It means "to *do*" for the "Hip Hop *cause*."

In his first verse, J.U. defined "the Hip Hop mike that we sort of rock" as "breaking, graffiti, rapping, DJing." The first three – break-dancing, graffiti writing, and rapping – are the core practices of Hip Hop, to which J.U. has respectfully added *DJing,* the art of *turntable dexterity,* of scratching and mixing vinyl records on paired record players. These practices *alone* constitute Hip Hop, "not the dissing bullshit": for J.U. dissing stood outside the defining practices of Hip Hop, operating only to "divide." The continued performance of the true practices, their *doing,* was the proof of the viability and vitality of the local Hip Hop Community. The ability to produce a narrative of the maintenance of these practices in performance over an extended period of time (well over a decade) operated as proof that Hip Hop had a local tradition, and therefore a substance as an authentic, enduring cultural form, rather than being (merely) a fad or (perhaps worse) a fashion. Further, the availability of historical narratives of the origins of these practices bound the local history of their performance to a global tradition transcending the local context.

Immediately following the battle, with evident satisfaction, J.U. offered the following précis of what had just transpired: "That's an old, an old Hip Hop tradition isn't it?" Miguel confirmed for his listeners that "if you've always wondered how people who listen to Hip Hop solve arguments and discussions and political differences that's exactly how it is. It's just the same as a conversation only it sounds better." J.U. and Mick shook hands, making a show of having appropriately resolved their disagreement:

J.U.: Thank you boys for steppin' up.
Mick: That's okay brother.

And that, supposedly, was that, although Mick later told me that he thought that the contest had not been fair, and that he had in fact rapped better than his adversary: his *flow,* he suggested, the overall relationship of his rap to the beat, had been superior to J.U.'s, notwithstanding the latter's apparent ability to produce a greater volume of rhymes on the day.

That this battle took place at all, as Miguel's summary above indicates, and as far as J.U. was concerned, served to affirm the legitimacy and sustainability of a local Hip Hop Culture, a culture demonstrably authentic because of the observance of, and participation in, "an old Hip Hop tradition." Its having happened was ultimately as significant as its material outcome.

And yet, having won the battle, J.U. spoke with Miguel for ten minutes, explicating for the audience his understanding, his vision, of the Sydney Hip Hop Community. He was involved, at the time that this interview took place, with Blaze, in opening a specialist Hip Hop record shop in Sydney's business district. As J.U. had mentioned during the battle, the shop was to be called the Lounge Room: "We hope to make the Lounge a little bit of a breath of fresh air, and make it welcome for everyone who's down with the Hip Hop Culture, which as I said in the rhyme is, we believe, graffiti, break-dancing or graffiti art, break-dancing and rapping, and anyone else who's actually interested in the music."

Having taken care to qualify graffiti as an artistic practice, J.U., perhaps with an eye cocked to his potential record-buying market (this interview was, after all, being broadcast), expanded the range of the Hip Hop Community from those actively involved in one of the three central practices, which, as he suggested, "*we* believe" *is* Hip Hop Culture, to "anyone else who is down with the music." (Note, too, throughout this account, J.U.'s use of the first person plural – "we"). "We want to make it . . . it doesn't want to be a place where there's any attitude or anything. If you're down with Hip Hop, if you're down with the Culture, we hope to represent it truly, because there's people out there in Sydney who don't represent it fully and truly, and they're not down with the Culture, and like that's just the truth, and so we hope to represent it and a bit more of a focal point."

A community must have a place. Even more particularly, Hip Hop is about neighborhoods, about belonging, representing (Decker 1993); here, J.U. was embarking on his own little piece of cultural strategy: locating himself at the geographical locus of Hip Hop. Having won what Mick had argued was, and Miguel had confirmed to be, the appropriate, authentic cultural "ritual," J.U. now spoke as representative of the Community and could start to "legislate" the boundaries of that community: "I've heard the term sort of flipped 'elitist' on me.[7] That's crap. Anyone that comes down that loves the music man, they're down with the Lounge, and you want to be down with the Lounge to be down with Hip Hop . . ." Even Mick and E.S.P., both silent now, slumped back in their studio chairs, would be welcome: "We hope to see the Illegal Substance boys there bringing their skills to the battle with the whole crew, and that's cool, because that's the way that we do shit in the Hip Hop Community . . . you can come and battle if I'm behind the counter. Anyone who thinks they can rhyme can come up there any time of the day and battle, that's cool." J.U. was in full stride.

> The thing is about Hip Hop, to us it's a Culture. It's not just the music . . . to some people it's the music and that's cool, they come as well, they get the music off us. Maybe they'll see a bit of the Culture. Hip Hop is all those things that I said, it's all integrated into the music. It revolves around or it might revolve around graffiti art, it might revolve around breaking for you. All that's the culture for us and we'll be living it and we'll be hopefully trying to display different, you know, the different aspects of that Culture, representing it fully, and that means that we will be having . . . it's not just going to be a record store, it's gonna be, it's a Culture, there's a culture behind it.

There is a place for everyone in Hip Hop. The record shop *represents* it; J.U. and his friends will be "*living* it." And *it* is "all integrated into the music."

The Lounge Room would cater for all aspects of the Culture. Graffiti, for example "will be represented there. We'll be hopefully trying to cover that with some dope mags, videos and stuff. We might try to get some copies of the older videos on um you know new tapes and stuff and so we'll cover that aspect of it." The shop will be a pedagogical institution, offering what amount to "master classes" from two of the most renowned exponents of break-dancing in Sydney: "There'll be a bit of lino there if you wanna break. There'll be lino there for all the boyz from out west all the Def Wish boys. I hope that Simon and Matthew are—" . . . having dropped the big names, J.U. had to correct himself and use their *tags* . . . "actually Def Wish and Mr E—are giving free lessons."

To claim access to such personalities, and to take care to extend the sphere of inclusion to "the boyz from out west," was to attempt to further establish the centrality of the Lounge Room to the putative Hip Hop Community, and to legitimize the right of those that speak for the Lounge Room to speak for all Hip Hop.

THA BOYZ: SUBCULTURES AND GENDER

J.U. concluded his account with a final invitation: ". . . so anyone who's down with our culture, come down to the Lounge Room we'll all kick it as

brothers man if you're down with Hip Hop then we'll roll, you know . . ."
Miguel didn't let this slip past: ". . . and hopefully some time very soon,
some sisters too . . ."

But despite Miguel's careful gesture toward the possibility of women's
participation in the project of Hip Hop Culture, there's no way around
this one. The Hip Hop world I encountered was for the *boyz,* a masculinized, even phallocentric, world in which young men performed, rapped,
breaked, boasted, *bombed,* leaving their *phat* tags to mark their presence,
hung out, strutted, posed with their legs thrust out and their hands
hooked in low-slung pockets, fingers brushing their groins. Where young
men talked about *their* Community, Culture, Nation.

In 1980 Angela McRobbie pointed out both the absence of studies directly addressed to female youth culture, with, as a result, the implicit
masculinization of the category "youth," and the absence of reference to
female behavior (and experience) in the youth subculture literature. "In
the literary sensibility of urban romanticism that resonates in most youth
cultural discourses," she wrote, "girls are allowed little more than the
back seat on a draughty motor bike" (1980: 40). The domestic space of
the family home, she argued, was completely missing from the "classic"
texts (Hall and Jefferson 1976, Willis 1978, Hebdige 1979); analysis did
not proceed past the doorstep, a methodological bias perpetrated, she
suggested, by a deep-seated leftist anxiety about the complicity of "the
family" with class oppression. There was a distinct lack of reflexivity on
the part of the researchers, a failure to address their own "politics of selection" (McRobbie 1980: 39) that allowed a superficial identification of
left-wing male researchers with working-class males to pass without critique. These biases reproduced in the resulting analyses the patriarchal
structures apparently invisible to the analyzers in the first place.

By 1993 McRobbie, responding, she wrote, to the realpolitik of dealing
with her own teenage daughter's engagement with the rave scene, was
reassessing her back-catalog of polemic against the implicit (masculine)
gendering of "youth" in the subculture theory "classics." Alongside a
recognition of the "unfixing" or "unhinging" of the "traditional gender
position" of young women in contemporary culture, McRobbie now reads
a fundamental shift in the nature of youth culture, dating from the late
1970s. "In fact," she writes, "things were never the same after punk"
(1993: 410); the distinction between "authentic" youth culture and "com-
modified" popular culture, demonized in the classic subculture literature,
could no longer be sustained. Further, throughout the 1980s, "the in-

creasing interest among a wider selection of the population in style . . . saw a situation develop where youthfulness became virtually synonymous with subculture" (410). I am particularly interested in developing this line of thinking, identifying what I think of as a media-driven "incitement to subcultural being" as being a key determinant in shaping the way that the people I researched understood their social being.

Theorists of youth culture have moved with the times; "class no longer underwrites the critical project of cultural analysis . . . ideology [is] also recognised as too monolithic a category (McRobbie 1993: 409). Analyses based on notions of class and resistance carried with them the romantic discourses of "authenticity" that McRobbie had earlier (1980) identified in the "politics of selection" of the early Birmingham theorists: the selection of the working-class lad as ersatz revolutionary vanguard, of (male) youth as the new Agent of History.[8] Such approaches were only able to read the processes of consumption in terms of discourses of "commodification" and "depoliticization"; witness the fundamentally pessimistic, depowering trajectory of the "classic texts," in which gestures of youth resistance are always already recaptured by the all-encompassing logics of capital and labor: "imaginary solutions to real problems" (see Frith and Goodwin's précis, 1990: 40).

More recently, McRobbie suggests, there has been an increasing alertness to "the more micrological level of dispute and contestation" toward what she calls, after Laclau, "the dignity of the specific" (1993: 410). In preference to an analytic orthodoxy in terms of which "so much attention was put on the final signifying products of the subculture and the permutations of meaning produced by these images, that the cultural work involved in the their making did not figure," McRobbie argues for an ethnographic approach in which the practical processes of selection, of interpretation, and of the reinscription of meanings are foregrounded (411). Thus Hebdige's "semiotic guerilla warfare" (borrowed from Eco, in Hebdige 1978: 105) might be witnessed in practice, rather than as a *fait accompli,* as a fixed system or structure of signification (magically) in place, and available for analysis. McRobbie argues that only through an attention to process will the role of women in the making of cultures become visible.

Further, accounts rooted in synchronic relations lend themselves to "homology" theories: a semiotic snapshot, frozen in time, seems to "be structured" and yields reductive explanations. Because a structuralist approach does not understand semiotics as an interpretive, social practice (or rather, because a structuralist semiotics reserves this practice for the privileged, panoptic analyst alone), social agents cannot "appear" in analysis: they may be "read" as texts, as images, but their accounts count for naught. The phenomenological pragmatics of Peirce can help here – particularly his understanding of semiotics as a process of interpretation (see Weber 1987), in which, *in time,* social agents create, fix, dispute, and negotiate meaning, forming contingent, useful consensuses, engaging- with a material world that offers resistance to the free flow of semiosis. The diachronic, experiential dimension of social being can not only be re- instated in analysis, but also foregrounded.

In my experience of Hip Hop in Sydney, women tended to win *respect* through the adoption of specifically masculine embodiments and *habitus,* by becoming what in other contexts would be known as "tomboys." Even the most broadly respected female writer coded her own femininity into her graff practice, writing "Sugar" and "Spice."[9] Women were often pres- ent, but silent, and my own access to the girlfriends of rappers and writ- ers was carefully monitored, and frequently resisted by the women them- selves. Methodologically, I decided that I didn't want to incite people into discourse, to press people for their accounts, preferring to observe, and to learn from those whose accounts were forthcoming.

Talking with Miguel, though, J.U. responded to the unintended exclu- sion of women from his vision of Hip Hop: "Oh oh . . ." Miguel offered him a way out: "That was just a *faux pas* wasn't it?" Allowing J.U. to explain himself: "Well yeah, brothers, is like a unity thing. I wouldn't be saying brothers in a racial term [sic] – it means my brother you know, my friend, you know, my, my homie. Mate, I've seen some I've seen girls who can wreck the mike but they know who they are out there as well . . ."

And, with this final subsumption of race, color, sex, gender, and dif- ference to the all-embracing discourse of Hip Hop, the interview ended.

THE METAPHYSICS OF HIP HOP

Donna Haraway quotes Karin Knorr-Cetina's account of "the world" as "science" sees it: "[T]his 'world' is the outcome of a process of in- quiry constructed *generatively* and *ontologically,* rather than *descriptively* and *epistemologically*" (Haraway 1989: 182; emphases mine). J.U. and his friends, like the scientists described by Knorr-Cetina, apparently under- stand themselves as being engaged in a (cultural) process of representation, rather than creation. The same implicit metaphysic girds the Hip Hop understanding of the relationship of practice to cultural essence. Practice, for J.U. and his friends, *represented* a preexisting, "ideal(-ized)" cultural essence. Hip Hop is not created by individuals doing things, the total of which *is* Hip Hop; Hip Hop is always already there, waiting to be *done.*

The moment of representation is in fact a moment of production, of what Judith Butler calls "essence fabrication" (1988), creating a "real," a transcendental signified, perhaps, that can then stand as the "alibi" for a logic of representation founded on the sharing of a belief of its real-ness. By placing "interpretation" at the heart of this account, the aspirations, beliefs, and accounts of the individual agents engaged in these processes will be privileged. These agents operate co-creatively within a partially constraining field of determination, a field that to no small extent structures experience, but must ultimately be understood as itself consisting of "instituted," and therefore reinterpretable, negotiable, contestable orthodoxies.

MAKING CULTURE

Here's how I want to understand this battle. J.U. was *making a real.* He was making a move in a real-making game; he was engaged in a (micro)political struggle. He was attempting to institutionalize his own interpretation (Weber 1987) of the real, hegemonizing the field of interpretation of Hip Hop by excluding dissident readings or understandings of just how that field might *be* (Laclau and Mouffe 1985). He was "articulating" to a genre of music (to be distributed from his "place") particular values, meanings, interpretations (Middleton 1985). He was claiming that in that music could be found a truth, that of Hip Hop, a truth that could be found *in* that music. He was seeking to enroll other agents to this (his) truth (Clegg 1989), by claiming authoritative knowledge of that truth and of the means of accessing it. Claiming the right to speak for the community, as well as claiming an access to "the truth" of that culture.

In this introductory section, just as I have avoided directly addressing the important questions of race and class, I have expressly avoided offering any "definition" of Hip Hop, other than allowing J.U., Mick E, and Miguel to speak for themselves. In the pages that follow, I will elaborate on these ideas. Key insider concepts that have already appeared will reap-

pear, to be supplemented by other accounts from other social agents engaged (antagonistically or otherwise) in the same field of the social, to be
examined more closely; other performances, embodiments, discourses,
texts, images, sounds, and narratives will be discussed, with a view to understanding the grounds on which, and the means by which, this labor of
cultural production, this making of "Hip Hop," takes place.

part two
Locations

"Fads don't last ten years!"

. . . announces Ser Reck of Def Wish Cast, as DJ Vame warms up the turntables (*the ones and twos*). I am at Site nightclub in inner-city Kings Cross. The event is the launch of the Australian Broadcasting Corporation (ABC)'s Open Learning Cultural Studies and Popular Music course, to which I have contributed a piece on Sydney Hip Hop, and Def Wish Cast have been invited to perform for the assembled academics and ABC suits. They and their friends are uncomfortable as they wait for their set: a clutch of boys and girls in baggy jeans and sweatshirts having to explain who they are every time they ask for a (complimentary) drink. They decide that this is the perfect opportunity to "represent": to state who they are, and to promote not merely their project as a group of performers, but their cultural project, Hip Hop. Hence Ser Reck's précis of his commitment: "Fads don't last . . ."

Ser Reck's *tag* (graffiti name) is Unique. He has been *writing* (graffiti) for . . . well, ten years. He gets paid to do it these days. He is twenty-four years old.

In performance, Def Wish Cast simply *kick*. On this particular night, they pull out all the stops, *wrecking the mics* with the anthemic "A.U.S.T. (Down Under Comin' Up)"; launching into the chorus of "Runnin' Amok": "Is that your head or did your neck throw up?" Three or four of their friends bounce up and down on the dance floor chanting, "West Side, West Side . . ." The ABC suits take steps backward, pressing the smalls of their backs to the bar. Def Wish Cast continue to *rip shit up* as they produce an *a capella* beat box rap; and then the show stopper: Def Wish's *syllable ballistics,* a sixty-second burst of ragga rap, an unbroken stream of raucous, burbling rhymes delivered at the speed of sound. Finally, each of the three rappers takes to the floor to break as DJ Vame scratches and cuts the vinyl on the ones and twos. A few circling steps, a lunging move onto the floor, and the break-dance moves appear: flurries of arms and legs, spinning torsos, before finally returning to the microphones to once again proclaim the *real*ness and, what I always find fascinating, the fundamental benevolence of the Hip Hop culture of (Western) Sydney.

The three chapters comprising this section of the book will examine how Hip Hop in Sydney variously *located* itself: that is, how the agents engaged in the local Hip Hop Community emplaced themselves, first, within historical narratives of Hip Hop; second, within (and as contributors to) a global mediascape; and finally, geographically, by endowing (their) particular place with what might be termed a Hip Hop *identity*.

3
Origins

The search for origins is typically a subversive
activity. Its usual purpose is to discover precedents
that justify claims of one sort or another, inevitably
at someone's expense. One has the suspicion that if
such justifications were not needed, the search for
precedents in the form of pedigrees, genealogies,
myths of origin, and the like would be of no great
interest. . . . Not only do people use genealogies to
validate existing social relationships, they use these
relationships to prove the genealogies, modelling
the form of the latter on the former. This genealogical
argument is a kind of petitio principii, *an illicit*
use of causality, mechanism of managing and often
reordering history to find support for present
purposes. In whatever form, the search for origins is
usually an illicit mode of justification because it
always sends us back to itself as its own first principle.
—James Holston, *The Modernist City* (1989)

Here is the standard narrative of Hip Hop: rapping, the historical precedents of which can be found in the singer-historian/faith-healer of
sub-Saharan Africa, inflected through the forced orality of slavery and
the more benign evangelism of southern Baptism, (re?)united with the
rhythms of Africa via the Caribbean, collided, in the late 1970s, in New
York, with the Latino-American tradition of quasi-combative dance and
(also Latino) urban idiographics, morphing into what Brewer calls "Hip
Hop Graffiti" (1992). The standard account of Hip Hop traces its "origin"
to this moment in time and space, that is, the Bronx in the late 1970s,
when these three key practices coincided, at which point, apparently, a
"culture" was, if not born, then at least discernible.

Subsequently, rap as a musical form went through a number of what
R. J. Stephens (1991) calls "waves," starting with the "Boogie-Woogie" and
"message rap" of the period up to around 1982: the Sugar Hill Gang, Kur-

tis Blow, Grandmaster Flash, and Africa Bambaataa. Influenced by new synthesizer technology and the electronic music of European artists such as Kraftwerk, this "old school" Hip Hop is most readily associated with break-dancing. The second wave, extending through to the middle of the 1980s, Stephens suggests, was the increasingly commercialized "Rock 'n' Roll" Hip Hop of L.L. Cool J., Run DMC, Big Daddy Kane, Eric B and Rakhim, and the 2 Live Crew. Sexuality was foregrounded, with boasting and battling emerging as driving forces in composition. By the mid-1980s, what Stephens calls "hard-core hip-hop" emerged, with crews such as Public Enemy and Boogie Down Productions moving toward an expressly didactic politicization of their audience. Cross's account (1993) of the Los Angelino scene sketches out the parallel evolution of West Coast rap, with its origins deep in the Watts Poets tradition of ghetto-realism; Ro (1996) subsequently maps out what he reads as the distortion of this movement into the "gangsta" rap of the early 1990s.

Versions of this story abound in print. Toop (1991, an update of 1984), Hager (1984), and Rose (1994b) are the strongest; Fernando (1994) and, less satisfactorily, K. M. Jones (1994), offer more accessible, but somewhat celebratory accounts of the same story. Spencer (1991) includes R. J. Stephens's historical overview of "the three waves of rap music" (1991) among a patchy collection of essays, one of the best of which is Peterson-Lewis's fine response to Gates (inter alia)'s defense of obscene rap lyrics (1991).[1]

Beyond this history of Hip Hop from the mid-1970s to the present, Gates (1988) argues for a cultural continuity: an African-American oral tradition, traceable through the Middle Passage back to the sub-Saharan *griot,* elaborated by the experience of slavery. Gilroy's remarkable analysis of the African-American "experience" as a counterculture of modernity (1993) is an important corrective to the essentializing (but strategically significant, perhaps) pan-Africanism of Gates's work; Cross's archaeology of the Los Angelino Hip Hop scene (1993) usefully augments (and compounds) questions of "origin," as does Flores's important contributions (1987; 1994), stressing the Latino influence, particularly in regard to break-dancing and graffiti.

Authenticity emerges as the key theme around which the practice of Hip Hop (and much of the academic work *on* Hip Hop) has been organized. The "commercialization" of Hip Hop, for example, is a notion that is predicated on a narrative of cultural forms as pure expression of a substratal structure (see Watson 1983), distorted by capital or otherwise constituted hegemonic interests (Light 1991, Blair 1993). Arguments about rap and Hip Hop constellated around questions of authenticity need to offer an account of the moment of coincidence of breaking, rapping, and graffiti in New York in the late 1970s, leading to the extended archaeological projects of African-American theorists such as Gates, in which "the African-American experience" coheres these practices into a "cultural" whole. These archaeologies then feed back into the field of cultural production: witness the pan-African rap of, for example the Native Tribes Posse, A Tribe Called Quest, Queen Latifah, et al. (Gilroy 1993: 85), or the more militant Islamo-national rap of which Public Enemy is perhaps the most accessible example (Gilroy, 84; Perkins 1991).

As well as being a key analytic at work within the discursive world of Hip Hop, "authenticity" is an axis around which an industry of academic popular musicology has organized itself (see, for example, Goodwin 1990), particularly as popular music studies and ethnomusicology encounter each other over "world music" (Feld 1994a; Erlmann 1996; Neuenfeldt 1994, Mitchell 1992). Essentializing accounts of origin invest massive cultural capital in ideas about "authenticity," reflected both in the ethnographic Hip Hop scenes (in their various diasporic forms), wherein "authenticity" constitutes a core feature of the Hip Hop "ideoscape," and in academic writing on Hip Hop and rap; see the usual "insider" (that is, African-American and related studies) suspects: Rose, Gates, K. M. Jones, Fernando, Decker, Spencer, et al. There are also some interesting takes from outside (European) perspectives: Fornäs 1994 and Cloonan 1995, in particular, are able, because of their geographical and cultural distance, to offer perhaps more critical reflections on these questions.

THE POLYCHROME PACIFIC

Paul Gilroy has figured the "rhizomatic, fractal structure of the transcultural and international formation" of the African-American experience through the spatio-temporal trope of the "black Atlantic," that transitional zone across and through which the dialectic of modernity's encounter with its (black) counterculture was enacted (1993: 4). For Gilroy the enduring continuity of "black Atlantic political culture" can be accounted for in terms of the "ways in which closeness to the ineffable terrors was kept alive — carefully cultivated — in ritualised, social forms" (73). I am concerned, similarly, with the keeping alive and the cultivation of social forms. In the Australian case, however, the continuity of the experience of slavery, or the geographic continuity of the (black) Atlantic, is not available as a ground on which the social forms are "kept," or cultivated: there is, instead, a radical discontinuity of experience (and, of course, geography, a discontinuity that also manifests as a temporal disjunction) here, productive of the specificity of the "Australian Hip Hop experience." Hemispherically displacing (and thereby disrupting the geographical contiguity of) Gilroy's metaphor, we may discern a *polychrome Pacific,* through and across which the discontinuity of the encounter of (the standard narrative of) African-American Hip Hop with the experience of young people in Australia, in the early 1980s, might be considered.[2] "Authenticity" for the geographically discontiguous, isolated, and multicultural social agents engaged in Australian Hip Hop could not subsist in a discourse of historical continuity, or even in a shared diasporic experience, grounded either in a remote historical myth of lost identity or in an identity of suffering or oppression. Instead, the story of Hip Hop in Australia largely turns on the possibility of ascribing to local performance an authenticity that had to be articulated to a discontinuous, geographically remote narrative of origin. It is to the efforts to effect this articulation of, in Bhabha's terms, pedagogy to practice that I now turn. This articulation involves a cultural labor, applied to sustain a *felt* contiguity between the idea and the practice, the labor of producing a *habitus,* and, more importantly, ensuring that meanings are maintained over time. This involves less the rigorous maintenance of a system than the capacity to reconcile practice to discourse, to produce, over time, a *fit* between what is done, or is being done, and the narrative of "culture" within the context of which the actors understand their practices.

■ Here is how Mick E and E.S.P. explained the authenticity of their Hip Hop practice. I had asked them about a "drive-by" shooting in Far Western Sydney, about which they had recorded a rap:

> E.S.P.: Friends of ours were performing there [Villawood] and we went to see them and after the show, after everything was finished late at night . . . inside there was a fight, between the Lebs and the Blacks, and the Lebs got kicked out, and they came back and did a drive-by.
> Mick E: I mean *that's* American . . .

44

E.S.P.: *That's* very stupid . . .

Mick E: . . . the drive-by, but then it happened in Australia, therefore I wrote a rap about it as an Australian issue.

E.S.P.: Cos to start with, things do happen in Australia that do happen in America, like the drive-by and all that, like people say, mate, I dunno they say like, they'd call Australian rappers fake, but . . .

Mick E: Nah, we're not, because we're talking about things that happen in Australia, even though they may be American things happening, but they're happening . . .

E.S.P.: They did happen in America, but they're happening here. (Maxwell 1994a: 4)

I'll flesh out this evocation of a suburban landscape of "blacks" and "Lebs" below. What I want to note here is the assertion of a claim to Hip Hop authenticity through complementary ontological and epistemological moves: the simultaneous predication of a (the) "real" — the (mean) streets where "things happen" — and the positioning of the rapper as the figure able to see, understand, and report on this reality. For Mick E, this principle could be extended into an aesthetic of Hip Hop music: "hard core" (a term expressing an unreserved aesthetic approval) raps simply involved telling things as they are. The Mick E and E.S.P. double act explained that Mick (the rap-writing half of the equation) writes ". . . things that I saw that happened in the city."

E.S.P.: Realistic things . . . straight to the point . . . not hiding things, straight out, straight to the point . . . Especially if you go out one night and something happens, and you spin out "wow" . . .

Mick: Like the drive-by, I wrote about it the day after . . . You've got to write a story . . . I'm *saying* things. I'm talking about experience. I'm telling stories because . . .

E.S.P.: That's Hip Hop . . .

Mick: Yeah, Hip Hop is . . .

E.S.P.: Self-experience, self-expression . . .

Mick: . . . telling your story.

There are echoes here of Public Enemy's Chuck D's styling of rap as "Black America's CNN," and the arguments of Gates (1990),[3] Morley (1992), and Stanley (1992) defending "obscene" rap lyrics: "telling it like

45

it is." These are well-rehearsed models for the understanding of what it is to be a rapper: to play out this role, to adopt these attitudes, then, is one way to assert Hip Hop authenticity.

There are many ways in which Australian Hip Hoppers might assert the authenticity of their project. Some argue that the experience of being a member of an ethnic minority in Sydney is sufficiently comparable to that of the oppressed African American to allow an intersubjective identification. The number of Anglo-Saxon youths I met professing allegiance to Hip Hop, however, would appear to militate against this being the dominant mode of what I will provisionally call "identification," begging, perhaps a more generalized notion of "otherness" or marginalization around which a desire to "be" Hip Hop might constellate; racial or ethnic otherness might then be considered a special case of a more general sense of otherness, the specificity of which might take any number of forms: recall the appeal of rapping to the "pretty chubby kid" who was, he told me, "no good at sport." Blaze claimed to be an outsider because he "didn't like guitars" — the synthetic, sampled sounds of old school rap offered a more satisfying alternative. On this kind of account, Hip Hop stands as sort of a reservoir catching the misfits of (schoolyard) society — this, indeed, was a theory put to me by a number of insiders, sometimes bluntly (I was taken aside one night and had it explained to me that Hip Hop tended to appeal to those who were "not too bright"); more often it was couched in terms of a "they" or a "mainstream" that was unable to understand the "reality" to which the "outsider" figure had immediate, unmediated access.

Political solidarity is often cited: to believe in the emancipatory values espoused by key African-American Hip Hop figures — peace, brotherhood [sic], antiracism, and so forth (in other words, the standard occidental litany of self-evident liberties) — constituted sufficient grounds for claiming a Hip Hop authenticity. The discourse of the right to self-expression is closely related to both these lines: rap (along with graffiti) was held to constitute a means by which otherwise silent (silenced) voices could be heard. A discourse of youthful rebelliousness often accompanied this: it is not an ethnic or politically marginalized group that seeks emancipation from "the (corrupt) system" — it is *youth*. Still others argue that simply participating in the same activities as putatively original or authentic "Hip Hoppers" sufficiently qualifies one as similarly authentic.

I will return to these discourses later. My argument is, in part, that the massive labor of effacing the irreducible discontinuity of experience between (a perceived) African-American Hip Hop and the local experience relies on the fabrication of an idea of an abstractable, reified *essence* of Hip Hop, an essence evidenced, and thereby given credence (the term used within the scene is "represented"), by the public, visible, sustained practice of rapping, writing, and breaking.

This is not to deny that the forms of expression through which this essential Hip Hop-ness are expressed originated in a culturo-historical specific — in the African-American inner-cities of the United States. However, I am not interested in adjudicating the relative "authenticity" of an Australian "take" on these practices. To simply dismiss an Australian Hip Hop as "imitative" or derivative, while on its face arguable, misses the point. It is not my intention (I cannot state this often enough) to understand the phenomenological subjects of my ethnography as being anything other than precisely that: genuine, phenomenological subjects, furnishing themselves and their practices, with narratives and knowledges that *they experience as genuine,* as *real.* It is certainly not my intention to "reveal" these subjects as being in a state of disavowal, or as constructing phantasmic identities out of an imitative *ressentiment.* That may be an argument for another writer; it is not one that I am interested in.

A STORY OF HIP HOP IN SYDNEY: SOUND UNLIMITED'S NARRATIVE OF THE "ORIGINS OF SYDNEY HIP HOP"

> . . . hip hop autobiographies are accepted at face value, simply because they perpetuate a collusive myth that feeds artists, fans, scholars, newshounds and self-appointed moral guardians alike.
> —Hip Hop historian David Toop writing on the death of Los Angelino gangsta-rap figure, Eazy-E, in the *Face,* May 1995

In a comic-book-style booklet circulated in clubs, pubs, venues, and cafes, the Sydney rap outfit Sound Unlimited, or rather, their publicists, in 1993 produced a narrative in which an early 1980s Sydney "scene," in "dire need of an energy boost," is saved from a "dismal future" by the arrival ("enter the future," the caption reads) of "three graffiti writting [*sic*] break dancers and a singing school girl captivated by the funk." The "funk" was hip-hop [*sic*]. In the Sound Unlimited narrative, "gangs would congregate west of the city, engaging in break-dance battles." In this environment, Kode Blue and Rosano were introduced to each other by "Penguin, a mutual friend from back in the dayz." Together, they formed the United Break Team, dancing in clubs, touring with the Rock Steady Crew ("one of the highpoints of this period"). "Phase Two" of the story concerns the dispersal by the police of outdoor break-dancing parties, and the "outlawing" of "Hip Hop Culture" and the subsequent channeling of "b-boy energy into the ever-expanding graf-scene." Rosano meets Vlad (later the Sound Unlimited DJ) and forms the Future Art Beat (FAB) Four bomb squad.

As the "graf scene exploded," DJs were honing their skills in their bedrooms "out west." Unable to get club gigs, these turntable instrumentalists threw small parties outdoors, using petrol-generated sound systems, drawing larger and larger crowds. "It was these jams that gave birth to Australian rap"; with the "def jams held by the West Side Posse," "the emergence of this street culture forced clubs to re-evaluate the situation and open their doors to that fat sound of hip-hop" (see Maxwell and Bambrick 1994 for an extended reading of this booklet).

This comic-book version of the story of Sydney Hip Hop circulated throughout the scene, arousing a degree of antipathy. Some felt that it was somewhat self-serving and self-important and failed to sufficiently respect the contributions of others. Others (older, wiser heads, perhaps) recognized the hand of the marketing executive and were able to assimilate the document to the narrative of commodification (and even *selling out*) that was more and more frequently applied to Sound Unlimited (and against which Sound Unlimited was determined to defend itself; see Maxwell and Bambrick 1994 and Blair 1993). The point is not, however, for me to legislate on such matters; indeed, allowing for poetic embellishments, and the tendency of the account to anachronize various ideas (the Hip Hop personae spring into the story fully formed, already, within the narrative, referring to an anterior golden age, "back in the dayz," constituting within the logic of the story just the kind of *petitio principii* Holston identifies at the heart of any genealogical project; Maxwell and Bambrick 1994), Sound Unlimited's story is, in fact, fairly accurate. However, its appearance in the form that it took was seen as an attempt to bestow on it a logocentric authority, an authority that, to others in the scene, both failed to *represent* the contributions of other important figures and was inappropriate, given Sound Unlimited's straying from "true" Hip Hop into the realms of commercial and aesthetic compromise. Sound Unlimited was, in a very real sense, perceived as having made an inappropriate grab for what Sarah Thornton has called "subcultural capital" (1996), if not actually "inventing tradition," to borrow Hobsbawm's phrase (1983), then at least certainly bending history to their own ends.

Indeed, while there is no disputing the influence and involvement of the members of Sound Unlimited on the early days of Hip Hop in Sydney, during the course of my research their star was somewhat on the wane. On its release, their album was condemned critically by both the mainstream press and by Hip Hop aficionados. Its slick, heavily instrumental production and the claims made by the crew to represent Sydney Hip Hop were sticking points for many people in the scene. One rapper I spoke to took me to task for writing about Sound Unlimited, claiming that "they're not the real thing, man"; others would only talk to me about Sound Unlimited "off the record." Still others, generally the younger members of "the new (Sydney) school" simply dismissed them out of hand, suggesting that although respect was due to the West Side Posse, the members of Sound Unlimited were out of touch, "up themselves" or simply "wack." Poor sales of the album, and the subsequent financial burdens imposed by a major company record deal, resulted in the dissolution of the group in 1993 and the reformation of the crew under the name Renegade Funk Train the next year. Their comic book history, in this light, can be understood in terms of a generational crisis: an attempt to seal their place in a history that was, in a real sense, moving along without them.

Behind the narrative pyrotechnics of Sound Unlimited's historiography, of course, there are oral histories for which the comic book hyperbole stands less as fabrication than as a poetically exaggerated trope. In the following pages, I will focus on a particular "ur-moment" recurring in personal narratives, and over time elevated to the status of foundational myth, about "the origins of Sydney Hip Hop," and the nature of the appeal of this "culture" to particular individuals. It is a moment that makes the Sound Unlimited claim to have "come" from "the future" to save a moribund scene seem a little less unlikely; a moment in which geographic distance (in which America is "somewhere else") was displaced into temporal difference (in which America is "ahead" of us in time), and in which temporal difference (the sequence of cultural "events" unfolding over time in America) was collapsed into a pure moment of transmission (a video clip on Saturday morning television).

49

THE "STANDARD NARRATIVE"
OF SYDNEY HIP HOP

Tricia Rose takes care to sort the three key Hip Hop practices into a chronological sequence: New York experienced graffiti first, then breaking, with rapping "the last element to emerge," around 1979 (Rose 1994b: 51).

In Blaze's account, however, Australia got all three as a "package deal," a couple of years later. Wark's maxim, that "we no longer have roots, we have aerials" (1995: xiv), is, in this instance, entirely apposite. Across the polychrome Pacific (by way of Chelsea High Street) came Malcolm McLaren's "Buffalo Gals" and, more importantly, the film clip that accompanied the song.

McLaren had been lurking around New York in the late 1970s, seeking out "hip" new acts, bringing break dancers and rappers from the Bronx projects into downtown clubs to support his New Wave acts (Toop 1991: 132). The New York punk/new wave scene, and the related avant-garde art scene had been quite attentive to the nascent Hip Hop scene in the late 1970s. In 1980 New Wave group Blondie released "Rapture," which included a rapped vocal (K. M. Jones 1994: 50), a number 1 hit in Australia; in 1981 Talking Heads spin-off funk group the Tom Tom Club released "Wordy Rappinghood" and "Genius of Love," the latter being in turn sampled by Grandmaster Flash later that year ("It's Nasty") (Fernando 1994: 67, 69).[4] Nelson and Gonzales preface *Bring The Noise* (subtitled "Guide to Rap Music and Hip-Hop Culture") (1991) with an interview with seminal Brooklyn "hip-hop renaissance man" (v) Fab 5 Freddy, in which he recounts how he brought "hip hop to the down town bohemian culture" in 1980 (vii). Toop accounts for the appeal of "rap" to the punk/downtown bohemian scene in terms of its being "irresistible as a genuine street culture created by disaffected youth . . . [having] . . . the double virtue of being romantic and daring yet easily packaged" (Toop 1991: 134).[5]

"Buffalo Gals," a perky novelty hit from 1981, included McLaren's nasal quasi-rap over a funky backbeat, a delivery owing more to rural American square-dance calling than to the urban raps of the Sugar Hill Gang or Grandmaster Flash and the Furious Five. Toop, interestingly, describes the song as "a hip hop inspired melange of rap, Latin, Appalachian and Zulu music" (1991: 134), already effacing the syncretic nature of rap, positing it instead as an originary form on a standing with "Latin," "Zulu," and so on.

However, for audiences in Sydney, what apparently most stood out about this clip was not the music, but, at least in the first instance, the break-dancing, and then the graffiti art that formed the background against which the dancing was shot (Bil Blast's "Sky's the Limit" is pictured on pages 20–21 of Henry Chalfant and James Prigoff's 1987 book *Spraycan Art*). I asked Blaze how, at the age of fourteen in 1983, he first encountered "Hip Hop" and what it was that led him to reach a level of involvement with what he calls "the culture of Hip Hop" that enabled him to make the claim, in 1992, that "I don't *think* any other way [than Hip Hop]." It wasn't the music that appealed: "[T]he song was [only] okay — 'three buffalo girls go round the outside'" . . . this Blaze recited somewhat unenthusiastically; but the *dancing* . . .

It's hard to explain — I mean, I just got into it because the dancing was like nothing I'd ever seen in my entire life, I just couldn't believe that you could do that — roll around on the ground, it was astounding . . . Malcolm McLaren . . . it was just like no way in the world . . . it was like, whoah, how do you do that?

And the graffiti: "[T]here was a guy in the background like painting this big painting with a spray can and it was like, uh, what?" These things appeared to "go together":

Here's two things in one clip that I'm freaking out at and I then realised what he was doing was painting, and I realised that what the guys were doing on the ground, like watching it over and over again — thank god we had a video recorder in those days — and I kept hitting the rewind and it was like nothing that I'd ever seen in Australia . . .

Mediascape and technoscape[6] coalesced for a moment: the technology was available for Blaze to record and to replay the break dancers, iterating the (fictive? McLarenesque?) space of Manhattan in his family lounge room, effortlessly (re)-territorializing his bedroom floor, soon to be awash with album covers, clipped articles, penciled outlines, and eventually his own page layouts, and in the school yard, where he burned his back and joints copying — no, not copying — *performing* the break moves he had studied.

There followed the "realisation," he explained, that all of these practices were dimensions of "the one culture." This perceived cultural totality bound breaking, rapping, and writing together, allowing multiple points of entry into that "culture," as I have suggested. "Hip Hop," as this "cultural" substrate became known, "offered something to everyone": if you couldn't break, you could write graffiti; if you couldn't write, you could rap.

Blaze grew up on Sydney's Lower North Shore, an affluent, middle-class part of the city, and attended a private Catholic boys' school. The "otherness" of this vision of the Bronx put together by McLaren had instant appeal. For Blaze, the local music "scene" (Straw 1991) held no attraction: "[A]ll that sort of Aussie rock and roll guitar stuff, smoking dope down the street—I mean, I just can't stand guitars—but *this* . . . it [the world of the video clip] was just totally, it was so *alien* . . ."

Blaze went on to recount how he and a handful of friends set about teaching themselves to break. The breaking in the clip is primarily the Bronx-style break-beat, Latin-influenced acrobatics, with exciting ground moves and spins, as Blaze's account suggests. He explained that "everybody got into it for a while." Those who, like Blaze, felt a particular attraction to breaking took the trouble to "research" it a bit more and "to learn the skills." The research was abetted, Blaze told me, by a handful of local DJs who, broadcasting on the ABC's "alternative," or "youth-oriented" radio station 2 JJJ, played the latest rap tracks (often late at night, on specialist programs, thereby contributing to a sense of "underground"). Commercial radio stations, of course, would not touch the stuff.

The need to "research" Hip Hop recurs in accounts like Blaze's. Another rapper explained: "We've been into the culture for a while we know what we're talking about. I don't want people to come up to me and say 'man you're not black you can't rap,' man that's bullshit man I can prove that I've got skills and I've analysed the culture, you know, I've *studied* it, it's a part of me and I respect it for all it is."[7]

For many, the interest in breaking or graff flagged; for them it was, in the words of Def Wish Cast, "just a faze" (from "Perennial Cross Swords" on *Knights of the Underground Table*). But Blaze and his friends, and the hundreds of other Hip Hop aficionados spread across the suburbs, often in isolation, would meet at the few record shops that stocked, or were prepared to import, the Sugar Hill or, later, Def Jam and Tommy Boy recordings. They would start to hang out together, formed crews and posses based on the New York models of Hip Hop social organization (see Castleman 1982). Blaze and others argue that rather than being the cultural tabula rasa on which the mercantile hand of American cultural imperialism inscribed commodity desire, they *created* a demand for high-top shoes, shell-tops, and track pants: the soon to be ubiquitous Nikes and Adidas runners. This argument, forcefully stated against a perceived "mainstream" accusation of cultural imperialism, holds that the commodification of these styles came later.

Tags started appearing, and then pieces; breakers met in parks, rolling out strips of lino, or on the smooth outdoor terraces of office blocks to bust moves to the latest cassettes. One famous venue was a newly constructed block in the satellite business district of Parramatta, close to the geographical and demographic center of Greater Sydney. The architects had thoughtfully provided external power sockets: boom boxes and ghetto blasters could be plugged in; and the smooth granite surface was ideal for the ground moves of the burgeoning local break-dancing scene.

This was the halcyon golden age of Sydney Hip Hop: the quasi-mythologized underground "dayz," prior to "sell-outs" and the "divisions" that, as we will see below, supposedly characterize more recent attempts to maintain the scene. Like any golden age, it is remembered as a time of *unity,* despite the (rather embellished) accounts of *rumbles* and inter-crew rivalry. (A famous episode was recounted to me several times: a massive "war" in a central Sydney square, involving — accounts vary — between 200 and a dozen b-boys stepping to each other. As near as I could tell, it would seem that the latter figure is closer to the truth.) Within the discourse of Hip Hop, of course, such rivalries are markers of authenticity. The geographical diffusion of Hip Hoppers across the vast expanses of Greater Sydney militated against the rigidly observed territoriality of inner-urban (African)-American Hip Hop, although a specific Hip Hop geographics did emerge, mobilizing discourses of socioeconomic marginalization to privilege the Sydney's Western Suburbs as the authentic originary site of Sydney Hip Hop: the experience of the ghetto, the discourse of 'hood and homies was translated to this sprawling landscape of quarter-acre blocks and freestanding homes. The train lines laced across this topographical space became the trajectories or vectors of a displaced territorialization: writers strove to become "king of the line," the suburban trains carrying their tags hundreds of miles around the city.

One of Sound Unlimited's rappers, Kode Blue, offered an account of his first encounter with Hip Hop that is virtually identical to Blaze's: "The first thing that got me into it was the first time I saw that video for 'Buffalo Gals.' I saw the breaking. I guess just physically, you know, being a kid, being into sports, I straight away picked up on the dance."[8] Vlad, also of Sound Unlimited, confirms the account: "I think most kids had their first exposure to Hip Hop from the whole 'Buffalo Gals' thing." The third male rapper in Sound Unlimited was Rosano (El Assassin) Martinez. As they did in Blaze's account, rock music "scenes" appear in his account of Sydney in the early 1980s: "All the people that I used to know living around the city used to be into rockabilly and other forms of rock music . . . the same sort of kids . . . I see them now in the clubs dancing to Hip Hop, so I guess it took awhile to actually hit the city. And people like that used to knock, make fun of what we were into, and the same sort of people are into it now."

Several important features emerge from these accounts. First, Rosano makes a claim for the longevity of Hip Hop: similarly to Blaze, he suggests that "Hip Hop" is categorically distinguishable from other scenes. That is to say, he implicitly premises that there is "something more" to Hip Hop, evidencing this through a claim to Hip Hop's apparent longevity: the fact that it has survived proves that it exists as a culture, as it were.

Second, the references to "the city" point to the specificity of the Sydney Hip Hop scene, manifested in the "regionalization" of the sprawling urban expanses of Greater Sydney into (allegedly) distinct pseudo-neighborhoods: what I shall call the "West Side" phenomenon. The project of bringing the Western Suburbs of Sydney into visibility has been one of the more interesting and extraordinary aspects of the local Hip Hop scene. It is a project grounded in discourses of "the urban" borrowed from those circulating throughout African-American Hip Hop, and has, necessarily, socioeconomic dimensions. I will return to this in some detail later, as the negotiation of this suburban context of Sydney Hip Hop with the folklorically recognized inner-city "ghetto" "origins" of Hip Hop has informed the subsequent development of the scene. Additionally, the tension set up between those in the local scene who claim a socioeconomic identification with urban African-American Hip Hop (that is, constitute themselves in their discourses as members of disadvantaged, discriminated against, or even oppressed class, ethnic, and geographical populations) and those who are perceived as having more "middle-class" backgrounds has considerably informed the micropolitical negotiations and conflicts that continue to shape the scene, negotiations that circulate around the perceived relative "right" to claim status within the ambit of the putative "true" Hip Hop Culture.

Third, in Kode Blue's account, the reference to sporting prowess invokes the specifically masculinized nature of the Hip Hop Culture. Rosano's sister, Tina ("T-Na"), was also a member of Sound Unlimited, and she took pains to make it clear that the early days of the Hip Hop Community in Sydney did not exclusively belong to the boys: "There were girls that break-danced, and popped, and rapped, and were into the whole thing, yeah . . ."

Other writers have explained to me that girls were less likely to get involved in graffiti because "you have to be able to run fast to get away from the transits [police]." Another (female) informant explained to me that boys only got into rapping to attract girls, an idea supported by a writer who told me that one of the main benefits of being a bomber was that whenever he and his crew went to a nightclub, they would attract attention: "You'd always pick up . . . there'd be fifty wogs and three of us bombers would walk in and all the girls, you know how girls go for the rebellious ones."

The same female informant, Heidi, also suggested that girls involved in the scene tended to get pregnant and were unable to maintain their commitment to the scene. Heidi was one of the original active break dancers and writers, "into" Hip Hop "from the beginning," as she told me. Now in her early thirties, Heidi has turned her back on Hip Hop, pursuing a more general interest in "black music" as an importer, distributor, and broadcaster. When I spoke to her, she was quite dismissive of "the Hip Hop Community," adopting a nostalgic tenor. The new generation of rappers and writers claiming to be "the Hip Hop Community" were mere shadows of those committed in the old days. Rhymers such as the Lounge Room crews (she didn't name names, but the implication was clear) were really only playing at being rappers: "None of that freestyle stuff is really improvised," she told me.

When I asked her how and why people, and particularly boys, originally "got into" Hip Hop, Heidi explained that "it's a psychological thing . . . they're all missing something. You look at them . . . most of them come from broken families . . . and they tend to be not very intelligent." The discourses of community/belonging and self-expression that circulate within and around Hip Hop, then, on such an understanding, have a tangible appeal, providing a kind of surrogate family, as well as a sense of creativity and expression or, in Heidi's terms, a justification for what she now thinks of as puerile self-aggrandizement (rapping) and (at best) mediocre art and vandalism (graffiti). There certainly is something in this explanation, although Heidi was perhaps being a little harsh; since her own days as a breaker, she had become a devout Christian and married her long-standing boyfriend, who has put his own writing days far behind. They still spoke fondly of the old days, he of the warrants still outstanding for his arrest, of the midnight chases and the breaking battles. But they both admitted that many of the stories of huge gang wars and so on were exaggerations.

■ In all these accounts, Hip Hop in Sydney enjoyed an initial florescence, involving a period of broad, faddish appeal. Over time, *half-steppers* fell by the wayside to follow the next (fashionable) "thing" that came up. Only true believers remained, and they were often persecuted for their commitment. Forced *underground,* misunderstood, working hard to stay true and to maintain the Culture, these people felt their commitment to Hip Hop to have withstood a series of tests. That they had remained true, they would explain; they had demonstrated the truth of Hip Hop and had earned the right to tell the story to subsequent generations.

Holston's comments, quoted above, regarding the "illicit" nature of genealogies" are certainly overstated. Perhaps "suspect" would be a better word. Since Foucault, of course, it has become if not an orthodox, then at least a commonplace methodological procedure to subject historiographical projects to a contextualizing scrutiny. Recent reactions to the influence of what are styled as French critical theoretical perspectives have argued that implicit in such positions is a desire to "kill" history. Keith Windschuttle (1994), for example, argues that a fashionable "historical relativism," derived from what he calls "the salons of Paris" pervades cultural studies, anthropology, media studies and history departments. He argues a media-friendly "common-sense" counterposition: writing history is simply a process by which "facts" are established, a process that "we" (historians) are getting better at over time. Against this reactionary current, it is important that I clarify exactly why it is that I do not want to concern myself with a verifiable, documentary history of Hip Hop in Sydney.

To place the question of the "history" of the Sydney Hip Hop experience under erasure, as it were, is not to deny the "truth" or otherwise of events, moments, or biographies constituting that history. Rather, I simply want to argue that what is most significant, for my purposes, about the history of Sydney Hip Hop is the manner in which a historical narrative is adduced in the ethnographic present, in order to locate particular agents in positions of authority and within a discourse of authenticity. An accepted, or "instituted," history becomes an orthodoxy, *the* history, which can be used to define generic boundaries, excluding some texts, practices, or agents, while including others. This is an ongoing process, negotiated in a developing field of flux, characterized by change and overdetermined by a number of discourses and interests. I argue that what I style as the "standard narrative" of local Hip Hop holds a particular significance, constituting one of the principle determinants of this process.

My account of this "standard narrative," then, is not concerned with what "actually happened" as much as it is with what is generally held, by the "community of investigators," to have happened. "Authority" within the scene to a large degree derived from this kind of historical subcultural capital: either a claim to "have been there" or a double claim: first, to have *knowledge,* albeit secondhand, of what happened, and second, to argue that one's current practice ad-equates to, or is consistent with, that history. Obviously, a claim to firsthand experience is very powerful; such a claim, however, can be challenged on a number of grounds: the person claiming to have been there is often accused of simply lying ("they wouldn't know . . . they weren't really there . . ." and so on). Alternatively, a person might be accused of embellishing or romanticizing past events, endowing them with a scale or significance that, it might be counterclaimed, they did not deserve. Additionally, it is also the case that "standard narratives," once in place, generate novel recollections, which over time substitute for personal remembrances. There is nothing deliberately "illicit" in such cases: the "false" memories are recollected in a mode of genuine belief: it is with these beliefs and their material impact on the ethnographic present that I am concerned.

One such instance is the central role played by the McLaren clip in the standard narrative. It is almost impossible to verify whether every claim that a viewing of this clip was the catalyst for a devotion to Hip Hop is "true." It was, however, generally accepted that this event had such an impact. Writers and rappers who would only have been three years old at the time "recall" this moment: "Well, it all started with the 'Buffalo Gals' thing . . ." In effect, this collective recollection is synechdocical, the film clip standing as a signifier of origin.

This access to narratives of origin, and, more importantly, the possibility of locating one's self in that narrative, had a particular repercussion on the scene shortly after my fieldwork ended. One night, a "freestyle" session held at an inner city club, described by Miguel d'Souza, in his weekly column in the street magazine *3-D World* as "the public unveiling of Sydney's new school, young rappers, too young to ever recall the origins of Sydney's rap scene and the irrationality and occasional violence it was associated with" (*3-D World*, 17 October 1994, 26), was disrupted by a DJ and rhymer who apparently claimed that the organizers were not the "real thing," that they were, more or less, imitating a lost authentic Hip Hop practice, available, apparently, only to those who were "there" originally. The evening ended in violence, fulfilling the fears of the club management, who had offered their venue on the understanding that rhymers and aficionados "these days" were more interested in pursuing the aesthetico-cultural aspects of Hip Hop than with hard homeboy attitude.

This was quite a significant event. The organizers of the night in question had hosted a series of very successful freestyle nights at the Lounge Room. These monthly gatherings had proved so popular, in fact, that a new, larger venue was required. The popular understanding of rap music and Hip Hop as being associated with violence, however, meant that very few venues were prepared to take the risk of hosting a rap night. This association of rap with violence, of course, is a commonplace (see the section on media images of rap, below). Many within the scene, particularly those promoting Hip Hop as "Culture," argue that it is "all media hype," or at least exaggerated scare mongering (while, it must be admitted, enjoying the aura of *hard*ness that such hype lends them). The violence (a microphone allegedly stolen, a scuffle, threats, and a door demolished with a baseball bat) at the Good Bar that night confirmed the worst fears and effectively ended the burgeoning freestyle scene.

Clearly, the antagonistic DJ, a figure of some renown from the early days of Sydney rap, felt that his own position, his own authority, was under threat from the self-styled *new school* of freestyle rappers. This new school took its lead from recent developments in West Coast and New York rap and understood itself within a developmental paradigm, interpreting Hip Hop as an "evolving" culture, recognizing earlier mistakes, and presenting Hip Hop in a "positive" light. This was understood, from some quarters, as a usurpation, as being not sufficiently respectful to those who had "been there" from the beginning.

It is also significant that the divide between these generational factions was also marked in terms of, on the one hand, an appeal to straightforward experience ("we were there, you weren't"), and, on the other, an appeal to superior knowledge ("that may be how it *was,* but what it *should* be is . . ."). Cutting across this set of arguments was a discourse of class: the older generation would argue that while their Hip Hop practice had been authentic because it emerged out of a genuine privation (the under-resourced West, and so on — see chapter 5, "West Side and the Hip Hop Imaginary," below), the members of the "new school" were engaged in the culture at the level of the dilettante, were from markedly more middle-class backgrounds, and were only interested in Hip Hop now that it was more accessible, respectable, and mainstream, claims hotly disputed. There was no risk, now, of being "into" Hip Hop, unlike "back in the dayz." The "new school" exponents argued that they were closer to "the spirit" of Hip Hop, that their authenticity derived from a superior understanding of what Hip Hop meant.

The processes of establishing a history of the local Hip Hop scene was critical in terms of supporting the thesis of "Hip Hop as Culture," rather than as "fad." It has not been my intention to produce here a "correct" historical account of the period following the watershed Malcolm McLaren video. I am less concerned, for example, to determine *absolutely* the circumstances of the role that the "Buffalo Gals" clip played in creating the possibility of a Hip Hop Community in Sydney than to note and assess the discursive fact that the clip has come to stand for a moment of origin, in which, to borrow the metaphorical schema Rose uses to describe the totality of the Hip Hop experience, the smooth flow of genealogical history, so contested and debated by academics and Hip Hop historians alike, is interrupted, displaced, relocated to the Antipodes, in a moment of pure "rupture in line" (Rose 1994b: 38), or, to use Appadurai's (1990) term, of "disjunction." The specificity of the development of the Hip Hop scene in Sydney also militates against a reading within the paradigm that understands the specificity of subcultural phenomena as direct "expressions" of underlying, determining contradictions in the economic base. This is not, of course, to deny the contributory impact, and the partially constraining and determining effect, of the socioeconomic context, but to suggest that dynamics other than those of class were at work. The point here has been that local experience was, effectively, gauged against, "read" in relation to, informed by and generated from cultural material "arriving" from another place.

In the next chapter, I want to turn to Appadurai's model of the generation of cultural phenomena that recognizes this increasing significance of mediation and disjunctions operative at a global scale for the production of local "worlds." Through the course of this examination, I will turn the Appadurian model inside-out, demonstrating that social agents are not merely subject to the global flow of cultural material, but also become the (active) subjects of texts and practices that enter into complex, co-creative relationships with that material, as part of the ongoing process of making culture.

4

Global Cultural Flows

A human life is seldom a blind recapitulation of givenness, but an active relationship with what has gone on before and what is imagined to lie ahead. . . . Culture cannot be set over or against the person. Rather, it is the field of a dialectic in which the sedimented and anonymous meanings of the past are taken up as a means of making a future.
—Michael Jackson, Things as They Are *(1996)*

In many ways, Australia offers a signal case study of the effects of globalization. Geographically isolated from the Northwestern Hemisphere, settled as series of convict colonies — a process that might also be thought of in terms of invasion and dispossession — and only federating under its own Commonwealth government in 1901, Australia has, throughout the twentieth century, enjoyed an awkward development toward its present status as a sophisticated multicultural nation-state. Predominantly Anglo-Celtic at the turn of the century, by the late 1960s Australia was casting aside an Anglophile obeisance (famously labeled the "Cultural Cringe" by A. A. Phillips in 1958). Successive waves of Mediterranean and northern European immigration following the Second World War and East Asian immigration in later decades substantially broadened the national demographic, and the left-leading Labor governments of the early 1970s, 1980s, and 1990s entrenched multiculturalism as state policy. In the 1990s, much was made by then prime minister Paul Keating of Australia's status as "part of Asia," a position that has subsequently been subjected to a conservative backlash. Nonetheless, it is probably fair to say that, notwithstanding an appalling failure to acknowledge and atone for the massive injustices and violence visited on Indigenous Australian peoples by the colonists, a decidedly racist past, and (the perhaps) inevitable tensions present in any such society, Australian multiculturalism has not been attended by the violence and social foment apparent in some other countries.

Historically a primary producer, in one sense, Australia has always been profoundly global in outlook. For Australians, globalization is not at all a new phenomenon; they have always been aware of their economic and cultural reliance on societies on the opposite side of the world, building relationships initially through colonial allegiance, engagement in colonialist/imperialist conflicts from the Boer to the Vietnam Wars (and beyond), sport,[1] and, more recently, mass media. The colonial/imperial patron has, of course, changed over time — from Mother England to Uncle Sam. Habituated as we are to a sense of outsiderness and remoteness, and having known as a lived reality for several generations the forces now being recognized as those of "globalization," we are not as surprised by the growing awareness of the complexity of the global flow of cultural material as are theorists working from closer to the (lost) cultural centers of the Northern Hemisphere.[2]

For the purposes of this book, which takes as its focus the immediate, lived experiences of a local "community," I am less interested in advancing a general theoretical position about globalization. At the same time, however, I would hope that this account of the way in which such a local community negotiates its engagement with globalized cultural material, and recombining that material to create new texts (simultaneously, as this chapter argues, claiming to be expressive of a unique, "non-mainstream" cultural identity, while effectively reproducing a set of "ideals" commensurate with Appadurai calls "the enlightenment worldview"), might contribute to the burgeoning accounts of that phenomenon. Among the plethora of recent writings about globalization, Appadurai's formative work is preeminent, and it is to that I now turn.[3]

The "modern world . . . is now an interactive system in a sense that is strikingly new" (1990: 1). So massively new, Appadurai suggests, that by comparison the effects of the development of print technologies on the development of the modern nation state (Anderson 1991) are "only modest" (Appadurai 1990: 2). Reading Meyerowitz's less than celebratory account of cultural processes in the age of mass media against McLuhan's premature communitarian optimism, Appadurai looks toward a spatial metaphorics borrowed in part from Deleuze and Guattari, in part from Jameson, and in part from Pico Iyer. In moving beyond a conventional Marxian understanding, Appadurai displaces political economy from its status as determinant of cultural processes, opening up the possibility of an understanding of those processes as being informed by a "much subtler play of indigenous trajectories of desire and fear" (3).

Appadurai proposes an "elementary framework" for exploring the "new global cultural economy." This framework seeks to determine the specificity of any given cultural formation in terms of the discontinuities constituted in each specific circumstance through the "relationship between five dimensions of global cultural flow": ethno-, media, techno-, finan-, and ideoscapes (1990: 6–7). The specificity of any given "imagined world," defined as "the worlds which are constituted by the historically situated imaginations of persons and groups," is given by the play of difference and disjunction between these -scapes as they pertain to a given context. "[T]he individual actor," then, "is the last locus of this perspectival set of landscapes, for these landscapes are eventually navigated by agents who both experience and constitute larger formations, in part by their own sense of what these landscapes offer" (7).

The mismatches between, for example, the "ideoscape" of (African-American) Hip Hop, carrying with it particular discourses of ethnicity, and the ethnoscape of contemporary Sydney is an absolutely critical axis for analysis, not simply to weigh the respective scenes, or imaginaries, against each other with a view to discussing "authenticity" or "culture" in a reified sense, but because these disjunctions are experienced as impediments (or points of contact, to be sure) to processes of identification, requiring of interpretation and reconciliation. Or, as Appadurai has it, of "navigation."[4]

This model addresses the inadequacies of both an orthodox Marxian reductionist account of cultural processes (what Appadurai [1990] calls the "globalizing marxist analysis") and of "post-modern" understandings predicated on an assumption of free textual play. The bulk of cultural theory from Marxism through to postcolonialism has privileged class or race, or a combination of the two, as the determinants of cultural phenomena. One of the main trajectories of Birmingham-school subculture studies was toward a "double-articulation" of class and race as determinants in the final instance, a move subsequently developed through, in particular, McRobbie's (among others') sustained assertion that sex/gender should also be factored into such accounts. Appadurai, on the other hand, allows for a range of determinants to operate within a particular cultural field without a necessary reduction in the final instance to an ontologically privileged ground, although, as Appadurai argues, one specific dimension may exercise a contingent dominance at any particular historical moment.

The analysis below will be primarily of the mediascape of Sydney Hip

Hop. Before moving on to that substantive analysis, however, I need to address the matter of race and color — that dimension of global cultural flow Appadurai subsumes under the rubric of "Ethnoscape." In this discussion I do not want to enter into a polemics about identity and authenticity. Instead, through emphasizing a radical ethnic disjuncture, I want to be able to clear the ground for an analysis, in the final chapter, of the performative, embodied means by which various agents attempted to bridge that very discontinuity in order to claim certain experiences as being indexical of a core identity capable of transcending sociohistorical, geographical, and racial difference.

ETHNOSCAPE

On Appadurai's account, the "ethnoscape" is "the landscape of persons who constitute the shifting world" (1990: 7). Now, Appadurai's work specifically deals with displaced populations, "tourists, immigrants, refugees, exiles, guestworkers"; his analysis is expressly concerned with these and other "moving groups," qualifying this concern by noting that "[t]his is not to say that there are no relatively stable communities and networks, of kinship, of friendship, of work and of leisure, as well as of birth, residence and other filiative forms" (7). But everywhere, he continues, "the warp of such stabilities is shot through with the woof of human motion."

It is possible to view all but a tiny minority of the population of contemporary Australia in terms of such an understanding: a population of displaced peoples, all, to a greater or lesser degree, immigrants. And although this may be, perhaps, a stretch, it will be an illuminating one. The main benefit for my purposes of introducing this category is to isolate questions of ethnic origin, displacement, marginality, belonging, identification, and so on as one critical dimension along, through, or across which the labor of cultural production takes place. Discourses of ethnicity, color, racial origin, and of the racial etiology of specific practices figure largely in academic, popular, and insider discussions about and accounts of Hip Hop; I have already touched on them. Here is one Sydney writer's testimony: "A lot of kids can associate with the Hip Hop Culture because with like young Afro-American kids they see their heroes in the States doing the rhymes and stuff like that, and then Hispanics and Filipinos and stuff like that and Anglo-Saxons — wherever you're from it's like been part of who you are." This writer offers an interesting take on the origins of Hip Hop: "[W]hen Hip Hop first came out it didn't really matter where you were from, you know, it was like what you did. Then it went through a phase where the Afro-Americans were into strictly blackness, Public Enemy, X-Clan came out and it was like if you were white and were doing Hip Hop music you were a fake you know . . ." We have already seen Mick E and E.S.P.'s take on this (chapter 3, under the heading "The Polychrome Pacific"). ". . . [B]ut now it's returning the old school: people starting to learn their history. People don't really care where you're from as long as you represent what you've got, you know. I mean I don't really care if a rapper is black or white if he grabs the mike and he's got the skills I'm going to give him respect."

I want to argue then, on ethnographic grounds, against too ready a reduction of the "causes" of a local, Australian interest in "Hip Hop Culture" to an effect of class or race (or both). Here is a grab from a *Time (Australia)* color piece titled "Northern Exposure": "Paul . . . is a Greek-Australian who talks like an African-American . . . [who makes] black American music, in accents borrowed from the ghetto, in a brick veneer home in Melbourne's western suburbs" (Button and Lyall 1993: 52).[5] This is the standard media take on Hip Hop down under: ethnic, working-class kids borrow or imitate American culture. "McKenzie Wark . . . says rap first gained followers in Sydney 'among ethnic kids from the suburbs who identified with the outsider element'" (53). This is, however, only part of the story. For a start, one need not have been "ethnic" or "suburban" to have been interested in rap. There are, perhaps, other ways to be "other." My own research confirms the breadth of appeal of rap music, across various socioeconomic and ethnic (including "Anglo") fractions of the population of Sydney.

However, things are more complicated than even that, for this kind of discourse, accurate or not, circulates within the scene. Debates raged over the appropriateness of people from what were perceived as being middle-class backgrounds claiming Hip Hop authenticity, while those not from the "West Side" (see below) argued vehemently that socioeconomic status was irrelevant: that what counted was being "true" to the "ideals" of Hip Hop. This kind of assertion necessitated the finding, or the creation, of an "ideology" of Hip Hop that literally transcended race and class; take, for instance, Mick E's subsumption of ethnic determination to a more abstract discourse of "respect": it actually doesn't matter whether or not you are *black,* as long as you are "representing . . . what you have got," and do so with "skill."

At the same time, the figure of the funky black street dude loomed large. Invoking a discourse of desire that just barely masks a frank erotics, Mick explained that "all the little kids go for the American stuff straight away . . . they want to be black too." Why? "Because black has now been portrayed as cool, and you know, the beautiful body . . ." E.S.P. listed the black movie and sports stars who are role models, and Mick confessed that "I remember when I was young [laughs]. I was the same, when I was getting into it all, I was um, I'd wish that I was black because then I could rap."

The construction of the Western Suburbs as either analogous to the African-American ethnic ghetto, or, as Symonds (1994) and Powell (1994) argue, simply *as* an ethnic ghetto, has a particular significance for a discussion of the potential appeal of Hip Hop, allowing for a straightforward mapping onto the Sydney context of discourses of African-Americanness, and facilitating a "folk theory," particularly evident in popular print and electronic media readings, of the appeal of Hip Hop to Australian "kids" (as they are inevitably styled; see, for example, Guilliatt 1994, Gripper and Hornery 1996). This account understands Hip Hop's appeal in terms of its providing a subject position for otherwise marginal, unvoiced, ethnic minorities, and tends to effect precisely a mapping of ethnic otherness onto "the west": the demonized western suburbs of Sydney (see chapter 5).

And it is not only the "mainstream" press pushing this line: Miguel d'Souza's articles in *3-D World* stressed this angle as well. Miguel himself, as a second-generation Pakistani,[6] had a particular investment in a politics of color, and I do not want to deny for an instant that ethnicity was a significant feature of the Hip Hop Scene in Sydney; plenty of Lebanese, South American, and Pacific Islander (in particular) young men got into Hip Hop, performing raps in Arabic, in *Spanglish,* and so on.

Ethnic-based groups such as the infamous Sons of Samoa (s.o.s.) and the United Tongan Boys (u.t.b.) styled themselves as *homeboys,* listened to gangsta-rap, and tagged, but they were generally considered as being not appropriately "into" Hip Hop by those "in" the scene: their commitment was understood as being not to Hip Hop per se, but to their own ethnic loyalties. The Hip Hop Scene that I encountered took pains to distance itself from these *gangs,* claiming that *the media* was generally too ready to misread what were actually superficial "appearances," that the ethnic *gangs* were merely adopting the styles and bad-boy imagery of gangsta-rap without taking the trouble to understand the *culture* behind it. When I asked about these groups, it would be explained to me that they were at odds with the inclusionary ideology of Hip Hop and gave Hip Hop a bad name. It was also claimed that the media and the police alike seemed to have great difficulty in distinguishing the relatively trivial criminal transgressions of *crews* of "writers" from the big-league criminal activities of *gangs*.

There were as many, if not more, "Anglo-Australian" boys involved in the Hip Hop Scene I encountered. Importantly, it tended to be these individuals who would promote the subsuming discourse of an ethnicity-inclusive Hip Hop Nation as a model for Hip Hop communality. This inclusive model frequently broke down: a group of Islanders rang up Miguel at his radio show and, not realizing that he himself was a Pakistani-Australian warned him against playing hip hop because "it is a black [that is, *their*] thing," and Miguel himself would argue for the value of Hip Hop in encouraging otherwise unvoiced ethnic kids to follow the example of the similarly marginalized urban African-Americans and to articulate (express) themselves. Anglo-Australian Ser Reck assures me that "they'll tell you it's a black thing, man, but it isn't . . ." — fixing me with his gaze, index finger jabbing once, emphatically — ". . . it's *our* thing" (see Maxwell 2001).

Elsewhere, Miguel had argued that "records from African-American rappers are to the Hip Hop Community a documentation of . . . missing histories, and so it is through Hip Hop that the culture is obtaining its black history" (from Miguel's radio documentary "Hip Hop Culture in Sydney").[7] Miguel suggests that this "studied respect for African-American culture" has enabled "Australian Hip Hop fans" to "interpret their surroundings with the benefit of a black aesthetic." By way of an example, Miguel points out that "Def Wish Cast have in the past incorporated Koori [Aboriginal] words into their raps."

I saw two Aboriginal crews perform, both consisting solely of female members. The Aranta Desert Posse, from the Alice Springs area of Central Australia, performed at Sydney's Powerhouse Museum as part of an exhibition on the history of popular music in Australia. Three teenage girls, faces painted in "traditional style," walked onto the stage and performed a number of "traditional" dance moves and read poetry, before repairing to the back of the stage to change into checked shirts and beanies, translating themselves, somewhat awkwardly, into a video-clip-informed embodiment of the urban "Hip-hopper."

Closer to the imaginary of the ghetto, Black Justice lived in inner-city Redfern, one of the most concentrated centers of Aboriginal population in Sydney. Goie Wymarra and Paula Maling, who were politically active in their local area, rapped about the White Invasion of Australia and AIDS (see Browne 1992):

Taking our land our souls our beliefs
Rape, murder and all the white lies
Resulting in black genocide
Clear the land with whiteman tools
With the land the stars the moon and the sun
They should have left us alone
40,000 years of living in peace
And now 200 years that peace has ceased
Motherland no longer smiles
Vanished bushland around for miles

They told me of Public Enemy visiting "The Block," a ghetto precinct in Redfern; Chuck D spending hours with the black kids, giving away T-shirts and encouraging them to get political, while Flavor Flav sat in his limo and talked on his mobile phone. (In concert, P.E. had flown the Aboriginal flag from the stage). However, Black Justice had their tapes produced by a funk-dance musician, and were, Blaze explained to me, despite their adoption of black nationalist rhetoric and air-punching hard core performance embodiments, "not really *Hip Hop*."[8]

Rap music did appeal to Aboriginal youth; the manager of the only record shop in Redfern told me that rap records were popular with younger Kooris, but did not sell as well as country and western music! However, it is probably best not to overemphasize any relationship between Hip Hop and Aboriginal Australians purely in terms of a logic of the color of skin. Perhaps Miguel's assessment is to the point: the benefit of the experience of (African-American) blackness afforded through and by the encounter with Hip Hop was that of giving "white Australian youth an understanding of repression, isolation and blackness that they haven't been privy to" ("Hip Hop Culture in Sydney").

"Class" (loosely defined), then, and "ethnicity" *did* count; they did have tangible effect on the contested field of Hip Hop in Sydney. Moreover, these discourses often become entwined, race and class double-helically informing and contradicting each other as the protogenetic material generating the form that a "social" will take. And, indeed, the articulations of various subject positions within these ontologies are *used* as discursive weapons in the struggle for (sub)cultural capital within and across that field (as do, it must be noted, sex and age), informing a fluid, arcane subcultural algebra — could Miguel's blackness, for example, compensate for his middle-classness? However, although they do offer powerful figurations for the construction of communal identity and belongingness to a social imaginary, neither "class" nor "ethnicity" alone can offer either a determination in the final instance for the social phenomenon in question or a satisfactory account of the feeling of belongingness experienced by all those whom I encountered.

HIP HOP MEDIASCAPE

The other terrains within or across which Appadurai considers the flow of global cultural material are, he writes, two "closely related landscapes of images" (1990: 9). The mediascape, Appadurai writes, refers to both "the distribution of the electronic capabilities to produce and disseminate information (newspapers, magazines, television studios, and film production), which are now available to a growing number of private and public interests throughout the world, and to the images of the world created by these interests" (9). He continues: "What is most important about these mediascapes is that they provide (especially in their television, film and cassette forms) complex repertoires of images, narratives and ethnoscapes to viewers throughout the world in which the world of commodities and the world of news and politics are profoundly mixed" (9).

These images, Appadurai suggests, tend toward blurring the "realistic and the fictional" in proportion to the (presumably both spatial and temporal) distance, giving rise to imagined worlds that "constitute narratives of the Other and proto-narratives of possible lives" (1990: 9). The interplay between these territories is dense and almost inseparable. For now, however, I want to abstract from the mélange of imagery the term "mediascape" to isolate some, and hopefully most, of the textual, visual, and sonic sources that inform and surround — and provide recombinative material for — the social agents operating within the Hip Hop Scene.

■ Already we have seen that Hip Hop in Australia was constructed not through a continuity of experience or history with African-American Hip Hop Culture, but through the active engagement with various forms of media. The frequency with which "media" images recur in the insider accounts of the Hip Hop Scene, for example, has already been noted. From the ur-status accorded to the Malcolm McLaren "Buffalo Gals" film clip to the Monk's dismissal of those boys who copy b-boy fashions (and the embodiments appropriate to those styles) from "their TV shows" and "what they see in the magazines," it is clear that the most distinctive feature of these social agents' construction of the world within which they operate is its thoroughly *mediated* nature.

Now, Thornton notes the idea that authentic culture that is somehow born "outside media and commerce is a resilient one" (1996: 116). She continues: "In its full-blown romantic form, the belief suggests that grassroots cultures resist and struggle with a colonizing mass-mediated corporate world." Following Bourdieu, Thornton argues that "contrary to youth subcultural ideologies, "subcultures" do not germinate from a seed . . . only to be belatedly digested by the media. Rather, media and other culture industries are there from the start" (117). And while "[s]ubcultures often define themselves *against* the mass media," those same media "are *integral to* youth's social and ideological formations" (116, emphasis added). The Hip Hop Scene in Sydney had just such an ambivalent relationship with the media, both drawing on and rejecting it in its various forms. Perhaps the most consistent feature of the relationship of people in the Hip Hop Scene with the media, however, was that they understood themselves as competent navigators of the media, able to distinguish "the truth" from "hype." In the words of Ser Reck from Def Wish Cast: "A lot of it's all blown out of proportion with all the media . . . how can they [the public] learn the truth if they get fed lies, and with the media always wanting to, like — how can you say it? — [the media] always want to be on the main view thing, the view of bad things, you know? Bring it out, like all the bad violence, and people straight away are relating it to Hip Hop because they [Hip Hoppers] wear a baseball cap."

When I first met Blaze, he established in no uncertain terms his suspicions about my project: "I hate journalists . . . they always want a quick story" and don't take the time to "get the facts." His problem, he explained, was that journalists would never listen to what he wanted to say, wanting instead to treat him as a symptom, as a passive cipher for generalizations about youth culture, and so on. Never, he felt, did journalists treat him as an intelligent, thinking human being, or actually listen to what he had to say.

Thornton describes at length what she calls "the editorial search for subcultures" (1996: 151); fired by "sociologies of moral panic" (119; Stanley Cohen 1972/1980 is the seminal text in this field), youth culture makes for good copy. In Sydney, throughout the 1980s and 1990s, the print and electronic tabloid media and the broadsheets alike seemed to work on a biennial cycle; every twenty months or so, feature writers would be sent out to "investigate" and write frankly terrifying reports of the youth cultures of the mean streets. Powell, in her analysis of the media demonization of Sydney's Western Suburbs, describes this genre of reportage as "slummer journalism": self-styled "social explorers" braving the fringes of society in order to offer up the spectacle of the lower classes for the delectation of a bourgeois readership (1993: 18–35).

MORAL PANIC: HIP HOP IN THE NEWS

Two often-conflated themes have dominated media accounts of Hip Hop in Australia. The first concerns criminality, with particular reference to graffiti and "gangs." Reports of graffiti-related deaths (Cameron and Crouch 1990; Skelsey 1992; Papadopolous 1992; Uncredited 1992e), vandalism (Harvey 1990; Carthaigh 1992; Cameron 1993) and disruption (Uncredited 1991a; Olsen 1992) were tempered by reassuring reports of the efficacy of police response (Roberts 1992; Uncredited 1991a, 1991b, 1992a, 1992b, 1992f and 1993; Morris 1994). The second theme, generally presented as analytical or "investigative" journalism, affected a critical view of the "Americanisation" of local youth culture. Guilliatt's 1994 feature piece in the prestigious Saturday feature section of the *Sydney Morning Herald* particularly rankled with the Lounge Room crews, with whom he had spent a few days, in that they claimed he had completely misrepresented what Hip Hop *was* (see Maxwell 1994a). In a similar vein, a series of articles and editorials lamented the increasing popularity of American sports heroes. Jon Casimir (1994) noted that, as the headline of his article put it, "For the Jordan Generation, Footy Doesn't Make the Grade," while, over the summer of 1993–94, the editor of the *Sydney Morning Herald* regretted that cricket, the "national sport," was in danger of becoming "just another sport"; and a sportswriter suggested that American basketballers enjoyed a higher local profile than test cricketers (Derriman 1994).

Both these strands of journalism characteristically presented apocalyptic visions of Sydney sinking toward a future state of terror, characteristically emblematized by images of contemporary Los Angeles (Uncredited 1992d). A series of pieces in the Sydney *Daily Telegraph Mirror* in

November 1994 were based on a report on youth gangs, commissioned by the New South Wales Police. Prepared by a company named Pulse Consultants, and subsequently leaked to the press, the report itself played down the significance of the alleged gangs, suggesting that there was no reason to believe that the American urban experience of gangs was being reproduced in Sydney's suburbs (see Godbee 1994). Among the consultant's conclusions was a warning that one of the surest ways to precipitate a "gang problem" would be to allow the media to "beat up" the story.[9] In November 1994, the *Telegraph Mirror* ran a front-page article titled "City Street Gangs Crisis" (McDougall 1994a: 1). Two pages into the paper, a double-page spread headed "Special Investigation" was accompanied by a list of alleged gangs, more than half of which were annotated "not active" or "degree of activity unknown," framed by a graphic consisting of knuckle dusters and flick knifes.

Deeper in the newspaper, near the editorial and comment pages, was another piece, illustrated by a photograph of a gang. The caption read: "Sydney's swelling street gangs are reminiscent of those depicted in the film Colors, in which the 21st Street Gang (above) roamed LA, terrorising anyone and anything in their path" (McDougall 1994b: 11). This caption alone offers several levels of "reification" (Keil 1994: 227). First, "Sydney's swelling street gangs" are presented as *fact*, the tumescent imagery of the seductively alliterated process verb ("swelling") removing from this statement (that is, that Sydney street gangs *are*) any possibility of questionability. Second, "reminiscence" ties this "real" phenomenon to a "real" movie. Third, the use of the process "depicted" positions the reader within an economy of representation by which the fictional world of the movie is predicated to, and actually retrieving, a reality that precedes it. The final clause closes the circuit, ambiguously referencing both the filmic, "fictional" gang and the real L.A. gangs that that gang "depicts." Fiction (the movie gang) and "reality" ("Sydney's swelling street gangs") become entwined in a seductively logical inevitability: there are gangs in Sydney; they will remind you of those you saw in *Colors;* that film (accurately) depicted/reproduced/represented what happens in L.A.: viz., "terrorising anyone and anything in their path." A virtually identical article, also subtitled "Special Investigation," appeared in the *Sunday Telegraph* in 1990, describing graffiti gangs "copied from the cult . . . made famous by the film *Colors*" (McEvoy 1990) and the members of these "color gangs" as being "devoted to American rap music." Rap music, in such analyses, is read as being simultaneously symptomatic and causative of these processes of cultural contamination.[10]

A further set of articles attempted to cast more favorable light on Hip Hop. In 1992, the *Sydney Morning Herald* started to print a regular Hip Hop CD review feature, as well as pre- and reviewing concerts by visiting rap/Hip Hop acts (Casimir 1992; 1993a, 1993b; Danielson 1992). Other stories attempted to understand graffiti as an "artform" ("Vandals Learn Art on Govt Grant" rang Monaghan's 1988 banner; see also Mostyn 1991; Cochrane 1991; Danielson 1991; de Vine 1991; Best 1991; Visontay 1991; Ingram 1992; Wingett 1992; Pearce 1993; Christie 1994).

The electronic media offered tabloid journalism aplenty, with current affairs programs presenting alarmist images of allegedly burgeoning street crime. When presented with statistical evidence to the contrary, such reports were still able to point to what was claimed to be a growing "perception" of terror, of a "lack of safety" (see Castleman 1982: 176–77), perceptions fueled by the credulous interviews conducted with visiting rappers on prime-time television (see Maxwell and Bambrick 1994: 3).

THE COMMODIFICATION OF HIP HOP

Beyond the moral panic genre of current affairs shock journalism, the electronic media also produced images of rap music both in television drama and in advertising. An episode of a locally produced series thematizing racial tensions and teenage angst in a "typical," multicultural secondary school, *Heartbreak High,* concerned a female character, a newcomer and outsider to the core cast, who raps. An opening shot shows her, accompanied by a beat box, rhyming attitude-drenched verses in an American accent, about the various injustices to which high school kids are subject. Chorusing "the school is on *fi*-er" to an appreciative crowd of students, who punch the air and shout their approval, the rapper is silenced by an approaching teacher, striding across the playground to disperse this potentially . . . (dangerous? un-Australian? inauthentic?) gathering. Sullen faced, muttering, the kids disperse in a sea of baseball caps and high-fives, and there always seems to be either a Vietnamese or a Polynesian face in the shot immediately behind the protagonists. "Rap" is immediately constructed as being subversive, counterhegemonic, dangerous, and somehow intuitively appealing to the young, susceptible audience. Urgent staff meetings are convened; conservative teachers warn against the insidious power of rap to twist young minds, while younger, more liberal staff members defend the right of the girl in question to express herself. The argument is rendered moot, however, when suddenly graffiti appears all over the school, vandalism increases, and the student body takes on an aggressive, anti-authoritarian mood. In the best tradition of hour-long series dramas, by the end of the episode, "sense" prevails: the headmaster, revealed to have been an "angry young man" activist in the 1960s, is adjured to allow this group of students the right to their own "rebellion"; here is the narrative of the generational return of rebellious youth. Rap is allowed, and the closing credits roll over a sequence in which the groovy young teachers and hoary old conservatives alike rock their heads to the (substantially mellowed out) flow of the male lead(!), as the female protagonist sings(!) the chorus ("Ho ho, hey hey, it's Valentine's Day") behind him.

This episode (screened in late 1993) rehearses several of the then-current popular discourses about "rap": its insidious, "underground" quality; its association with (an idea about) "American" cultural imperialism, a discourse that could only account for any local (Australian) manifestation of rap as being inauthentic or, at best, derivative; a narrative of the ineluctable slide into criminality; and so on. Characters sympathetic to the young female rapper couch their defenses in terms of the by-now familiar discourses of the right to self-expression ("Express Yourself"), and even that of the appropriateness of youth rebelliousness.

Ser Reck laughed about this episode. He told me that he and the boys had got together to watch it and couldn't believe how *wack* it was. Its "surface" approach bore, he claimed, no relation to the Culture as he understood and practiced it. It affirmed, for them, the failure of the "mainstream" to understand Hip Hop.

Not that such a response should surprise. One can hardly expect someone who has invested so much to a "culture" to concede that a television drama has captured that culture in all its supposed "truth." A lifetime's commitment, I was told, was deserving of more respect: I have already shown how the ideas of "paying dues," of continuity of commitment, and of dedication figure in the construction of Hip Hop. Such ideas demand a degree of reserve, implying a kind of *mystery,* rites of passage that require sustained *practice* (as I shall suggest below) and *experience* as criteria for understanding. It is into this quasi-mystical realm that committed Hip Hoppers have recourse in attempting to explain why representations of rap such as the one in question have no credibility. The important thing about these representations of "rap" in the popular mediascape is that they are interpreted by those aspiring to Hip Hop Culture as *misinterpretations:* they stand as "what we are *not,*" constituting a negative image that, in practice, obviates the necessity of positing, let alone defining, a positive image of what we *are.* "Hip Hop" can only be "understood" through an experience of commitment and practice; it cannot ever even hope to be represented by people who have not had those experiences, who have not *practiced* and, by extension, *demonstrated* their commitment.

Television advertising also created images of something that looked a bit like "Hip Hop Culture," images once again received with scorn by the insiders. Throughout the mid-1990s, more and more advertisers, from Coca Cola and the Australian National Basketball League to the Roads and Traffic Authority (producing road-safety material), used rap music and rapped vocals to sell their products and messages.

Mobilizing rap music to market soft drinks to a demographic is the inevitable result of the general extension of rap into the mainstream of popular music. This popularization of rapping as a mode of vocal delivery created particular problems for those wishing to claim a Hip Hop particularity. I will discuss this later in the section concerned with the notion of "hard core," that label constituting a shifting, unfixed aesthetic category, or, perhaps, genre, with which insiders could negotiate musical texts, strategically including or excluding them from the Hip Hop canon. The point here, however, is that the enrollment of Hip Hop to advertising was viewed less than favorably, although the criticism leveled at particular advertisements often circulated less around concerns with the politics of commodification than with the failure of the advertisers involved to engage "real" rhymers for the jobs.

At the same time that the episode of *Heartbreak High* described above went on the air, a prominent burger chain screened an advertisement in which a denim-clad boy is seen busking to an appreciative audience, a happy cross-section of middle Australia. Rolling his head, pursing his lips and screwing up his face, his trembling fingers (those vibrato-signifiers of "heartfeltedness") wring a heart-felt blues from his guitar. All of a sudden, this wholesome enjoyment of the fresh-faced young man ("He's *cute,*" whispers a nine-year-old to her friend) alone with his guitar, strumming authentically, is shattered by the arrival of an angry-looking teenage boy, baggy-clothed, crop-haired, baseball-capped, and bearing a beat-box. The first shot of this interloper is of spastically splayed feet in oversized boots; his whole embodiment is coded as aberrant, as dysfunctional. Stabbing the play button of his ghetto blaster, this figure starts to execute a series of distorted, pseudo-break moves, shadow-boxing and leering at a pair of elderly ladies to an in-your-face techno beat. He moves jerkily, slack-jawed, overtly hostile. The crowd shrinks away, the soundtrack fills with their sharp intakes of breath and expressions of horror.

Outgunned, out-amplified, his crowd driven away by the interloper, the young hero is all set to pack up, strumming a final electric *ssstrkkkk* that ends up in a hammily exasperated shrug . . . Whereupon, out of the crowd steps a nice-looking man, who, opening up his own guitar case, straps on his axe, and, flashing a winning smile, with a flourish strums off a catchy acoustic chord. The young boy's face lights up, and, to the sighed approval of the crowd, the pair of them improvise a virtuoso duet, utterly blowing away the b-boy wannabe, who skulks off, no doubt to wreak his sociopathic mischief elsewhere.

But it doesn't end there. The pay-off comes later, when the young boy and his guitarist friend, walking off after their successful defense of musical probity ("Nice doin' business with you," the older dude offers), encounter the breaker-boy, and, in a gesture of open-hearted reconciliation, extend to him an invitation: differences aside, all three are last seen walking into a McDonald's family restaurant (see Maxwell 1994b).

THE MASS MEDIA AS REPERTOIRE OF IMAGES

Def Wish Cast's *Knights of the Underground Table,* as its title suggests, uses the Arthurian legend as an extended trope, a metaphor mixed with the popular construction of Australia as the (geographical) "down-under." The album's cover illustration shows the four members of the crew, photographed from ground level, framed by a sandstone arch (signifying "old," possibly even "ancient"). All four are scowling, striking tough b-boy poses, legs apart, wearing beanies, shell-tops, and runners. They bear a selection of weaponry: shields, swords, a battleaxe (borrowed, I read inside, from the "Nepean Ancient and Medieval Re-enactment Society"). The Arthurian "text" that is drawn on throughout the album's lyrical, sonic, and visual imagery is not however, the literary imagery drawn from, perhaps, *The Sword in the Stone,* but that of the 1983 Holly-

wood movie *Excalibur*. One rap in particular is explicitly gleaned from the
screenplay of the film: a passage in which the sword Excalibur is embedded in a stone by the dying king, caught in an ambush. It is Def Wish's *a
capella* rap "X-Crin":

> Back in the Dark Ages there was a king ambushed,
> Holder of the X-Crin, — a golden mic with power to deliver
> Fast aggressive lyrics that murder
> This king, dying, took the X-Crin — threw it in a stone
> In which it was embedded in
> For hundreds of years, no one could free it.
> Alone, I stumbled upon it, released it from the stone.
> Knights gathered around, — no-one saw me do it.
> So I put it back. Yeah I knew it!
> — Up stepped a half-stepper knight, he shoved me
> Aside, tried, X-Crin didn't budge.
> People cried out "let the boy try." The noise
> Died. — Silence as I took my grip, I prayed.
> Some sneered laughed in dismay.
> Eyes wide, the golden mic gave way, — pulled it from
> The rock, set on my way to unite the land
> And be a part of the underground table and the Saga. (Def Wish 1993)

Def Wish's ontogenetic narrative doesn't really need any explication. It
parallels exactly the scene in the film. The "fit" of the Arthurian story, the
applicability of the Arthurian world of that film to the Hip Hop (self-
styled) demimonde, derives from the discourses of battling and dueling
that are part of the common Hip Hop cultural history of practices such as
break-dancing and rapping, a combative discourse extended to the ongoing war with authority: the graffiti police. Other tracks on *Knights of the
Underground Table* include "Battlegrounds of Sydney," "Perennial Cross
Swords," and the extended "posse" track "Saga." Short linking tracks include sampled grabs from the movie *Excalibur*: swelling orchestral scores,
signifying chivalry and honor; the clashing of swords, galloping hoofs. I
should note that there is certainly a playfulness at work here: a familiarity with other "Arthurian" films, particularly Monty Python's *Holy Grail* is
apparent. The playfulness is, however, tempered by a seriousness of intent: Ser Reck is simply not kidding when he talks about battling with the
transit police, about his own "perennial" battle with them.

Other film genres are sampled throughout the album, including schlock-horror films such as those of the *Halloween, Friday the Thirteenth,* and *Nightmare on Elm Street* cycles. The opening rap on the album is a three-part meditation on the relationship of sleep and dreaming with poetic creation: a kind of post- or neo-romanticism in which each of the Cast's three rappers takes a verse to explicate his own theorization of the artistic process. For Ser Reck, sleep is a "Dream chamber," in which he is "my own author." His girlfriend wakes him, telling him that "ya rappin in ya sleep," whereupon, in the morning, he raps the "lyrics I wrote the night before / During the night I had my memory on store." The potential threat that this discourse presents to the Hip Hop discourse of self-expression is resolved in the final line of the rap: "my skull as my barricade." Wherever these lyrics come from, they are still *his.* Die C's verse constitutes the dream as a territory, a realm through which he, identity intact, fully self-aware, travels: "cross a bridge to a warzone . . ." He wakes, "sweating," confused; "back to reality where I'm lost . . . was that reality?," to "rewind back what I recorded on my deck." He reassures himself by feeling that his "bones are still in tact [*sic*]." Finally, Def Wish deploys a physiological trope: his brain is "infected, diseased with rhyming words."

When asked, none of the boyz was familiar with Coleridge, Shelley, or Blake. The source text here is, in fact, *Nightmare on Elm Street,* in which teenagers' dreams and "reality" merge and become indistinguishable: the quoted "to sleep, perchance to dream . . ." that introduces the track is less Shakespeare than schlock-horror.

The album was recorded and mixed in a garage studio in Penrith. The producer, Dave Laing, who also distributed the album through his company Random Records, explained to me that most of the samples were taken directly from video tapes borrowed from the local video store: the relatively poor quality of production on the CD is a direct consequence of this. The image, however, of teenage boys in the Far Western Suburbs, consuming "mass culture," navigating their way through it, cutting it and pasting it to produce their own texts, is a compelling, exciting one.

In early 1994, Def Wish told me that the next Def Wish Cast album was going to have "an intergalactic theme," based on George Lucas's *Star Wars* films. For various reasons, the album was not made, although writing was well under way (I never heard any of these galactic raps in subsequent Def Wish Cast performances, either). I asked Def Wish whether there was any particular reason for choosing that theme. "Nah, not really

. . . we just thought that it would be cool." After the success of the first album, it seems, Def Wish Cast had been alerted to the possibilities of using genres or themes inventively and creatively, without needing to look
for specific thematic iconicities or indices.

MEDIA AS PEDAGOGY

A subset of mass media images, including social-realist films and documentaries, pertained directly to Hip Hop and to African-American urban
culture. Video copies of a couple of documentaries that screened during
the period of my research were keenly watched, circulated, and discussed.
These included "Melvyn Bragg's Southbank Show: Lenny Henry Hunts
the Funk,"[11] screened in October 1992, the 1986 BBC series *The Story of
English*, one episode of which was titled "Black on White," and which was
repeat screened in Australia, in 1994.

Key films were avidly watched, studied, consumed, and digested (and
I use the metaphorics of incorporation advisedly), often repeatedly.
These ranged from the documentary and *cinéma verité*-style records of
the New York Hip Hop Scene of the late 1970s and early 1980s (such as
Wild Style [1982] and *Style Wars* [1983]; see Fernando 1994: 18), through
the Hollywood take on the new dance styles (*Flashdance* [1983], *Break-
dance* [1984], and *Beat Street* [1984]; see Toop 1991: 134), Dennis Hopper's rap-sound-tracked *Colors* [1988], to the John Singleton and Spike
Lee features of the late 1980s and early 1990s. Such films provided kinetic elaboration of the rapped and written accounts of "hoods" and "the
streets." The early breaking movies provided, as I suggested above, "ideological" constructs about "Hip Hop Culture" and kinetic material; recall
Blaze with the aid of a home VCR freeze-framing breaking moves and
practicing them at home.

The later Lee/Singleton movies provided contextual material: images
of streets, neighborhoods, more embodiments, more *habituses*. Sometimes these films produced jarring disjunctions: surprise was regularly
expressed, for example, at the "suburban" feel of the L.A. streetscapes of
Singleton's *Boyz N the Hood* (1991) and the Hughes Brothers' *Menace II
Society* (1994); the imaginary Los Angeles, gleaned from the gangsta-raps
of NWA, Ice T, and other L.A. crews, appeared to take the form of the
dense, tenement-style brown tones and projects, familiar from media

representations of New York. "When I got there [Los Angeles]," one writer told me after a trip to California, "it was just like the western suburbs [of Sydney]."

The visual-kinetic texts with perhaps the most important impact on the local Hip Hop Scene were, of course, video clips. People would collect tape after tape of rap videos, recorded from late-night weekend music video shows screened either by the national broadcaster (the ABC) or on free-to-air stations.[12] Music videos were also programmed for the early weekend youth audience, although these basically consisted of Top 40–type material: only the R'n'B end of rap, becoming popular by the early-mid 1990s, made the cut.

The significant feature of many rap video clips was, of course, the construction of a street realism. Rose writes of the specific "style and genre conventions" of "rap video" (1994b: 9), centered on "rap's primary thematic concerns: identity and location" (10). This emphasis on "posses and neighborhoods has brought the ghetto back into the public consciousness" (11), the locations that figure, Rose argues, as the "lurid backdrops for street crimes on the [U.S.] nightly news" (scenes that also appeared, when lurid enough, on the Australian nightly news) (11). Rose goes on to problematize this ghetto thematic: "ghetto" becomes a symbolic marker for "authenticity," and therefore a sign deployed by any crew, regardless of their own "location," wishing to establish their authenticity.

And so, when Sound Unlimited came to produce videos for its own releases, the crew headed off to Sydney's red-light district, to be shot cruising past strip joints, drunks, prostitutes, the usual freak show of underclass lowlife (and at the same time, New Zealand's Lower Hutt Posse were strutting down Auckland's equivalent, K Road, high-fiving and hanging out). Here is Tom Horton, director of one of these videos: "We had gang scenes where gang members were walking down alleyways, with hoods, real street dudes. Which people don't think exist in Australia, but they [Sound Unlimited] just made a few calls and we had a hundred hoods hanging out in a corner block in Newtown. It was a fantastic" (Maxwell and Bambrick 1994: 15). Even the director takes representation for reality, apparently: the members of Sound Unlimited call up their friends to make a (generic) rap video clip, friends who certainly are able to embody (generically) "hood," and the director (mis-?)takes them for "hoods, real street dudes."[13]

HIP HOP RECORDINGS

Hip Hop releases from North America became available through specialist and import record shops in the early 1980s, generally in response to a demand created by "alternative" radio broadcasts on radio stations such as the Australian Broadcasting Corporation's "youth network," 2 JJJ. Key record shops are often remembered as the place where crews first coalesced, and began to hang out, as private listening habits found kindred spirits, riffling through the import shelves, gleaning narratives and glossaries from the cover notes of Rock Steady Crew and Run DMC albums.

Sales increased, and North American acts toured to Australia throughout the period from 1984 to 1996 (Run DMC in the mid-1980s, Public Enemy toward the end of the decade and again in the early 1990s, before the onslaught of acts throughout the mid-1990s — Ice Cube, Shaq, Naughty by Nature, Cypress Hill, the Beastie Boys, Coolio, Arrested Development, and so on). Each of these tours and album releases was accompanied by a rash of publicity and interviews. Crews such as Sound Unlimited were able to meet, do support gigs for, and spend time in the studio with Public Enemy and Run DMC, accruing to that group a certain status and access to subcultural capital, as well as the opportunity to learn and develop certain performance and recording skills (for Sound Unlimited, leading directly to a contract with Public Enemy's recording company).

The accounts of the "origins" of Hip Hop gleaned from these sources, and the recognition of the generic articulation of these origins both in the recordings and on the packaging surrounding the recordings, are of commensurate importance: these materials were at once sources of information and models for the production of local accounts. These recordings, collected as fetishized vinyl in hundreds of bedrooms, rerecorded onto compilation cassettes of favorite tracks, to be played at parties, on a car tape deck, in a Walkman. The raps of LL Cool J, Public Enemy, Ice T, even the old-school raps of Grandmaster Flash and the Furious Five, constitute the oral history of the putative Hip Hop Culture; a postindustrial, mass-mediated, but, nonetheless, profoundly pre-(or perhaps counter-)literate mode of pedagogy.

In addition to, and often prior to, this level of historico-oral pedagogy, local rappers and DJs learned and honed their "skills" listening to these records. "Skills" and "listening" are here, importantly, modes of embodiment: to listen is, in this milieu, to move; skills are techniques, practices, performances. Without the cultural context of street parties, or the "street" milieu of inner-urban America, with its historical emphasis on oral exchange (see, for example, Abrahams 1970, 1976, 1992; Abrahams and Szwed 1983; Gates 1988; Leary 1990), the site of the learning of these embodiments in the local, Australian context was the suburban family home, and specifically the privacy of a bedroom (Thornton 1996: 14–25). Surrounded by images of (black) men, with a set of headphones, or perhaps a cranked-up CD player and speakers shaking the walls of the bedroom (you can hear now the parents pounding the door and shouting: "Keep it down!"), the proto-rapper would rap along (I've done this myself), learning how to control his (or her) breathing, how to stretch his oral apparatus around the sounds and syllables (try it: harder than you expect), and *how to move.* Thornton writes of youth "carv[ing] out virtual, and claiming actual, space . . . by *filling* it with *their* music" (1996: 19, italics in original), but it is more than just this: the bedroom was a rehearsal space, in which the strange new embodiments could be tried out, where the young fan might (perhaps with the help of a blunt or two), experiment, move, *embody;* they laugh about using hairbrushes as microphones, about copying gestures and movements, striking poses.[14] And as I will suggest below, it is this embodiment, long after the work of embodying itself has been forgotten, that "feels" simply *real.*

DJs collected vinyl, spending hour after hour *cutting, scratching,* moving, *flexing* their *skills,* all metaphors of embodied practice. DJs talk of "manual" or "turntable dexterity"; the flipping, slicing, flicking motions of the DJ are echoed in the movements of the rappers, flexing (the same word is used in this context) their verbal skills, their "syllable ballistics."

And when the crews come together to write, to party, to break, the same tunes pervade their bodies, setting up a shared *habitus.* And when a favorite rap is played, a dozen voices will rap along, bodies ducking and weaving, trying out moves, mirroring each other, informing each other as the mimetic moment, structured around these musical texts from another place, another time, another set of experiences, is superseded, or develops into a local, embodied practice.

And, of course, the model of the rap as oral history (or as urban reportage) generated local counterparts. In local raps, various materials from the mediascape come into dialogic play with each other, constituting a key feature of the mediascape itself. Producers sampled particular sounds or dialogue from rented videos or a B-grade horror movie, a rhythm track from a favorite old school record, and a rap drawing stylistically on the latest West Coast freestyles, with lyrics referencing whatever television series was currently enjoying "cult" status within the scene. Entering circulation, such a recording might assume status as a "style," perhaps a genre, thereby figuring subsequent releases, and perhaps privileging a certain account of the scene, and elevating certain figures (from the scene) who might be referred to in the raps themselves or receiving "shout-outs" or "props" in the liner notes.

Among a clutch of recordings, two local releases stood out during my period of research: Sound Unlimited's *A Postcard from the Edge of the Underside* (1992) and Def Wish Cast's *Knights of the Underground Table* (1993).[15] The CD/album *A Postcard from the Edge of the Underside* was hailed as a breakthrough (not least by Sound Unlimited's own publicity): the first signing to a major label of a local Hip Hop act (see Maxwell and Bambrick 1994). Slickly engineered, and aggressively marketed and distributed, the Sound Unlimited album contrasts with the low-tech, handmade, self-distributed Def Wish Cast product. Both crews, from Sydney's Western Suburbs (see below), take pains to assert their "authenticity," both in their lyrics and in their discourses about themselves. I want to read an example from each album, in which the crews narrate their engagement with the developing Hip Hop Scene, locating themselves within that development. These verses constitute a kind of oral history, contributing to (an often-contested) folkloric, historical microknowledge of that scene.[16]

Sound Unlimited's track "Tales from the West Side," for example, is basically a claim that "we were there at the beginning"; three raps delivered in the distinctively American-sounding voices of the MCs Rosano and Kode Blue:

Let me tell ya now about the West Side
I'm talkin about comin up on the West Side of the eastcoast
No need to brag or boast
As some feel the need to state in every second sucker song
West Side was a force so strong . . .
Hardcore no longer for the mindless
Set out the lyrics with meaning and define this history
You see some neglected but cannot cover the truth
No matter how protected West Side was in 87 on the record
But further back in '83 who rocked the party?[17]

Little explication or comment is needed here. A quasi-mythologizing refrain follows: "These are the tales the tales of the West Side," delivered in a deep, rumbling sampled voice, to which an antiphonal chant responds: "Go West Side go West Side." As to who "rocked the party," way back in '83 . . . well, after the chorus, across the breakbeat, crew members Kode Blue and Rosano, not rapping, but in "street" voice, enjoy this exchange:

> Rosano: Yo Blue remember back in the dayz we had a supreme style
> man we were out there . . .
> Kode Blue: Yeah West Side Posse was definitely the crew . . .
> Rosano: That was it, man . . .

The final rapped verse elaborates the history:

> Let's get back
> I'll start at Burwood Park
> Hip Hop breakin' after dark
> Many crews would join the fray
> Travel from east to west upon the train
> Some to break some just to inflict pain
> You had to be down you had to use your brain aim
> Aim to watch or aim to lose
> Aim to perform or aim to bruise
> Some had no choice
> Some could choose
> Me I was a breaker in the UBT [United Break Team] crew
> Those that were there you know who you are
> A tale from the West Side from one who remembers

Elsewhere on the album, the familiar themes appear: calls to unity, appeals to "knowledge," accrued through having "paid the dues back in the days." The historiographical theme of these raps and of the album itself was developed in the publicity material prepared by the members of the crew and distributed free in pubs, clubs, and venues throughout Sydney.

Def Wish Cast's raps emphasize the importance of "commitment," constructing a narrative of a glorious past, fondly remembered and romanticized. Die C raps on "Perennial Cross Swords": "Many just tried it once, jumping on the bandwagon," advocating the wearing of "shell top Adidas and Puma Clydes," items of "authentic" b-boy wear that "will never go out of style." Reflecting on the heady days since passed, he continues:

We stare at brick walls and parked cars smothered with broken
   down art
Only flakes of old days remain, where the heart prevailed
Unity eroded and found the Hip Hop scene in Sydney
A part of a battleground
Zonal wars, writers rebelled
Breakin was just a dying craze to the majority, but a minority survive

Ending on a positive note, the rap echoes the upbeat "tomorrow belongs
to us" theme of the rest of the album: "The unstoppable scene that's
growing stronger and flourishing."

Def Wish Cast's publicity material, distributed by their manager during the period following the release of the album, similarly stresses the
right of the members of the crew to claim Hip Hop authenticity, premised
on continuity of involvement in and, by extension, commitment to the
scene. The biographical notes included in the publicity material were
written by the four members of the crew themselves. Eponymous rapper
Def Wish (age twenty) notes his own "dedication to Hip Hop in the last
ten years [which] is still proven by his involvement in break-dancing and
graffiti writing" (Xiberras 1994); Die C's "involvement of eight years" included "joining forces with Def Wish four years ago [that is, at age six-
teen], still under the name of Def Wish Posse. They started a small but
very strong following around the west of Sydney" (Xiberras 1994). Four
years older than the other two, Ser Reck also takes care to state his "ten
years dedication" to Hip Hop.

These self-narrativizations (of both Def Wish Cast and Sound Unlimited) were important moves in the game of accruing (sub)cultural capital. These stories of origin, of commitment, and of authority ("we were
there") circulate in and around the Hip Hop Scene, constituting a narrative orthodoxy into which neophytes are introduced and, to no small extent, inculcated. That such narratives are recorded (in the case of the
raps), sold, and printed on lyric sheets accords them a quasi-documentary
status: it is in this respect that they can be said to constitute a significant
part of the local Hip Hop mediascape.

The CD insert cards, in addition to supplying lyric sheets, offer an
opportunity to "shout out" to the rest of the Hip Hop Community. The
shout-outs on Def Wish Cast's album run to over two hundred names. In
addition to other crews (Intense Quality, Finger Lickin Good, Mamma

Funk, the Noble Savages, Home Brewd, 046, Capital Punishment, the Brethren Inc, Sound Unlimited, Voodoo Flavour, Fonkke Nomads, Urban Poets), writers (Reskew, Frenzy, Atome, Scram, Kade), and "to all the true Melbourne, Adelaide and Sydney crews for their support and staying true to the real Hip Hop Culture cause we all know that the breaking writing and rappin wont die, hardcore is something more than just wearing the freshest clothes and owning one hardcore tape and the rest, well you know, its something thats in your blood, you live and breath it, cause blood is thicker than water . . ." Then: "I must give a huge shout-out to the west of Sydney for it's constant support, cause soon the west will rise. To all the non-believers, doubters and straight-up suckers who did'nt [sic] think that 4 youths from out west had the heart and ability to put out this album and rock crowds around Australia, well this ain't for you. It's for and from the west." The triumph of commitment over adversity, of the outsiders (the west), *representing.* The notes conclude: "If there is anyone we forgot, it's only because there is so many to remember." This last sentiment was frequently voiced over the air during Miguel's weekly Hip Hop broadcast (see chapter 2), as guests ran through their "shout-outs," taking care not to slight anyone by omitting them (or, of course, deliberately doing so).

Sound Unlimited's album, in addition to individual acknowledgments to parents and families, includes a triple-column page, "send[ing] the mighty props to da following . . ." This list extends beyond the "community" to which Def Wish Cast's shout-outs were explicitly addressed; as well as covering breaking and bombing crews, Blaze and *Vapors,* rapping outfits such as Def Wish Cast and 046, Sound Unlimited locates itself within the global Hip Hop genealogy: amidst all the local names we find Afrika Bambaataa and Public Enemy (with whom su had recorded and performed in Australia). Further, the shout-outs go to a host of local artists such as Midnight Oil, the Allniters, Dig and Swoop. Sound Unlimited, clearly, was working the "big end" of the music biz: Def Wish Cast, for example, spoke only disparagingly of the "pub rock" scene from which bands like the Oils came; Dig and Swoop were funk-oriented outfits making hay out of the mid-1990s "acid jazz" craze. Dig featured a rapper whose rhyming efforts were considered risible by "true" hip hoppers.

046's 1995 album *L.I.F.E.* was produced and distributed by Dope Runner Records. Dope Runner was set up by Shane Duggan (DJ Vame) after his departure from Def Wish Cast and was financed by a number of "sponsors," including a local (Campbelltown) pharmacy and newsagent, acknowledged in the inset notes. Shout-outs go to the same collection of Western Sydney crews, with an appeal to "end the bullshit fights [and] wake up and unite." The familiar formulae are here: "A super huge peace out to the true followers of hip hop, the real people that are never scared to express themselves to the fullest," "picture this if we change the way we think, we could even change the world." The most striking feature of the album notes, however, is a number of memoria to "the Graf artists who died for our culture, Mase, Rasem, Dizmel . . ." Throwing up RIPs or full pieces marking the death of a writer is a long-standing practice among graffitists. Here, 046 extend this respect to late family members and another friend "killed outside a Campbelltown nightclub." One track is in fact titled "R.I.P." The rest of the shout-outs are prefaced by thanks offered to "the All Mighty Lord for giving us the strength an[d] power to be the people we are today," echoing the almost de rigueur expressions of (often Islamicist, or, less frequently, post-Baptist) faith found on North American Hip Hop releases from Public Enemy through to Arrested Development. The effect overall was to emphasize the *seriousness* of the crew's commitments: Hip Hop has martyrs, tragedies, deals with the big questions of faith and death.

HIP HOP MEDIA: INTERNATIONAL

The *Source,* subtitled "the Magazine of Hip-Hop Music, Culture and Politics," published monthly from New York, reached local (Australian) newsstands and record shops a couple of weeks later. Along with the London-based *Hip Hop Connection,* the *Source* contained reviews, interviews, letters, feature articles often concerned with political issues and Hip Hop history, fashion and music advertising, and editorial writing that emphatically reinforced the understanding of Hip Hop as Culture, Community, and Nation. Both magazines were read widely by the local Hip Hop Community, enjoying a high "pass-along" rate.[18] I often saw both publications being read, or at least skimmed through, collectively; a reading practice through which "meaning" and "values" are negotiated and consensuses arrived at. Advertisements for new album releases, for example, might provoke discussions about the rappers' past releases, their skills, an assessment of their styling, and so on. The importance of this collective reading practice and its impact on determining consensual interpretations cannot be overstressed. The Lounge Room, for example, kept back copies for browsing, and many people have collections totaling dozens of issues.

These publications became important sources of subcultural capital: the latest news, the latest gossip (which rappers were in jail, who was producing whom, and so on), critical argot, and street slang. Subcultural capital accrues in terms of a logic of scarcity: getting hold of the most recent edition of the *Source* early in itself marked one as an authority of sorts (at least for a while); a subscription was highly desirable. Advertisements provided important information about the most recent fashions and, even more importantly, how to wear them: how to embody the "attitude" of Hip Hop (or, once again, at least the latest version of it).

I do not want to dwell on the content of these publications in any detail, other than to stress the ubiquity of each, and their major role in the dissemination of Hip Hop history and current trends. The reviewing and writing styles, particularly those of the *Source* informed those of the local (Australian) publications, to which I will turn below.

THE AUSTRALIAN HIP HOP PRESS

"Perennial Cross Swords," on Def Wish Cast's *Knights of the Underground Table,* details the exploits of graffiti writers in the "battlegrounds" of Western Sydney, in which the writers are pitted against the *transits:* that special arm of the law officially known as the "Graffiti Task Force."

The rap itself is preceded by a dramatic sonic composition, in which two writers working on a piece (the distinctive rattle and spray of the aerosol cans is preeminent in the soundscape) are disturbed by a train. They urgently try to finish off the piece as the rumble of carriages drowns out their exchange of terse instructions ("it's too dark . . . fresh, man . . . I just want to finish it and get out of here"). As if the intrusion of the train isn't enough, just as the noise dies away, one of the writers shouts, "fuck, transits: run!": the graffiti police have arrived. It is too much for the other writer (it is Ser Reck's voice), who has been pushed too far: "Stuff this . . . I wanna duel . . . c'mon . . . let's get it *on!*" In keeping with the combative discourses of Hip Hop, and in the immediate discursive context of the Arthurian thematics of the album, a metal-on-metal sword duel follows (sampled from *Excalibur*), complete with orchestral backing and grunts. After fourteen seconds of furious combat, the writer is victorious, and (you can almost see it), breathless and faint, leaning on his sword, he announces that "it's the end."

The mix returns from this noisy, mythological ur-scene to the sonic purity of the studio present, and Ser Reck offers his analysis of the confrontation: "We won the battle 'cause we have the underground network that's controlling the world with graff mags such as *Vapors, Bits and Pieces, Zest, Full Effect, Hype,* the original *I.G.T.s*[19] from New York, *Flashbacks, The Bomb, Fat Cap, Tommy T,* word, *On the Run, Sneak Tip, Bomber Mag, True Colours, From Here To . . . , Can Control, Beat Down, Over Kill, Underground Productions;* just a few underground graff mags that keep Hip Hop alive, word." That transnational imaginary, the Hip Hop Nation, is here shown to exist as something more than a phantasm: the name-checking of the graff mags affirms its tangibility. The metaphors of networking, of the underground, even the fanciful counterhegemonics ("Controlling the world"), are grounded in the empirical, indisputable fact of the ubiquity of these publications.

Ser Reck's dedicatory comments segue into a sampled grab from a B-grade science fiction movie: "The day we have long feared is upon us. A small but extremely dangerous band of killer humans have invaded our planet . . ." Engaged dialectically with the mediascape, enjoying, as so many did, the frisson of playing out the role of the outsider, the track is teasingly playing with what we have already seen as the media construction of the graffitist as gang member, as harbinger of a Los Angelinesque urban dystopia (Davis 1990, 1992).

Locally, as Ser Reck's tribute suggests, there were several fanzine-type publications produced within the Hip Hop Scene, the two most significant being *Vapors,* written, published, and distributed by Blaze in North Sydney from 1988 to 1992, and *Hype,* published by various editors from the Brisbane writing scene from the mid-1980s to the present. Both titles refer to the magazines' concern with graffiti: "vapors" and "hype" are expressive of the corporeal effects of spray paint, a sickly, chemical sweetness that "hypes," producing a kind of low-grade glue-sniffing high experienced after extended exposure to paint fumes.

I want to quote liberally from a number of issues of both of these publications throughout the section that follows. Lest this be taken as being overly logocentric, too academically concerned with text, perhaps, I want to qualify this approach by, in the first instance, noting the centrality of writing and words to Hip Hop, whether that writing is graffiti writing, the

practice of which involves literally writing one's name on a public surface, or the writing of rap lyrics ("It's all about the words, man," J.U. told
me once), or the production of textual discourse in specialist publications
such as *Vapors* and *Hype*. Lyric sheets are pored over; Internet bulletin
boards contain hundreds of carefully transcribed raps, downloaded,
printed out, and circulated ("It looks just like poetry, doesn't it?" reflected
one Net-surfing b-boy after printing me out the lyrics of a new NAS
recording); local rap improvisers talk about their compulsion (addiction
is a common trope for both rhyming and graffiti writing), their constant
rhyming: Sleek the Elite talks of spending all day driving around the city
(he works as an air-conditioning mechanic) composing "similes"; Def
Wish raps "my brain's infected, diseased with rhyming words" ("Rappin
in My Sleep" on Def Wish Cast's *Knights of the Underground Table*); other
rappers show me school notebooks filled cover to cover with rhyming
couplets, with "metaphors" (this term is in common circulation). The
scene is characterized by a palpable will to discourse, a veritable logo-
centrism. This also means that often the fact of the magazines' existence
is as important as their content; the magazines themselves function as indices of the vivacity of the scene itself: "Like any nation" writes one contributor, the Hip Hop Nation "has history, traditions, fashions, culture,
language . . ." (*Vapors,* no. 8, April/May 1992: 9). And, I might add, a
popular press.

Second, important themes and discourses can be gleaned from a reading of some of these print texts. Key Hip Hop discourses of Nationalism,
Community, Culture, Truth, Respect, Knowledge, Representation, and
the various attendant discourses of race, geography, individualism, and
the right to expression emerge.

Third, I want to reproduce in this somewhat up-market context some
imaginative, passionate, playful writing, allowing the many voices to be
seen and read (if not literally heard) as they twist and distort ("signify
on," as Gates [1988] would say) language, typography and orthography,
the variations in which I have preserved in all quoted passages. Blaze's
journalism and review writing in *Vapors* in particular offers a model of
the appropriation of stylistic and generic conventions from "mainstream"
media, conventions refracted through the specific sensibility and politics
of his scene.

Finally, I should note that early in my inquiries, it was a detailed reading of *Vapors* in particular that facilitated my own engagement with the
Hip Hop Scene: it helped me to understand the performances I was see-

ing, filling in context, explicating assumed knowledges, and so on. In now turning to these publications, I am, I suppose, recapitulating my own journey into the scene.

Vapors

From a photocopied pamphlet, *Vapors* became a forty- to fifty-page black-and-white magazine, sold for four or five dollars (issue 7 carries a warning: "don't be a victim & pay more than $4.00 for this mag") at record shops and through Blaze himself. No less a figure in Sydney Hip Hop than Def Wish had echoed the regard with which Blaze was held, in his assessment of the same incident, telling me that Blaze knew "95% of what there [was] to know about Hip Hop," and that whatever he did not know was "not worth knowing." One had to respect him, Def Wish said, for that, if for nothing else. Had anyone dissed Blaze to his (Def Wish's) face, he told me, marveling at J.U.'s restraint (in the battle sequence described in the Prologue), "we would have bashed him."

Though not without challenge, as Mick's diss evidenced, Blaze's contribution to the Hip Hop Scene and his commitment—"body and soul," he assured me—were widely recognized. Blaze had spent many of his teenage days on the wrong side of the law, mainly because of his love of graffiti. Of Anglo-Finnish descent, to his mother Blaze is Jason Murphy. When I first arranged to meet him, in 1992, he was twenty-four years old. I had expected . . . well, a baseball cap wearing hood with an attitude, I suppose. Instead, when he knocked on my door (he had offered to come to see me, as he needed to photograph some graffiti in my neighborhood) I met a rather "normal"-looking young man, largish of frame, with a goatee, wearing a T-shirt and oversized shorts. The only identifiable element of "rap" attire he wore, or rather, the only article of clothing that he wore that I was able, at that time, to read as "Hip Hop wear," was a pair of ankle-length sports shoes: Nikes, I think.

Blaze was fairly dispirited: the effort of publishing and distributing *Vapors* was getting him down. He was also reaching his middle twenties, was worried about his future, and was perhaps a little rueful about his decisions in early life. As we negotiated my own project, he mentioned to me that he would have liked to have studied sociology, had he been to university, but thought that it was too late, and was now aware of the deadening effect of living on welfare: I got the impression of someone who felt quite powerless, who felt that he understood how the world worked, and that there was no place for him in it. He told me that he didn't think that he would ever be able to get a "real" job, that he had no skills that would ever earn him money.

Vapors was largely a labor of Blaze's love of his culture: he pretty much wrote, laid out, printed and distributed the magazine alone, despite the repeated crediting of the "Vapours Collective."[20] A box in issue 5 acknowledging "The Hip Hop Scribes of the Vapors Clique," credits editorial, layout and design, record reviews, and articles to Blaze: *Vapors* was a one-man show, with occasional contributors. Blaze's frustration in respect of this emerges sometimes in the pages of the magazine. "A bedroom floor conspiracy," reads one editorial page, "masterminded, & acted upon by BLAZE (producer, editor, layout, etc)" (no. 6, July/August 1991: 3).

One result of this was that *Vapors* tended, throughout its eight issues from late 1989 to 1992, to pursue a consistent editorial line. Hip Hop was Blaze's utopia. *Vapors* is probably best read as Blaze's attempt to, in a sense, ennoble, legitimate, or to give "meaning" to his decade of commitment to that ideal.

"What is Up?," for example, appeared in the final issue (no. 8, April-May 1992) and was, Blaze explains, "written almost off the top of my head (& it shows) by a pagan, heathen, agnostic come atheist, non god believing human with soul, Blaze." Over four sections, headed in turn "the angry shit . . . the getting heavier bit . . . the had it up to here shit . . . [and] . . . the afterthought section," and after calling on his "Hip Hop brothers" to "take heed" in the face of the misinformation perpetrated by "this supposed "Hip & yeah, we know what's happening "music industry,'" Blaze works through a number of concerns ranging from the "fuckheads who write for the weekly musical rags" — consigning rap to "the columns of dance music" — to an analysis of the hypocrisy of censoring rap lyrics.

"I have never read anything [about rap in the "weekly musical rags'] that hasn't been condescending, ignorant, malignant, stagnant or Hip Hop illiterate," Blaze writes, then distinguishing "those fatly obscene beats of real Hip Hop grooves" from "dance floor fodder." Stressing the importance of actually buying the material, a theme that he returns to time and time again ("support Hip Hop . . ."), Blaze claims that "nobody I know" purchases Hip Hop records "for the sole intent of body gyratics." "It's all about the words, man," J.U. told me on another occasion. Blaze accuses those who buy, judge, or review records for their dance value as "inactive brain carrying mutants" who "just wanna relax & not think about other people's problems" claiming of rap that "it's too deep to enjoy."

For Blaze, this is the product of a pervasive misrepresentation of rap as "just racist, sexist, mindless crap that glamorises criminal behaviour" by the media. His analysis proceeds: "A few rhymes are usually either taken out of context & expanded into an image (for the mass populous) that conjours up a frightening army of mind marauding teenagers that will subvert the youth of today with an unblinkered knowledged-up brain." He develops this argument further: "What are they afraid of, people thinking for themselves? Damn! Can't have that shit! I mean, the powers that be would lose control."

The image of the "powers that be" and the discourse of rap as counterhegemonic media was most prominently developed and circulated by New York rappers Public Enemy. P.E. toured Australia several times, and were perhaps the highest profile crew throughout the early 1990s. Blaze pushes his analysis further, developing a theory of false consciousness to account for the popularity of "crap" music, music responsible for "hiding the real life everyday issues under a gloss-encrusted carpet."

Addressing a favorite Hip Hop issue, Blaze ends this article by condemning the hypocrisy of "censorshipping butterheads," whom he labels "the immoral minority." Censorship is the key mechanism by which the powers that be deny us access to the truth.[21] He wonders why the Geto Boys are subjected to censorship while "the works of the Marquis de Sade are praised." "Why," he continues, "are children allowed to read the subtle racism of Enid Blyton or Capt. E. W. Johns, yet told that Public Enemy is regarded as subversive?" He compares "the reality" of Ice Cube's lyrics to "the bloodthirsty theatrics of most opera," rhetorically asking whether "the verbal expulsion of expletives [will] be the downfall of modern society." "No," he concludes, "I don't think so." And Blaze's *coup d'analyse* comes in the final paragraph: "This may be a bit of a wild notion, but societies problems wouldn't have anything to do with ignorance, greed, selfishness, power, instead of the recordings of individual thoughts, would it now. Be them on film, in book or on audio. I hardly think that Robert Mapplethorpe, Gus Van Sant, George Batille, Ice Cube, will lead us to damnation. No. In all likelihood an ordinary god fearing family man in a conservative suit probably will."

Another editorial confronts the question of the influence on the local Australian cultural field of an imaginary "America." The issue here is the beating of Rodney King by the Los Angeles police in March 1991 (see Cross 1993). Blaze weaves his own narrative of this episode, drawing on CNN reportage ("A recent survey from C.N.N. television said that 86% of

African-Americans feel that they are treated unfairly in the court system, while only 36% of white Americans say that African-Americans are treated unfairly"), the "real-life" genre of television verité ("What we see on shows like COPS is the police in action . . . with a video camera following their every move. They have to be on their best behaviour then, don't they?"), and making links between the King episode and police violence in Australia (Blaze's reference here being to a then recently broadcast exposé screened by the ABC), before moving on to a generalized critique of colonialism and patriarchy. The evidence that Blaze collects to justify his "Soured Rage" (the title of the article) is presented under the subtitle "A Confirmation of Theory."

Note Blaze's sources, the imaginary of global geopolitics he constructs and, with it, his construction of his own location and position, and, finally, his reconciliation of this imaginary with his cultural (Hip Hop) project. He explicitly draws on CNN, an ABC documentary, and "reality" television to construct his narrative. All three are understood as offering a direct access to "reality," the CNN broadcast offering hard statistical data with which Blaze develops a thesis about the persecution of African-American minorities. The "reality" here is, of course, the physical reality of the beating of King. Scopocentric metaphors abound: "The whole world had seen the videotape of the King beating & with their own eyes had formed an opinion that what they had seen was an obvious criminal act . . . Yet still after several days deliberation, **12 jurors** failed to see what the rest of planet Earth saw . . . the basic fact what this naked eye saw. **KING** was getting the shit beatin' out of him." The blinding obviousness of the barbarity of this act that directly leads Blaze to posit a conspiracy: "This whole debacle confirms that the American legalsystem is one huge m/f of a joke, *that* is unfortunately not funny for a lot of minorities. . . . Then again the whole process started before the jurors gave their stupid verdict (corruption anyone?)." Blaze's uncredited source for the hard information he is disseminating, for his urgent street journalistic style, and for his positioning of his own writing practice in this role of disseminator is, of course, the *Source.*

I have reproduced Blaze's typography. His use of italicized, boldfaced, and capitalized text stylistically quotes tabloid journalism: breathlessly urgent, the bold type guiding the reader through the text, marking out key characters, emphasizing dramatic moments, unabashedly partisan. From his observations about the specifics of the King jury, Blaze leaps into a political analysis, in a paragraph that needs no glossing:

His right royal wankness president **george bush** (little capitals for a little man) said that the "system worked" & "all people should have respect for the law," while later another Republican (read ultra-conservative) wannabee president, **pat buchanan**, said that the jurors had courage. Courage schmourage. Of course Bush's answer to the melee in LA was his usual knee jerk reaction of "send in the troops" & "restore law & order." At least Democratic presidential candidate **Bill Clinton** realises that prevention is the best cure, by addressing attention to the social, economic & racial difficulties that need to be fixed, instead of Bush's "shoot first, questions later" approach.

Rhetorically asking how people like Bush stay in power, he concludes that "that is not a hard question to answer":

> Why is it that less than 50% of Americans who are eligible to vote do vote? Why in Hell's name don't the other 50% vote, are they so apathetic to their own plight that they will let the actual voters rule their lives. Why don't they get off their flippin' butts & move things? Imagine if all the poor, oppressed, downtrodden etc went to the polling booths & voted for the "good & trustworthy" candidates, then maybe things will change. **Get into it & get involved!**[22]

Blaze rounds off this piece with a fleeting reference to comparable police violence in Australia; specifically, the "DAVID GUNDY affair," which involved the mistaken point-blank shotgun shooting of an Aboriginal man in a dawn raid on an inner-city house in Sydney, and to the ABC's controversial documentary "Cop It Sweet," which had recorded and broadcast evidence of a police culture of systematic brutality and abuse directed toward urban Aboriginal populations, demonstrating, Blaze concludes, to "the cosy lounge room living mostly ignorant public that our own Police force aren't exactly heaven sent angels."

Finally, Blaze offers an extended critique of what he understands as the androcentric colonialism of Western discourse. Blaze offers an account of the United States of America ("the most oppressive, sexist, prejudiced, racist, bigoted, greedy, destructive, etc . . . nation on this Earth") as the heir to the British Empire's tradition of "butchering & colonising of "savage native peoples' land." Blaze is quite certain: being involved in Hip Hop does not entail a slavish devotion to all things American, notwithstanding the popular media's attempts to institute such an analysis. Blaze's postcolonialism is coherent and sophisticated. In the aftermath of the 1990–91 Desert Storm operation, Blaze here speculates about the failure of establishment America to address concerns on their own doorstep:

Send half a million troops to defend an extremely rich country like KUWAIT, but yet they turn away a few thousand refugees from their poor & politically unstable neighbouring HAITI. Hey if HAITIANS were rich with lots of gooey black stuff then maybe things would be different, oh and maybe if they weren't voodoo worshipping black folk then maybe they would be welcome. But they don't & they're not of the pale persuasion. So they get the bozack from the "The greatest democratic nation in the world." Keep another country afloat while your own is sinking. REAL GOOD LOGIC?

"In reality," Blaze says, "the United States of America, as a whole, doesn't mean shit to anybody. The Americans, in their over indulging patriotism think that their country is the greatest democratic nation in the world, well we know that is a crock of shit. The good ol' U.S. of A. is nothing but a sick puppy." Blaze concludes that "the world is made for & by the middle aged white man," and wraps up with another solicitation for contributions:

DESTROY INEQUALITY NOW. Please send in letters on the subject of racism for the next issue & we will print them. We want to know your views from a Hip Hop perspective. This magazine is your outlet so please feel welcome to write what you feel.
WE WANT TO HEAR FROM YOU.

The assumption, or positing, of a thing called "a Hip Hop perspective" is striking. It is a central feature of this somewhat intellectual side of the Sydney Hip Hop Scene that it posited the possibility of its truth as Hip Hop without predicating that claim on a simple identification of skin color, of shared blackness. The attribution of authenticity to blackness, a version of Orientalist discourse, is alive and well in Hip Hop in general (see Gilroy 1993: 33–34, 82–83), and in the local scene. However, Blaze's own whiteness necessitates the finding of another ground on which to assert his belongingness to this culture, just as his maleness places him, prima facie, in a relationship of complicity with those whom he identifies as the enemy. Of course, mobilization of a class discourse can help him out in this respect: although he cannot claim to be "working class," Blaze's ethnicity places him, for the purposes of establishing a Hip Hop authenticity, "on the outer." Blaze's desire that Hip Hop can be a place from which to speak, a "point of view," recapitulates the social consciousness discourse of politically aware rap. His flood of discourse attempts to paper over the experiential disjuncture that denies the possibility of a linear, genealogical connection between an Antipodean Hip Hop and an African-American one by predicating a community based on an affective affinity, rather than on blood descent.

Vapors also featured review pages: masses of them. In issue 8, Blaze reviewed well over a hundred recordings: around 26,500 words. "Our mission," he writes, slipping into a magnanimous first-person plural, "is to provide you, the listener, [with] a complete guide to what is released so that you will have a permanent record of what to choose from. We sort the WACK from the DOPE. *WARNING*. No pop rap/hip-house/swingbeat reviewed . . ." (38). Blaze used a star rating system, providing the following key:

☆☆☆☆☆ Doper than dope. Buy it.
☆☆☆☆ Fat. An essential purchase.
☆☆☆ Gettin large. Only if cashed.
☆☆ A waste. Goin' downhill fast.
☆ We don't review shit this wack.

Eighty-four albums were reviewed, in three sections, each alphabetically ordered, spread over some ten A4 pages in single-spaced, ten-point type. Artists' names appeared in bold capitals, and an attempt had been made to reproduce (black-and-white photographs/bromides) album covers for each review, a total of twenty-eight illustrations, throughout the various pages, some canted at about fifteen degrees to the text, to effect a sophisticated graphic design. Following this main album review section were two pages of twelve-inch single reviews — twenty-nine reviews, averaging ninety words (albums got two hundred words).

A third review section, titled "Via the U.K.," covered eleven albums and eighteen twelve-inch singles over three pages. Once again, the albums received generally longer reviews, averaging three hundred words to eighty words for the singles.

The final review section catered for "records that are either re-issues of classic 70's funk or of modern albums that don't quite fit into the Hip Hop category. The emphasis is on the GROOVE." Titled "Jazz Funk/Rare Groove/Breakbeats," this two-page layout reviewed twelve albums, each in about two hundred words.

Seventeen albums, rating at least four stars were recommended as "essential purchases." A further forty-eight, rating at least three, were re-commended for those who are "cashed [up]."[23] Four received the "doper than dope . . . buy it" five-star rating. Blaze's critical appraisals are well worth quoting at length, offering as they do a lucid insight into Hip Hop aesthetics:

> . . . dope cutting & scratching . . . an unmistakable and original vocal quality . . . drop[ping] science with obvious knowledge & lyrical tal-ent . . . real undiluted rap attacks . . . the real deal . . . true to their music . . . no hip-house, no ballads, no new jack-shit, no rubbish, just pure Hip Hop that is enlightening & well, it basically sounds dope . . .

Truth, knowledge, "real"-ness, purity, and individual style are valued positively. Another rave review turns on the notion of self-expression, foregrounding the ". . . funky, creative, original . . . inventive and indi-vidual . . . frenzied scratch inflicted positively puzzled jam against . . . slow piano clinking . . . dopest flute break . . . ," as does this:

> . . . unique . . . [E]xtremely distinctive & exciting with the micro-phone skills being the most apparent & dynamic feature . . . earth moving fortress like vocals . . . sentence ending exagerators . . . This is the shit . . . The production is flipping A . . . I have never heard so much variety in so many songs, damn! . . . the music just never stands still . . . I'm sure that the audio equivalent of a kitchen sink has been thrown in for good measure . . . mind crunching crazily cooking wood-burning . . . human beat boxing over one crunchy shuffling break . . . bizzarely spun nonsense . . .

Clearly this recording was a favorite; Blaze's enthusiasm erupts into an apostrophic "damn!," his carefully tuned Hip Hop ear isolating "variety" in a musical form usually condemned for its repetitive nature (over a pe-riod of months, my own ear became similarly, if not as sophisticatedly, tuned; I went from having no Hip Hop aesthetic sensibility in 1992 to by 1995 at least having favorite recordings). Blaze's alliterated excitement is palpable, the motile force of the music being reproduced in both his as-sessment ("the music just never stands still") and in the form of his writ-ing, with the relentless layering up of imagery, the headlong rush of his syntax, the onomatopoeic viscerality of the repeated "crunch."

A final example offers as close to a musicological definition of Hip Hop as one could hope to find: ". . . the b-b-b-b-basics . . . A phat beat, a booming bassline, a simple hook & dope lyricists & hey presto, waddya got . . . Raw hard edged Hip Hop . . ." Blaze is at his musicological best here, developing his analysis from the "primary musical text" through the discourse of a (Hip Hop) musical purity under threat of dilution. Here, at the heart of Hip Hop, we find exactly the same discourse of cultural imperialism, of "authentic" culture under threat, that circulated around the question of rap and Hip Hop in the popular press: "The simplicity of the grooves provides an antithesis to the majority of musically overcrowded Rap . . . The only squabble . . . a few of the drum tracks are too similar . . . fortunately this is overlooked when one hears the powerful double-bass tugging at one's ectoplasm . . . they say what everyone feels, except they always say it over a true unadulterated musical base which remains unadulterated by current trends . . ."

At the other end of the scale, two albums received no rating at all. One appears to have been reviewed as an afterthought, described as "not a Hip Hop album," but instead "an R & Bish, bluesy keyboard infested lightweight smoky club number," and therefore receiving no rating. The other review closes with the damning words "I hate to say anything bad about a Hip Hop act that means well, but hey it has to be said."

Six albums received two stars, and one, possibly through a typographical error, no rating at all. Those recordings worthy of less than two stars don't receive a published review, Blaze explaining that "we don't review shit this wack."

Blandness, inoffensiveness, lack of social comment, commercialism (the dreaded "cross-over"), and femininity emerge as the demons in the reviews of two-star raters ("A waste. Goin' downhill fast"). "Happy, tinkly drum machines," "girly keyboards," and "melodic singing" consign one album to "inoffensive" mediocrity. "Female singing" is doubly distressing, apparently, and a slightly homophobic line is also apparent: "fairy key board melodies" are antithetical to the "rawness" and "hardness" that characterize the favored recordings. Otherwise, among these recordings, Blaze finds ". . . bland recipes . . . rock infested . . . productions are boring & very very dull . . . simplistic and unadventurous . . . cliched and uneventfull [B]oring drum machine . . . woven with cliched vocal samples . . ."

A recording featuring sexually explicit raps is dismissed as "cliched." Blaze actually found it quite hard to reconcile his own distaste for sexually explicit lyrics with the pervasive Hip Hop discourses of reportage, of "telling it like it is," of the right to self-expression having moral precedence over concerns of political correctness. Here, he deflects his concern into a judgment based on the album's lack of originality, its clichéd nature, thereby saving himself from having to pass a judgment on the lyrical content.[24]

The feminization of negatively valued musical features is also noteworthy. In fact, among the mass of reviews, only three albums are by female rappers. Although this was roughly commensurate with the proportion of releases during the time *Vapors* was published, Blaze's critical discourse about these rappers is revealing. Yo Yo's *Make Way for the Motherlode,* for example, receives three and two-thirds of a star. She is, in Blaze's opinion, "the best female artist to come from the West Coast & not just because she has production & assistance from Ice Cube . . ." This is not the only time that a favorable review of a female rapper is qualified by the citing of a male producer. Queen Latifah's *Nature of a Sista,* for which, Blaze writes, she has "an entourage of [male] producers to give her a wider range of musical styles," "pleasantly assaults" the listener's ears." Overall, Latifah's album is favorably received: "it's not bad for what it is . . . [A] bit too many love tracks for the harder listeners . . . Three and a half stars."

Most female rappers, Blaze writes, citing Latifah, Lyte, Salt'n'Pepa, and Antoinette, are "watered down or compromised." On the other hand, Yo Yo's "main strength comes in the form of an empowering voice, a quality that makes one sit up & listen." This review and one of Nikki D's *Daddy's Little Girl* are both favorable; in both instances, however, Blaze highlights the rappers' concerns with feminism. Of Yo Yo he writes:

> [B]ut it's her lyrical direction that is in favour of the female population. Hardhitting strong Hip Hop . . . cuts like the straight to the point *"Put a lid on it"* which tells girls to watch their mattress activities or *"Girl don't be no fool"* which tells females to watch their men closely & *"You can't play with my yo-yo"* which reflects a strong minded "take no shit" persona, are indicative of her feminist-like stance . . . A push comes to shove type of a gal.

Nikki D is commended for dealing with

> contemporary female issues in an insightful way . . . she goes on to attack free and loose women on the EPITOME OF SCRATCH production *"Wasted pussy,"* adultery . . . on . . . *"Your man is my man"* . . . phatly

pumped . . . a fuckin' dope "cut the beat" ending . . . kick n'tha head . . . NIKKI rips her bi-sexual lover to pieces. NIKKI is a good strong vocalist.

As long as female rappers are "hard" or "strong," as long as they address a kind of feminist concern that is predicated on claims to such qualities, implicitly coded as masculine, and as long as they are guided by male producers, it seems that their work is considered worthy. If they "sing," "melodically" about "relationships" . . . well . . .

By the eighth issue of *Vapors,* Blaze was feeling the strain of maintaining the projects of both publishing the magazine and maintaining Hip Hop as a culture. Ten years after Malcolm McLaren's video clip for "Buffalo Gals" had set him breaking in the school yard, Blaze was still, as he told me in late 1992, "eating, breathing and sleeping Hip Hop." The difficulty he experienced in trying to get an issue out every two months militated against establishing a subscriber base: the last issue of *Vapors,* number 8, the first with a color front-page and color photographs, was circulated in April/May 1992. Thereafter, Blaze's energy was directed toward establishing the Lounge Room.

Hype

Hype was a hand-assembled, cut-and-paste magazine, generally around thirty-six pages in length, with a color cover and inserted color pages. For a while distributed nationally through newsagents, from issue 20 and into its subsequent second volume, *Hype* was available by subscription and through selected retail and record shops.

In contrast to the monologic *Vapors, Hype* was markedly heteroglossic. The letters, interviews, photographs, articles, advertisements, and editorials offer a tumble of discourse from a multitude of contributors, and there were often internal debates that circulated between various sections of any given issue: an ongoing "discussion" about the appropriateness of techno music as an accompaniment to graffiti writing, for example. Where Blaze maintained a clear editorial line, in which divisiveness within the community was referred to obliquely or displaced into commentaries on social problems, in *Hype* the heterogeneity of the scene is manifest on the page: an article calling for tolerance, for example, is found juxtaposed to an article advocating the beating up of Hip Hop "pretenders."

Three main themes emerge: first, the global orientation of the magazine; second, its concentration on graffiti; and, third, an ongoing concern with themes of "unity" and "divisiveness" within the Hip Hop Scene.[25] I will discuss each in turn, before turning to the correspondence pages.

Primarily a graffiti magazine, "produced by the writer, for the writer" (cover, vol. 2, no. 1), *Hype* was modeled on a number of similar 'zines from across the world, many of which were advertised on its pages in reciprocal cross-promotion. Advertisements, alongside letters from correspondents in the United Kingdom, Germany, and the United States, affirmed a sense of the global Hip Hop Community. Feature articles included interviews with (usually) European graffiti writers, who were often able to name local, Australian writers when asked to list their favorite graff artists. Sydney comes in a creditable fifth on Danish writer Bates's list of the "Top Ten Aerosol" cities, after New York, Copenhagen, Amsterdam, and Los Angeles, although he does concede that "this was the first [list] that came into my head" (*Hype,* no. 19, February/March 1993: 5). Nonetheless, Sydney and Australia *rate.*[26] Bates can even name some Sydney writers: "Merda, Puzler, Atome, Unique, Tame — There are so many out there, some I don't even know about" (5). Mr Rens, also from Denmark, offers this: "U.S.A. is TOP! Australia is fresh too . . . I heard a lot of stories about what was going on there . . . and still is. before I saw HYPE I didn't know shit about graff in Australia. Many good artists there" (12). Engaging in a bit of cross/self-promotion, the interviewer asked Mr Rens whether he likes "the Hype magazine . . ." The answer was "HYPE is 'HYPE!' First magazine I saw with colours! Sure Fresh!" (12).

Every issue of *Hype* featured a list of addresses "to write or swap flics." Potential correspondents hailed from Germany, Spain, the United States, and Britain, as well as from all over Australia. There *was* a demonstrable global community of writers, and it appears to have crossed international boundaries, substantiating claims to a Hip Hop Nation.[27] Pictorials included spreads of "European Trains" ("bombin' is so strong on Dortmund trains at the moment that EVERY train is pieced") (*Hype,* no. 20, 1993: 18). Another layout was accompanied by this text: "Brisbane's KASINO and Sydney's ATOME have arrived back from their world tour. First stop New York and then off to Europe. During their travels they pieced with writers such as RENS, BATES, POEM and loads more. Plus several successful wholecars and top to bottoms in Germany" (*Hype,* no. 20, 1993: 7).

The possibility of traveling to Europe and America and being able, on arrival, to both collaborate on a graffiti work and be welcomed into strange homes "like a brother," as one writer put it to me, was often cited as evidence of the Hip Hop Nation. Accounts of such experiences emphasize the feeling of being brought together by shared *styles,* shared enjoyment of the experience, mutual "respect" brought about by the circulation, in magazines such as *Hype,* of photographs, and, of course, the thrill of *getting up* on the other side of the world. A sense of a global project, reinforcing the strength, ubiquity, and realness of the Hip Hop Nation and Sydney and Australia's belongingness to it, leaps from these pages.

In the pages of *Vapors,* Blaze discouraged writers from sending in drawings: "Please send photos. NO OUTLINES. It's kinda safe & easy to draw on a piece of paper, isn't it? Piecing takes skill and plenty of practice. Ie: walls, trains, etc . . ." (*Vapors,* no. 7, March/April 1991: 18). But the editors of *Hype* solicited photographs of both completed pieces and outlines. *Hype* devoted most of its page space to graffiti, with a cheeky disclaimer appearing on almost every page of the pictorial layouts: "NOTE: HYPE MAGAZINE DOES NOT ENCOURAGE THE PAINTING OF TRAINS. These are reproduced for the interest of our readers only" (*Hype,* no. 20, 1993: 18). Celebrating the petty criminality of graff, a feature on "Mel-burn (Melbourne)" announced in gleeful tones: "The [train]lines are thrashed, 90% of pieces from Melbourne we receive are on the lines and illegal" (*Hype* 2, no. 1, 1993: 13). On the opposite page, "a collection of old school shots from Sydney and Melbourne ('84–'87)" placed the contemporary "thrash" in an almost art-historical context: a discourse of progress and genre in which graffiti passes through periodicized "schools."

Another set of pictures documented a train that was "vandalized top to bottom" by Brisbane crew K.O.C. (*Hype* 2, no. 1, 1993: 20). Immediately beneath one of the "*Hype* does not encourage . . ." disclaimers in issue 19, the editors urged the reader to "watch out for HYPE's Metal Monster issue coming out soooooonnnnnnnn . . . (*Hype,* no. 19, 1993: 14): an entire special issue, in color, documenting train after train covered in top-to-bottom pieces. As a guide to circulation numbers, an advertisement for this special issue warned that there will "only be 2000 printed" (*Hype,* no. 20, 1993: 30).

Linking the local bombing scene to the rest of the world, an article titled "German Train Bomber RIO Is Still on the Attack" told of a "bad German guy" calling himself RIO. RIO had written a letter to *Hype,* enclosing photographs, explaining that "the vandal squad is on our asses very bad. They tap our phones, search our homes and observe us . . ." to which the *Hype* editors added ". . . Sounds like home" (*Hype* 2, no. 1, 1993: 24).

Affinities were negotiated across the globe, unities effected in the face of an "oppression" that was, perhaps, of their own making.

And, finally, another media critique, under the title "Something to Laugh At . . ." Editor "Broke" wrote in issue 20 of a dispute that threatened to take *Hype* off newsagent shelves, before commercial pressures actually did so:

> Recently I had to talk live on a South Australian radio show, in order to comfort a City Council and some newsagencys that HYPE does not encourage illegal graff. Well I don't know about that but I know there is magazines available a lot worse than ours. Such as pornography, is this encouraging RAPE? And how about violent sport and gun zines, what do they encourage? Any kid can walk in and pick up a newspaper, HYPE looks like a Golden Book[28] compared to these. Stop and think, is art a crime compared to murder and rape? Stupid Old FOOLS! Stay Hyped! (*Hype*, no. 20, 1993: 31)

A familiar generational rhetoric shores up a somewhat flawed logic. Nonetheless, the argument presented here recapitulated "freedom of speech" arguments put forward to defend the right of rappers to perform and record misogynous lyrics (see Morley 1992; Stanley 1992), alongside the notion of "graffiti as art." And while Broke was quite right, perhaps, to question the strict logic of arguments that read directly from representation to practice, he quite clearly enjoys the petty criminality of his "art": it's not as bad as rape and murder, but one still detects the pleasure the writer takes in what he freely calls "illegal graffiti."

In the first issue of volume 2, Katch wrote of the "'differing opinions on where to hang out or what is cool or fashionable at the current time," lamenting the centrifugal forces that appeared to be threatening the coherence of the scene. Calling for "open minds," Katch suggested that if people stop trying to "compete with each other, then the original essence of Hip-Hop can be discovered" (6). Significantly, this full page article could not offer much of a clue as to what that essence might be, other than to say that it "is one of unity and acceptance not of elitism," and that although there will always be "personal differences," matters of personal choice, "there will always be binding similarities, that lots of other people will not recognise, whether it's Aerosoul Art, Breaking, Hip-Hop or whatever . . ." (6).

One of the issues that had precipitated this attempt to reconcile differences had been an extended debate about the relative merits of techno and rap music. Seiz had written, "I like to breakdance to techno . . . it's fast and energetic . . . is not new . . . this might stun a few people, but Techno music is similar to Rap music in many ways" (*Hype*, no. 18: 8). Seiz and Katch both produced genealogical arguments to legitimize techno in the contemporary scene, adducing evidence of "old school" breakers dancing to the high beats per minute electro-funk (see Toop 1991) in the early dayz, before techno gained its "bad commercialised reputation." Wrote Seiz: "[I]t's not a part of the scene today. But it is. A large number of respected writers are listening to today's techno, myself for one. It brings back memories . . ." (8).

Seiz seemed to be wrestling with a contradiction that ought to have brought his sense of cultural being crumbling down around him: "it" (techno/electro) is not a part of the scene, because it is "commercialised," and therefore is not "rap." However, it *is* part of the scene: he had the empirical evidence of his own practice to prove that. The recourse to a common tradition solves the contradiction in one way: his listening to techno, he argued, is actually *more* authentic in Hip Hop terms because it harks back to the "old school" days. He claimed to have superior knowledge, mobilizing his subcultural capital — "this may surprise some readers/students, but . . ." — and used his authority within the scene (as a "respected writer" who can remember the old days) to renegotiate cultural meaning.

Katch argued that his own tolerance of a music form that he personally "couldn't give a fuck for" is demonstrative of the Hip Hop ethos of acceptance, identified before as partly constitutive of "the original essence of Hip-Hop." He added: "I respect breakers for the artform they practice." This discourse of respect for the artist is central to Hip Hop thinking and is intrinsically linked to ideas about "representation" and "self-expression."[29] Katch continued his article, suggesting that "breaking is still part of the Hip-Hop culture and must keep evolving as it has for the past decade, and if breaking to techno is the next step in the evolution then good luck and stay strong" (*Hype*, no. 18: 8). The "Culture of Hip Hop" is a simple given. "Evolution" is change within the ontology of a cultural essence, a cultural essence that will be recoverable whatever happens, rather than itself being subject to the vagaries of evolution.

Not all the writers in this same issue of *Hype* seemed to be quite as accommodating of techno. GNOME One writes: "It seems the Techno scene has kicked in with a big boot, and its sucking once devoted Hip Hoppers into becoming freaks" (*Hype* 2, no. 1, 1993: 8). Clarifying his position, he continued: "Now I'd be a hypocrit to diss Techno, cause I attend raves and also bust rhymes in a Techno outfit . . . and honestly, I don't mind the shit. But no way am I crossing over to the Techno genre and it's sad to see writers selling out to a scene that is so plastic" (8).

Techno tended to be associated with crass commercialism, with mind-altering drugs (as opposed to the merely facilitative high of the blunts, I suppose), and therefore was understood as being "false," "plastic." But to attend raves and to rap with a Techno crew was apparently not the same as "crossing over" to what is (only?) a "genre," a subset, not a fully formed "culture": "Remember, Techno is cool, but in no way can it replace the unforgiving culture of Hip Hop" (*Hype* 2, no. 1: 8).

The Hip Hop god, apparently, was a jealous god: once you "crossed over" the generic Rubicon, there was no coming back. GNOME One's article continued its round-up of Hip Hop happenings in the Brisbane scene, warning against "a large number of half-stepping toys turning up . . . Sadly these wannabe's associate themselves with Hip Hop." To "half-step" was to not be fully committed to the Culture, to be a weekend Hip Hopper. Gnome's solution? "Half-stepping bashers might have to become the flavour of the month!": beat the wannabes up! He urged his readers to "support Hip Hop!" before signing off with a nasty postscript, directed, I assume, at Sydney crew the Brethren, who had recently visited Brisbane and told me afterward that they had been refused permission to perform at a Hip Hop night at a club. Gnome writes: "Christian half-stepping P-funk wannabe sellouts weren't shit back in the day and they still ain't shit!" (*Hype* 2, no. 1: 8).

An uncredited article on the penultimate page of the first issue of volume 2 placed the question of techno music within the rubric of *representation*. An article had been published in *Zest!* magazine, apparently claiming that "Brisbane's Hip Hop Community have sold out to Techno, that nothing has been happening" (*Hype* 2, no. 1, 1993: 31). The *Hype* article denied this categorically: "Well, you on the Gold Coast [where *Zest!* was published] have misrepresented the Brisbane scene. It is dedicated to graff with a constant flow of pieces and bombing" (31). To *misrepresent* was a cardinal sin within Hip Hop, on a par with *disrespecting* and *capping* (disrespect to another writer's art). The article continued, offering just about the closest thing to a formulaic definition of Hip Hop Culture available: "There seems to be a never ending complaint about what we all should listen to. If you paint, break, DJ or MC, you are Hip Hop involved and supporting your culture . . . we will always believe piecing is the strongest dedication to Hip Hop, because of the risks involved for something you believe in" (31). Once again there is the invocation of the key Hip Hop practices and of the subordination of self to the cultural essence, the sense of self-sacrifice, and commitment to the greater glory that is Hip Hop. And again that sense of nostalgia, here couched within a discourse of cultural dilution or contamination: the article was titled, and closed by repeating, "Stop the Rot."

Finally, it was not merely the local scene that seemed to have fallen from its originary unity, prey to infighting, as SIAMONE, the correspondent from New York suggested: "The violence and disrespect towards each other must cease. Graff is a world-wide movement, black, white, asian, hispanic or whatever, we're all in it together" (*Hype*, no. 20, 1993: 28). The Brisbane graffiti scene in particular had a reputation for violence. I spoke at length with two self-styled "Hip Hop Promoters" from Brisbane, Felicitè and Andrew, together calling themselves 360 Sole Massive. They had edited *Hype* until October/November 1992, Felicitè subsequently producing another magazine, *Zest!* They told me that *capping,* the deliberate defacement of another writer's tag, throw-up, or piece, was rampant in Brisbane, and that fights had broken out, homes been ransacked, and people hurt as a result. A conspiracy theory circulating in the scene suggested that the police were the perpetrators, precipitating violence to facilitate arrests. This divisiveness, whatever the cause, is manifested throughout *Hype*. Locations of photographed pieces are not revealed; there are recurring exhortations, as we have seen, to unity and a return to shared, originary values.

The letters page in *Hype* offered a variety of perspectives (and degrees of literacy). Echoing SIAMONE's sentiments, "FLOTER & DLEMR" from Sydney crew "T.S.P." recounted the damage being done to pieces in Sydney, including "even the 'Pots' dedication" (a piece marking the death of a young writer). He called for an end to "all the bullshit between writers . . . Peace and unity, have respect, be respected" (*Hype*, no. 19, 1993: 27), before crediting *Hype* for its pedagogic function: "you've got everybody in Sydney who's anyone schooled." Another correspondent concurred: "Your mag is so dope, whenever I flick through it, I just get high off the stuff in it. I've just started to piece, and I'd like to congratulate you guys on helping me by having a sketch page. I learn my style off it" (Uncredited, *Hype*, no. 19, 1993: 27).

Another letter explained that the writer had just been released from a detention center and had decided to "give up illegal graffiti and just stick to legal graff." He also took the opportunity to notify readers that he was changing his tag to "TAO," before calling on everybody to "STOP THE POINTLESS VIOLENCE IN HIP HOP . . . we're meant to be about peace to your brother, writer and art." Tao's letter seems to be a heteroglossic return of some of the rhetoric of Nelson George's 1990 illustrated book, well known in the scene, titled *Stop the Violence,* a text about a project involving several prominent African-American rappers, including Public Enemy, advocating "brotherhood" and an end to gang fighting in urban America.

A poignantly named writer from Perth, Western Australia, credited *Hype* with "keeping hip hop alive and kicking" ("Loner," *Hype* 2, no. 1, 1993: 25). The next letter on the same page was from Adelaide in South Australia: "The scene here goes off" (Faulter and the Blackwood Boys, 25). "Taoist" wrote in to inform everyone that he had moved to Coonabarabran ("chillin' with the country bumpkins") in rural ("outback") New South Wales, and needed pen pals to keep in contact with him. From each corner of the country, these words claimed a belonging to the culture, casting out their nets of "shout-outs" and "respects to," lists of crew and tag names. In issue number 20, a correspondent admonished writers to whom he had sent photographs of his own work, anticipating an exchange: "at least have the decency to send something back!" ("Never," Brisbane, *Hype,* no. 20, 1993: 28). This appeal to "decency" echoes Unique's assertion that to respect someone else's work by not capping it is simply "the common sense thing to do"; the code of conduct informing graffiti practice was founded on values that were held to be self-evident: the values of polite, middle-class society, revolving around the right to expression and, of course, proprietary rights over the products of that expression.

From "Unsolved Mysteries" came a letter replying to Broke's comments on representations of violence and pornography (quoted above). "We are not murderers or rapists," the correspondent wrote, they are the real perpetrators of violence in society, not graffiti writers"; then followed the familiar call for unity: "If all writers could get down with real hip hop and not violence imagine the results. Could you?" (*Hype,* no. 20, 1993: 28). This is the discourse of "coming up," the vaguely proselytizing dream of a unified Hip Hop sensibility releasing an unrestrained creativity on the world that doesn't want to understand.

Before leaving *Hype* behind, I want to quote in full a favorite article: a piece that appeared in issue 19 (28), uncredited, center-justified, and surrounded by a black border in which the words "push style to extremes" were repeated half a dozen times:

on a mission
title: the nameless language
word - read this openminded! - it's part of the universal truth
about a language createt by indivisually destructively
recreating/transmutating the alphabet to a phenomenon called
"style." the communication through the alphabet in daytimelife
failed on every level (state, race, social a.s.o.). our
indivisuallanguage is global, colorfull, independent, the
outsideworld couldn't understand it and gave it the name
"graffiti." they named a phenomenon that couldn't be named for it
has no limits butthe state of mind of the creator. to give it every
kind of name means to give it limits. every wrighter is able to
see the same creative spirit as within himself in every tag,
throw-up and piece (simple or complex). important for us is what
style is sayin' to us and what we can say through style! the more
we realize the harder it will be to give it a name. let them
outsiders call it graffiti, as soon as they wanna become or became
insiders they will realize that this phenomenon has no
name/limits. we don't have to be accepted by an "art" trading
gallerywhorehouse world. their oppinion is of no segnificance for
us. our culture stays strong within itself. it's alive on trains, walls
and canvases. as long as we are consiess of what we are doing, as
long as we don't fight over biting, who has better style, crossing
or who is up most for we all learned from that, we're able to see
that we're not fighting against each other, the cops or society but
within it for more tollerance and understanding between each
other. at that moment we'll realize that this struggle is
nameless/endless. the important thing is what we do with it not
how we call it. stop wasting your time and energy on dissin,
going over, betraying, realize what can be done with
style/spraycan; expand it, pioneer it, innovate it, bomb it, teach it
and give respect to those who did this before you–peace to the
roots and all styleaddicted junkies worldwide–the fantastic
partner scum! division wild west germany is out?

The piece appears to be a contribution from a writer called "Scum," recapitulating several of the themes I have addressed above: the salutary calls for unity, the self-sufficiency or completeness of Hip Hop as a culture, the marking of a boundary between Hip Hop insiders and outsiders. What draws me to this piece of writing, however, is the concern with the innominate, innominable center of Hip Hop Culture. The construction of the idea of "culture" here is frankly theological, and I recall Spivak's introduction to Derrida's *Of Grammatology:* "Heidegger makes it clear that Being cannot be contained by, is always prior to, indeed transcends signification. It is therefore a situation where the signified commands, and is yet free of, all signifiers, a recognizably theological situation" (Spivak 1976: xvi).

The refusal to speak Hip Hop's (real?) name is recapitulated in the rhetoric of transcendence, the almost archetypically mystical language of the newly converted, and in the discourse of the universal creative spirit, recognizable in each and every piece, large or small.

Other Fanzines

Three other publications are worth noting in passing. *Zest* was published from the Gold Coast (Queensland) by the aforementioned Felicitè Prior, sometimes contributor to *Vapors* and ex-editor of *Hype*. A small format (A5 size), black-white-and-green publication selling for AU$4, *Zest* focused on music, DJing (particularly advocating the purchasing of vinyl records), and interviews, rather than on graffiti. Each issue included an "update" column from each major Australian city, detailing Hip Hop events, or the lack thereof. *Zest* carried limited advertising from record shops and mail-order spray-paint distributors.

Slingshot was published in Sydney and, until 1993, was distributed free to sympathetic record shops and clothing retailers on photocopied "100% hemp paper"[30] by Trent Roden. This 'zine was addressed to skate boarders and to Hip Hop enthusiasts: an interview with Ice Cube was reproduced in part from an upcoming edition of *Slam* skateboard magazine in which Ice endorses/legitimizes/authenticates the "connection between skate culture and hiphop music," reporting that "I have a brother in law who is 14 who doesn't leave the house without his skateboard" (*Slingshot,* no. 3, n.d. [1993]: 13).

A letter in the same issue, in a section titled "Voices from tha Street," recapitulated the "true hip hopper" versus "half-stepper" debate seen in

Vapors and *Hype:* Observing the fashionable ubiquity of "fat jeans" (noting that even *Vogue* ran a feature on "fat fashion"), the purchasing of "the humble and honerable Puma Clydes and Adidas Gazelles" by "anyone with money in their pocket," and the "biting" of "our vocabulary" by everybody from "newsreaders to taxidrivers," the letter-writer (calling him/herself "The silent partner") reassures the reader that "obviously these bandwaggoners will fall off and the true hip hoppers will still be around so there's not really anything to worry about."

The discourse of progress, of Hip Hop as culturally developmental, reappears here in the midst of a reflexive analysis of "society's" qualms about the scene: "hip hop is angry music (mostly) so as a result hip hoppers are angry people (mostly) therefore society fears us and sees any attempt to seriously gain recognition for ourselves as musicians, artists, dancers or whatever as half cocked." Recall J.U.'s claim that "we're not angry people" (chapter 2, "Enter J.U."). The tension between the discourses of counterhegemonics and those of recognition are among the hardest for Hip Hop advocates to negotiate. Similarly, the tension between the oft-stated proselytizing desire to expand, "come-up," and grow and the need to retain a degree of exclusivity necessitated a constant labor of genre-boundary policing, as I have suggested, and as this letter further illustrates.

Using a disconcertingly media-stereotypical metaphor, the letter proceeded: "We got the finger on the trigger but we're only firing blanks. This attitude only makes it harder to achieve any growth let alone an uprising of the Australian hip hop movement." Once again, the plea for a Hip Hop Community free from violence: "we're past that stage now." Instead, "the creation of unity and friendship" will lead to "the uprising of our culture fired with both barrels." This need not entail, however, forsaking a *hard core* attitude: "Look at Bretheren or Def Wish Cast they both hit hard as a motherfucker on stage but off stage they're mellow and genuinely peaceful." Echoing Blaze's discourse of tolerance, the correspondent asked: "What's the point of dissin or cleanin up someone who's not a bomber or straight up B Boy, that's just a different kind of racism, and aren't we all against that." What is important is, again, the quality of being true to one's self, and, concomitantly, respecting those who seek merely to (honestly) express themselves: "Why beat down someone who rides a skateboard or a horse even, or listens to thrash music? As long as they keep to them self and are true to the game there shouldn't be a problem . . ."

Often I was the beneficiary of this discourse of respect for people being true to themselves, to their own thing. After hanging around long enough for people to understand that I wasn't a journalist looking for a sensational angle, or attempting to diss the scene, and establishing my self-stated desire to "know what is going on," the perceived "genuineness" of my project was reciprocally "respected."

The letter concluded with the familiar peroratory flourish: ". . . for every true hip hopper . . . there's probably twenty and a half steppers out there just aching to be 'In there.' Peace to all the real peoples out there bringing on the change and the uplifting of hip hop culture." The editor had appended a note to this contribution: "More like a short story than a letter, but worth it anyway."

Finally, at the end of my research, another Hip Hop publication appeared, this time at newsstands. *Raptanite,* published from Cessnock, a coal-mining community some 180 kilometers north of Sydney, promised to "express the words and thoughts of the hip-hop culture," this first issue manifesto/editorial going on to solicit contributions: "As ya flow through the following pages please remember YOU have to make this 'zine work" adding that "RAPTNITE is completely uncut, raw and uncensored."

Among the record reviews (guest reviewer DJ Vame), interviews, and graffiti photo-spreads, a feature article addressed the question of *respect.* Promisingly opening with a promise to "define the word hip-hop" the writer conceded that "[a]lthough everyone has a different definition, to those who are a part of it hip-hop means a way of life." The three key practices — writing, breaking, and rapping — get a mention as "aspects of this culture," to which was added "the general attitude." Again, the discourse of Hip Hop expansionism was activated, here expressed as an almost evolutionary necessity, global in its dimensions: "With this lifestyle becoming ever-present in most societies around the world, everyday people are starting to sit up and acknowledge its characteristics." Note the echoing of Arrested Development's massively successful 1993 release "Everyday People."[31] There is also the familiar discourse of revelation: "sit up and notice," lamenting the misrecognition of *the facts* about Hip Hop: "Those who don't know a whole lot about hip-hop discount the music as a "faze" or "fad," when in fact it has been around for almost two decades and still going strong." The failure of "society" to acknowledge and respect Hip Hop is attributed to "the media," which dwells on rap's alleged promotion of "misogyny, violence and racism," rather than on "the positive side of the culture."

ORGANIC INTELLECTUALISM

Throughout my research, Miguel d'Souza published a weekly column in a free newspaper, *3-D World,* distributed through shops, cafés, and clubs. Nestled between other genre-specific columns (a header lists "house, funk, ragga, bhangra, reggae, soul . . .") and titled "Funky Wisdom," the column was illustrated by a succession of piece outlines by Mr E and later by another writer, Loco. Principally a review column, covering foreign and local releases, "tha Wisdom" also operated as a switching point for a mass of information about what was happening in the American scene, what was on locally, and the promotion of Hip Hop as a culture.

Miguel enjoyed a close relationship with the Lounge Room scene, promoting it as *the* place to shop for records, and often quoting Blaze as an aesthetic authority. He was particularly excited by the freestylers based around the Lounge: "Freestyling continues to be the creative literary scene that has expanded the creative potential of many of Sydney's young rhymers; it all began at The Lounge Room, the idea of Blaze and J.U., who lent their store over to be inundated by all sorts of lyrical wizards" (26 September 1994: 28).

Repeatedly asserting the vitality of the local scene, Miguel responded to a fellow columnist's lamenting the apathy of the Hip Hop Scene: "in reality there is plenty of activity . . . there is no need to fret . . . if you scratch the surface of what appears to be a very bland city, there is an amazing amount of diversity and activity in hip hop . . . Rappers like the Sleeping Monk are aiming for the future, working on the downlow, on the grassroots excursion, building up support from people who really appreciate their talent and quality" (25 July 1994: 24).

Again, the familiar discourses: a teleological, authentic Hip Hop "coming up," full of promise. "Genuine," "underground," "real," "authentic" recur as leitmotifs throughout Miguel's journalism. Condemning one local crew's album for "intertpolat[ing] their sound with references to authenticity to keep the feel of reality . . . it's not that I doubt the reality of government neglect, racism, snobbery . . . crime and frustration that exists in Sydney's Western Suburbs," Miguel remarked: "it's just White Boys' *West Side* doesn't do any justice to the realities faced daily by youth there." Later in the same column, Miguel identified "the real thing": 046's album wasn't "posing or posturing," but expressive of a "genuine identity," evidenced by the "rough" quality of the recording. Miguel discerned in this roughness a "lack of technology," the "limits of small scale production" requiring a compensatory "inventiveness" that bespeaks authenticity (29 May 1994: 26).

Miguel's column functioned as an interface between theory and practice, a site from which academic thinking about youth culture was brought into contact with that culture itself. Arguing that "maintaining an underground culture relies . . . on the transmission of . . . alternative perspectives through the magazine medium," for example, Miguel quoted and glossed three long sentences from Tricia Rose's *Black Noise.* "We aren't just talking vinyl, magazines, walls, free street papers," Miguel continued, offering his own précis of the Hip Hop mediascape, "but an ever growing number of media including the Internet" (5 June 1995: 28). Reviewing Lawrence Stanley's collection of rap lyrics (1992), Miguel explained that "so much of hip hop's lyrics are part of an underground dialogue that is often so culturally bound and coded . . . that to examine them with no reference point . . . is stupid" (22 August 1994: 24). He also critiqued the mass media's approach to Hip Hop, one column taking Richard Guilliatt's review of the Americanization of Australian youth culture to task (Guilliatt 1994), and arguing instead that the perceived imitation is in fact "an expression of the solidarity that youth in Australia feel with minority youth in America" (4 July 1994: 22).

I could write another ten thousand words on Miguel's output, but won't. Instead, I will turn to the final dimension of the Hip Hop mediascape, where we will find him again: radio.

In mid-1994, the ABC's "youth network," 2 JJJ-FM, put Public Enemy's new album on high rotation. Miguel was furious, writing that he was "well and truly sick of the hand job dished out to a substandard PE product being flogged on the 'Js.'" "This station," he continued, "has been hard at work play-listing some of the most substandard music posing as hip hop . . . simply accepting and pushing the product that the record companies want them to."

But it hadn't always been that way. Recall Blaze's account (chapter 3, "The Standard Narrative of Sydney Hip Hop): it was on the "Js" that Hip Hop was first broadcast with any regularity, on Tim Ritchie's Saturday night new releases show through the early 1980s. And in 1990, amidst a furor over their playing of NWA's "Fuck tha Police," the staff of JJJ (including Ritchie) *took themselves off the air,* replacing scheduled programs with an endless loop of another NWA track — *Express Yourself.*

Rap forced its way onto commercial play lists in the early 1990s as artists such as MC Hammer, Salt'n'Pepa, and Vanilla Ice made inroads into the charts. Public Enemy, Ice T, and later Naughty by Nature, Ice Cube, and Arrested Development all received attention from JJJ, although commercial stations tended to revert to adult-oriented and nostalgia-driven play-listing from the mid-1980s. Even JJJ focused more on "alternative-indie-grunge" into the 1990s. The only place to hear Hip Hop was on specialist programs on public broadcast stations.

In addition to his weekly column, every Tuesday afternoon, Miguel broadcast his Hip Hop show from 2 SER-FM, a public station based in the tower block of Sydney's University of Technology. Blaze also hosted a fortnightly Hip Hop show on another similar station, 2 MBS-FM: *Funkin' Lessons* went on the air in the wee hours, featuring wall-to-wall beats. Miguel's broadcasts were more magazine-like in format, featuring new releases, guest DJs and selectors, interviews with visiting artists and local rappers, writers, and breakers, and, particularly through the latter part of 1994, freestyles live on the air courtesy of the Lounge Room crews. The studio would often hold half a dozen b-boys, relishing the opportunity to strut and swear to a live audience: it was at one of these sessions that the battle between J.U. and Mick E took place in mid-1994.

Shortly after that episode, Miguel put together a radio documentary titled "Hip Hop Culture in Sydney." Over the course of an hour, editing together freestylee grabs and his own on-air interviews, Miguel presented his analysis of the scene, arguing that "in the Australian context, Hip Hop's movement has come out of the ranks of suburban and migrant youth whose dissatisfaction with the isolation of suburban living, unemployment, racism and the Anglo-Saxon dominance of Australian culture has caused them to identify with similar sentiments coming from African-American rap." Hip Hop's popularity, he continued, "rests on its adaptability, in that youth who are already familiar with substantial slabs of American culture but who see themselves as existing on the fringes of the mainstream of society readily identify with the anti-establishment sentiments of rappers from the underdeveloped inner-cities of the United States."

Word had got around, and Miguel's documentary reached a surprisingly broad audience within the scene, being met with general approval. Many expressed the feeling that they had been put "on the record" and that Miguel's on-going efforts were going quite a way toward redressing the "mainstream" media's misinformation about Hip Hop Culture.

ACADEMIC WRITING ON HIP HOP

Many ground-breaking ethnographies are providing us with timely and
ironic reminders that for the most part human beings live their lives
independently of the intellectual schemes dreamed up in academe.
—Michael Jackson, *Things As They Are* (1996)

One day I told a writer, who was wondering what I was doing, that I
was writing a book about the local graff scene. "Oh," he responded. "Is it
like a subculture thing?" The air was thick with the heady, sweet chemical smell of aerosol paint, metallic rattles, and sibilant hissings, the ever-
present soundtrack of the spray-can artist. "Cool," he said. "I'd like to be
in book about graff . . . there are heaps of people who'd buy it . . . I tried
to find some books about graffiti at Liverpool library," he told me. "But
there weren't any in the art section. I found them in the culture section."

Jackson is wise to qualify his assertion that "human beings live their
lives independently of the intellectual schemes dreamed up in academe"
only *"for the most part."* The human beings with whom I had contact in
the Sydney Hip Hop Scene were, as a general rule, very well acquainted
with the schemes that people like me have dreamed up to account for
their ways of doing things.

In the final issue of *Vapors* (no. 8, April/May 1992), Blaze reviewed a
couple of Hip Hop–related publications, one of which was Costello and
Wallace's *Signifying Rappers: Rap and Race in the Urban Present* (1990).
After a full citation, including the ISBN number, suggesting a writerly
concern with "review as genre," Blaze, in front of the readers' eyes, as it
were, negotiates Costello and Wallace's text: "This is not your everyday
non-fiction expedition, instead it is a published manuscript written by 2
Harvard educated males [. . .] in a style & format that is totally unfa-
miliar & somewhat bewildering to this un-colleged reader." Blaze remarks on Costello and Wallace's (admittedly at best prolix and often ob-
fuscatory) prose, claiming that "on nearly every 2nd page I had to reach
for my 'Superior persons" dictionary to find the meaning of words like:
bregma, decoct, ephebes, phylogenic, semioticizing, synecdoche, etc . . ."
He draws a contrast between the language of the observer-scholars and
the authentic "linguistics' of the street: "No slammin, def, dope, hype,
krushin street slang in here. This makes it a tad heavy & a mighty involved read, with language that seems somewhat estranged & far removed from the raw urban linguistics of the ghetto, of which the subject
matter is derived." Blaze, however, pushes on in his analysis, expressing

his amazement at the extent of the Hip Hop mediascape: ". . . what totally bugged me out about this piece of literature, was the fact that this essay/critique manifested itself into book form & ended up in an inner city suburb of Sydney." He then considers the methodological issues implicit in such an academic project:

> But more bugged, was the fact that it was written by 2 26 yr old white boys in Boston, Massachusetts [. . .] While both share an enthusiasm for this music called Rap/Hip Hop, they realise in their analysis that their upscale middle class whiteness would give a different overview than that of a young urban black male. So they knowingly take a cautious approach as "outsiders" in their interpretation of the validity of Raps many attributes, negative and positive. Outsiders, in regards to the fact that although they know the history of the music & have high praise for "serious rap," they aren't exactly disciples of the Hip Hop Nation.

Blaze regards Costello and Wallace's methodology with some bemusement, describing their analysis as using "an allegorical format that can throw one of[f] curve many times"; their "disection" of a Jazzy Jeff and Fresh Prince track — sampling the theme from the 1960s sit-com *I Dream of Jeannie* ("Girls Ain't Nuthin' but Trouble"; see Costello and Wallace 1990: 61–67) — stretches a point. Costello and Wallace's attempt to conjure "imaginatively woven storylines" out of what to Blaze is an "innocent and facile use" of source material is "a most peculiar slant on pop culture."

Remarking that "on the whole the book is full of interesting points more theoretical than factual," Blaze indicates that his methodological sympathies evidently fall on the side of ethnography: "Apart from all the brain examinations, they thankfully also manage to deliver some first hand observations. The setting for these anecdotal exploits is not The Bronx, Brooklyn, BedSty or any other N.Y. borough, instead its Roxbury, Boston." The book, Blaze continues, follows the career of "a local & as yet unsigned female rapper," noting that the album in question "is available now," drawing an immediate link between this clearly alien text and the Hip Hop milieu of his readers.

Quoting the text (and furnishing his own parenthetical explication), Blaze also finds reaffirmation of something he feels to be blindingly obvious — that "rap music on the whole has been given a bum rap": "critics & writers so far have done a shitty job of countenancing (approving, encouraging –Ed.) the decade's most important and influential pop movement." As far as Blaze is concerned, this is good stuff. He sums up: "For their research they plowed through hundreds of essays & reviews from major periodicals in the CD ROM Data Base & discovered that 'fewer than a dozen pieces are critical attempts to come to terms with the music itself.' The rest associate Rap with rape, crack, gangs & 'lost generations.' An observation that we had already noticed."

Having examined its premises and methodological bases, Blaze endows the text with a provisional authority, an authority that he now extends, finding in the text an affirmation of something that he, the *true* authority, already knows; something that the insider doesn't need books, CD ROMS, or scholarly articles, to find out. "The only gripe I had against this exposition," he concludes, "was their failure to come to grips with the constructive & creative process behind the use of sampling. They constantly refer to it as 'theft' & as a lack of originality. Obviously the whole concept behind it has escaped them. I thinkz they may have mizzed the point mizelf."

Finally, Blaze offers some (good) advice: "[T]o be fully understood, it [the book] is best read twice. Includes a discography [. . .] No photos." The book's ISBN is added to this final, terse formula, rounding out the generic markers of the book review.

To understand Blaze's positioning of his own authority in the opening section of the review, it must be remembered that Blaze's concern in publishing *Vapors* was overtly didactic. "It has to be done . . ." he told me, "so that correct information is disseminated to the audience," adding that "there are focal points for everything in life . . . a home to go to." This concern with "place" will also reappear throughout this analysis, generally in the context of a concern with "neighbourhood," rather interestingly translated from American inner-city contexts to the broad reaches of outer Sydney. Blaze explained the necessity of opening a specialist Hip Hop music store in terms of establishing a central place for people to meet, to hang out, to network. Significantly, in the months following the opening of the Lounge Room, it quickly became as much an information center as a retail outlet. Note also Blaze's use of the imperative form: "it [the dissemination of 'correct' information] *has* to be done." This construction recurred throughout my experience with those "dedicated to the culture," further reifying an assumed cultural essence capable of motivating activity; the individual merely has to "commit," receive *knowledge,* and in return will receive direction.

Blaze treated me with a fair degree of suspicion during our early meetings. As I have noted, he was contemptuous of journalists, whom he felt wanted to deal with only the "sensational aspects of Hip Hop," ignoring its "cultural aspects." Many writers were simply not interested in having their names in print, lest the police catch up with them — not many were prepared to be quoted directly for this reason. When I attended graffiti workshops with a video camera, I had to take pains to be introduced to all by a respected senior writer, and even then I met occasional no-go areas; Unique one day, for example, let me look through his "piecebook" (graffiti portfolio) on the condition that I did not video or photograph any of it.

Many other academic and quasi-academic texts circulated in the scene. Henry Chalfant's graffiti photojournals (Cooper and Chalfant 1984; Chalfant and Prigoff 1987) and, to an extent, Craig Castleman's *Getting Up* (1982) were widely read and circulated in Sydney Hip Hop circles. It was a standing joke, related to me by writers and the transit police, that these books could not be found in libraries: that they were *racked* by writers as soon as they were put on shelves. Chalfant's books, in particular, offer brief histories of graffiti and its association with Hip Hop Culture. His *Spraycan Art* (Chalfant and Prigoff 1984) is a worldwide survey of piecing, featuring a couple of pages of photographs of Australian work. The local writers could easily locate their own practice within a global and historical framework, a critical contribution to the sense of belonging to, and being part of, a Community, Nation, and Culture.

Other, more scholarly books also circulated. Miguel reviewed and promoted, on his radio show and in his weekly column, a Penguin collection of rap lyrics (Stanley 1992), which included an introductory essay, "Rap as American History" (Morley 1992), as well as Stanley's own preface defending the right to free expression in the face of moral majority objections to obscene rap lyrics (see Peterson-Lewis 1991, Gore 1987). The book itself, titled *Rap: The Lyrics,* was immediately popular; even the long essays seemed to be consumed with zeal. Miguel also offered brief reviews and recommendations of books by Fernando (1994) and K. M. Jones (1994).

On occasions when rappers or writers visited me in my apartment, they would fall on my bookshelves. Brian Cross's 1993 collection of interviews with Los Angelino rappers and Hip Hop identities was an immediate success, as was Toop's panopsis (1991). Toop's book enjoyed an enduring popularity in the scene; Jones's (1994) and Fernando's (1994) books were easily digestible, and were enthusiastic about Hip Hop to the point of being elaborate fanzines. Both were avidly read and circulated in the scene.

These books not only repeated, once again, in an authoritative manner, the historical narrative of Hip Hop, offering validation of facts, names, dates, and so on, but, in so doing, confirmed their significance and importance as the objects of academic discourse. My own project was understood within this context, at once affirming the value of Hip Hop Culture and offering, it was thought, the opportunity of (a limited) fame: Castleman had mythologized New York writers; why shouldn't Maxwell do the same for *this* local cultural vanguard?

After J.U. read one of my published papers (Maxwell and Bambrick 1994), he was particularly concerned that I "see the real thing," taking me to task for writing about Sound Unlimited, and telling me that "the thing is . . . they're not Hip Hop." Def Wish rewarded me with his approval after hearing me speak about his scene on the radio: "You know as much about Hip Hop as Blaze," he told me (high praise indeed).

In addition to taking account of these exchanges between the ethnographic population and academe, it is important to understand their being within or, perhaps better, their engagement with a mediascape in which "youth subculture" had assumed reified, ontological significance. "Youth subculture" is, in such a mediascape, a horizon of analysis and, therefore, of possibilities for being in the world. It is a constraint that both subjects persons *to* particular assumptions about ways of being and produces persons *as* subjects: hence the pervasive understanding, current both in the Hip Hop Scene and in general discourse, that a subculture gives, frees people into, or allows them their "identity," their voice, thus enabling them to "express themselves." Everyone, it would seem, belongs to some subculture; they choose it, or it chooses them (the direction of flow of this process is determined by the analyst's own agenda), and if someone doesn't, that person is "a loner."

A documentary screened on the ABC in 1994, for example, dealt with three separate "youth sub-cultures" (including Hip Hop), suggesting explicitly that *this* is simply what youth *does;* that youth *is* tribal, that being a teenager is about selecting one's subculture. A double-page spread (with a front-page lead article) in the *Sydney Morning Herald* addresses "Generation S"; a post-*Simpsons* take on Coupland's 1991 *Generation X* (the periodizing logic rolls relentlessly onward, demanding ever new epithets). The *Herald* journalists suggest that "it seems that there is no such thing as the typical backyard-and-beach Australian teenager any more," and that "teenagers have always been attracted to tribes as a way of expressing identity" (Gripper and Hornery 1996: 10).[32] This is what I call the "Ted Polhemus analysis": see in his 1994 *Streetstyle* the sections titled "The Supermarket of Style" and "The Gathering of the Tribes," along with his "flow chart" of youth subcultures (128–37). These kinds of analysis largely originated from, and were certainly popularized by, the Hall/ Hebdige/Willis nexus of the Birmingham Centre for Contemporary Cultural Studies in the 1970s, becoming grist for journalistic mills: user-friendly, powerful, analytical tools. Emptied of the too-difficult Marxian theorizing, this model of being/doing/performing youth has been reified to the point that Polhemus is able to suggest, in his eminently readable, illustrated text[33] that subcultures are, simply, tribes, and that "the tribal imperative will always be a part of human nature" (1994: 14).

There is a clear "trickle-down" (to use a somewhat politically and spatially loaded metaphor) from academic takes on "subculture" to "the street." Miguel was one important nexus through which this material was disseminated. Significantly, Blaze et al. took pains to distance themselves from what they understand as the "faddishness" of youth styles, dismissing *half-steppers,* or *weekend warriors,* extending respect only to other "cultures." And this is critical: Hip Hop was not understood as a subculture, but as (the one true?) Culture, with a capital C.

Blaze's negotiation of Costello and Wallace's difficult text, his effort to locate and translate it for his readership, in effect returns the gaze of the cultural theorist. Indeed, the figure of Blaze seems to be looking over my shoulder now as I write, as it has throughout my period of research. The review reminds me, in a very tangible way, that the field that I have looked at is in no way a "pure" object of research, and that Blaze, and J.U., and Def Wish, and Unique, and the Monk, and any number of people that I have spoken to in this scene are alert to *my* project.

CONCLUSION: THE HIP HOP IDEOSCAPE

Ideoscapes, Appadurai says, are "concatenations of images" that are "often directly political and frequently have to do with the ideologies of states and the counter-ideologies of movements explicitly oriented to capturing state power or a piece of it." Ideoscapes are characteristically "composed of elements of the Enlightenment worldview" (1990: 9). This

"Enlightenment worldview," Appadurai continues, involves a "master-narrative" (cf. Lyotard 1986) that presupposed "a certain relationship between reading, representation and the public sphere," was constructed with a certain internal logic, and involved certain key words and images, "including 'freedom,' 'welfare,' 'rights,' 'sovereignty,' 'representation' and the master-term 'democracy'" (10). Appadurai recognizes that these words, and the concepts entailed by them are not, of course, fixed, but are subject to pragmatic and semantic fluidities. Processes of translation, from linguistic, geographical, and temporal contexts result in misrecognitions and deliberate appropriations ("captures," as Appadurai puts it, 11).

In the mass of discursive and ethnographic material discussed above, it is possible to discern a *Hip Hop Ideoscape,* an ideoscape that, I stress, is not only *my* analytical construct, but is also discernible ethnographically: references were made to "the ideology of Hip Hop," the "ideals of Hip Hop," the "meaning of Hip Hop." Hip Hop was understood as having an "ideological" dimension, as simply being ideological.

We might, then summarize this "ideology" of Hip Hop: One gains *respect* from one's *brothers* in the *community,* by being *true* to one's self, by *expressing yourself,* and by being *true to the music.* When you are being true, you will *know.* Individuals are discrete, sovereign beings, are *free,* and have *rights* (to expression, to be free from oppression) that transcend race, nationality, even religion ("sex" is not generally on the agenda as a political issue). *Knowledge* is *rationally* derived from first-hand *experience* through the application of *common sense.* This *experience* is available from or on *the street, the underground,* from the margins, from positions of disempowerment. The shared experience of, or the ability to empathize with, oppression of any form (particularly racial and economic; sexual oppression is not really in the picture), allows social agents to transcend their differences, and to *share* a globally inclusive *culture.* Through an attention to the narratives of oppression — that is, an attention to getting *knowledge* — and the sharing of practice, white middle-class teenagers can empathize, at a distance, with what happens to African-Americans in the Bronx, and can therefore participate in the *culture* of Hip Hop. Further, the vast majority of people in our *slippin' society* no longer have access to true *knowledge,* or misrecognize it. Are brainwashed. Hip Hop, because it is *from the streets,* coming *from the underground,* is able to redress the false ideology consuming the world.

Hip Hop should be *united,* not *divided.* Members of the *community* should support each other and nurture their *culture*. Recall the letter writer to *Slingshot* (no. 3, n.d. [1993]: 13): "As long as they keep to them self and are true to the game there shouldn't be a problem . . ." And they should *represent* themselves and their culture.

The use of the term *representing* simultaneously invokes at least two "meanings" of the word: a "political" meaning, grounded in a sense of liberal democratic processes, and what I will call a "semiotic" meaning, grounded in particular assumptions about the relationship of practice to meaning itself.

In the first sense, a rapper *representing*, for instance, is understood to be "standing-in-for" his (or, less frequently, her) absent colleagues. "Sydney Hip Hop representing," said J.U., claiming this status as representative, as one holding the right to speak for, or on behalf of, a *community*. The rhetorical, or strategic, value of such a gesture is clear, as I hope I have demonstrated.

Above, in chapter 2, I stressed the strategic dimension of this practice. I suggested that J.U. was attempting to effect a hegemony of the Hip Hop discursive field, to position himself (and his "party," perhaps, the Lounge Room scene) as authority, as legislator of what is and is not authentic Hip Hop. I want to emphasize again that I am not necessarily reducing the phenomena in question to "power-relations," for there is also a ludic dimension to such moments of self-narrativization, as I have suggested: serious fun. It feels good to locate one's self in an important context, as a "representer." There is a certain gratification in the sense of participating in a grand project, and doing so as a central representative of that project.

There are any number of empirical, quantitative questions about the sustainability of assertions to representation: how many Hip Hoppers *are* there? how "logically" or "practically" sustainable is such a claim to representation? how organized are they? how "political" are they? just how "oppositional" is Hip Hop Culture? and so on. I am less interested in such questions, particularly those that tend toward an academicized agenda of enlisting youth cultural forms to positions of progressive political agency, however, than I am in understanding the assumptions about cultural processes within which such assertions are made. For in claiming to represent in this way, J.U. and his friends are importing into their discourse a raft of understandings, of assumptions about the sovereignty of the individual, about "self-expression," about "freedom." Values identical to what Appadurai calls the ideoscape of the "Enlightenment worldview." In the next chapter, we will see Blaze's claim to rationality: "Be rational . . . ," he wrote, an exhortation to his readers to search out knowledge, to be smart, not to fall for the ideological misrepresentations of "the powers that be."

The second sense of representation being used, that which I have called the "semiotic" sense, is closely related to this first, liberal humanist political sense. To break, to rap, or to write is to *represent* the *culture*. "Representation" is that of a cultural essence by a visible, demonstrative practice, understood as reproducing, in the present, something that already exists prior to the moment of the demonstrated production. That which is represented is absent: the paradigm is the same as that implied in the "political" use of representation above. In his critique of the political economy of signs, Baudrillard (in the days prior to his becoming the pin-up boy of postmodernism) described this process as that of providing an "alibi": the always absent referent "guaranteeing," in its privileged status as transcendent, necessary, ontological "presence," the "meaningfulness," or even the *possibility* of meaningfulness, of the sign (Baudrillard 1991).[34] Practice "makes sense" because behind it stands the (never seen, always elsewhere) thing represented by the practice.

Thus in the context of democratic politics, the absent body politic and the attendant will of the people is represented by a present politician, the absent Hip Hop Community/Culture/Nation is represented by the present rapper. In the context of cultural production, the absent cultural essence is represented by the present evidence of a practice. In each instance, the logic is identical, and, within the given cultural contexts, self-evident and therefore persuasive. And yet, cause and effect are inverted: it is, rather, the persuasiveness of the argument that yields the self-evidence of the logic, where, to effect an admittedly vulgar distinction, persuasion is the realm of strategy. It is this putatively self-evident logic that is being invoked by claims to representation.

In other words, then, the ideology, the *ideoscape,* of Hip Hop is more or less identical with that of "the Enlightenment worldview" described by Appadurai. The Hip Hop Scene I encountered offered no ideological critique other than positing that the rest of the world has *fallen* from the "ideals" it purports to follows. In this respect, Hip Hop is deeply *conservative.* The discourses of *Community* and *Nation,* of *self-expression* and *representation,* and of *Culture* that are invoked are, far from being *post*modern, discourses of highest, capital *M* Modernity.

5

West Side and the Hip Hop Imaginary

Def Wish Cast shows started with Def Wish himself, a slight, crew-cut, somewhat boyish figure in an Adidas shell-suit, T-shirt, hi-tops and a baseball cap bearing his crew's logo (a cartoon bomb in the shape of a map of Australia, its fuse sparking, ready to explode) — the only baseball cap, he assures me, that he'd ever countenance wearing. Grabbing his microphone (preferably a radio mike, but more often one trailing several meters of cord) in both fists, Def Wish would take a massive breath, hauling his shoulders high, up to his ears, and then, abruptly, lunge forward and downward, bending over the mike, launching himself into an a capella ragga rap, usually the thirty-second introduction to "They Will Not Last." The words (Blaze memorably reviewed Def Wish's style as "syllable ballistics") tumble out, Def Wish interpolating burbling grabs, rolling his tongue, using the plosive effect of the release of air tongue-dammed against hard palate. The effect is of a series of jack-hammer explosions, punctuated by the shrieking intake of a fresh breath, his body lurching upright, ribs visibly expanding inside his T-shirt, and then plunging down and forward again, seemingly squeezing every last gasp of air from his body, wringing the words out.

In half a minute it is over, and Def Wish, sweat dripping down his face, his oversize T-shirt wetly flapping from his shoulders, is joined by the other MCs. Ser Reck is older, bearded, his long hair pulled back into a pony tail. He wears, as a rule, a Def Wish Cast T-shirt and baggy black pants. Die C is completely bald, except for a thin "rat's tail" falling from the back of his clean-shaven pate. Angular, shorter than he appears on stage, he more often than not wears a dark T-shirt and black track pants. Both leap onto the stage; their talk is always of making an "impact," of "hitting" the stage and audience. Throughout the performance all three rappers stalk the stage, trailing spaghetti trails of microphone leads as they cross and recross each other.

I most often saw DWC perform in small club venues, often supported by four or five other crews. A tiny raised stage was generally provided, and, upstage, DJ Vame would work at his console, a calm, measured counterpoint to the frenzy of the rappers downstage. At the back of the room a sound engineer ran the DAT and monitored microphone levels. The exchange between the rappers and DJ on stage and the sound engineer at the opposite end of what was usually a small, dark, sweaty, smoky, and noisy room was a feature of virtually every performance I saw: "Stop the DAT . . . stop the DAT motherfucker . . ." or "louder . . . *louder*" and so on.

Throughout this period DWC had a standard performance list: five or six tracks, each of which included a verse from each rapper and serious cutting and scratching from Vame through the breaks. As each rapper launched into his own rhymes, the other two would move upstage, loose heads nodding to the pulse, loping around whatever space was available, flicking and tugging at leads, eyes often closed, mic held down next to the solar plexus. The choreography was not particularly sophisticated, but questions of focus and the directing of the audience's attention had certainly been taken into account. Every rapped line would include at least one syllable "punched" by the other two rappers: their upstage stalking would momentarily halt, microphones brought up, touching lips, all three striking fleeting friezes, which I now recall as a series of strobe-flashed tableaux: Def Wish drops to his haunches, arm outstretched, palm open to the audience, his face shadowed under his laced-up hoodie; the others stand behind him, to either side, pressing to him, outside arms extended upward and outward, palms open, an expansive, open-chested gesture, eyes turned to the heavens, into the spotlights as, in unison, they shout "west-*side*," and the tableau immediately dissolves into more pacing ("like a panther," raps L.L. Cool J), more convulsive downstage rapping. A rapped reference to the DJ ("DJ Vame / going sick as a renegade!") sees all three lunge upstage, dropping to their knees, gesturing to the console as Vame, calmly, methodically, his wrists loose, almost elegant, or even *dainty* (he would love my saying so) flick and flip and twist and fly, cajoling halting, stuttering rhythmic squeaks, rasps, gurgles, and squeals from the vinyl on the turntables. The boys turn downstage, striding back toward their audience.

And this audience, when the crew is on song, *thumps*. The dance of choice for DWC shows is a frenetic pogo, harking back to unremembered days of punk. The boys commented on this, laughingly — they don't know how it started — "in Melbourne, or something," offers Def Wish. It's almost a mosh-pit, but more dangerous. Down at the front, it is all boys in flannel shirts, usually soaked with beery sweat. As the night progressed, they'd be drunker and drunker, the slicked, big-boned youths careering into each other in boozy imitations of Australian Rules footballers "hip and shouldering"[1] each other, falling over, sometimes hitting each other, dragged apart, spilling over into (and scattering) the more sedate outer ring of spectators in a domino-effect-like chain reaction.

Such displays inevitably fueled venue managers' antipathy toward rap acts, confirming fears of the inherent violence and "gang"-orientation of the scene. As a result, few venues were willing to risk hosting Hip Hop nights, although this had as much to do with the minimal revenue such evenings could generate: a bunch of late-teenage/early-twenty-something Hip Hoppers simply don't have the spending power of a similar crowd of university students or "straight" folk.[2] Such roughhousing, although unpleasant to experience, was not necessarily any more marked at Hip Hop nights than at any number of pub rock 'n' roll gigs.

Between raps, the crowd punch the air in unison, playing out its half of the antiphonic banter as the crew sorts itself out for the next track, chanting, "west *side!* west *side!* west *side!*" or "whoa-*oh!* whoa-*oh!*" Further back in the crowd there are more women, and people move to the pulse (it demands it of you), carefully negotiating the occasional pogo-melee. A surprising number of people of both sexes rap along to every verse, the whole room exploding into a manic *crush* as the crew belts out the glorious, broad-accented, quintessentially *suburban* chorus of "Runnin' Amok":

Runnin' amok!
Is that your head or did your neck throw up?
Runnin' amok!
Is that your head or did your neck throw up?

Runnin' amok!
Is that your head or did your neck throw up?
Runnin' amok!
Is that your head or did your neck throw uuu-uup?

And then, sometimes, often, Ser Reck would point to the floor in front
of the stage, and shout at the crowd there . . . the first time I didn't know
what was happening . . . a fight? An injury? (There is always a fight and
an injury.) But no . . . Def Wish dives off the stage, and he's breaking,
there, amidst all that spilt beer and cigarette butts and broken glass and
god knows what. Hardly anyone can see his performance as they strain
over each other's shoulders, laughing, cheering, clapping. Then it's Die
C's turn, and Ser Reck's, and Vame is still *going sick,* cutting it up, smiling,
building a stack of used records on the piece of tatty carpet beside the
console (surely, I used to think, they must take more care of these
records?).

And in the panting breaks between tracks, as the sound engineer
struggles to cue the DAT, and the microphone lead tangle is unraveled,
one of the rappers (it's usually Ser Reck) will announce what they are *doing:* "Sydney Hip Hop!" or "Support Australian Hip Hop!" or simply "Representing all the crews!!!" Cheers go up, the tape is ready to roll, and the
room is flung into the next four minutes of driving beats.

STAGING HIP HOP IN SYDNEY

Given that they are "imagined" communities that cannot be experienced
empirically in their totality, and whose identity is often contested, nations
cannot be understood outside the relations of power that give certain groups
the possibility of simultaneously representing, constructing and . . .
staging the nation.

— Ghassan Hage, *Republicanism, Multiculturalism, Zoology* (1993)

In the previous chapter I mapped out the vast field of media(ted) images and discourse from and within which Hip Hop in Sydney created its
own discourses and narratives of belonging and identity. In Part Three,
below, the focus will move into and around bodies, sound, and movement. First, however, having located those bodies within a global mediascape, I want to now locate them in *place:* the *where* of Sydney Hip Hop.

To understand this where-ness involves an understanding of how this emplacedness sustained and, even before that, grounded the possibility of agents in the scene thinking of themselves as *representing,* and being, a community, as a culture, and as a Nation. In this chapter, then, I will first examine the claim to Hip Hop Community, understanding it as the ongoing process of integrating practices of performance, embodiment, and the production of various forms of discourse into a somewhat ineffable organizing concept: that of Hip Hop. Central to this process, I argue, is the articulation of those practices to place — in this case, that place generically referred to in Sydney Hip Hop as the West Side. The chapter will then examine the articulation of this emplaced sense of community, within the context of Australian nationalism, to broadly circulating discourses of Hip Hop (trans)-Nationalism.

THE HIP HOP COMMUNITY

Robert Walser has remarked on the difficulties presented to ethnographical methodologies by "industrial societies": in such societies "there is no single 'local' to be studied" (1995: 291). In purely empirical terms, the Sydney "Hip Hop Community" was rarely, if ever, experienced in its totality. It is hard to even put a number on its size; my inquiries along these lines were usually met with indirect responses suggestive of, perhaps, a desire not to admit the empirical fragility of the concept. This indeterminacy, this nonempirical status of the community had distinct advantages: it allowed any substantial gathering to claim that it "was," or at least "represented," the community. So, when crews from Brisbane "went over" a number of pieces on the sea wall at Bondi Beach in late 1994, the gathering of writers that went back a fortnight later to reclaim the wall space was able to name itself as "the community."

In simple terms, what I encountered was this: a number of people, mostly young adult and late teenage boys, from various socioeconomic and ethnic backgrounds, participating in a number of activities. These activities included listening to "rap" music, talking about rap music, judging rap music, rapping, making "beats" and recording their raps, improvising raps, writing raps, performing raps, DJing, painting graffiti, sometimes legally, or on commission, often illegally; looking at pictures of graffiti, and hanging out with each other, in their parents' homes, less often in their own homes; occasionally break-dancing, practicing breaking moves; smoking dope, reading magazines, drinking, stealing spray paint, going to work, going to school, watching videos, raising their children.

They dressed and wore their hair if not similarly — if not, to an outsider, immediately identifiably — then at least in response to and consistently with an ever-shifting, negotiated, but shared sensibility: that which has been labeled in subcultural studies, since the pioneering days of Hebdige (1979) and, before that, Melly (1971), a *style*. They shared a language, a critical vocabulary, a set of aesthetic values and embodiments — related to, or consistent with, at any given time, the consensual set of interpretations of these "Hip Hop" practices. None of these, of course, was fixed: words floated in and out of circulation; aesthetic standards were negotiated. Force of character (or something like that) could impose or delete a set of preferences as power, or access to subcultural capital was exchanged, accrued, resisted. They shared a folk history, a set of knowledges about the "origins" of these practices in far-off places and about their local manifestation over a period of a decade (a long time indeed, both for the young men involved and for a nation of barely two centuries' standing).

What they were doing, these people suggested in their discussions (with me, with each other, in the articles they published in small-circulation but broadly distributed magazines, in the course of radio broadcasts, in their raps, in their addresses to the audience between raps, on their album covers, on their cassette and compact disc inserts, in interviews — in short, in any forum to which they gained access) was participating in a "culture": specifically, something called Hip Hop Culture. To participate in one of these activities, and especially in one of the three central practices — rapping, writing, or breaking[3] — was, in the frequently used expression circulating in the scene, to *represent* this culture.

This participation in this culture constituted what they called "the Hip Hop Community." This community was qualified variously as the "Sydney" Hip Hop Community, the "Australian" Hip Hop Community, and in its broadest form, simply "the" Hip Hop Community, a transnational community of like-minded folk also commonly referred to as "the Hip Hop Nation.'

Of course, not everybody who rapped, who wrote (graffiti), who break-danced, DJed, and so on identified with these discourses. For many, graffiti writing was unrelated to anything called Hip Hop Culture. They did not understand themselves as participating in a "Hip Hop Community." They hung out with their friends. They wore shell-tops, Adidas runners, hooded jackets, baseball caps, baggy jeans, sharp dos, called themselves "homies," or "homeboys." Listened to rap, R'n'B, new jack swing. Listened to techno, perhaps. Used the argot. Smoked dope. Threatened passersby. Acted tough. Provoked letters to the editor and tut-tutting feature articles in the daily press. Went to school, didn't let their parents know where they were, and so on. In an interview, Miguel asked the Sleeping Monk about the look identified with Hip Hop:

Miguel: [When you see kids] wearing hi-tops and that . . . does that all mean that all of them are into rap?

The Monk: Hah. They see the image on their TV shows and they see the image. Basically, to be cool, like back in the days when I was at school you know it's like you had to wear the freshest stuff and like, you'd wear your Starter cap and your sneakers and that and people say "yeah, that's cool"; that's what they see in the magazines, but it doesn't necessarily mean that . . . I used to go up to kids at school who, you know, perceive themselves to be b-boys, [and] would ask them questions and they wouldn't have a fucking clue about what they were doing. (d'Souza 1994)

"Half-steppers" adopted the "appearance" of "true" Hip Hop aficionados without "committing" themselves to "the culture." "Homie" became a broad-brush label for anyone adopting what insiders saw as the superficial trappings of Hip Hop style. My concern is, however, with those individuals for whom it was, for whatever reason, of critical importance to subsume those (Hip Hop) practices, those *habituses,* to these narratives of community, culture, and nation. Those who *did,* in the Monk's phrase, "have a fucking clue about what they were doing."

And here is the slippage from a discourse of "community" to one of "culture." Cultures are not, of course, *a priori,* coherent wholes (S. F. Moore 1989: 38); they are, rather, sites of negotiations, inclusions, and exclusions. Here, the Monk is, effectively, policing cultural boundaries, regulating the traffic of cultural material. Hip Hop Culture here is a "reality . . . still in the making," where this "making" consists in "conflicting political struggles" (Hage 1995: 61).

The main evidence, however, offered to support the idea of the Hip Hop Community was that of an unambiguous presence. A gathering, whether for a gig, or to piece, or to hang out, was presented as incontrovertible evidence. *"Here* is the community," I would be told: our friends, these people sharing our ideas and values. A well-attended gig or freestyle session constituted evidence of the "strength" of the community. The ability to name people in the scene further demonstrated that the community existed: the "shout-outs" that would go on the air whenever Miguel hosted rappers or crews on his weekly broadcast. "So many, so many" muttered one DJ as he attempted to not omit anyone in the scene; to miss out somebody's name was a cardinal sin, liable to be interpreted as a diss. This "namechecking" is the aural, electronic counterpart to the graffiti practice of "tagging": the covering of any available surface with one's tag, creating a set of constantly updated traces of self across the suburban rail network. These naming practices, whether in spray paint, over the ether, on record covers, or in magazines do not constitute simply a "re-presenting" of an existing "community," but rather *are* the performative acts of producing, of *presenting,* that constituency. Graffiti, one writer told me as pieces flashed past outside the train window, is a "sign of life . . . I see it and I know that someone has been there." Writers "know" each other through seeing each other's tags, before they meet. The shared practice is taken as evidence of a shared being.

On a social organizational level, graffiti writers "hung out" in "crews," or "posses" (not gangs). A crew was simply a group that might have gone to school together, lived in relative proximity, hung out in the same place. As crews came into contact with other crews there was a degree of interaffiliation: writers from different crews might join up to tag or piece together. In the Sydney graffiti scene, there was little violent rivalry, although there was always a degree of braggadocio, and reminiscing about the great intercrew battles of the old days. Crews tended to be semiformalized and governed in their internal and external relationships by discourses of "respect." Transgressions; "going over," "dissing," and so on; were dealt with by ostracism, perhaps "small-scale" violence (fistfights and pushing and shoving: I came across no evidence for the *use* of knives, firearms, or other weaponry), and attempts to resolve disputes through the invocation of "appropriate ritual": J.U. and Mick E's battle.

And yet, the gathering of a number of writers and crews at a given site constituted very powerful affective grounds for claims to "community." As does, for example, a show: a night at an inner-city bar with all the "west-side posses" in attendance, pogo-ing to DWC, having made a sixty kilometer journey from the far western suburbs for the occasion, clearly demonstrates, or is taken to demonstrate, a shared experience, a shared desire to be part of something.

The problem confronting these folk is, however, precisely that of *place.* As I have suggested, discourses of place were central to Hip Hop as it emerged and developed in inner-urban North America (Decker 1993): rappers come from a place, a "hood" that is named, which they claim to represent. The majority of rap or Hip Hop albums will have at least a passing reference to the geographic point of origin of the performer: NWA's "Straight outta Compton" literally put that Los Angeles district on the map.

This is one of the most distinctive features of the Sydney Hip Hop Scene, a feature that is responsible for the massive effort put into the discursive production of the "Hip Hop Community": a geographical dispersal. A massively sprawling city, Sydney lacks the dense inner-city "hoods" of Hip Hop folklore. The city center is a grid of tower blocks and a handful of entertainment precincts; people live in the suburbs, tens of kilometers distant. Sydney Hip Hop is decidedly — assertively and proudly — suburban. Crews "operate" (that is, "hang out") in isolation, encountering each other through the traces of tags, at (very) occasional Hip Hop nights at clubs, or not at all. Hence the pressure to tag up as often as possible: otherwise, one is, literally, invisible. Crews, which are, after all, only a small group of friends hanging out together, rather than gangs "claiming territory" or marking out turf possessively, get their tags up whenever and wherever possible. Tagging itself is a reason for a trip to the city, or for an afternoon "bombing" expedition around the rail network. Absent members of the crew will sometimes have their tags, or interpretations of them, put up.

In Sydney, then, there was no Hip Hop Community that "simply" *appeared,* organically, out of neighborhood localities. If not for the constant effort of generating the "representation" of this community, it would not be found at all. All that would remain would be clutches of individuals hanging out together, leaving graffiti for . . . well, for no one, really. The *idea* of the Hip Hop Community, somehow unifying these disparate groups lends these practices meaning, renders them coherent. Further, in rendering the "Community" thinkable, this "idea" holds out the promise of a possible, future, union: the Hip Hop Community is an idea suspended between a halcyonic past and a deferred future (re)completion.[4]

And in order to sustain the idea that there is a community, it would appear that there needs to be a place: the West Side.

WEST SIDE

To be national is to "possess" a territory, without which there is no national existence.

— Ghassan Hage, "Nation-Building Dwelling-Being" (1993)

While U2 were talking about "The Streets With No Name," Eazy [E] and [Ice] Cube [of the Los Angelino crew Niggaz with Attitude (NWA)] were talking about Crenshaw, Slauson, Gauge and Figeroa. U2 may have meant well with their liberal rhetoric, but they missed the kind of naming that occurs from below, even when there are no street signs. How else do you find your way home? Hiphop in many ways is a map for precisely this purpose.

— Brian Cross *It's Not about A Salary* (1994)

You look at the main thing of Hip Hop and every group and everything they represent their area and they represent their neighbourhood it's the same with us our friends are around where we live where we live that's like our home we know it so well like the back of our hand and so yeah, we represent the people we see every day you know what I mean and plus the people like that live somewhere else, yeah, like we class Sydney as one, but the West as our home really.

— A Sydney writer (anonymous)

Here comes that chorus again . . .

A.U.S. Down Under Comin' Upper . . .

In the slamming break between Die C's and Ser Reck's verses on "A.U.S.T.," Vame has sampled an African-American MC antiphonally responding to the voices of the crew namechecking the suburbs of Sydney's far west:

St Claire's
in the house
St Mary's
in the house
Mt Druitt's
in the house

. . . culminating in the climactic

Aaaah . . . *Penrith's*
in the house!

It's tempting, but perhaps just a little too smart, to read this moment as one of the negotiation of cultural contexts: the African-American voice brought into play with the overcoded "Aussie-ness" of the chanted suburb names. In performance, in classic Hip Hop call and response form, Def Wish Cast's pogo-ing audience anticipates the rappers' appearance on stage with an air-punching chant, again sampled by Vame as the introduction to Def Wish's ragga rap tour de force, "Stupid Kind of People":

West Side! West Side! West Side!

And among the fantastic "syllable ballistics," Def Wish raps:

I'm takin the time to perpetrate the slammin' style of raggamuffin commin up from the west of Sydney doing it, doing it properly to the beat . . . [a] rappar coming from the W.E.S.T. . . .

Again and again this place appears in the raps of Def Wish Cast: "The [definite article] West," "The West Side," "the W.E.S.T.," "far west," and so on . . . The West that "runs amok," that constitutes the readership of graffiti on trains ("A piece seen by the whole West-side," raps Die C, celebrating the power of writing on "Perennial Cross Swords"), the West that constitutes the Hip Hop Community, for whom the crew raps. Def Wish calls his rhymes "the saga from the suburbs . . . that's The West . . . ." On the same track ("Battlegrounds of Sydney"), another rap offers a street-level counter to the pervasive spatio-temporal tropes of Australian cultural anteriority, the "Australian Cultural Cringe" (Phillips 1958); Die C challenges all those who claim that Australian Hip Hop is "behind":

That might of been the case before
But Def Wish Cast has redefined their way of thinking
People come out here throw flames at our nest of crews in Sydney
But they never got to hear The West!

And so, Def Wish Cast's Aussie Hip Hop is emblematic of the

Down under comin' up!

This is an attempt to institute Sydney's western suburbs, or, more specifically, Sydney's *far* western suburbs, as the authentic "home" ("hood") of Sydney Hip Hop, in the context of two convergent discourses about communal identity. The first is that identified by Homi Bhabha in terms of the "recurrent metaphor of landscape as the inscape of national identity" (1994: 143); this is the impossibility of thinking "nation" without thinking "place." The second, perhaps a subset of the first, is Hip Hop's concern with "place" (see Decker 1993; Cross 1994), manifesting as a (generic) injunction to write "place" into raps and to assert a (geographical) point of origin and (therefore) a population or constituency from which, and for whom, that rap is spoken. This is, in turn, bound up in the Hip Hop discourse of "representation" (see Maxwell and Bambrick 1994: 6–15). The experience of living in a periphery, an "under"-place, can be equated with the Hip Hop discourses of origin in the Bronx, or in an imaginary downtown Los Angeles, or in Philadelphia. Such narratives, graphically portraying the decayed inner-city zones of North American metropolises, circulate in the Hip Hop mediascape, from the more "highbrow literature" (K. M. Jones's 1994 celebration of the Bronx is exemplary) to hundreds of raps and magazines where the identification of specific places of origin is, as Decker (1993) notes, celebrated. The qualitative aporia, the vast, almost, one would think, incommensurate empirical differences between the experience of growing up in the dense hoods of the Bronx and the sprawling outer suburbs of Sydney, characterized if anything by a lack of a sense of "neighborhood-ness," is subsumed under the posited assumption of a shared experience of neglect.

The corollary of the Hip Hop concern with time and place identified by Decker is a generic encouragement of the discursive production (and adduction) of specific place, and the attendant discourses of "representing," to which I shall turn below. From the earliest days the American raps that circulated in the Sydney scene named districts and neighborhoods. That local raps followed suit is no surprise. The problem was, however, to name the neighborhood that a local rap practice could be said to represent. The construction of the West Side, and the privileging of the western suburbs of Sydney as the "place" of Hip Hop in Sydney is an attempt to authenticate Sydney Hip Hop by "demonstrating" both that this Hip Hop speaks for a "real" constituency and that this constituency is somehow identifiable with, or commensurate with, an African-American urban underclass. Sydney Hip Hop thereby was able to stake a claim to a counterhegemonic, if not underclass, status and to understand and present itself as being an "authentic" expression of, or response to, the experience of oppression. In this translation of the inner-city North American experience to the sprawling outer suburbs of Sydney, the marginalizing Hip Hop discourses of "the streets," "the underground," and so on, are literalized in terms of geographic peripherality: Sydney Hip Hop becomes "postcards from the edge of the underside," or tales from "the underground table." The rappers of Def Wish Cast assert their Hip Hop authenticity by rhetorically adopting the position of the mouthpieces of a downtrodden lumpen class denied access to cultural capital, marginalized by a "mainstream'/centralized bourgeois culture that has lost touch with "the street," that is crippled by false ideology, populated by *suckers* and *perpetrators,* by *half-steppers* and *sell-outs,* and that fails to recognize a reality accessible only through remaining in touch with the street.

■ Sydney is massive, its population of around four million sprawling nearly seventy kilometers from the glamorous scenery of the northern beaches to the green swath of the Royal National Park in the south; the same distance lies between the picture-postcard sweep of Bondi Beach on the eastern seaboard and the floodplains of the Nepean River, at the foot of the Blue Mountains, the westernmost extremity of the Cumberland Plain. To the southwest, dormitory suburbs, by now satellite cities, have sprung up along the axis of the road and rail trunk routes to Canberra, the national capital, and Melbourne, a thousand kilometers to the south.

"The City," notes Shirley Fitzgerald, is, for Sydney residents, that "bit in the middle" (1994: 79), a place that one goes to for work, to shop, to go to the cinema, but in which (at least until the state government's push in the early 1990s for "urban consolidation") no one lives. Ringed by Victorian workers' terrace suburbs, gentrified in the 1970s and 1980s and now populated by the professional classes, the "City" itself is the hole in the demographic doughnut.

In the narrative of mid-1980s Sydney Hip Hop, the "City" figures as the *empty* center, "played-out" (Sound Unlimited: *Tales From the Underside* publicity material 1992), populated by suburban kids "going into town," night clubbing, and often affecting Hip Hop style. These are the "weekend warriors," the "half-steppers," understood as following trends rather than "committing" themselves to the culture: the City, then, is coded as a site of pretence and inauthenticity.

In the early days, I was told, there were attempts to locate Hip Hop in "the City": "everyone would go to the City and hang out," one writer explained; but the effort required was too great: ". . . from there, um, it sort of died out." Hip Hop flourished, instead, "in the suburbs . . . on the streets": authentic, fresh, *real*. Inverting North American Hip Hop, in Sydney it was the suburbs that were conflated with "the street," with "the real": the suburbs became Hip Hop's "place.'

THE WESTIE SYNDROME

Sydney's Western Suburbs (capitalized, prefixed by the definite article) are best understood less as a geographical locus than as an imaginary "other," a periphery constituting the grounds against which central "cosmopolitan" Sydney is constructed.[5] Diane Powell's *Out West* (1993) traces the development of this demonization, demonstrating the prevalent public (that is, media) discourses of the Western Suburbs operating to erase difference, homogenizing a vast, complex range of peoples and lifestyles into an imaginary population characterized as being working class and of primarily "ethnic" background. From her extensive analysis of print media (in particular the daily broadsheet the *Sydney Morning Herald*), Powell argues that life in Western Sydney is portrayed in terms of lack and excess: lack of facilities, beauty, culture, refinement, taste, health; excess of crime, violence, poverty, broken homes, single mothers, unemployment, welfare recipients. Any positive aspects, she argues, are played down. Further, locals tend to be portrayed as passive victims, unable to help themselves, but nonetheless culpable for their inferior condition. Building on Powell's analysis, Symonds recognizes the contributory significance of demographic features, while arguing that a materialist analysis cannot account for the depth, the intensity, and, often, the irrationality of the mythical construction of the western suburbs as being "uncivilised," as being "so bad as to be 'impossible'": impossible to live in or with, impossible to understand. This myth creates a monolithic "West" erasing difference and constructing "a significant portion of Sydney's geographical area as a negatively valued, homogeneous entity" (Symonds 1993: 64).

And it *is* a significant portion. A 1988 review of urban planning policy (Spearritt and DeMarco 1988) offers a geographico-historical overview, defining "Western Sydney" as "the area extending from Parramatta to the Blue Mountains and from Hawkesbury to Liverpool . . . [having] a young population and a high proportion of non-English-speaking migrants . . . [and] average household incomes . . . lower than in the Sydney region" (65). These are dormitory suburbs built largely since the Second World War to cope with the rapid influx of migrants, largely from Mediterranean Europe. Developed by real estate, finance, and construction institutions with little regard for coherent planning principles, these suburbs sprawl for dozens of kilometers, the expanse of privately owned (or, more correctly, mortgaged) free-standing, quarter-acre-block brick homes broken occasionally by ill-conceived public housing estates, such as those in Campbelltown and Mt. Druitt (Spearritt and DeMarco 1988: 67).

Ser Reck was fond of telling me that the Western Suburbs are "the future." The 1988 Australian Bureau of Statistics growth projections for the Sydney region bear this out, anticipating that "Western Sydney" will constitute, by 2011, 37.7 percent of the overall population, up from an estimated 30.9 percent in 1986 (in Spearritt and DeMarco 1988: 66). The Sydney Region Outline Plan of 1968 identified Mt. Druitt, Penrith, and Blacktown as "three new towns" on which Sydney's expansion would be centered (Spearritt and DeMarco 1988: 67).

Symonds's analysis considers the conventional materialist reading of such demographic data: the narrative of a working poor pushed into the hinterland as the Victorian working man's terrace houses of the inner-city neighborhoods are gentrified. To characterize the Western Suburbs as "working class" however, is overly simplistic. Symonds argues that "there are two basic problems" with predicating a "middle-class, materialist basis" for the popular, denigrating mythos of the Western Suburbs, suggesting that at least ethnicity (Symonds adds "and gender" without any elaboration) also has significant effects. Furthermore, "'the west' is not just poor and working class (as opposed to the seeming uniformity, according to Edward Soja, of Los Angeles). There is wealth and a strong middle-class self-consciousness amongst many western Sydney residents" (Symonds 1993: 65).

Industrial development — with concomitant employment opportunities — has not kept up with the rapid population growth in the west. Using the results of the 1986 Australian Census of Population and Housing, Horvath et al. (1989) note that the period of the development of the far western suburbs as residential zones was also a period of the radical deindustrialization of Sydney in general: "In 1971 Sydney was a manufacturing city with a large industrial working class. . . . In 1986 blue-collar workers comprised only twenty-one per cent of the labour force" (48). "The overall pattern," they conclude, "is one of industrial decline" (44). The period from 1981 to 1986 saw a 17.3 percent reduction in workers involved in manufacturing across Sydney, growth being experienced in the sectors of "Finance, property and business" (23 percent), "Community Services" (15 percent), and "Recreation and Personal Services" (12.6 percent) (44). The main industry in the west has been, in fact, construction: the building of the suburbs, and the provision of services for the growing population.

Heavy industrial activity, such as refining and steel making, tend to be located along coastal strips to Sydney's north and south (the port cities of Newcastle and Wollongong/Port Kembla respectively). There are few economy-of-scale advantages to be gained from locating industry in the west, although there has been some manufacturing development in the Liverpool-Minto-Campbelltown corridor, where government incentives were used to attract investment. By 1976, for example, twenty-two major industries, including Comalco, Volvo, and Pirelli had established manufacturing plants in the Minto Industrial Estate (Spearritt and DeMarco 1989: 73), while over 5,000 jobs had been created in the Macarthur area (centered on Campbelltown) by 1986, contributing to a total of 27,000 jobs in 425 industries in the area (76). In light of the massive influx of population to the region noted above, however, it can be seen that demand for work would exceed supply, requiring aspiring job-seekers to travel outside the district (using an inadequate transport infrastructure), and resulting in a chronic unemployment problem.

As Symonds argues, "the ethnic heterogeneity of the population, its dispersal over large areas and the lack of centralised industry mitigates against an analysis of the Western Suburbs in terms of it being 'working class'" (1993: 65). He also makes the point that there are large areas of "middle class wealth and sensibility" among the "western suburbs." The discursive construction of the Western Suburbs as "working class" is precisely that: an imaginative construct, rather than an empirical socioeconomic fact. Notwithstanding Horvath et al.'s identification of Sydney as a city experiencing a general pattern of "industrial decline," the vast bulk of the development of the Western Suburbs has taken place subsequent to this decline.

That the population of the Western Suburbs in general constitutes an "underclass," however, is a more sustainable proposition. Horvath et al. "essentially identify working class Sydney" as forming a triangle "from the outer western suburbs around Penrith–Mt Druitt to the outer southwest (Campbelltown) and then to the northern tip of Botany Bay" (Horvath et al. 1989: 48; see Spearritt and DeMarco's definition of "Western Sydney" above): in other words, precisely what Def Wish Cast calls "the West Side." The public housing areas of Mt. Druitt and Campbelltown are characterized by "extreme concentrations of poverty" (58), while the Census Districts of Airds (near Campbelltown), St. Marys, and Penrith ranked two, three, and four respectively in a listing of "Relatively Poor Sydney" (Horvath et al. 1989: 86).

An economic corollary of the service-industrial base of employment is a vulnerability to economic downturn. Areas populated by high densities of people from non-English-speaking backgrounds suffer first and recover last from extended recessions, such as those of 1982–83 and 1987–90, creating a vast pool of long-term unemployed. The major concentrations of unemployment in Sydney can be found in Airds, Cabramatta, and Fairfield (Horvath et al. 1989: 52), with unemployment tending to be a direct function of distance from the Central Business District (of Sydney itself). Horvath et al. go on to note the concentration of youth unemployment "in outer-suburban areas, particularly in areas with large concentration of public housing such as Mt Druitt" (52). The locating of a major university campus in Penrith is one governmental response to these problems: plans for Chifley University (realized as the University of Western Sydney) were announced by the Federal Government in 1987 (Spearritt and DeMarco 1988: 66). Def Wish's father expressed to me in late 1993 his desire that his son complete his undergraduate work in graphic design at this campus. The university union also offered occasional performance opportunities for Def Wish Cast and other crews in the early 1990s.

The important point is that the (sub)urban landscape of Sydney's Western Suburbs is not so much "postindustrial" itself: there has been no collapse of industry, of the body politic; rather, it is a landscape that is very much the product of a postindustrial world, a world in which the "industrial" bit happened elsewhere. The Western Suburbs are a massive, very recent encampment of displaced, ethnically heterogeneous populations: it is this sense of displacement, of not-belonging, leading to a "yearning" for community (Hage 1993a), rather than a socioeconomically grounded class-identification, that is ultimately of significance. However, in terms of the present discussion, the argument that Symonds is making is that the demonization of the Western Suburbs is not adequately accounted for in its totality in strictly materialist terms.

An alternative explanation for the depth and intensity of "the westie syndrome," suggests Symonds, lies in a long-standing tradition in Australian literature of deriding "the suburbs" as boring, uninspiring, and isolated (and often, on the other hand, peaceful, clean). Barry Humphries, for example, derives much of the humor of his character Dame Edna Everidge from her suburban *gaucherie*. When it comes to the Western Suburbs, however, Symonds argues, even the positive aspects of suburban life are removed. Peacefulness, leafiness, cleanliness: all these are absent. Instead, the west is violent, polluted, sparsely ugly, a wasteland where gangs roam, and youth is suicidal.

A third account of possible determinants of "the westie syndrome" is derived from feminist, psychoanalytic, and postcolonialist theories of the Other: the Western Suburbs as the Other to Sydney's center. The west here is considered as the formative contrast to the cultural ideal of the Sydney center. Symonds argues, however, that the preeminent theories of otherness — those of de Beauvoir, Lacan, and Said — are informed by the notion of desire: the desire for the Other. However, this doesn't really seem to fit with the west, argues Symonds, pointing out that "[i]t *all* [the West] is to be spurned. There is no fascination, no sense of the exotic or of sexual attraction. Certainly it is heavily investigated, measured and studied as an empirical case study by well-intentioned academics, but the 'westie' mythology holds no such attractions" (1993: 67).[6] He even argues that the usually favored "others" of the Anglo center, such as Aboriginals and migrants, actually become dull when placed in the Western Suburbs; although well over half of Sydney's Aboriginal population lives in the west, they lack the "appeal" of those inner-city ghetto Aboriginals or the tribal Aboriginals. Similarly, inner-city migrants are valued for their "fine food, writing and sensitivities," while westie migrants are "mostly reduced to loud cars and houses with balustrades. . . . The western suburbs seem to envelop the[se] groups so that they lose the standard, theoretical desirability" (67).

Symonds argues, then, that the west functions as the Sydney center's cultural colony. On this account, the shaking off of the "cultural cringe" in the 1970s was paralleled by massive expansion into the Western Suburbs. A cosmopolitan center developed as the west exploded — Sydney grew and divided itself materially and culturally. The center saw the development of a powerful artistic-intellectual elite — opera companies, dance, theater, films, books, an academic milieu, and so on. Sydney became a center, able to rival overseas centers. The reproduction of local European and American cultural models could fairly successfully challenge British colonialist ideas about Australia as materialistic, cultureless, without manners and learning, as still inhabited by violent criminals in a hot, dreary landscape.

Not only were the cultural forms of the Northern Hemisphere reproduced; so too was the colonial cultural relationship. The Western Suburbs became cast in the same relationship to the center as Botany Bay had been to London. "Part of the British myth of Australia was almost exactly reproduced by the Sydney myth of 'the west'" (68). Symonds goes so far as to suggest that the west can be seen as Sydney's excrement—the convict stain removed from the center by grafting it onto the population of the west.

A historical argument accompanies this analysis. Symonds suggests that Australia missed out on the European experience of the Enlightenment and that the late 1960s through to the 1980s are understood as Australia's Enlightenment—an indubitable assumption of progress of culture and ideas. Enlightenment is paralleled by a condemnation of all that went before—all that went before, in this respect, was seen to live on in the west—"History" argues Symonds, "was spatially located and separated from 'the centre,' as a contrast to its own progress" (69).

The overall conclusion that Symonds comes to is that the Western Suburbs now constitute, in the Sydney imaginary, what the center once was—a pre-modern convict colony. Suffering in this place is pre-modern. The Western Suburbs, then, is still enmired in a battle with nature. True, modern consciousness, the argument goes, can only be formed in the cosmopolitan swirl of the city. The west is coded in discourse as a place where, by definition, the modern subject, who is free, equal, and rational, cannot exist.

Symonds concludes his survey by arguing that the Western Suburbs should be recognized as a center, or a place with many centers. Quoting Raymond Williams, he poses the possibility of this place as a subject position, rather than as an object: if the west is being judged from the center, it, the center, should be judged from the west. This is a matter of "reversing the mythology and seeing what is valuable in the eastward gaze back to the shining towers of the coast" (71). This "returning of the centre's gaze," Symonds continues, will always operate within a field of contradictoriness, informed by a simultaneous desire for the center's ideas, money, and culture and a contempt for the its achievements.

THERE'S NO THERE, THERE

The Hip Hop imagining of the "West Side" follows Symonds's redressive prescription to the letter. The almost parodic series of self-marginalizations and self-otherings is in effect an active inversion of the "othering" of the Western Suburbs, a reversal of the popular demonization of the

Western Suburbs troped by Symonds as "the westie syndrome." This inversion is not without its contradictions: the "down under" of DWC's rap is valued insofar as it is "coming up," thereby maintaining a logic privileging up over down. "Down" is recoded, however, as "in-touchness": "the street," "the underground," and so on all become indices for "reality," and the practices of "streetness" are epistemological, even when nobody really "hangs out" on any literal streets (hanging out is more likely to happen in bedrooms, as will be discussed below). The logic of other discriminating binarisms are more completely inverted: the City's (colonizing) gaze is returned, privileging the periphery over the center, the "west" over the "east," through this epistemological gesture: the City is mistaken, deluded, subject to false ideologies (witness Blaze's editorials). And as the rhyme above suggests, the temporal mapping of the Western Suburbs into a position of backwardness is displaced by the predication of the west as a site of literal cultural avant-gardism: the West Side is reinscribed as being in touch with global currents, a connection maintained through processes of dissemination (Bhabha 1994) or contagion (Deleuze and Guattari 1987) that completely bypass the linear logics of center-periphery or top-down pedagogies.

But there is more going on here, too. The West Side is also (a) *home.* Indeed, Symonds recognizes the assertion of "homeliness" as being one of the first strategies of redress in the face of the center's demonizing of the Western Suburbs (71). But as Hage argues, being at home always involves a process of "feeling at home" (Hage, 1997): that is, home is an affective space, the building of a home an affective practice. Hage's Heideggerian analysis ontologizes this *process* of dwelling — of building a dwelling — in order to argue that nationalist projects are "existential dramas" that can never be complete. Hage evokes the figure of the nomad as the archetypal " postmodern" figure, mourning whatever traces of stability he [*sic*] can find in his wanderings (1993a: 102–3). From this figure he develops an ontological premising of a fundamental "homesickness" (103) or "yearning" (102) as the horizon of a human being, a being whose being can only be understood, after Heidegger, in terms of the activity of dwelling: that is, Hage suggests, in the contemporary context, of the building of nations.

Def Wish explained to me, one baking summer day as we sat at St. Mary's station, that he and his crew had "put the west on the map . . . people from Melbourne, Adelaide, Brisbane, they all know about the West Side now." "So," I wondered, "what do you show someone who wants to see 'West Side'?" "That's it man," he replied, almost too poignantly: "there's nothing here"[7] (Maxwell 1994a). But he means it literally: there is the train line, a bullet-straight link stretching from the low ridge of the Blue Mountains, marking the by-now transcended limit to the suburban sprawl (suburbs now march right up the once-prohibitive slopes), to the postcard Sydney of Harbour, Opera House, Bridge, and Beaches, some 60 kilometers to the east. There is "Australia's Wonderland," an amusement park set on a scrubby eucalypt plain, adjacent to the Eastern Creek motor raceway. There are the postmodern consumer palaces of Penrith, in the shadow of the mountains: the Panthers entertainment complex, a vast, stranded ocean liner of poker machines, restaurants, bars, and recreational facilities, and the glistening shopping malls of the Penrith CBD. There is Rooty Hill, with its massive RSL Club[8] and hotel accommodation. A clutch of cinemas in Penrith. A suburban rugby league ground (for the Penrith Panthers), a theater (the Q), and, now, a university (the University of Western Sydney). Otherwise, there is housing: vast expanses of free-standing bungalows, carpeting the Cumberland Plain, occasionally visible, over the top of wooden and concrete baffles, or through wire-mesh fencing, from the freeway that parallels the train line. The importance of this single pair of rails cutting across the plain is impossible to overstate; linking the West Side to the radial latticework of the "Sydney System," the eight-car trains carry tags and pieces across hundreds of kilometers of territory, threading together the far-flung community that is not one: the act of recognizing someone's tag on the other side of the city becomes in itself a community-constituting practice. The appeal to the young bomber is obvious.

Def Wish is Ghassan Hage's nomad. Or rather, a young man named Simon Bottle, of Anglo-Celtic descent, is the nomad, living now in the tract housing of a sun-burned gum-tree plain, surrounded by the ghosts of the Dharruk (the Aboriginal inhabitants of these plains, whose words, borrowed from the Macquarie Dictionary, he inserts into his raps). Feeling the emptiness around him, Simon *invented* Def Wish, taking a new name from his graffiti practice (bear in mind Baudrillard's description of graffiti as "free publicity for existence" [1988: 21]), and he also *invented,* after a fashion, belongingness to a nation, with which he could negotiate his own being in, and colonization of, this strange, alien place: not simply making a home by being in a place, but also *being* by making a home there.

What is at stake in making a claim to community? Recent work at the University of Western Sydney's Research Centre for Intercommunal

Studies provides some useful ways to approach such a question. Rejecting "those analyses of community or communities that conceptualise these social forms as static and unproblematically conceived entities interacting with each other," Hage and Johnson suggest that communities "be investigated as temporary, conjunctural manifestations of on-going processes of communal formation fuelled by internal struggles for the very creation of, and the right to speak in the name of, 'the community'" (1993a: v). Community, on this account, is understood as an ongoing accomplishment, undertaken in a mode of desire, through which individuals define their own collectivity in relation to and against other collectivities — recall the policing of communal borders going on in the pages of *Hype* and *Vapors,* above[9] — and through processes of struggle and negotiation within the boundaries of the putative collective.

COMMUNITY

I will return, below, to the master trope of nationalism in Hip Hop; now I want to briefly turn to what Hage and Johnson call "the conditions of emergence of new forms of social identification and communal formation" (1993: v). In addition to taking into account the ideas about Hip Hop Community, Culture, and Nation circulating within the mediascape examined in the previous chapter, we will need to understand how such discourses permeate the more general, public sphere.

Indeed, one of the conditions for emergence of the Hip Hop Scene was in fact, the ubiquity of such discourses in the public sphere within which that scene was located. Ferdinand Tönnies, writing in the late nineteenth century, is generally recognized as having introduced the term "community" to sociology, identifying *gemeinschaft* with "organic life," "intimacy," and privacy. In this sense, "community" designated "closely knit networks of people of a similar kind, with intimate relationships, with face-to-face relationships . . . [The community] was seen as serving the needs of its members with warmth, strength and stability" (Skrbis 1994: 8). The implicit discourses of authenticity and of consensual democratic politics that inform such an understanding are the very features that facilitate the taking up of the word itself by a range of individuals and groups. Skrbis notes that Hillery, writing in the 1950s, was able to list ninety-four definitions of the word "community," concluding that "all of the definitions deal with people . . . beyond this common basis there is no agreement" (8). Skrbis accurately suggests that "community" has become "a mythological construct in everyday language as well as in the scholarly literature" (8).

In a collection of essays titled *Community in Australia,* Lucy Taksa reviewed this ubiquity of use of the term "community." To the apparent dismay of anthropologists and sociologists, for whom, Taksa argues, the term loses any analytic specificity, "community" is attached to any number of social groups and services. Thus it is possible on any given day to pick up a newspaper and read of "the Sydney Lesbian and Gay Community," "the Greek Community," "the Vietnamese Community," "the Arts Community," "the religious community" and so on. Taksa reads, in this discursive ubiquity "a romantic and positive orientation in regard to moral duties which supposedly arise out of shared 'group interests,' shared identity, mutual support and so forth" (1994: 24).

Terms such as "community" and "culture" certainly have attached to them a certain *cachet:* to go out spray-painting train carriages late at night with a handful of friends, for example, is fun. It is illegal, clandestine, and therefore exciting. One might be chased by the police, get arrested, or escape, running all through the night, collapsing hours later after traversing a dozen kilometers of train lay-up yards, storm-water channels, housing estates: a grand cops and robbers game played out (for real) across the reinvented graffiti-geographics of Sydney's Western Suburbs, this is a rhizomatic remapping of the city that traverses, overlays, and underpasses the conventional radial-arboreal geography of freeway and railway corridor. To be a bomber is to be tough, to have a blast, to fight a guerilla action against a uniformed, or poorly, laughably inadequately disguised plain-clothed "transit." And at the end of the night, there is a beer or a bong with your mates, and the possibility of seeing your piece, your "throw-up," or at least a few dozen of your tags "running" on the day's commuter trains. Finally, as one writer told me, there are always the girls ("they love the bombers, man").[10]

Dozens of accounts testify to this; listen, for example, to the breathless raps of Def Wish Cast ("Perennial Cross-Swords," the account of the eternal struggle between the writer and the transit police), or read the frankly exhilarating account of a "whole train" piece by the legendary writer Lee of the 1970s New York–based Fabulous Five in Craig Castleman's *Getting Up* (1982: 2–17). Castleman's transcription of Lee's story is buoyant, intoxicating, thrilling—almost (and significantly) required reading in graffiti circles.

How much better is all this if you can make a case that not only is it good fun, but it also is part of a "culture" — if you are both "expressing" yourself and "representing" your community? What if you are able to justify these activities in terms of a discourse of rebellion, able to claim that you are fighting the powers that be? Even more: what if there is a researcher asking you about it? *Studying* you? You can push the affective side of it right out of sight . . . sure, it's fun . . . but it's *more* than that . . . *"it's a culture, man"* . . . It is a vocation, a job. And it's not only "speaking" on behalf of your proto-community. It's speaking for (variously) "youth," "the west," "the underground," the dispossessed, the unvoiced, the oppressed.

This is all a big part of it, particularly when understood in this context: several of these people (remember, the Hip Hop subcultural elite) have been doing these things for *a decade*. They have police records, have spent time in prison. They have children, some are married. *They have invested their entire adult life in these practices.* They live, breathe, sleep these things . . . they have a marked (this is too weak a term) interest in these activities *meaning* something. Their being is Hip Hop. Why "concede," or admit, perhaps, that it is fun, when it can be more than that, when it can be everything?

There was a contradictory tension within Hip Hop: the pervasive understanding within the scene that Hip Hop, as a "street" "culture," and as a "world" community is able to access otherwise occluded, dissembled, or otherwise inaccessible truths, is often accompanied by a kind of teleological, quasi-Attalian millenarian discourse, in which a developing musical form prefigures a future social order (Attali 1985). Ser Reck, for example, repeatedly asserted that "Hip Hop is the future." In a less dramatic form, witness Def Wish Cast's ecstatic assertion of the Australian Hip Hop's imminent ascendancy on the world (Hip Hop) stage: "A.U.S.T. down under comin' up . . ."

The use of the term "Hip Hop *Culture*" was significant; many were aware of the use of the term "subculture" to describe youth cultural activities, but did not use it as a label to be applied to their own practice and beliefs. Blaze, for example rejected the idea out of hand, claiming that Hip Hop is a culture in its own right, implicitly not "sub"-anything. "Members" of the Hip Hop Community *understood* their communal being not as a hierarchically delimited subset of an overarching public sphere. Insiders understood this culture as being *counter*- rather than *sub*cultural.

Taksa notes that "community" "tends to be used in such a way that suggests a totality" (1994: 24): a consensus of opinion, implicit in the discourse of organicity around which "community" is constructed and elaborated as a mode of socio-political organization. At the same time, however, "[t]he denial of internal differences implicit in the word [community] . . . can have fundamental socio-political ramifications" (24).

Skrbis, echoing Walser's observation, warns against the potential methodological pitfalls of an approach predicated upon an a priori concept of "community": "in reality it is very hard to locate an ethnic community" (1994: 10). Skrbis is concerned with what he calls "community labelling": the processes by which a discourse of "community" is mobilized by an elite to develop its own interests. Community-making is the product of strategies of exclusion and inclusion, through which the elite effect "multiple fluctuations of boundaries" in order to discipline the segmented, contested space of the proto-community. Not everyone is immediately included within the community boundary, notwithstanding their ethnic, religious, class, sexual, gender (and so on) status. Rather, inclusion is determined in relation to situational factors; whoever is able to legislate on the fluctuating rules of inclusion or exclusion is thereby able to determine who or what *is* the community.

Of course, from the "outside," Skrbis argues, the space of the community appears to be uniform. The (early) sociological and, by now, popular understanding of the term "community" as *gemeinschaft* implies an a priori homogeneity, in the context of which difference appears as an anomaly: as evidence, more often than not, of the "inauthenticity" of the rival group claiming the status of community. Such an *appearance* of homogeneity is precisely what is at stake in making claims to "community." The refusal of the Hip Hop Scene to conform to homogeneity in its empirical, lived dimension was a recurring theme: witness the calls for "unification," the complaints about those who wished to divide the scene.

All claims to community are, then, predicated on a set of micropolitical circumstances, dependant on an existing hierarchy, or elite, but also on "loyalties, interests, envy, gossip, scandals and demands that take place within a group at any given moment" (Skrbis 1994: 11). Skrbis offers a generic experience from his fieldwork (he was researching Slovenian and Croatian "communities" in South Australia at the time of the Balkan wars of the early 1990s), an experience I shared on many occasions: "While conducting my fieldwork, I was told by individuals from 'both sides' that 'their' particular arguments were the right ones. When I commented, 'Oh, I didn't know that' or 'I am surprised to hear that,' I was openly told that this was so because I did not frequent their (correct) side of the community" (11). I think here of the "battle" between J.U. and Mick E, and the subsequent concern on the part of both parties to set the matter straight in my mind. Weeks later, J.U. was to tell me that he was glad that "now you've seen the *real* thing."[11]

Skrbis uses the word "hierarchy" to designate the social elite, arguing that this need not designate a fixed structuring of power relations in which power is a quality held by some (the power*ful,* the "elite") and not by others (the "subjects," perhaps). Rather, following Foucault, Skrbis suggests that power circulates within and around a given context, informing, being exchanged within, producing and disciplining every moment of discourse — gossip as well as "official" discourse. It is these qualities of power — its ubiquity, elusiveness, supplementarity, its tendency to overflow, to be generative, those aspects of power rendered in the French as *pouvoir* — that inform the exertion of disciplinary power (*puissance*). The formation of a "hierarchy," such as that of the Sydney Hip Hop Scene, requires that the ubiquity of "*puissance*" be somehow disciplined into regulatory discourses. In order for such discourses to have an effect, however, requires that those to be subjected to them are "enrolled" within a particular closure of what Laclau and Mouffe (1985) call the "field of articulation."

Stewart Clegg borrows the term "enrolment" from Callon's "empirical sociology of power" (Clegg 1989: 204). Callon's model neither reduces action to the intentions of fully self-aware agents nor to the effects of a structure, thus negotiating both "subjectivist" and "objectivist" accounts of social practice in a manner somewhat similar to that advocated by Bourdieu (Bourdieu and Wacquant 1992: 11). Callon (as well as Clegg) suggests that "networks of interest are actually constituted and reproduced through conscious strategies and unwitting practices" (Bourdieu and Wacquant 1992: 11). The schema Callon employs to analyze such processes seeks to "map how agents actually do 'translate' phenomena into resources, and resources into organisation networks of control, of alliance, of coalition, of antagonism, of interest and of structure" (11).

For J.U. to establish his "leadership" in the Hip Hop "field," he does not merely have to "beat" Mick E; he first has to establish that Mick E and himself are operating under a set of shared assumptions or understandings about what constitutes their "field." Only once Mick E has been so "enrolled" does the battle have any "meaning." J.U. "wins" by "translating" the resources at hand into "networks of control" and so on, successfully "positing the indispensability of [his] 'solutions' for ([his] definition of) the other's [Mick E's] 'problems'" (Clegg 1989: 204). In other words, as soon as J.U. convinces Mick E that he (Mick E) should battle J.U. in order to solve the problem of Mick E's transgression, then J.U.'s "worldview," his fixing of what Laclau and Mouffe (1985) call "nodal points of discourse," *effectively* (and the stress here is important, for we are not dealing with questions of what *is*, but with questions of what is *acted on*) establishes, no matter how contingently or fleetingly, the social reality within which these agents are able to act.

Bourdieu argues a similar point: "The symbolic efficacy of words is exercised only in so far as the person subjected to it recognizes the person who exercises it as authorized to do so, or, what amounts to the same thing, only in so far as he fails to recognize that in submitting to it, he himself has contributed, through his recognition, to its establishment" (1991: 116). Substitute the word "practice" for "words" in this passage; the symbolic efficacy of the battle was exercised only in so far as Mick E recognized J.U.'s authority to subject him, Mick E, to it. Although he may well have been reluctant to cede to J.U. the status of someone he should have to "prove" himself *to* (by battling), Mick E, in terms of Bourdieu's argument, contributed to the establishment of J.U.'s status. J.U.'s "victory" in the battle was not simply that he out-rapped Mick E.; the real victory was his establishing of himself as someone who had to be battled, as an authority.

This sense of community as a site of struggle, as I suggested above, extends beyond micropolitics into a broader set of ideas about community/nation as an always incomplete project. Hage, for example, suggests that the nationalist dream of homogeneity is an impossible project, and that this impossibility in fact structures nationalism itself (1993a). A similar incompleteness structures the experience of the Hip Hop Scene in Sydney: the completion of the Hip Hop community-as-project was perennially deferred, both temporally and, perhaps concomitantly, ideologically. Recall the implicit eschatology of the discourse: Australian Hip Hop was, in Def Wish Cast's words "comin'," but not yet completely "up"; Hip Hop was repeatedly described as being "the future"; Unique/Ser Reck is convinced that a kind of scaled-down apocalypse of the Western Suburbs is imminent. "Struggle" was thematized as the fundamental "being" of the "culture," as it fought to resist dilution, appropriation, commercialization, and so forth. Discourses of authenticity, couched in arguments about lineage or, just as frequently, about lived experience, bore out the affective, phenomenological dimensions of "living and breathing" the culture (Blaze), of being "true to the music" (DWC). The latter discourse often takes the form of the subdiscourses of self-expression, the right to a voice: the undeniably immediate sensation of rapping, writing, breaking, and so on. Such discourses frequently rely on a predication of the embodied experience of music (particularly, of course, Hip Hop, with its deep, corporeal beats) as being unmediated, as immanent and immediate.[12] All these discourses are produced, circulated, enlisted to the "struggle."

Recall, too, the article in *Hype* (no. 19) on "the nameless language," addressing the impossibility of naming Hip Hop "for it has no limits but the state of mind of the creator." To name it is to limit it; to know more about it is to realize the impossibility of naming it; and so on. Hip Hop as an essence cannot be demonstrated, cannot be named. This impossibility, however, is not a limit; rather, it constitutes the possibility for thinking about experience as community — an argument I will develop in the final chapter. Here, I will only point to Peirce's understanding of the coherence of any system of meaning being grounded not in a demonstrable transcendental signified, but, instead, within a "community of investigators," themselves oriented toward a future (deferred) consensus of belief/ knowledge (Maxwell 1997a).

HIP HOP NATIONALISM:
A.U.S. DOWN UNDER COMIN' UPPER!

In considering what he calls "the mechanics of the presentation of the national self," Hage uses Goffman's 1959 analysis of the double space of the performance of group identity. Refracting Goffman's Durkheimian analytic of the sui generis "team" through a Bourdieuan concern with symbolic politics, Hage argues that "nations" must be understood within "relations of power that give certain groups the possibility of simultaneously representing, constructing and most importantly . . . staging the nation" (1993b: 126). The space for such an analysis of nation- (or collective-) building as being determined by power relations between groups within teams is opened up by Goffman's observation that there are two dimensions of performance of identity: the "front" space, where fostered impressions are played out; and the "back" region, which is understood not only as the place where less than favorable aspects might be hidden or suppressed, but also as the place where "illusions and impressions are openly constructed" (Goffman in Hage 1993b: 127). The discourse of the Hip Hop Community is commensurable with the "front" space of the performance of identity, a discourse produced and mobilized within the "back space" of power relations, contestation bestowing on the emergent "elite," in Hage's words, "the possibility of simultaneously representing, constructing and most importantly . . . staging the [Hip Hop] nation."

The genealogy of Hip Hop Nationalism lie in the early decades of this century; the nascent "ideology" of the Nation of Islam, and the (strategic) construction of an absolute racial identity and the subsequent use of "Nation" in what Gilroy has called the "pedagogic" rap of crews such as KRS-One, X Clan, and the Poor Righteous Teachers, and the "ludic Africentrism" of other crews such as the Jungle Brothers and De La Soul (Gilroy 1993: 84–85). In Australia, the discourse of Hip Hop Nationalism resonated with a generalized concern with (and a de facto state ideology of) questions of national identity, with republicanism, and with the negotiation of a national postcolonial status, involving subdiscourses of multiculturalism and tolerance — fertile ground for the affectively appealing discourses of Hip Hop Nationalism.

This context, and the disjunction and discontinuity between it and the North American urban experience, is productive of the specificity of the oxymoronic identity known as the Australian Hip Hop Nation. The Black Nationalist tropes were "refracted" through the "internal structure" (Bourdieu) of Australian nationalist discourses, resulting in a moment of discursive and cultural syncretism, resolved in terms of a "both/and," rather than an "either/or," relationship, offering a concrete example of what Hage has referred to as the fundamentally dialogic structure of all nationalisms.

While it certainly is the case that the discourse of Hip Hop Nationhood tended to figure most frequently in the more institutionalized texts that circulated within the scene — *Vapors, Hype,* Miguel's weekly column and broadcasts — and in accounts offered to me as a researcher; that is to say, in more overtly, consciously "discursive," textualized moments; no one involved in the scene was unaware of the "Hip Hop Nation" as a dominant, recurring trope for the Hip Hop social imaginary, or of the import of such a trope for the positioning of their "Hip Hopness."

Here, I want to unravel the complex entanglements of the nationalism to which the Hip Hop social agents are laying claim: the heterogeneous progeny of an overarching, global modernist incitement to nationalism that is amplified in the jingoistic Australian fin de siècle proto-republican ideoscape and the elaboration of a pan-African Islamicist nationalism, inflected strategically through the African-American experience, woven into the heart of the Hip Hop standard narrative. The "Nation" emerges, in this cultural/discursive milieu, as an unproblematically "positive" category, constituting both a grounds and a horizon for the thinking of collective and individual identity.

COMING UNDER NOTICE

At a particular stage of history, Hage writes, the nation "becomes the preeminent mode of collective being, where a collectivity can no longer be if it is not formed into a nation." He quotes Hegel's observation of this status of "the nation": "In the history of the World, only those peoples can come under our notice which form a state . . . it must be understood that all the worth which the human being possesses — all the spiritual reality, he possesses only through the State" (1993a: 77).[13] Hage elaborates on Hegel's theme, suggesting that the question of "coming under notice" is of "often forgotten" importance in nationalist thought. Above, I suggested that an idea about "community" figures in contemporary discourse analogously to "the nation" in these quoted passages; in the contemporary Australian public sphere, informed and circumscribed by (often contradictory and contested) state and popular discourses of multiculturalism and republicanism,[14] "community" can substitute for "nation" in the above quoted passages. Thus, in the postmodern, postcolonial context, "only those peoples can come under our notice which form a community."

Coming under notice, Hage continues, involves questions of "presence, existence and direction" (1993a: 77). It is also a matter of coming under the notice of an "us"; "our notice": "there can be no nation [community] without a 'community of nations [communities]'" (78). In Hage's schema, the becoming of the "Hip Hop Community" would be seen as being predicated on a certain desire to come under the notice of a meta-community of communities. The Hip Hop Community exists within an economy of other communities, and it occupies, within that field, a privileged place, in that Hip Hop claims a specific, "authentic" lineage, tradition, and so on.

Within a broader cultural context, one in which, as Annette Hamilton observes, the problem of distinguishing a national self exists as a virtually ubiquitous incitement to narrate one's self as a national, Hip Hop Nationalism, along with other tropes of communal identity circulating in the scene, is precisely a response to lack of a "sense of national, ethnic, local, class or trade-specific" identity in contemporary Australian urban culture, nourished by a seemingly ubiquitous incitement to particular ("multicultural," "egalitarian," "cosmopolitan") Australian nationalisms (Hamilton 1990: 16).

FEAR OF A BLACK PLANET

Where, then, does the idea of the "Hip Hop Nation" come from? In genealogical terms, one line of antecedents can be traced to the Afrocentric discourse of Nation of Islam ideologists such as Elijah Mohammed, Malcolm X, and, more recently, Louis Farrakhan. Perkins (1991) argues that a familiarity with the racial doctrines expounded by these teachers is essential to an understanding Public Enemy's extraordinary 1990 album, *Fear of a Black Planet*. Drawing in part on the monographs of the early 1970s pamphleteer Frances Cress Welsing, who argued that the (degenerate) white race actively oppressed non-Caucasians as a response to "pigment envy," P.E.'s album was a high point, if not the culmination, of the "message rap" Hip Hop subgenre, a subgenre traceable back to Grandmaster Flash and the Furious Five's "The Message" (1982). Accounts of the Nation of Islam can be found throughout the academic and popularized accounts of Hip Hop (Fernando 1994: 119–152, and particularly 144–45 for a brief historical account of the development of the Nation of Islam; Rose 1994b: 103, 118–19; Toop 1991: 130, 190),[15] and it is not my intention to go into specific history in any depth. It will suffice to note that by the early 1990s, "message rap" had transmuted into what Paul Gilroy identified as one of the three emergent strains within Hip Hop: "Africentric" rap (1993: 85), which invoked lyrically, visually, temperamentally, and discursively an appeal to a lost, benevolent, "tribal" pan-Africanism as an alternative to both the more militant self-conscious racial pedagogy of rap drawing on the redemptive power of Islam and the "affirmative nihilism" (84) of the West Coast gangsta rap of NWA, Ice Cube, Snoop Doggy Dog, Dr. Dre, et al. (see Ro 1996 and Decker 1993).

Gilroy's analysis of the "radical utopianism" of the Africentric Hip Hop movement (exemplified by such artists as those constituting the Native Tongues Posse) is apposite to my concerns. He argues that in premising a pan-African nationalism based on "pure ethnicity," it "corresponds to no actually existing black communities" (1993: 87). A famous piece of Hip Hop lore, recounted by Toop, concerns seminal figure Afrika Bambaataa, inspired by the fiery rhetoric of Malcolm X and the visible good works of the Nation of Islam, changing his name and forming his "Zulu Nation." When he was growing up, Bambaataa explained, "[t]here was no land called negroland. Everybody in America—when they came here knew what country they was from" (in Toop 1991: 58). The turning point was in the early 1960s: "The Zulu Nation. I got the idea when I seen this movie called *Zulu* which featured Michael Caine. It was showing how when the British came to take over the land of the Zulus how the Zulus fought to uphold their land. They were proud warriors . . . fought like warriors for a land which was theirs" (in Toop 57; see also Fernando 1994: 6–7).

Once again, a cultural genealogy is predicated on a mass-mediated ur-moment, a moment serving as a catalyst for a subsequent labor of cultural production: in this instance, the genealogizing of the contemporary African-American experience to an originary (mythical) pan-Africanism. Bambaataa was instrumental in forging a close practical and ideological link between the emerging Hip Hop Scene in New York in the late 1970s and the Nation of Islam. With what in hindsight looks like rich irony, for example, he sampled grabs from the speeches of Malcolm X and Martin Luther King over extended mixes of the particularly Aryan-in-appearance German proto-techno group Kraftwerk's "Trans-Europe Express" (Toop 1991: 130). Subsequent generations of rappers and producers throughout the 1980s also drew on the recorded speeches and rhetoric of the martyred heroes of the 1960s, as well as iconographic visual material: KRS-One's album from 1988, titled "By All Means Necessary" (this quote itself later appropriated by George Bush), reproduced the famous image of Malcolm X, gun in hand, peering through a curtain. Instead of the shirt-sleeved, pistol-toting Malcolm X, in this version KRS-One wears a shell-top jacket bearing his crew's logo ("BDP" for "Boogie Down Productions") and a baseball cap and totes an Uzi, the iconic signifier of the late 1980s urban gangbanger (Toop 1991: 196). The density of signification layered up even further four years later when Spike Lee staged the same moment in his film biography of Malcolm X. The repertoire of images builds up; a polydimensional chain of intertextuality in which "the original," or "the real" is, indeed, if you were to follow Baudrillard's nostalgic postmodernism, "lost," subsumed to a logic of hyperreality and representation.[16]

While Gilroy's tripartite typology of rap music (the "pedagogic," the "affirmative," and the "ludic') suffers from the ongoing processes of sub-generic bifurcation and syncretic discontinuity over time, he points to a fundamental "looseness" in the use of the term "black nationalism," arguing that the ontological essentialism of such discourses generates "overintegrated conceptions of pure and homogeneous culture which mean that black political struggles are construed as somehow automatically *expressive* of the national or ethnic differences with which they are associated" (1993: 31). The "nation," on Gilroy's analysis, stands as a fundamentally modernist trope deployed to provide a "supposedly authentic, natural, and stable 'rooted' identity" (30), one that "masks the arbitrariness of . . . political choices" (31) with the decided advantage, Gilroy argues, of being able to subsume differences of class, sexuality, gender, ethnicity, age, and political consciousness (32). A few pages later he refers to the lure of "those *romantic* conceptions of "race," "people," and "nation'" (34, emphasis added): the discourses of nationalism exert a mighty pull; enough, as Benedict Anderson remarked in his seminal book (1991), to send tens of millions to their graves in its name.

This subsumption of difference to a powerful, seductive, affective, and romanticized discourse of belongingness constitutes the appeal of discourses of Hip Hop nationalism to the local, Australian context. Overcoming the lack of an organic, "neighborhood" basis for the sustainable production of a discourse of "community," local proponents of Hip Hop communality have recourse to the more abstract, inclusive, transcendent category of "nation" in order to explain their togetherness.

THE *AUSTRALIAN* HIP HOP NATION

Here is the oxymoron. Hip Hop in Australia is it once part of the global Hip Hop Nation and distinctly *Australian.* The inclusionary, *outernationalist,*[17] discourse of Hip Hop as global community and the distinguishing, competitive discourse of Hip Hop as subsumed to a geopolitical (Australian) national identity are activated simultaneously. But not necessarily paradoxically, as I will suggest below.

Let's take a couple of sets of texts with a view to unpacking some of the complexities of the encounter of discourses of Australian nationalism with those of Hip Hop nationalism. The first will be some writing in *Vapors,* in which we can see the refraction of the Hip Hop nationalist tropes through the specifically local metaphorical structures of jingoistic Australian nationalism. Blaze, as editor, pushed quite didactically what he understood as "the ideology" of the Hip Hop Nation, deploying this idea rhetorically as a "call to arms" and constituting in his various texts and conversations a nationalist teleology: a Hip Hop "project." This is perhaps what Feld (1994b) would call the "up-town" version of Hip Hop nationalism, or what could also be called, perhaps, allowing the nationalist metaphor to take root, the Hip Hop "state ideology." Taking the show "downtown," DWC's celebration of "Australian Hip Hop," the anthemic "A.U.S. Down Under Comin' Up(per)" offers what they would themselves describe as a less cluttered, if no less self-conscious, evocation of a distinctly "Aussie" nationalism.

ADDRESS TO THE HIP HOP NATION

"The Hip Hop Nation comprises many cities, built out of individuals, ideas, attitudes, and beliefs . . . All have their place . . . All have equal status in the nation." This is "Fibular" writing in *Vapors* issue 8 (1992). The operant understanding of nationhood here is that of the sovereign state as a collection of sovereign individuals, each guaranteed fundamental equalities and rights. And when you examine these "citizens" in order to see what they have in common, suggests Fibular, you notice that they "all are individuals whose personality shine through in their art. The collective is comprised of salient individual accomplishments . . ." The individuals are, almost without exception in these texts, men. Brothers, Brethren. Blaze, for example, in an article accompanying Fibular's text warns that "[s]uckers are on the move & encroaching on the space that was once occupied by the Rap fraternity" and suggests that the reader should "[h]elp your brother & he will help you."

Here, then, is a distinctly liberal-democratic post-Enlightenment state, reminiscent perhaps of high school modern history accounts of, for example, the "rights of man" as enshrined in the revolutionary and nation-building constitutions of the late eighteenth century. The discourses of society, the nation, and culture are bound up here, inextricably, with those of "self-expression" and "accomplishment." These two key aspects of the post-Enlightenment ideoscape manifested themselves, completely intact, within the rubric of the Hip Hop Scene in Sydney, as horizons of human and social being: specifically, the idea that performance ("accomplishment," for Fibular) *represented* the (already existing, transcendent, or substratally essential) *culture* was fundamental to the scene. Simultaneously, one's practice or performance ("accomplishment" again) was a pure expression of *self:* to learn to rap is, for example, in Hip Hop terms, to lay claim to one's voice, a voice characteristically understood as being somehow denied; to write (graffiti) is to at once "get [yourself] up" and to "represent the culture/community/nation."

Throughout this "Address to the Hip Hop Nation," Fibular deploys an extended set of geopolitical metaphors as he negotiates the problem of defining the boundaries of Hip Hop: "the real deal." Fibular's analysis proceeds by elimination. For starters, he suggests, we can be sure that Vanilla Ice and his like ". . . are certainly not within the geographical boundaries of the Hip Hop nation . . ." A series of discourses are conflated here in the course of a single paragraph: the geographical metaphor collapses into the mercantile metaphorics of the business page: ". . . nor does he [Vanilla Ice] even reside in its major trading partners . . ." Here is an image in which can be seen the echo of the contemporaneous economic discourse dominating the public sphere: the Australian Balance of Payments "crisis" that dominated political and corporate discourse throughout the late 1980s and into the 1990s. The economic metaphor gives way to a *heimat* image of the Nation as (homely, mothering) village (Hage 1993a: 79–80). Vanilla Ice, Fibular continues, "wouldn't even trim the hedges in the Hip Hop village." The geographical and mercantile imagery then comes together in a full-blown geopolitical discourse: "Vanilla Ice and his insulting counterparts reside within the boundaries of the Hip Hop Nation's traditional enemies." These enemies are possessed of a "moral economy" that can "only be described as third world." The evidence for this? Well, Fibular continues, this "enemy status" has arisen "out of a total disrespect and green-blooded, wanton thievery and mockery of the customs and tradition of the [Hip Hop] nation, which are held in the highest esteem by its patriotic inhabitants."

Here is an example of what Hage and Johnson (1993a) understand as the fundamental "intercommunality" of communalism: any nation can only exist in the context of *other* nations. Fibular extends national status to the "many other nations who trade regularly with it [the Hip Hop Nation] . . . Rock and Roll . . . Jazz . . . Reggae." But, of course, fundamental to nationalism is the understanding that one's own nation is the "true" nation: that it alone has a destiny toward which the national being is striving. Indeed, Hage argues, it is this striving that is the essence of the nation: "Nationalist discourse . . . rarely refers to an existing achieved national order, a full-fledged motherland and fatherland. Rather it is always referring to their non-existence while arguing at the same time for their necessity" (1993a: 97). Hage's analysis, drawing on Lacan and Heidegger, also offers an explanation for the repeated lamentation of "divisions" within the Hip Hop Scene, both throughout the pages of *Hype* and *Vapors* and in everyday conversation. The need for "unity," the calls for "getting together," and so on are suggestive of an ongoing process of the preparation of the "Nation": "Nationalist discourse is above all a discourse articulated to the practice of nation-building as an on-going process. *It loses its significance if this process achieves its aim and comes to an end*" (1993a: 97; emphasis added).

Here is an unedited text of Blaze's editorial in the issue of *Vapors* in which Fibular published his "Address to the Hip Hop Nation":

> The Hip Hop Culture is like a participant sport. It needs team players to survive. And the Australian Hip Hop Nation needs those players. We need people that are active & dedicated to the culture for it to live. Mind you, it will live, no matter what! No matter how many obstacles are laid down in front of it. No matter how many fuckwits try to internally destroy it. No matter how, where, who, why, what! It will persevere through thick & thin. . . . We know that the Australian Music industry doesn't give a shit about our culture. Does this worry us? No not any more. We have travelled their paths & have seen no future. So what is the solution to this problem? The answer is simple. YOU! You are the solution. We have too many back seat drivers & not enough people actually manning the wheels. Unification & dedication is all we ask of you. We can't do this ourselves, we need your input. (*Vapors,* no. 8, April-May 1992: 3)

The sporting team metaphor eloquently encapsulates the dominant mode of thinking about Australian national identity in the contemporary Australian public sphere, a nice little example of the local refraction of the outernationalist discourses of Hip Hop nationalism.

Hage argues that nationalists, of course, do not understand the impossibility of the completion of these processes; if they did, they would not undertake the project of nation-building (1993a: 99). In Blaze's text, the possibility of (Hip Hop) national failure is dismissed as soon as it is articulated: "Mind you," (you can almost hear Blaze bellowing, finger stretched out in a Kitcheneresque *I want you* gesture) "it *will* live, no matter what!"

In order to sustain the *possibility* of the nation, Hage argues, an "other" must be found to maintain a logic of obstruction, thus sparing the nationalist of the anxiety of the impossibility of the goal. This "other" can be constituted, as above, by internal schisms (such as "the Battle") or by those who have lost the faith: "some people have turned their backs on a cultural form that prides itself on self-development & artistic expression instead of pill popping & allnight dancing." In the example of Fibular's text, this "other" is constituted by ". . . a lot of impersonators . . ." who, ". . . in light of 'Raps' new popularity . . . are knocking on Hip Hips door and trying to get in with false IDs . . ." Blaze (and others) call these "impersonators" "halfsteppers" and "perpetrators . . . Usually the ones with the most expensive showy clothes are the disciples of falsehoods . . . Halfsteppers who only dress & act as though they are down with our cause." While, on the other hand, "a true Hip Hop pupil is 100% loyal, not a weekend warrior or a part-time purveyor." Vanilla Ice, for example, "is nothing more than a return persona of the black and white minstrels . . . a white man donning a black mask — where white audiences could 'legitimately' identify with the pathos of a black character, while being distanced from real blacks" (*Vapors*, no. 8, April-May 1992: 9).

So the question of "blackness" makes an appearance. Obviously, for the predominantly white Sydney Hip Hop Scene,[18] this blackness needs to be negotiated. For Fibular, the problem is simply this: how can Vanilla Ice, a Caucasian impersonating a black man, be excluded from the Hip Hop Nation, without this also disqualifying Fibular, presumably also white, from citizenship? The solution is to identify an authenticity deriving not from color or race, but from a notion of truthfulness to one's self. It turns out that it is okay to be white and into Hip Hop as long as you don't *misrepresent* who you are, as long as you do not simulate blackness: this, it seems, is where Vanilla Ice goes horribly wrong. In *pretending* to be black, in claiming a "street/black" history that he apparently fabricated, he is not being "true" to his "self."

Once again, this discourse of truth to self, bound up with that of self-expression, emerges as a powerful horizon of analysis. "Selves" are simply givens, retrievable and expressible: the nation is a collection of these individual sovereignties, and *knowledge,* as I will suggest below, is something that can reveal the truth about those selves and is simultaneously predicated *on* them: the truth is something that the rational, clear-thinking individual will be able to apprehend through the application of common sense, as Blaze suggested.

Corollary to these discourses (and to those of tolerance: Hip Hop is "probably the most accepting racially diverse culture that exists today," writes Blaze) was the notion of *respect*. Respect was *due* to those who were true to themselves. I was accorded respect, for example, because I didn't pretend to be anything other than a research student investigating a cultural phenomenon. Respect is always reciprocal, of course: it was incumbent on me to demonstrate my good faith, to respect the scene myself.

Fibular, in elaborating these ideas, deploys two key tropes: "masking," as used in the excerpt about the minstrels above, and "naturalness." The media and popular perceptions of rap and blackness are also culpable, in the eyes of Fibular, as once again he confronts the problems of "half-steppers" and "weekend warriors": "The libelous actions of these pseudo street artists, are adaptations of a painfully stereotyped view of rap, which lacks any soul or heart and the casual naturalness which is really the only ingredient necessary in Hip Hop" (*Vapors* no. 8, 1992: 9). So, it is not the "blackness" of African-American Hip Hoppers that constitutes their authenticity; it is their "naturalness." Therefore, to be white and into Hip Hop is fine, so long as you, too, are "natural."

Fernando's account of the development of Hip Hop nationalism from "Nation of Islam" ideology is framed by ethnographic material taken from one Kam, a Los Angelino rapper and "gangbanger turned Muslim." Kam supports Fibular and Ser Reck's hypotheses, by completely displacing color from the discourse: the Nation of Islam is "not about white this or white that. . . . It's not about skin color, it's about the mentality behind the skin colour." It *is* about being oppressed, he continues: "We victims, you know . . . 438 years of slavery . . . we the victims of all this" (Fernando 1994: 144).

So there's one way of forging a shared citizenship, a shared nationality: the nation is constituted by the shared struggle of social agents to maintain the specific enjoyment of their being in the face of those (others) who want to take it away from them (Žižek 1994): witness Blaze's utopian imagining of the harmony that is so close, yet denied by the "Racism/sexism/culturism/ageism/homophobia" of our "slipping society" (about which more is said below), or the laying of claim to a "voice" characteristic of accounts of the development of rap in the United States. The members of the Hip Hop Nation are bound by this contingency: an implied identity of an essential idea about oppression, able to be abstracted from its specific circumstances, its realpolitik.

Much effort, then, must be expended in demonstrating an "oppression," and therefore an oppressor, against which this claim to national identity (with the African American) can be constructed. In claiming a specific oppression, or status as a victim (of sorts), the Sydney Hip Hoppers are able to authenticate their claim to Hip Hop nationality.

Here, though, Blaze and Fibular offer an alternative account (it is perhaps useful to note that Blaze himself came from a *relatively* affluent background on Sydney's Lower North Shore: for him, a reduction of oppression to a simple logic of class was not a credible option). For these writers, belongingness to the Hip Hop Nation needed to be predicated on a more abstract, and more generalized model of oppression, in which you need not necessarily belong to a marginalized class, race, gender, sexuality, creed, and so on. In fact, Blaze suggests, Hip Hop is "probably the most accepting racially diverse culture that exists today." Emerging from this account is the idea that the Hip Hop Nation is actually the "true" trustee of enlightenment values: there is no radical critique in all this of those values; only the assertion that the rest of the world has got it wrong, is "slipping," has fallen from (Enlightenment) grace, has been corrupted. Only Hip Hop sees with clear eyes.

KNOWLEDGE KICKS TO THE HEAD

Kam explains that "the most important thing that's taught in the Nation of Islam is knowledge of self . . . it's a school of knowledge" (in Fernando 1994: 144–5). Knowledge, or, as it is referred to, "science," is central to the notion of Hip Hop nationality. Blaze understands knowledge as the telos of the Hip Hop Nation: "We live, breathe, die for the evolution of the Intelligent Nation." And this is where we can see most explicitly the development of the idea that other "nations," including the nation-state complexes of the "mainstream," the "powers that be," have "got it wrong." Blaze calls on his brothers (*sic*) to "wake up!": "To understand why, is to know why. Don't be stupid. Be rational & logical. If you have questions, ask them. Seek out information. As BDP [Boogie Down Productions] said 'You must learn.' Whether it be in school or on the streets" (*Vapors*, no. 8, April-May 1992: 8).

At stake here is a society that Blaze describes as "slipping": "[W]e must find answers to the head-smacking problems that circulate in our slipping society. Racism/sexism/culturism/ageism/homophobia [these rammed into each other, building up a vast, polysyllabic monolith, a single word] etc. . . . . should be eliminated because they don't promote harmony, they only encourage conflict." Blaze is addressing the media representation of rap and Hip Hop as being inherently violent. A "bullet in the head" does not, on Blaze's account, constitute "an answer" to these "pressing problems." Instead, he advocates "a *knowledge* kick to the head" (emphasis added). The agent of this moment of historical awakening is to be "youth," which "must/should hear a variety of opinions from various locales/races/religions, so that they can examine/disect [*sic*]/interpret on their own time." Truth, then, is at a premium. The Hip Hop Nation can be distinguished from both the monolithic, hypocritical "powers that be" and from its "enemies" by its fundamental commitment to *truth*.

Hip Hop operates epistemologically: it is a way of knowing. Through Hip Hop, one can find truth. Hip Hop, coming from "the streets" — that is, drawing on an unmediated, empirical experience of the world — is free from the cluttering ideologies of the mainstream. It *kicks reality*. Blaze's analysis here is one of a "false consciousness" against which Hip Hop is mobilized. He attacks, for example, "crap" music that is responsible for hiding the real life everyday issues under a gloss-encrusted carpet" — taking care, however, not to deny the "right" of others to make such music; tolerance, after all, is a fundamental Enlightenment/Hip Hop discourse.[19] The problem is, rather, a question of priorities. Big budgets, Blaze claims, are wasted on "wack artists" offering "fake happiness/smiles/cover-ups/safety," budgets that could be spread around to artists offering, instead, "insights/intelligence/controversy/originality."[20] Hip Hop can offer all of these, in spades. You see, Blaze says, "we as a people of this world have a responsibility to undertake. To make this land a better land (but not in a religious sort of way) . . . [w]e need to progress . . . Conformity is degression and stagnation."

There can be no clearer summary of what I frequently heard referred to as "the ideology" or "ideals" of Hip Hop. The discourses of knowledge, originality, progress, and self-expression define the essence of Hip Hop, according to this discourse. This discourse (of the essence of Hip Hop Culture), I have suggested, is identical to that which Appadurai calls the ideoscape of the "Enlightenment worldview." And yet, within Hip Hop, this ideoscape must define Hip Hop as being somehow fundamentally different. Apologists for Hip Hop must argue that the discourses of free-

dom, progress, and so on informing "mainstream society" operate ideologically, to conceal that mainstream's real aim, which is to render the
"mass populous" docile. Alternatively, less damningly, Hip Hop can argue
that, for whatever reason, the mainstream is simply incapable of recognizing the real and that the real can only now be retrieved or represented
by the phenomenologically and epistemologically privileged few.

Blaze is, of course, speaking what he understands as "common sense."
These are what politicians call "motherhood issues," assertions with
which one is unlikely to find an argument. What is interesting here, however, is the passion in Blaze's writing: the very fact that he feels so
strongly that the world is *not* governed by such ideals. The centrality of
"youth" to his concerns echoes that desire to construct youth as the agent
of radical social change that Harris (1992) identifies in post-Birmingham
cultural theory: the recruitment of a putatively "alienated" or disaffected
youth to fill the aporia in Marxian analyses left open by the failure of the
working class to fulfill its (orthodox) historical destiny. Def Wish raps: "A
perfect example of youth overtaking the system /Are trains running with
panels and the release of our album" ("Runnin' Amok").

There is, of course, always a discontinuity between discourse and
practice. Blaze understands that homophobia and sexism are *bad,* but often his own critical practice, as we have seen, strayed into the pejorative
use of "homophobic" or "sexist" stereotypes. And while the discourses of
tolerance and respect were pervasive throughout the scene, the Hip Hop
world was one that decidedly privileged the masculine over the feminine.

So that's the "state ideology" of the Hip Hop Nation. Miguel's weekly
column in *3-D World* also frequently invoked the Nation as a form of Hip
Hop social imaginary. His written texts, spilling over with dynamic prose
and grammatical inventiveness colorfully develop these ideas about tolerance, belongingness, knowledge: the inwardly directed subdiscourse
of nationalism that, following Hage, I want to characterize as nurturing
(feminized) and inclusive. The other subdiscourse identified by Hage is
that of the nation as Fatherland: a discourse directed outward, with a
view to projecting an identity into a community of identities. And there is
no better example of such a mode of nationalism in Sydney Hip Hop than
Def Wish Cast's showstopper.

A.U.S. DOWN UNDER COMIN' UP(PER)

"A.U.S.T." . . .

. . . three verses of what Def Wish describes, in his rhyme, as "a simpler b-boy kind of rap," punctuated by an incantatory refrain:

A.U.S Down Under Comin' Upper
A.U.S Down Under Comin' Upper
A.U.S Down Under Comin' Upper

First, Def Wish himself raps over DJ (and producer) Vame's slammin' mix:

It wont be too long before we're breaking down the doors
of record companies who ignore the fact that hip hop
down under is just as strong . . .

. . . the backing track hangs in suspension, and Def Wish completes his condemnation of these ignorant, parasitical record companies, oblivious to the power and truth of this home-grown Hip Hop right under their noses: "but they continue to live off imported songs . . ." Die C's rhymes assert the inevitable success of the larrikin, upstart Aussie rappers:

A.U.S.T. defender Die C delivering strong and aggressive lyrics
    heard clearly
In every other barricade across the world
. . . an island that many never look twice at as being
associated with rap —
On Hip Hop charts they come across a new discovery
U.S., U.K., U.S., what? A.U.S.T.?

Def Wish Cast's first EP release, "Mad as a Hatter," I was told, went to Number 2 on the Norwegian Hip Hop Charts. Die C charges on:

Where's the pride? Many'd rather just step aside. See
what the rest of the world is doing and live their lives lounging.

Determined not to fall prey to simply "following," Die C's rap is a folk critique of the malaise identified by poet and critic A. A. Phillips in the 1950s as the "Australian Cultural Cringe" (Phillips 1958): a pathological national dependence on the canons and institutional structures of European high art in lieu of an identifiable "national" cultural identity.[21]

Hold up a new flag

. . . Die C continues, drawing on contemporaneous public debate about the desirability of removing the Union Jack from the Australian flag:

> The letters that stand alone
> Not in the shadow of any other country
> Def Wish Cast from the A.U.S.T.

It is absolutely critical to understand Def Wish Cast's national-cultural project in the context of Phillips's massively influential critique, the effects of which continue to ripple through the decades. Take the Arts Policy statement published in the final eighteen months of Paul Keating's (putatively) social-democratic Labor federal government in 1995. Keating, in the final term of his office, was promoting multiculturalism and republicanism as de facto state ideologies.[22] A self-styled champion of the arts, Keating's hand is evident in the construction of the *Creative Nation Commonwealth Cultural Policy* (1994). The document's introduction predicates a national "we," accessed through a "culture" that is fundamental to our understanding of who we are" (Commonwealth of Australia 1994: 5). And yet there is the same circularity of logic apparent in the discourse of the Hip Hop Nation: "Culture is that which gives us a sense of ourselves" (5). This is a discourse of immanence, almost tautological in its determination of the relationship between "culture" and "identity": culture both generates our "we-ness" and is (of course) the key to understanding who that "we" is. The *Creative Nation* document quotes Keating:

> The Commonwealth's responsibility to maintain and develop
> Australian culture means . . . that on a national level;
> • innovation and ideas are perpetually encouraged
> • self-expression and creativity are encouraged
> • all Australians have a chance to participate and receive [cultural
>   material] (90).

Keating, apparently, was using Blaze as a speechwriter around this time. I don't want to dwell any longer on state nationalist/cultural ideology; the point has been to demonstrate the (hardly surprising) neat fit between their respective discourses.

Creative Nation also identifies two centrifugal ideas about Australian national culture, the first being the aforementioned "cringe" (Commonwealth of Australia 1994: 5), the second an overcompensatory "cultural strut" (6). Def Wish Cast's jingoism is perhaps a manifestation of this latter tendency: "[M]ethinks the lady doth protest too much," as Hamlet said.

Ser Reck's contribution to the track offers an ethnographic account of the Australian Hip Hop Nation:

> Piece'd with Brisbane, drank with Adelaide boys
> Perth kicks, Melbourne society making the noise

— namechecking the components of the Nation, demonstrating its tangibility, its basis in experience. Ser Reck has been to all these places, gone bombing with people there, got drunk with them. It is the same argument used by writers to demonstrate the tangibility of the global Hip Hop Nation: they can exchange photographs, outlines, tactics, paint, handy hints, and so on, with other bombers across the world. They can, they told me, go to visit pen pals in Berlin, New York, or Copenhagen and be instantly "at home." Nation, again, as *heimat*.

Ser Reck's rhyme takes the other tack, however. This Aussie Hip Hop Nation is

> . . . trying to break out, it's like a marathon
> Engaging yourself in a market, takin' the world on

Once again, the mercantile metaphors conflate with those of sport. Australia, he concludes, is

> an island with more than just a dream
> With a stand in Hip Hop,
> A definate mark . . .
> A journey to embark on
> All bands on an outbreak not a remake
> A.U.S.T. on a path to overtake ya!

And the track leaps into its raucous chorus again . . .

The trope of the Hip Hop Nation, then, emerges as a mechanism through which this process of identification with geographical, racial, and cultural "others" can be negotiated. The imaginary Hip Hop Nation is predicated on a shared "otherness," rather than on a continuity of "national, ethnic, local, class or trade-specific identities." As I have already noted, the sense of "globalism," literally of "transnationalism," carried in the formulation "Hip Hop Nation" is evidenced in experience: the "universal language" of graff, for example, seems to transcend (conventional) national boundaries; bombers, I would be told, would be welcomed by other bombers anywhere in the world, a claim justified by the experience of those who had traveled to Europe or North America — or even interstate within Australia. The point is that what might seem like a particularly abstract "idea" had a basis in practice and experience. Indeed, this global aspect of Hip Hop was often cited to me as evidence for the vitality and reality of Hip Hop itself and as one of the "best things about Hip Hop," facilitating a sense of compassion, of tolerance, and, perhaps most importantly for the participants and "believers," of optimism and purpose: the ills of the "slipping system" could be, if not righted, then at least addressed, through, as Blaze put it, "probably the most accepting racially diverse culture that exists today."

Sydney writers doing a "day legal," 1998 (courtesy of Paul Westgate)

Piece by Spice/IBS, c. 1997 (courtesy of Paul Westgate)

Brethren, 1996 (courtesy of Paul Westgate)

Audience at a Sydney Jam, 1995 (courtesy of Paul Westgate)

"Door to Door" by Dream, 1996 (courtesy of Paul Westgate)

"Old School End to End" by CIS, c. 1985 (courtesy of Paul Westgate)

B-Boy Unique (courtesy of Paul Westgate)

*Def Wish ripping up the mic
(courtesy of Paul Westgate)*

*Ser Reck "getting picky on the flow"
(courtesy of Paul Westgate)*

Sydney jam: Def Wish, left, in striped shirt; Unique, right, in "Athletic" T-shirt (courtesy of Paul Westgate)

DJ Blaze (courtesy of Paul Westgate)

Piece by Unique/IBS (courtesy of Paul Westgate)

J.U. of the Urban Poets (photograph: Marcelo Pena)

part 3
performance

*Young people don't really get into the politics of Hip Hop — they're more
into like the rhythm of it . . .*
— Blaze

"Listen to this . . ."
A friend is in my apartment. "Listen to this," I tell her, and I put on a Souls
of Mischief CD, *93 'til Infinity*. I've taken to bringing this disc with me to
parties, slipping it into the mix and experiencing a mischievous *frisson,*
knowing that my friends are dancing to raps about *gangbanging,* about
bitches and *hoes.* It's dirty, funky: fluid, mellifluous bass riffs looping round
and around, generating a miasmatic throb; abrasive scratches punctuate
the drone, and across the foreground of the sonic space flow the sneering, nasal West Coast freestyles. Horn fills, guitar samples, a synthesizer-
wash flesh out the mix, an alien soundscape of sirens, alarms; stories of
street life in the San Francisco–Oakland Bay area. It is, simply, my favorite rap music. My friend watches me (me!) as I *groove,* the beats reg-
istering in my shoulders, in the rocking of my head, my lips, I'm sure (because by now I know these raps), mouthing all the words, and I'm
thinking, "Yes, this is what it is like, if I live this music, if I can inhabit it,
if it inhabits me, then I can get somewhere else, I can go to this alien place
where there are guns and gangs and hard, fluid bodies languidly hanging
out on stoops, on street corners, with my home-boys, doing all that lazy,
studied, cool hand-shaking and high five stuff."
And my friend looks at me and she says, "You know, when you listen to
this music, it's like you become another person."

■ Now, the final part, in which we get into (like) the rhythm of it: what is it that happens to someone — an *embodied* someone — that enables them to claim *this* is me. I am (in this instance) *Hip Hop*. My argument will be that whatever this thing that happens is, it is more than an idea, a discourse, a *belief* in the narrow, propositional sense of the word. More than all those ideas covered in the preceding chapters. Rather, it is a state of being, of affect. A performative experience, perhaps, articulated to a world of discourse, but, first and foremost, an event made flesh.

True to
the Music

We have seen the kinds of discourses, narratives, and genealogies circulating within the field of Sydney Hip Hop. Within or across this field, social agents engaged in struggles or negotiations in order to legitimate and authenticate their practices within various narratives of a continuous cultural tradition. These struggles were themselves informed by and grounded in discourses and values circulating within a broader public or cultural sphere: discourses, for example, of "community," "culture," "truth," "authenticity," "nationalism," "self-expression," and so on.

FROM PERFORMANCE TO *REPRESENTING*,
OR HOW TO MAKE (A) CULTURE

Now, I want to turn to a more specific consideration of the means by which the experiences and performances of these agents are articulated to these discourses. A useful way to approach this is through a term that circulated widely throughout the scene, "representing," which was used to describe the relationship of a given performance, artifact, or statement to a purported cultural essence: Hip Hop. The final two chapters examine some of these performances, artifacts and statements in order to demonstrate how the idea of a cultural essence (which existed for those who used it, of necessity, outside, or prior to, the vicissitudes of history) was sustained through strategies of explanation and narration. In terms of

Bhabha's analysis of the narration of nation, the potential semiotic open-ness of a performative action (an embodied event, experienced, in the first instance, affectively) is, in practice, linked to, and embedded in, a particular narrative — a "pedagogy" — to produce a meaning for that that event/experience.

Various practices held to *represent* Hip Hop were drawn toward each other; salient features were adduced, in discourse, implicitly or explicitly, pedagogically, by powerfully placed individuals in the scene, in order to construct logics of necessity, or homologies, that could then be used to support a thesis of causality. Through the ongoing process of, first, the se-lection of particular features from a given performance (a break dance, a piece of graffiti, a record scratch, a recording, a rap) and, second, the of-fering of an account of those features in terms of a narrative of "culture" and "representation," a cultural metaphysic was sustained: "that which has been represented." The constructed, *interpreted* nature of these ho-mologies, or the "iconicities of styles" across these practices, is obscured by the narrative of representation, in which the formal qualities of the practices and performances are understood, within the field (and often from without), as being *generated by* the substratal form of "the culture." Moreover, these processes of interpretation and the "institution of inter-pretations" (Weber 1987) generate further "iconic propagations" (Lewis 1992) as the interpreting community itself becomes institutionalized: the whole "thing" hangs together as a function of belief. The linkages, the intertextualities, the propagations, and iconicities between these prac-tices, established though everyday practices of interpretation, were sus-tained by shared aesthetico-critical languages (*hard core* can refer to breaking, writing, and rapping, as can *burner*) constituting what Hymes called "speech communities" (Hymes 1972) and the subcultural capital resources for the drawing of distinctions (Thornton 1996) within the field of "youth culture." Further, a broader assumption about the nature of cultural products operated to sustain the coherence of this cultural prod-uct: they were understood as being, simply, "representative," extensions of the same substance. In the words of one informant: "rapping, writing, breaking — they're all the same thing."

The issue, then, is this: how do various practices and experiences be-come, in very particular contexts, meaningful for cultural agents within those contexts? I am less interested, for example, in the "meaning" of break-dancing in terms of its cultural genealogies than in terms of how genealogies of break-dancing are adduced to account for the meaning of a given performance of break-dancing in Sydney, in 1994, by middle-class Anglo-Australians. The meaning was sustained by intensity of affect: the apparently irreducible evidence of pre- or superlinguistic affective states stands as the clearest, most incontrovertible evidence, within the field, of the very being of a thing called Hip Hop Culture.

TRUE TO THE MUSIC

"If you want, I can define it in two words," Blaze told me at our first meeting (I had asked him what "Hip Hop" *was*). This: *"fat beats, dope rhymes."* That's actually four words, which I mention not to make fun of Blaze, but to acknowledge the conceptual clarity of his formulation (and only later did I come across the deviant spelling *"phat"*); *two* elements were involved, each with particular qualities: the words and the music. Together, they are Hip Hop.

So, what are *fatness* and *dopeness?* What determines which rhymes are dope, which beats are fat? Or, perhaps, *who* decides, and by what authority? How are the distinctions made?

A musicological account of various rap recordings is not sufficient to enable a listener to make distinctions about *dopeness* and *fatness:* rap *attitude* can be faked, or interpreted as being fake. A Madonna track, for example, can be constructed out of exactly the same groove as a Public Enemy track (itself sampled from a James Brown track), but it will still not be "Hip Hop."[1] Any such assessment of the value of a given recording (or performance) is not made in a semiotic vacuum; many contextual factors are taken into account, and such processes of assessment are inherently social. To this end, it worth reiterating the fuzziness of these terms as aesthetic indicators. A definition of what is *dope* can be shifted to suit a particular context, a particular strategy of exclusion or inclusion.

However, this is not to say that a musicological analysis is not useful. Within a given interpretive community, "meaning" or "worth" will be ascribed to particular, identifiable musicological features and, often, to those features of the "primary text" (A. F. Moore 1993) that tend to escape the notice of conventional musicologies that stress the "extensional" (Chester 1970), notate-able quantities of pitch and meter, and are less able to attend, for example, to timbral and "intensional" qualities, such as those features of voice Barthes subsumed under "grain" ([1977] 1990).

In this chapter, I will look closely at two tracks recorded by Sydney crews in the early 1990s, one of which was interpreted within the scene as being "authentic," the other as a "sell-out" (or worse, "crossover"), in order to demonstrate both that the critical distinctions made can be sheeted home to musicological features and that in different circumstances the same musicological features can be "read" to opposite effect.

And we're back to "authenticity," a notion I am concerned to approach not in terms of a verifiable set of "truths," but in terms of modes of belief. The *music* itself figures centrally in this construction of belief because certain values and knowledges were held to be immanent in the musical texts. The rest of this chapter will consider how certain musical texts came to be understood as meaning in this way; how these recordings or performances were understood as being, in the expression that I heard time and again within the scene, *true to the music.*

STUDYING POPULAR MUSIC

From the polemics of the Frankfurt School to the present day, musicology's encounters with popular music forms make for engaging reading. Much work has been committed to the negotiation of a mode, or modes, of musicological scholarship appropriate for the task of analyzing popular music forms, most notably that conducted by Andrew Chester (1970; see also Chester and Merton 1970), Phillip Tagg (1982), John Shepherd (1982, 1987, 1991), Antoine Hennion (1983), Simon Frith (1987), and Allan Moore (1993), and in the essays (including some of those cited here) collected by Shepherd et al. (1977), Leppert and McClary (1987), and Frith and Goodwin (1990).

This is not the place to rehearse the debates between "traditional" musicologists and musicologists of popular music (see, for example, McClary 1987; McClary and Walser 1990; Frith 1987; A. F. Moore 1993). However, within the study of popular music, debate about the "meaning" of popular musics has ranged along a continuum from approaches that privilege the sociological context (for example, the work of Simon Frith and, in its most extreme statement, Hennion 1993) to those which advocate an attention to the "primary" musical texts themselves (A. F. Moore 1993). The questions revolve around the relationship of musical texts to their cultural milieu, and the participants in the debates draw on a variety of disciplinary (and institutional; viz. Harris 1992) contexts in order to construct their positions.

In his survey of this territory, Middleton starts to draw together various musicological discourses and those of the subcultural theorists emerging from the Birmingham Centre for Contemporary Cultural Studies (BCCCS) in the mid-1970s (1990: 103–26).[2] Middleton argues that two key concepts — bricolage (from Lévi-Strauss) and homology (via the ethnomusicological writings of Lomax and Keil) — were adopted from anthropological discourse by the Marxian scholars of the BCCCS in their analysis of youth deviance, in which they saw "one of the few remaining sources of popular discontent or protest" (155). Middleton draws out the influence of approaches (drawn in part from ethnographic and ethnomusicological sources, and from the successive waves of Marxian thought) that advocate a "tight homology" between a society and its music, exemplified by John Blacking, who argued that music "confirms what is already present in society and culture" (in Middleton 1990: 155), and those understanding cultural forms as the result of "individual interpretive choices, which, somehow, just happen to result in social and cultural patterns" (Middleton's gloss of Clifford Geertz). In the context of the Marxian problematic, the debate was argued in terms of the "relative autonomy" of the (cultural) superstructure from the (politico-economic) base. Gramsci had opened up the possibility of a dialectical, rather than a merely determinant, relationship between the political economy and culture; subsequent argument hinged on the exact nature of this autonomy: just how "autonomous" were cultural forms? What is the nature of the correlation between expressive forms and the underlying structures of a given society?

"The most persuasive position is somewhere between total correlation [Blacking] . . . and meccano-set pragmatism [Geertz]," suggests Middleton, approvingly quoting Lévi-Strauss: "between culture and language [or music] there cannot be no relations at all, and there cannot be one hundred per cent correlation either" (in Middleton 1990: 147; the quote is from Lévi-Strauss's 1972 Structural Anthropology). Middleton, through the course of his own work (and citing, among other precedents, Bourdieu's notion of a "third-order knowledge" negotiating "the ritual either/ or choice between objectivism and subjectivism" [A. F. Moore 1993: 123–24; see also Bourdieu 1977: 6; Bourdieu and Wacquant 1992: 10–11]), moves toward such an "in-between" position, recapitulating what Bourdieu and Wacquant describe as the "polarized antagonism between symbolic anthropology (Geertz, Schneider, Victor Turner, Sahlins) and Lévi-Straussian structuralism . . . on the one side, and cultural ecology . . .

and political-economic and Marxist approaches on the other" (Bourdieu and Wacquant 1992: 10–11).

Middleton takes as the "classical statement" of the early BCCCS work the collection of essays edited by Stuart Hall and Tony Jefferson, published as *Resistance through Rituals* in 1976. The "culturalist" position is manifest: culture is understood as "the patterns in which social groups organise their response to their experience" (Middleton 1990: 156). In responding to the fundamental contradictions of capitalist society, working-class youth produce, in the famous BCCCS formulation, "imaginary solutions to real problems" (Frith and Goodwin 1990: 40). Resistance to a dominating bourgeois culture builds up partly autonomous activity, constituting a class- and *generationally* determined "identity": youth subcultures.

This is where the concepts of *bricolage* and *homology* started to find their way into the analysis. The young people involved in a "subculture" make use of existing cultural materials. Existing "institutions, values, and objects . . . are taken over, transformed, reinterpreted, inserted into new combinations, combined to form a new *style*" (Middleton 1990: 157). "Homology" is the principle governing the choice, combination, and interpretation of objects and values (Hall and Jefferson 1976: 56), operating through the process of *bricolage,* Lévi-Strauss's term for the improvisatory cultural agent creating new meaning from "second-hand" cultural material.

In the burgeoning body of work on subcultures, however, these terms came to be used for divergent positions. In Paul Willis's seminal ethnographic study of biker and hippy subcultures (Willis 1978), participants in the cultures seek out (for example) musical forms that "reflect, resonate, and sum up crucial values, states, and attitudes for the social group involved" (Willis n.d. cited in Middleton 1990: 160). The range of material to be selected from is, of course, limited by the "objective possibilities" inherent in the given musical form and the historical context. The process of selection operates diachronically; the selection of music resonates with and affects lifestyle, and vice versa: material is drawn into ever tightening homologies through a process of "integral circuiting."

On this analysis, subcultural "style" is understood as being expressive of the given group's material position in society. The presumption of homologies, or "'structural resonances' . . . between the different elements making up the culture, consciousness, and social position of a particular social group" (Middleton 1985: 7), offers the cultural critic a powerful analytical tool, which, Middleton argues, produces a compelling circularity, leading to tendential readings of "subcultural" formations. Middleton takes pains to discuss both Willis's (1978) and Hebdige's (1979) seminal texts, pointing out the tendency in both to construct "pure" subcultures, and to overemphasize these subcultures' opposition to a putative dominant culture, concluding that Willis's work in particular is "flawed above all by an uncompromising drive to homology," laboring a supposed internal coherence that is in fact the premise from which his analysis sets out (Middleton 1990: 161).

Now, one of the reasons that I have dwelled on these ways of thinking about youth culture is that precisely such a theory circulated in the Hip Hop Scene I encountered: the base-superstructure model of cultural processes informing homology theory informed the interpretive practices instituted within that scene. The Hip Hop logic of representation *suggested* (and engendered) a belief in a form of structural necessity, in which a rap, a break dance, or a graffiti piece is a manifestation that could be read, within the interpretive community, as being determined by the immutable, underlying essence of Hip Hop: a folk homology theory, perhaps.

Sarah Thornton's recent positioning of her own work on the English club and rave scene recognizes a necessary debt to the work of the Birmingham theorists, while simultaneously offering a pointed critique of that same work. Aside from the important question of the reductive logic of class and resistance that underpins the work, and that leads to what Meaghan Morris ([1988] 1993) has recognized as the tendency of subsequent cultural studies to find "pockets of symbolic resistance wherever they look" (Thornton 1996: 93), Thornton offers three points of divergence in her own work from the Birmingham orthodoxy. First, she argues, the concept of "subculture" is empirically unworkable. As we have seen (in chapter 5, "The Hip Hop Community"), Walser makes a similar argument in reference to Hip Hop, suggesting that "ethnography in industrial societies poses special difficulties: there is no single 'local' to be studied; audiences are diverse and linked by mass mediation" (1995: 291). This leads directly to Thornton's second point: that the classic Birmingham studies (Hall and Jefferson 1976; Willis 1978; Hebdige 1979, for example) "tended to banish media and commerce from their definitions of *authentic* culture" (9, emphasis added). For Hebdige in 1979, for example, media and commerce are understood as incorporating subcultures *back into* a hegemonic, parent cultural "mainstream." I have already suggested that the relationship between youth and the media involves far more complex, co-creative feedback loops than analyses based on simple "authentic" versus "hegemonic" binarisms suggest.

Thornton's third bone of contention with the Birmingham studies concerns their focus on synchronic interpretation, at the expense of any understanding of processes of change. Angela McRobbie has similarly written of the tendency of subculture studies in the late 1970s to focus on the "final signifying products" (McRobbie 1993: 411), at the expense of an analysis of the material process of cultural production.

Thornton uses the Bourdieuan concepts of cultural capital to understand the process by which "youth imagine their own and other social groups [and] assert their distinctive character and affirm that they are not anonymous members of an undifferentiated mass" (1996: 10). Offering an alternative to vertical models of social structure, Bourdieu's schema, continues Thornton, "locates social groups in a highly complex multi-dimensional space," in which social status is conferred by differential access to various types of capital: cultural, economic, social; elaborated into subcategories such as "intellectual," "academic," "linguistic," "artistic," and the like. Thornton further extends this elaboration by positing "sub-cultural capital" as that which "confers status on its owner in the eyes of the relevant beholder" (11).

Middleton's break with homology theory is based on, in part, the Gramscian inflection of subculture studies in the latter half of the 1970s. In the late 1970s Hebdigian formation, "hegemony" is used to refer expressly to an idea of "dominant ideology," engaged in the ideological struggle to "win" the superstructural field of cultural production. The "youth subcultural" *bricoleur* assembles material from among the "straight world" to construct parodic and subversive "styles" that resist hegemonic worldviews. Hebdige also introduced a semiological dimension of analysis: "subcultural style" is seen "less as expressing a group's material position in society than as intervening in existing processes of signification" (Middleton 1990: 164). Middleton maps out, within Hebdige's 1979 text, a movement away from a consideration of what Willis called "the objective possibilities" determining, in the last instance, the homologous selection of material in the formation of subcultural styles, to a poststructuralist celebration of "polysemy" (Hebdige 1979: 117), in terms of which teds, punks, and skinheads are engaged in a free play of cultural "deconstruction," generating new meanings and constituting a kind of avant-garde disrupting of ideologically fixed positions. Fight the power.

Once again, these extreme positions need to be mediated. The constitution of subcultural styles must be determined by more than a simple
mechanism of homological generation, but a model based on the promiscuous recombination of cultural material cannot account for the
specificity of particular choices. Recognizing that the processes by which
cultural material is assembled is subject to "multiple determination,"
rather than responding to "a single expressive need," Middleton sought
to retain a "qualified" sense of homology (Middleton 1985: 6), based on
a principle of "articulation," a concept taken from the post-Gramscian
work of the political sociologist Ernesto Laclau. "The theory of articulation recognises the complexity of cultural fields," continues Middleton, in
order to develop a model of cultural formation in which the key organizing principle, in keeping with the Gramscian discourse of *struggle,* is that
of the *effort* required to contest existing conventions of meanings:
"[O]nce particular musical elements are put together in particular ways,
and acquire particular connotations, they can be hard to shift (8).

Meanings "exist" as the ongoing results of social processes; they are
"instituted" over time, by a "community of investigators" (Weber 1987: 13),
laying out networks of self-supporting chains or networks of interrelated
references without a final transcendental referent. Meanings are not "natural," "determined by some human essence or by the needs of class expression" (Middleton 1985: 8), but nor are meanings *un*determined. They
are, rather, *over*determined: meanings are sustained by a constant effort
of maintenance, interpretation, and institution, directed at arresting the
free flow of polysemy. Weber writes: "The formation and modification of
what Peirce described as 'habits' depend on collective traditions and institutions through which they transmit and reproduce themselves . . .
the institution of specific interpretations thus calls for the interpretation
of specific institutions" (17).

All languages, all semiotic codes, rely on contingent, spatio-temporally
specific *closures,* without which no communication would be possible.
Laclau and Mouffe describe this process as the "suturing" of the "field of
articulation": an interest group, they suggest, whether it be a class interest, a gender, or, perhaps, a group of rappers attempting to create and to
direct, as it were, a local "Hip Hop Community," do so by tying all possible expression (or performance) to a "sutured" set of meanings: a "closed
symbolic order" (Laclau and Mouffe 1985: 88n. 1). It is this sense in which
I argued, above, that J.U.'s battle with Mick E might be understood as
an attempt to "hegemonize" the Sydney Hip Hop Scene through a dem-

onstration of their respective subcultural capital. The reward for success in this struggle involved, as I showed, the "right" (or at least the opportunity) to assert a set of meanings, to institute a particular set of interpretations.

MUSICOLOGY AND RAP

Now, we are moving toward a model with which to understand the way in which certain musics can "mean." The next thing that we need is a language with which to describe the music itself. Tricia Rose isolates *flow, layering,* and *rupture* as being the defining musicological features of rap (1984b: 38). In both the examples below, the dynamic relationships between these dimensions of the sound can clearly be seen at work: the use of the backbeats, the polyrhythmic complexities generated by the layering of drum-machine tracks and samples, the construction of hypermetrical patterns interrupted by regular breaks, the sheer volume of sampled material, and the extraordinary melodico-rhythmic-percussive use of record scratches generates a genuinely complex musical text.

The most thoroughgoing musicological analysis of rap music is that undertaken by Robert Walser, who argues that "only the musical aspects of rap can invest [the rapper's] words with the affective force that will make people want to wake up" (1995: 291). Aside from the general musicological imperative to look "beyond the vocals" (Walser 1993), no small part of the argument here is that the sheer mass of rap lyrics[3] constitutes fertile ground for academic and popular analysis, producing a skewed emphasis on a demonstration of "rap's verbal complexity and the cultural significance of its lyrics" (Walser 1995: 291). I encountered the intellectualist bias toward textuality that Walser is addressing here: it was frequently assumed that I would be primarily interested in the *words* of the raps. J.U. told me one day, for example, that "it's all about the words, man." Although I don't want to suggest that he was simply telling me what I wanted to hear, there was a sense that it was important for J.U. to impress me with the value of (the "cultural capital" of) his practices. The words *were* important to J.U., but so was *the flow* . . . the affective thump of the bass.

After addressing a series of conventional musicological (and popular) positions that seek to define rap as "not music" (and with which I am not concerned), Walser explains how rap compositional practices generate

188

this affective power. Acknowledging first that "the lyrics and reception of rap cannot be detached from the music" (1995: 291), and later the dangers of adopting too formalistic an approach to the "meaningfulness" of individual (musical) notes, Walser sketches out the "solid but richly conflicted polyrhythmic environment" of Public Enemy's "groove" and the "polyrhythmic flexibility" of the rap (296). The interaction between these polyrhythmias produces a "non-teleological . . . complex present . . . containing enough energy and richness that progress seems moot" (296).

From this consideration of Public Enemy's "primary text" (A. F. Moore 1993), Walser is able to concur with Toop's (1991) archaeology of an "explicit" lineage to be drawn from the verbal and musical styles of present-day rap to "African music itself," finding in Public Enemy's music "the clash of rhythms" identified by one scholar as "the cardinal principle of African music" (Walser 1995: 297). However, this is immediately qualified by Walser's observation that "to trace the origins of a stylistic feature is not to account for its attractions and functions in later contexts" (298).

So, as we move toward understanding how rap music was understood by those who made it in Sydney, circa 1994, let's go back to that ethnographic context.

HOW TO MAKE A RAP RECORDING, SYDNEY, 1994

In "On the Fetish Character in Music and the Regression of Listening," his response to Walter Benjamin's famous essay "The Work of Art in the Age of Mechanical Reproduction," Adorno offers this thumbnail sketch of the fetishistic listener, that "eager [male] person who leaves the factory and 'occupies' himself with music in the quiet of his bedroom": "He is shy and inhibited, perhaps has no luck with girls, and wants in any case to preserve his own special sphere. He seeks this as a radio ham . . . He patiently builds sets whose most important parts he must buy ready-made, and scans the air for shortwave secrets, though there are none" (1992: 292–93).

Eighteen-year-old Steve Petridis, DJ E.S.P. of Illegal Substance worked not in a factory, but in an inner-city chicken shop. In his bedroom, with his keyboards and an MPC 60 sampler, E.S.P. was a self-styled *beat freak*, not dissimilar to the fetishistic listener described by Adorno, patiently building his set(-up) and scanning second-hand record shops, not the airwaves, for secrets of all lengths: long, short, but all *phat*. These are *the beats;* the grooves and breaks plucked from the vinyl with his MPC 60, slowed down, sped up, looped and layered, mixed for the tracks for DJ Mick E's rhymes. And where Adorno dismisses the futile effort of the ham radio operator's search for nonexistent secrets, for E.S.P. there were secrets aplenty, in the form of precious beats from thirty years of back catalogs, deleted, rereleased, hocked, borrowed, or pilfered records.

And there were plenty of professional secrets: once discovered, sources were carefully guarded. On the air at 2 SER, being interviewed by Miguel, E.S.P. was (playfully) asked where he got his beats:

E.S.P.: Um . . .
Miguel: You're not going to tell us are you?
E.S.P.: I made them myself. [Laughter]

On Illegal Substance's first album release, "Off da Back of a Truck," a production credit refers to "The Hospital of Hits." When Miguel asked where this studio was, E.S.P. said, "Ah, my bedroom." In the wake of the laughter that followed, he then offered an elaboration on this which again takes on Adorno's sketch: "Yeah, a lot happens in there [in his bedroom]." Miguel was running a radio show, so he seized the opportunity to make a joke: "What kind of surgery goes on in there most . . . I won't say nights . . . days? I don't want to know what goes on there at night . . . " Grinning slyly, but sidestepping the question of what Adorno coyly called "luck with girls," E.S.P. answered, ". . . just beat creating and tunes and that . . ."

Jokes aside, what do we have here? The distinction drawn, in African-American urban cultures, between the (feminized) private sphere of work and the (masculinized) public sphere of play has been remarked on by many writers; Abrahams and Szwed (1983: 13), Folb (1980), and Leary (1990: 12–13, 22–23) have used such a distinction to reflect on the public, communitarian development of the African-American oral practices (signifyin', the dozens, etc.), the precursors to "rap," "on the street." Such oral practices, on this account, are public performance, through which individuals accrue prestige and social status.

I have already shown how the discourse of "the street" informs the Sydney Hip Hop Scene. The "street" is coded as "the real": to claim to be in touch with the street is to claim access to (literally) unmediated knowledge and to be able to "represent" that truth. The expression "code of the streets," for example, would often accompany the performance of a rap. Accounts of the early days of Hip Hop Culture in Sydney and Brisbane often include references to public spaces, none more revealingly than one Brisbane writer's account of the early attempts to reproduce in that city a "street life" on the model of the street life (imaginary) of North America. Once again the reference here is to Malcolm McLaren's "Buffalo Gals" film clip: "It came out over that Christmas period, um, Rock Steady Crew, Malcolm McLaren and all that sort of stuff grew up and came out, every kid was trying to learn to break-dance, um, it was just something different to do, everyone sort of took to it, um, everyone would go to the city and hang out and from there, um, it sort of died out . . ." (interview with unnamed writer).

The urban geography of Australian cities is simply not conducive to hanging out: rapping, in Australia, is something that starts off in, and often stays in, suburban bedrooms.[4] One of Def Wish Cast's lyrics described the experience of being woken up by one's parents to be told that you are "rapping in your sleep." DJ Vame told me of the hours he spent locked away in his bedroom, practicing his DJ skills—cutting, mixing, scratching, sampling—illustrating his story by breaking into his mother's voice, "What are you doing in there?" and then laughing. On another occasion, I thanked the Monk for a particularly entertaining freestyle session at the Lounge Room. "No trouble, mate," he told me. "If I wasn't doin' it here I'd be doing it in my bedroom anyway." As Mick E put it:

> I started writing rhymes in my room, which was amazing because I didn't know enough about the culture, and they were alright you know, made them on my little portable CD tape thing and played them to Mum and she goes "it's nice dear, it's nice, just do your homework boy" and now [I] kept writing, persisted with it and then mum started saying "yeah the lyrics are quite good I like what you're saying" and so they sort of encouraged me a bit more, made me want to write more, [I] kept writing.

Blaze cut, pasted, laid out, and wrote *Vapors* on his bedroom floor. When I asked J.U. what the new Hip Hop shop the Lounge Room would look like, he replied, "Probably like Blaze's bedroom."

Phat Beats . . .

Here, then, is Sydney Hip Hop: rap music, recorded in bedrooms, while parents are kept in the dark downstairs. DJ Vame had no musical training, and he in fact argued that musical training ruins "the Hip Hop thing." Too much technical musical knowledge, he suggested, creates "cross-over" — you get synthesizers and, worse, real instruments.

Vame worked in a manner that he described as being "true to the music." This meant that he based his compositional and recording practice on the what he called "the original Hip Hop instruments: two turn-tables and a microphone." Well, he also used a sampler and a drum machine, but even these devices bestowed an aura of authenticity on a Hip Hop product: the distinctive sound of the famous Roland 808 drum machine was as much a mark of authenticity in Hip Hop circles as the Hammond organ is for Motown, or the Moog organ for particular New Wave pop genres (Goodwin 1990: 265).

Composing his tracks on software (worth around AU$1,200) running on a simple Atari home computer, Vame had complete technical mastery over his sounds, isolating waves, speeding them up, slowing them down, inverting them with the assurance of a Bach tricking up a fugue. The first step involved the selection of a "bpm" (beats per minute), constructing a big bottom end (in contradistinction to rock's treble-y sound): large, flattened-out bass tones. In describing the desired sound, Vame shook his tummy with both hands, demonstrating the effect of a *phat* bass. Another producer told me about the problems of mixing up the fat, almost atonal, subsonic bass notes: when he sent his tapes off to be mastered, they come back cleaned up — the word he used was "sweetened." Vame talked about the recording of Def Wish Cast's "Knights of the Underground Table." The sound engineer in whose garage studio they were working would constantly mix down the bass, and sessions would turn into the classic rock 'n' roll mixing scenario, with Vame sneaking his bass levels up whenever he could, only to later be played a tape that had been mixed when they (Vame et al.) were absent, and being told that this was the version they had agreed on.

E.S.P. described the whole compositional/recording process in similar terms: "Making a track, what I do is I come up with the beat first, drum beats, drum machine. I just like, get the beats, programme them in . . ." His rapper, Mick E, continued: "When Steve makes his beats, you can hear what the song will become, if it's gonna be a nice happy song, a slow, fast song, just by the speed of the song." The next step is to "muck around with the keyboard, come up with a bass line." To make a "hard core" track, he creates "*dark* sounds, that's all it is, the low basslines . . . The heavy bass, big bass, slow, heavy."

The process is guided, he explains, by *feeling*. And the metaphor here is iconic, rather than merely figurative. E.S.P. again: "It moves you. The hard core sound, it's like it really moves you. It's like 'wow,' you really like freak out over it. You just hear it and it's like, 'yeah, that's good.' If it makes you kick straight away it's good, if it doesn't, start again." This compositional process is improvisational: "I don't like to plan like okay, this song's gonna sound like this, so that . . . I don't decide on the music I'm gonna make. I just know that it's gonna be heavy, and it's gonna kick. And if it doesn't I'll change it to make it kick." Once the rhythmic fabric of the backing track was set down, the next step was to "get a few sounds and samples going through there."

The samples came from anywhere. Milk crates of secondhand records. Parents' collections. Television, rented videos. I watched another DJ, WizDM from the Christian rap crew the Brethren Incorporated, work his way through dozens of old jazz and blues records one afternoon, skimming from track to track, looking for a loop, a break beat. He explained his recording process, calling it *ping-ponging:* on a decidedly low-tech four-track mixing rig cobbled together from an electronics store, he would work for hours, reducing three tracks to one, and then repeating the process, layering up vast soundscapes of samples, piling on top of each other. It's not hard to "clean up" sounds, but, vitally, the sample had to retain the trace of its source — the snap, crackle, hiss of old vinyl proving not only the authenticity of the source, but the authenticity of the process by which the source was taken, appropriated, recomposed.

. . . Dope Rhymes

The next step in E.S.P.'s process involved talking with his rapper, his "partner in rhyme": "I call him up . . . ," he says, gesturing to Mick, who takes up the narrative, and together, they explain how a rap came about:

Mick: He goes "What do you think of this beat?" and I go "Yeah, awright, that's cool. That sounds like a song about . . . summertime" Boom! I wrote a song about summer.

E.S.P.: It's like we got a song, "Summer Holiday": it's like a cruising song, it's laid back, and really heavy and funky like summer, hanging out in your car, cruising about and it's sort of the like feeling you get out of that, so we wrote about it, you know, what's summer like?

Mick: He made the beat, and he played it to himself for three hours straight, just the beat, just that loop going through because it was such a . . . so relaxing, and he rings me up and he's just so mellow, going . . . talking about his beat . . .

E.S.P.: Hey . . . Didn't even have to have a cone [i.e., smoke marijuana].

Mick E: Like, "check it out, man." "Yeah, cool" very summertime feeling, I wrote all my feelings about summer.

Writing raps was a full-time business for these two, keeping notebooks crammed with *rhymes, couplets, similes, metaphors* (the terms they used). And while some rhymers preferred to improvise and others carefully crafted their lines, all shared the idea that rhyming was something that was done compulsively. The metaphor of addiction recurred: "I can't help it, man" (bombers used exactly the same language to explain their need to tag up any and every surface). "My mind is infected with rhyming words," rapped Def Wish. Sleek the Elite, a rhymer emerging in the Sydney scene just as I was wrapping up my research would speak of his obsessive need to "come up with similes" as he drove around the city in his work as an air-conditioning repairman.

Rhymers honed their "skills" by rapping along to favorite artists, learning lines by rote. I asked Mick E whether he studied poetry. "Nah," he sneered, dismissively, before correcting himself: " . . . Well I *do* study poetry . . . but it's got nothing to do with it."

Writing a rap could be hit or miss. Mick explained: "If it doesn't start off right, I have to stop, and like a take a deep break and start again, but it's got to be . . . if it starts off right, I can keep flowing, you know, keep going for a long time, but you've just gotta be in the mood." But "you can't just take two lines and go 'that will go well in a song.' You've got to write . . ." And E.S.P. finishes off the thought: "You've got to write a story . . . especially if you go out one night and something happens, and you spin out 'wow' . . . it's like it's all there and just waits and you just write about it."

So, the critical features of this compositional practice, as understood by those engaged in it, were, first, its grounding in a corporeal listening practice: the music must *feel* right, it must *kick*, be *fat/phat*. The music must bear the trace of its composition. Samples must sound like samples; the *grain* of the source must be retained, and could, supposedly, be drawn from anywhere. Fashions, of course, would change: Hip Hop ex-

periments with jazz sources, "authenticated" by the discourse of a historical continuity connecting, for example, bebop to Hip Hop. Vame told me
about one day teasing the rappers from Def Wish Cast by playing them a
track he had mixed using a sample from a 1970s pop hit that he referred
to as "that wack shit 'Oh What a Night.'" Only after they had started to accommodate to the idea did he "reveal" to them that he had, in fact, been
"tricking them." Vame almost got away with it through his own institutionalized status: there is no "formal" code that operates to exclude the
track in question from the bounds of Hip Hop, only a continually renego-
tiated consensus that is always open to challenge.

Sampling was also governed by a quite explicit code of ethics, explained by DJ E.S.P: "Well, like, rap samples rap, cool, they don't mind. If
rap sampled off someone else, they'd sue, all right, so if someone else
samples rap, what goes around comes around." It was not all right for
Madonna to sample Public Enemy, even though Public Enemy has long
since defended its right to use anything it wants, sustaining its ethical position on the grounds of a perceived ethno-political solidarity with the
group's sources. And, of course, looping in and around these discourses
of authenticity we also find the standard rock-and-roll narratives of the
sell-out (see Maxwell 1994b).

The successful rap track would also, according to Mick E, "tell a story,"
directly, mimetically related to "real shit that happens." Rappers simply
recounted what they saw. For Mick E, this was the defining feature of
"hard core." Additionally, the grounding of the content of a rap in reality
ensured that his practice as a rapper was not merely imitative of North
American rappers, and was therefore a guarantor of authenticity: if a rap
described a "real event that took place on "the street," then obviously,
self-evidently, it was authentic.

And although the "phat beats, dope rhymes" binarism suggests a strict
division of the musical text—the affective thrall of the music versus the
rational appeal of the lyrics—it's not that simple (see Walser 1995). Another rapper describes North American rhymer NAS's style: "They [the
"mainstream"] wouldn't understand that, that it's butter-smooth rhymes
and that, that stuff is just like originality and it's just like it's in its own
sense, you know what I mean they can't deal with that but it's like the underground, the underground know that, that NAS is like a . . . this guy is
so smooth and he's got rhymes that are like he's dropping science or like
they keep with it, you know."

The rap is *butter-smooth;* rhymers *flow.* It is an acquired taste: listeners must enculturate themselves, undergo what Feld calls "interpretive" moves (in Keil and Feld 1994: 163–64; Feld 1994c: 92) in order to make distinctions (Bourdieu 1984), to be able to tell bad from good.

To get a feel for *phatness,* though, we'll have to listen to some music.

LISTENING TO HIP HOP

To reiterate: the "meaning" of a given rap track can only be grasped through an investigation of the historically contextualized, sociological processes by which meanings are "articulated" to particular musicological features, these processes being determined in part by the play of interests, negotiations, and struggles as individuals attempt to enroll others to their "version" of social being. What is at stake in these struggles is not merely "power," although, of course, a certain power would accrue, for example, to J.U. in his (however fleetingly) successful closure of the Hip Hop symbolic order. What is at stake is the *having* of one's own affective state, of being able to understand one's pleasure, as Žižek would have it (1993): being able to offer an account of, and to give a name to "one's thing": the "real thing."

Let's listen to two recordings released in Sydney in the early 1990s. The first, from Sound Unlimited, was greeted with disdain within the Hip Hop scene, while the second, by Def Wish Cast, was acclaimed.[5] I will offer an account of the musicological features of these recorded texts, followed by an account of the articulation of value and meaning to those particular features. The varied reception of these recordings by the Sydney Hip Hop audience involves a range of considerations operating outside that "primary" musical text. Judgments about value and authenticity are informed by a number of factors — knowledges about the performers and the circumstances of the production of the musical text as well as the music itself, and particularly, in reference to the music, a timbral quality informing the recordings in their totality, rather than an attention to specific musicological features or systems at work within them. The key idea to be isolated, dominating questions of the aesthetic, the epistemological, the semantic, and, fundamentally, the ontological grounding of Hip Hop within the Sydney scene, is that tied to the expression *hard core,* and the related notion of a "truth" in the music — that somebody, or something, can be *true to the music.*

Sound Unlimited's Postcard
from the Edge of the Underside

After supporting Public Enemy and Run DMC on a couple of Australian tours in the late 1980s and early 1990s, Sound Unlimited landed a deal with Sony/Columbia in 1991–92. The massive recording and distribution contract was a breakthrough, and much was made by Sound Unlimited of the faith placed by Sony/Columbia in the community that SU claimed to represent (see Maxwell and Bambrick 1994).

The deal, however, involved SU's working with some in-house producers in Boston. The Antune brothers apparently listened to the SU demos and worked up the backing tracks on sophisticated recording equipment, using live instruments, before the rappers even got to the studios. The album, in keeping with the self-marginalizing discourse of Hip Hop, was called *A Postcard from the Edge of the Underside*.

Track six, "Kickin' to the Underside," starts off with five sampled voice grabs, punctuated by a percussive, synthesized chord and a DJ record scratch. The first is taken from an Australian pop hit from the 1970s, "Eagle Rock" by Daddy Cool, a recording that had been revived in the early 1990s. A voice, lifted from that track's introduction, intones, "Now listen," to which an echo has been added ("-isten -isten -isten . . ."). This segues into a second, similarly echoed sample, and a third, the three combining to construct the sentence "Now listen to this song" and the name-check "unlimited." The samples are crystal clear: the barest trace of the guitar figure and handclap beat from the Daddy Cool song, for example, is audible in the background; each sample is placed distinctly in the sonic space, located in clearly differentiated spaces, left, right and foreground. The sound quality is good, and the vocal tones are warm, resonant. The fourth sample is the immediately identifiable voice of Flavor Flav, the mercurial jester-rapper figure from Public Enemy: "That's right, from the Sound Unlimited Posse boy-ee . . ." The final sample is an American-accented voice announcing the crew's name: "Sound Un-*lim*-it-ed."

Then the backing track kicks in: a drum machine and a live slapped bass set up a brisk, funky common time beat at a punchy 114 bpms. Each measure is organized around the bass riff, which, played live in the studio, sets up a hypermetrical movement (A. F. Moore 1993: 39) across two- and four-measure groups. The drum track is dynamically even; a snare and high hat ride the beat, with a kick drum hitting the second and fourth beats (the backbeats).

The crew's three rappers take it in turns to deliver lines with a sort of mid-Pacific perkiness, neither identifiably Australian-accented nor American. T-Na, the female rapper, sings sections of the chorus, while elsewhere her voice catches and skips, almost playfully. All three vocals are timbrally colorful and tonally broad, although the dynamic of the male raps tends to be derived from a rhythmic observance of the emphasized backbeat.

The mix of vocals and backing track conforms to the standard pop-rock model: the vocals are foregrounded, placed in front of the music. The drums, particularly the high-range snares and high hats, are perhaps slightly more prominent than might be expected of a pop track, but the bottom end is not particularly emphasized.

When rapper Kode Blue rhymes "faster on the C U T . . . ," a rhythmic record scratch provides an iconic reference, placed high above the musical mix. A measure later, the rhythmic flow is broken; the drum machine and bass drop out, replaced by a percussive scratch and synthesizer sound as T-Na raps

. . . from the very first hook line and . . .

T-Na's syncopated delivery slides up the scale, anticipating a return to the tonic root falling on the final word: the music and the lyrics here combine again to effect a musico-semantic closure. After a brief moment of suspension, all three rappers, delaying their delivery just behind the strict measure of the beat, hit . . .

. . . sinker!

. . . the drum machine and bass kick in again, reestablishing the interrupted flow. The rhymers exchange lines again, until Kode Blue's final rhyme, where, once more, there is a small suspension, a kind of breaklet, the next rapper falling in just behind the beat to once again effect a musico-semantic closure. The chorus follows, a sampled flute figure from the early 1980s Australian hit "Down Under" by Men at Work.

The track proceeds through a standard pop-rock form: choruses and verses exchanged three times, a middle-eight break, another verse and chorus, a coda and chorus fade-out, the metrical and sonic pattern throughout complicated only by the addition of piano and horn samples and T-Na's sung track through the chorus.

Def Wish Cast's Knights of the Underground Table

Around the same time as the release of Sound Unlimited's album, Def Wish Cast released their *Knights of the Underground Table*, recorded in a suburban garage studio on a four-track, with no live instruments. Earlier releases on cassette and vinyl had recouped costs, and the crew was able to afford a small run of compact discs, distributed by Random Records. Twelve hundred copies were printed. DJ Vame produced the recordings, using turntables, a collection of old records, a VCR and rented B-grade horror movies.

"A.U.S.T. Down Under Comin' Upper" starts with a gritty sample, complete with a mass of background static. Across a low-level synthesized orchestral tone, generically identifiable as being taken from a horror movie soundtrack, we hear a male voice

and unlikely to bring anyone down there, so . . .

interrupted by a melodramatic chord and a screaming female voice:

no . . . No . . . NO . . . AAARGH!!!

The male voice completes the sentence

. . . *we're coming up.*

Abruptly, the ambience of the recording changes: the static hiss accompanying the samples disappears, and a synthesized drum track kicks in at about 104 bpm. The rhythm is a simple common time and conforms to a standard rock backbeat structure, the accent falling on the second (strongest) and fourth (second strongest) beats, while the first and third beats are weaker, the latter being the weakest, thus:

1	2	3	4
3d strongest	strongest	weakest	2d strongest

The second and fourth beats of each measure (the backbeats) are full notes, relatively uncomplicated drum sounds. The first and third beats are paired eighth notes, the third complicated by a range of drum sounds and the breaking down of the eighth notes into stuttering sixteenths, anticipating the final beat. As Walser points out, the layering up of different drum sounds, and the ability of the drum programmer to minutely anticipate or fall in behind the strict pulse, generates idiosyncratic dynamics within measures (1995: 295). The complication of the third beat constructs the particular momentum of this rhythmic structure, shared by

PERFORMANCE

many Hip Hop tracks, throwing the measure forward into the final beat, which, although it does not carry the dynamic emphasis of the second beat, is a single, sustained note. After the busy-ness of the third beat, the fourth beat is broader, fuller, and "feels" longer; it is this beat toward which the energetic drive of each measure is directed, on which the semantic content of the raps tends to be resolved, and on which the other rappers tend to "punch" into the rhymes. Thus, in broad terms, the second beat of each measure provides the impetus, and the final beat constitutes a point of arrival.

The drum track here is muffled, somewhat muddy and almost jangly, not placed anywhere in particular in the soundscape. For the first measure, this beat kicks alone, establishing the metrical figure sustaining the rest of the track. Into the second, third, and fourth measures, a record scratch is panned from left to right and back again, the turntables used as a featured solo instrument, developing a theme, rather than as a percussive or rhythmic fill. At the end of this solo, there is a short break: once again, the tonal, ambient surface of the musical text is disrupted as for a single measure the drum machine is mixed right down to the barest trace. Into the gap opened up in the rhythmic surface, Vame has sampled a deep male voice, saying, "Down-under."

Abruptly a cacophony of voices, samples, and drums tumbles into the brief hiatus: a mass of male voices chant the chorus "A.U.S. Down Under Comin' Upper," the drum machine fills back in, and, at the end of each chanted phrase, a synthesized orchestral horror movie chord stutters, sequenced to effect a braking, hiccoughing sound opening up over two beats and fading under the next vocal repetition. A rhythmic scratch and a garbled vocal sample accompanies the chorus: "A.U.S. Down Under Comin' Upper," repeated twice over four measures, the vocals, falling within the first and second measures, interacting in a kind of antiphonic dialogue with the samples in the second and fourth measures. When the chorus is repeated after the first rapped verse, the antiphonics become explicit: a sampled female (American) voice responds to each repetition of "A.U.S. Down Under Comin' Upper" with the words "I need something Hip Hop, you know what I'm talking about?"

The tonal shape of the vocal delivery is informed by the rhythmic structure of the measure noted above, thus:

1	2	3	4
3d strongest	strongest	weakest	2d strongest
A.U.S.	Down	Under Comin'	Up — per

200

The syllable "down" spreads out into a long, broad, bent vowel, a characteristically Australian diphthong; the final syllable fades away both in volume and down the tonic scale. The syllable "up" on the final beat is followed by the plosive release of "per," pronounced "paaah," trailing over the top of the vocal sample into the next measure.

The last repetition fades into the first verse. Die C and Ser Reck start the verse off, calling, "Who?," and Def Wish's delivery barrels in, overlapping this syllable. As he starts to rap, the drum pattern is augmented by a rhythmic, trebly guitar and bass riff, sampled and looped, becoming the rhythmic hook sustaining the rest of the track. The guitar figure is identical in rhythmic shape to the drum pattern: two eighth notes on the first beat, and a full note on the second, several tones higher than the initial notes. The pattern is repeated on the third and fourth measures, except that the eighth note doublet is broken down into a funk-rhythm: the drum track has been generated from this sample.

The vocal itself is unclear, textured into the rest of the mix. Def Wish's voice is ragged, rough, raw: a guttural scraping sound, and the other two rappers punch key words ("true to the music," for example). When he refers to his DJ, a record scratch falls in over the top of the mix. Halfway through the verse, there is a break in the rhythmic flow. The guitar figure, having been established as the device driving the composition forward, disappears, and Def Wish's rap trails off in intensity and drops down the scale into the resulting void, rapping, "But they continue to live off imported songs." The next handful of lines is delivered into a sparser musicscape: a backbeat on the upper end of the drum-machine kit, against which the rapper's voice is contrasted in high relief. Def Wish's voice has a distinctive epiglottal rasp, catching on each syllable. All three rap namecheck "Def Wish Cast," and the beat and the guitar loop return, now, after their absence, feeling even more dynamic and driving than before, and Def Wish launches into a ragga rap delivery for the final three lines, a climactic, breathless rush that delivers the track into a repetition of the frenetic chorus.

A basic dynamic of flow and arrest informs the rest of the track, with the alternative removal and reinstatement of the guitar and bass loop being the principal device used. However, as rapper Die C leaps into his verse, a new element is introduced into the sonic landscape: a deep, fuzzy, drawn-out synthesized bass tone spreading out under the mix, metabolic in its intensity. Operating as a rhythmic counterpoint slightly outside the strict meter of the track, it falls into the mix like a vast rubber ball failing to bounce, deflating on striking the bottom end of the sound-scape, at the lowest threshold of audibility.

It is in regard to this last musicological feature that the recording of *Knights of the Underground Table* is particularly interesting. In performance, this bass tone is extraordinary. I would *watch* the sound, the fuzzy color of the bass tone, shimmer across the broad backward and forward undulations of the woofers in the speaker stacks, driven by the high-quality DAT backing tracks. The CD release of the same tracks lacked this degree of resolution, resulting in a surprisingly (and disappointingly) tre-bly sound that is "noisy," with very little tonal dynamic in the mix: the mass of samples, synthesizer tracks, drum-machine tracks, DJ scratches, vocal grabs, and so on tend to blend together. The dynamic of the record-ing, as a result, derives more from the selective interruption of this con-glomerate sound, rather than from the placement of distinct musical parts in sonic space.

■ Both tracks conformed to standard pop-rock formulations: each is less than four minutes long (the Sound Unlimited track slightly shorter at 3'44", while the Def Wish Cast comes in at 3'55"); each uses a brief series of samples to lead into a standard verse-chorus structure, with a middle eight "break" section. Def Wish Cast fill out the middle eight with a namechecking call and response of outer Western Sydney suburbs, while the Sound Unlimited track moves into a complete *break-down,* complete with a cow-bell backbeat, a piano sample, and a voice interjecting, "Oh yeah!"—generically more in keeping with what Ronald Jemal Stephens (1991) calls mid-1980s "rock 'n' roll rap."

Def Wish Cast organize their verses around individual rappers deliver-ing their rhymes while the other two rappers punch into key words, usu-ally on the backbeats; all join in on the chorus. Each rappers' contribu-tions are informed by their own ability to sustain a *flow,* a key feature of which is their capacity to maintain their physical energy and capacity — in very simple terms, to not run out of breath. All three raps are reedy and scratchy in quality: tonally, the vocals are in the upper register, using head resonators rather than deeper, reverberative chest sounds, and a particular mobilization of the oral apparatus. In performance, they gri-mace and snarl, lips curling, mouths pursed and stretched. All three use a lot of syllables, particularly in Def Wish's "ragga rap" sections, in which he interpolates extra plosive syllables, tripping from word to word. The voices are frequently strained and hoarse (Def Wish in particular would often lose his voice, explaining to me that he was trying to use his diaphragm to punch the sounds out, but felt that he couldn't get the same effect). The reaching, shouting quality of these vocals was coded, within the scene, as being "authentic," as signifying "Aussie-ness" and a specifically Western Suburbs common speech. John Shepherd has identified a similar valorization in popular music forms of the high-pitched, straining male voice (1987: 166–67). Here, the rough, sandpaper grain of these voices was understood as not merely *signifying* authenticity, but as being, iconically, authentic. A particular metaphysics of the voice as self-presence informed these understandings (cf. Derrida 1976): the suffering voice is experienced by both performer and listener as (because *suffering,* because *felt*) "real." Other far Western Sydney crews, most noticeably Campbelltown's 046, pushed this vocal style even further, delivering shrieking, screeching raps, their voices leaping up into keeningly high registers.

In the case of Def Wish Cast, the valorization of this male voice is, on their own account, uncomplicated by any attempt to emulate "blackness." Indeed, the crew explicitly denies any suggestion that their work is in any way derivative of African-American musics. Def Wish took pains to tell me that his style is influenced by London ragga rap rather than North American rap, conceding the Afro-Caribbean "roots" of that scene, but carefully distancing himself from charges of imitation or of subjection to a putative American cultural imperialism.

The Sound Unlimited track involves a more atomistic breaking up of the verse: rappers exchange clauses, rather than verses. The voices are smoother, more colorful, as I noted, in terms of both tone and timbre. Where Def Wish Cast generates vocal dynamics through an inflection of the speed and syllabic volume of delivery and the energetic stressing of syllables, the vocalists from Sound Unlimited use a range of tonal and timbral inflections to create both musical and semantic differences. This results in a more subtle, inflectioned, "colorful" vocal, with each rapper being distinctively identifiable in the mix.

Walser's analysis of Public Enemy rapper Chuck D's careful negotiation of meter, as he sets up counter-rhythms and clashes in the rhythmic fabric of P.E.'s sound suggests a rapper of extraordinary sophistication. None of the Australian rappers I have described here approach this level of complexity in their relation to the beat. Although idiosyncratic relationships to the beat are discernible as rappers pull or push against the strict pulse, in general, the dynamics, as I have suggested, are generated by more conventional manipulations of volume, register, and tempo. Semantic and vocal emphasis falls regularly on the second and fourth beats of each measure; this is also where the other rappers, in the case of Def Wish Cast, punch in.

AUTHENTICITY

The discussion above of the Def Wish Cast rappers' own accounts of the relationship of their music and raps to an originary black musical tradition leads to a more general consideration of the cultural genealogies and contexts of these musicological features. As Walser points out, the explicit links that can be made between the musicological features of Hip Hop, the verbal form of rap and musicological and oral traditions in African-American cultures do not "account for [their] attractions and functions in later contexts" (Walser 1995: 298). The continuity between the sub-Saharan *griot* and Chuck D can be, and is, argued frequently; Toop (1991), Gates (1988), Gilroy (1993), and Rose (1994b) all offer variations on the theme. My concern with such accounts is that they start to fix certain meanings: Rose suggests, for example, that "[r]ap music uses repetition and rupture in new and complex ways, building on long-standing black cultural forces" (1994: 70).[6]

The problem here is that the qualities of flow, continuity, rupture, polyrhythmia, layering—indeed, *all* the musicological qualities associated with Afro-diasporic culture—are, so far as contemporary youth in Australia are concerned, part of a larger cultural repertoire, rather than being identifiably "black." Accounts such as that of Rose, grounding the possibility of a Hip Hop collectivity in a cultural politics of continuity and identification, could only ever understand an Australian Hip Hop experience as being inauthentic. And yet, Ser Reck, Def Wish, Mick E, Sound Unlimited, all understand their experience as being authentic. Although discourses identifying blackness with authenticity still abound in the local, Sydney context, "white" (and yellow, and olive, and brown) folk cannot assert a claim to Hip Hop authenticity through a simple identification with "color" or a biological or even a cultural continuity with African-Americans. They, in fact, recognize the decidedly mediated quality of

204

their relationship to what they know of as the "origins" of their (adopted) practices, and yet they are able to resolve this absolute difference by producing a discourse of cultural continuity that transcends the necessity for a causal, organic continuity. The point is that an individual in Sydney, Australia, in 1992, could, they claimed, *get* Hip Hop Culture from a television video clip, and that what they understood as being the *essence* of that culture is so pure, so transcendent, that the being-ness of an African-American was seen, in effect, as an expression of that transcendent ground, rather than the other way around. A white Sydney kid could claim to empathize with a black American kid through the shared experience of Hip Hop, which had an ontological primacy.

Within the scene, Def Wish Cast's album was approved for its "authenticity": its *rawness,* its graininess, its lack of pretension, its *truth.* The Sound Unlimited album, on the other hand, was heard as being inauthentic, as not being grainy enough, as being a sell-out, its sound cleaned up for mass consumption. In my analysis of tracks from the respective albums, it is possible to discern the musicological grounds for the making of this distinction, whereby "authenticity" is articulated to a particular mode of vocalization, as well as to a particular sonic quality, where "noisiness" bestows authenticity. The interesting thing is, however, that even these qualities are up for negotiation within the Hip Hop listening community. The work of the Los Angelino producer Dr. Dre, late of NWA, for example, was celebrated for its *smoothness* of production, for the *slickness* of its beats, its crystal clarity. NAS was celebrated for "butter-smooth" delivery.

What, then, appear as contradictions on the face of the musicological evidence are resolved in terms of a more abstract category, which is "read" as underlying the (contingent) features of the primary (musical) text: *hard core*–ness.

HARD CORE

With its implicit internal/external binarism, "hard core" is widely used outside Hip Hop scenes in pretty much the same way, more recently to refer to dance and techno music. However, in the Sydney Hip Hop Scene, the term bore a particular gravity. Break dancers doing floor moves on rough abrasive carpet or asphalt were referred to as being "hard core." A compulsive bomber would be described in identical terms; surveying a thrashed train carriage, a writer approvingly celebrates the tagger: "Man, he is *hard core.*"

Def Wish defended his decision to rap in a "simple b-boy style" on "A.U.S.T" by claiming that whatever style he uses, it will always be

. . . Hard Core!

'Cos hard core means true to the music . . .

I asked DJ Vame what "true to the music" meant. Simply this, he explained: it meant being "faithful" to the "original" "instruments" of Hip Hop—two turntables and a microphone. For Mick E, a track was "hard core" if it was based on a low, slow bass beat (he swings his body slowly, almost sensuously in order to fully impart the significance of this sound). DJ E.S.P qualified this definition: "Hard core means a really heavy sound, something that wouldn't be played on radio," and they both laugh, Mick adding, "[It] stays underground." Another (female) informant offered this: "A record is hard core," she told me, "if no one else has heard it yet," a perhaps more insightful definition, recasting the question of musical "meanings" into a sociological context, engaging with the Bourdieuan discourse of a logic of scarcity.

But perhaps the term is more usefully thought of in terms of its capacity to cohere a range of practices, articulating them to, and *signifying,* a central, substratal idea, without actually stating *exactly* what that idea is. Here, the semiotics of C. S. Peirce are a useful way to think about just what it is that is going on.

A PROCESSURAL SEMIOTICS

"A sign," for Peirce, "stands *for* something *to* the idea which it produces" (Eco 1979: 180). The emphasis here is on the "constructive" nature of signifying practices: ideas are *produced* by signifying practices, rather than simply *representing* social facts. Peirce called the sign a *representamen:* "something which stands to somebody for something in some respect or capacity."

For Peirce, then, a representamen has three references: "First, it is a sign to some thought that interprets it; second, it is a sign for some object to which in that thought it is equivalent; third, it is a sign in some respect or quality, which brings it into connection with its object (Peirce in Weber, 1987: 11). That is, a sign (representamen) is necessarily communica-tive, addressed to an interpreting thought, with a view to creating "in the mind of that person [to whom it is addressed] an equivalent sign." Peirce called this equivalent, or (better) sign [representamen], an *interpretant*. The second reference of the representamen, for Peirce, is to some *thing*, which he called an *object*. This object need not be a concrete thing, but, in Eco's words, "a rule, a law, a prescription . . . the operational descrip-tion of a set of possible experiences" (Eco 1979: 181). The third feature of the representamen develops this idea: the sign is *of* the object, bearing a quality or respect in which it is brought into relationship with the object.

In the example I am looking at, the representamen is the expression "hard core." In Peircian terms, this kind of (linguistic) sign is called a "sym-bol," a symbolic relationship being one of arbitrary convention. Peirce's analysis in this respect overlaps with Saussure's linguistic semiotics. However, while for Saussure and the structuralist tradition that built on his work language was the basic model for understanding all signifying processes, in the Peircian scheme the "symbolic," arbitrary relationship is a special case of a more general semiotics. Other signifying relationships, for Peirce, rely on relationships of shared quality (*iconicity*), or contiguity or causality (*indexicality*).

Now, the point of all this is that "the interpretant interprets by bring-ing the sign into a relationship of equivalence with an object" (Weber 1987: 11–12). It does so through a process of selection: the selection of a quality or respect through which the equivalence of the interpretant can be established. A sign stands for its object, suggests Peirce, "not in all re-spects, but in reference to a sort of idea . . . the *ground* of the representa-men." The "ground," explains Eco, is that which "can be comprehended and transmitted of a given object under a certain profile: it is the content of an expression and appears to be identical with meaning" (Eco 1979: 182). Eco concludes that "since it is impossible to define the ground if not as meaning, and it is impossible to define any meaning if not as a series of interpretants," then "ground, meaning and interpretant are in fact the same" (182).

That is, signification depends on a complex of relationships, signs, and interpretations both retrospectively, in terms of an "immense mass of cognition already formed" (Eco's "rules," "laws" and "proscriptions," but also conventions, frames, genres), and prospectively, in terms of the ad-dressee of any given representamen, on whose interpretation it depends for its efficacy.

The problem that arises, then, is that of the epistemological status of the sign, or the ontological status of the object. If signs only ever refer to other signs, how, to quote Weber, "can we distinguish between true and false interpretations?" (1987: 12). For Peirce, answers Weber, the *real* is that which, "sooner or later, information and reasoning would finally result in." Weber explains that here, "having eliminated the 'object' as the origin or foundation of cognition, Peirce . . . replaces it by a transcendental subject, the community of investigators. . . . [W]hen we appeal to the notion of truth, we are referring to the kind of future consensus described as the community of investigators: what is real" — and this is the important bit — "is that reference, not its existence (13). The "reality" of "truth," then, is the appeal to the future consensus about that truth, rather than the "content" of that truth itself.

Here is the attribution of not simply "a" or "some" meaning to "a" piece of, or "a" form of, music, but a general *meaningfulness* to music produced by these particular means. The potential openness of such a process of discrimination is, as I have argued, a powerful strategic tool, allowing a particular musical text or performance to be included or excluded from a generic canon.

In the relatively short period of my research into the scene, for example, I witnessed the acceptance of Hip Hop–jazz fusion recordings. Initially, albums such as Easy Mo Bee's collaboration with the late Miles Davis were generally given the thumbs down. As more "respected" figures such as Guru moved into the same territory with the "Jazzamatazz" albums, not only was the synthesis of rap and jazz accepted; its success was offered as proof of a cultural continuity. "Hip Hop *is* jazz, man," Ser Reck explained to me. Such recordings contained, as part of the music itself, a pedagogy arguing for such a continuity: listen to Guru's introductory and "half-way" commentary on the first "Jazzamatazz." Read the liner notes. These historico-cultural discourses quickly circulated through the scene. By late 1994, the injunction against live instruments was lifted to allow rappers J.U., the Sleeping Monk, Pewbic, and B.U. to rap over the acid-jazz band Ute at a Sydney jazz venue, the Basement. The scene momentarily underwent a subtle bohemianization, productive of distinctly Keroacian-Beat *habituses.*

Discourses of musical authenticity and signification within the Hip Hop Scene, then, were bound up in sociological processes that operated within the implicit assumption that the music (and the breaking and the writing) *represented* a preexisting, or at least ontologically prior, cultural center. Meaning is the emergent (never completed, always partial) "product" of ongoing negotiations and interpretations.

But that's still not enough. It's not just about negotiations, and meanings, and discourse. It's not even about *music*. Look at Blaze's words at the head of part 3 of this book: it's the rhythm of Hip Hop you "get into."

It's . . . *it*.

Recall J.U. impressing on me that "it's the words, man, it's all about the words." I have suggested that socially negotiated interpretations of particular musicological features, and the social institution of those interpretations, generate discourses of authenticity around those features, which in turn are used to support a transcendental signifier — the "essence of Hip Hop — which stands as the ground generative of representative expressions. But J.U. didn't think about it that way: for him, what was important was the *it*, in which the idea of Hip Hop communality and around which the discourses of Hip Hop communality constellated. It is to this *it* that is the name given to a state of affect, to a mode of experience, of embodiment, of rhythm (often articulated to discourses of authenticity entwined around essentializing blackness) that I now want to turn.

And, to look for rhythm, what better place to turn than to the dance floor. . .

Dance

What Hip Hop is about, you know, is respect, getting respect and showing people your talent, when you go out at lunchtime and break and the whole school's watching you like that's what you do it for, it's an incredible feeling, you know . . .

—A Sydney breaker

The evening had not been going well.

I was at "Rap City," a one-off event in a nightclub built into the foot of an art deco skyscraper in the business center of Sydney. The crews were, as they would say, "in the house": a collection of T-shirted and baggy-jeaned young men with cropped hair and a slightly lesser number of young women, the latter looking pretty much like any young women at a Sydney nightclub. The boys played pool; the girls sat or stood together, watching. There had been a ripple of excitement an hour earlier when Def Wish Cast, heading the night's selection of acts, and their entourage of West Side crews arrived, but, otherwise, nothing seemed to be happening. Everybody was drinking beer or spirits, and, as always at these events, a solid thump pulsed through the room.

The problem tonight was with the sounds. We had been waiting for an hour and a half for the first crew of the night to kick some rhymes, but each time they stepped to the microphones, a piercing tone shrieked through the speakers, and, scowling and cursing, they would retreat from the stage. Technicians with rolls of gaffer tape and heavy metal T-shirts crawled over speaker stacks, rewiring, tweaking, doing whatever it is that they could do to make the whole thing work, amidst a general air of exasperation and annoyance.

But at the turntables, unaffected by the technical problems, a DJ was cutting up a storm. In and around the wash of voices, the click of the pool games, the fuzzy, ever accelerating, rising rush of alcohol-lubricated conversation, shouts, laughter, the pulsing beats remained a constant. Each track would fade into the next, a continuous polyphonic flow of raps, voices, beats, merging into the one meta-beat, the DJ moving from track to track, dropping riffs and breaks over the top of instrumentals, cutting and scratching through the vocals, generating this seamless macro-beat, throbbing through the room.

■ How might I describe the sound, the *feeling* of the sound, as it thumped, pulsed, kicked through my body? I'm no fan, no dancer, but the phat, phat beats thrilled through my flesh. Bruce Johnson has written of the physiological intimacy of metaphors for the experience of popular music, citing examples from the argots of blues and jazz: "funky," "cooking" (1996: 100–101). For Hip Hop, as we've seen, the metaphors are no less visceral: the music "kicks," "slams," is "fat." But in this instance, the reference is less a metaphorical one than a literal description . . .[1]

For hours after Hip Hop nights I would lie awake — not with that intra-aural keening ring, the symptom of physical damage that you get from a pub rock gig — but from a kind of hypercorporeality, as if the deep, muscular core of my body had been massaged for three, four hours, its presence foregrounded by the echoes, deep in my chest, of the drums and the thudding, subtonal noise of the bass. Across and against the vast, deep somato-sonic territory of this almost subliminal, entrancing bass pulse is the staccato, off-beat kick of the snares, tick-tick-ticking me back from the potential danger of my own dissolution into the beat, snapping me upright, up, up, before the next moment, microseconds later, of miasmic intensity, when my being folds back inward and, inevitably (the spatial metaphor appears, unbidden), *downward*. A heightened feeling of corporeal being, my body alive, awake, now, hours later, in spite of my own efforts to lay it down, to make it sleep.

At Rap City, the dance floor was about half full: groups of boys and girls danced together. Others danced by themselves, some talking, leaning over to shout words into cupped ears, laugh, point out other dancers. Fluid, languid, sensuous, sweaty movements, people starting to groove, but still, identifiably, people; individuals arrayed across space. The music was tremendous: driving, throbbing beats below, the staccato snare and high-hat backbeats kicking across the top, and, somewhere in the middle of the mix, the rich, sonorous raps, sometimes getting busy ("I am the roughest, roughest, roughest / I am the toughest, toughest, toughest . . . "), then kicking back into a languid West Coast gangsta flow. I recall an interview with Public Enemy's Chuck D: "Gangsta rappers' sound is laid-back because their lives are hectic. I like hectic music because my life is laid back" (in Gonzales 1994: 49).

"It should be noted," offer Havelock Nelson and Michael A. Gonzales, somewhat redundantly, "that in African-American culture the art of movement is closely linked to the art of noize (be it blues, jazz or hip-hop); the image of Black bodies swaying to 'the beat, the beat' is as old as the motherland" (1991: 89). At Rap City, in this moment of what, for such Afro-essentializing accounts, can only be imitative culture, the energy level builds, as white (and yellow, and olive, and brown, but nowhere "black") bodies sway to a building "krush." The DJ was *goin' off,* the dance floor getting busier, as he dropped a snatch of Eric B and Rakhim's "Paid in Full" into the instrumental break of another track: a science-teacher voice (sampled from what sounds like a high school educational film) intoning, "This is a journey into sound." It is a virtuoso performance by the DJ, scratching the sample backward and forward over the primary track, dropping the grab . . .

this . . .
　　　(scratch)
　　　　　. . . this . . .
　　　　　　　(scratch)
　　　　　　　　　. . . this . . .
　　　　　　　　　　　(scratch)
　　　. . . [beats] . . .
this is a journey . . .
　　　. . . (scratch) . . .
　　　. . . [beats] . . .
　　　　　　. . . this . . .
　　　　　　　　. . . this . . .
　　　　　　　　　this . . .

and so on, tantalizingly, for fully five minutes, building the crowd up, waiting for the right moment to release the dancers into the whole rap.

And then, there it is . . . a sudden opening, a yawning gap in the sonic space: a moment of suspension as the flight of the music, of bodies in motion, reaches an apogee, a moment that feels freed from gravity. The thickness, the busy-ness, the dense chaotic energy of the mix seems to flee to the edges of the room and beyond, leaving an anticipatory void:

the room is in free-fall for the barest of moments, soaring, waiting, hearts racing, waiting for the

drop

. . . of the DJ's needle back into the groove.

And then, the massive, sensuous, broken-down and pared-back kick of "Paid in Full" thumps through the smoke and lasers: a roomy, *funky,* sexy, expansive, crisp, *metabolic* sound, grabbing hold of all those bodies, wrenching them out of that sublime moment of *waiting* . . . and they start to undulate, to groove, to melt into the pure fatness of one of Hip Hop's defining moments.[2]

Eight measures into the track, the sampled voice comes again: "A journey which along the way will bring to you new colour, new direction, new value . . ." And at once bongos start to tap across the territory laid out by the high-hat, bass, and tom-tom refrain. Another sampled voice slides in over the funky, funky bass, a female Arabic voice (Israeli pop singer Ofrah Haza "singing a Middle Eastern folk tune" [Costello and Wallace 1990: 143]), all half-tones and melismas through and around the beat, punctuated by staccato, slightly echo-enhanced tom-tom fills.

Through this, the tone of the dance floor had changed: the siren call of the Eric B and Rakhim track had drawn fifty, sixty more bodies into the crowd, pushing against each other, infused now by the insistent, metabolic drive of the beat. By the time Rakhim's smokily deep rap rumbles across, through, under and around the dance floor, the sinuous, snaky, sexy beat has everybody in its thrall. Lips move with the rap, eyes are glazed, bodies loose. By the time we get to the breakdown, just the kicking drum-machine track, some more dialogue samples, the room is simply grooving.

Again, the play between "flow," "layering," and "ruptures in line" that Rose identifies in this music: the creation, accumulation, and sustaining of "rhythmic motion, continuity, and circularity," which is abruptly interrupted. Rose hypothesizes in this music a blueprint for social resistance and affirmation: create sustaining narratives, accumulate them, layer, embellish, and transform them. However, be prepared for rupture, find pleasure in it, in fact *plan on* social rupture. When these ruptures occur, use them in creative ways that will prepare you for a future in which survival will demand a sudden shift in ground tactics (1994b: 39).

But I couldn't help but feel, there, watching the floor at Rap City, that such considerations were a world away. Sure, this emancipatory, guerilla discourse circulates around within this scene, but as an account adduced *after* the affective fact of the beat, of the break. I'm more interested in Rose's counsel: to "find pleasure in the rupture . . ."

Listen to this account, in David Toop's *Rap Attack*. He is quoting Afrika Bambaataa, seminal figure from the Hip Hop ur-scene in the Bronx of the early 1970s, talking about the "break," that fragment of a "Latin-tinged funk" piece that was "popular with the dancers." DJs like Cool Herc would play the percussive break, ignoring the rest of the track, sustaining the same few bars by skipping from one disc to an identical disc on the second turntable. Bambaataa explains: "[H]e just kept that beat *going* . . . that certain part of the record that everybody waits for — they just let their inner self go and get wild. The next thing you know the singer comes back in and you'd be mad" (in Toop 1991: 60). More than simply the release of an "inner self," in such moments there is a *loss* of self . . . "the next thing you know" . . . a departure from self, which can no longer know its destination.

Truly awesome, abyssal voids open up in Eric B and Rakhim's music. The flow stops, a yawning absence that is at once sonic and visceral looms, opens up across the room. Bodies lunge forward into the empti-ness, weightless, pure momentum. Hearts, blood coursing through veins and arteries, muscles, synapses, fall headlong with the somatic pulse still thumping, soaring, falling, tumbling until, with a crashing, thick, broad subtonal

!thump!

the beat returns, crashing through the sweat, the sinewy mass of move-ment, scooping up this contiguous throng of free-falling bodies, catching them deep, deep in the core, driving them further, longer, out . . . and it feels *good*.

■ Now we are getting closer, perhaps, to discerning the affective grounds for the thinking of *community*. This is Victor Turner territory: the forging of the raw material of collective being, *communitas,* through the ritual-ized sharing of experience. Indeed, for the seven minutes of the track all the bodies on the floor seem to meld into a continuity of being. In the sex-ualized imagery of Elias Canetti, this moment is "the discharge," when "in a crowd . . . man can become free of [the] fear of being touched," when social distances are broken down and the individual is dissolved:

"Ideally, all are equal here; no distinctions count, not even that of sex. The man pressed against him is the same as himself. He feels him as he feels himself. Suddenly it is as though everything were happening in one and the same body" (2000: 16). The crowd becomes the subject of affect and agency, rather than simply a sum of sovereign parts. It is the *crowd* that wants to grow; the *crowd* craves density. The *crowd* strains toward its (whatever) goal, on the attainment of which it will disintegrate: it is the deferral of the goal that maintains the possibility of being a crowd, just as, for Hage, it is the impossibility of the completion of the national project that is the condition of possibility for nationalism (1993a: 97). And good DJs know this too.

Bakhtin, too, wrote of these moments: the carnival crowd, which is "the people as a whole . . . organised *in their own way* . . . outside of and contrary to all existing forms of the coercive socioeconomic and political organisation" ([1965] 1984: 255). The grooving night club crowd is, indeed, carnivalesque, sharing its being in the emergent *funk,* the moment possessing a particular character that exceeds that of any given individual in the crowd of moving bodies: "[T]he pressing throng, the physical contact of bodies, *acquires a certain meaning.* The individual feels that he is an indissoluble part of the collectivity, a member of the people's mass body. In this whole the individual body ceases to a certain extent to be itself; it is possible to . . . exchange bodies . . ." (1984: 255, emphasis added).

Turner distinguishes between the calendrical, culturally integrated, "eufunctional," formally framed, liminal *rite du passage,* and the limin*oid:* "[T]he liminoid is . . . felt to be freer than the liminal, a matter of choice, not obligation . . . One *works* at the liminal, one *plays* with the liminoid" (V. Turner 1982: 55). At Rap City, the experience of the groove is decidedly not *liminal,* but liminoid: a moment Turner describes as being of "potentially limitless freedom," characterized by a sense of "flow" (54). The groove experience moves beyond a simple metaphysics of self-presence. It is a moment of blissful intensity, of suspension, of dissolution (and, it has to be said, of the experience of a kind of freedom).

Andrew Murphie, writing about the phenomenology of the dance floor, describes the power of what Deleuze and Guattari call *the refrain* to "territorialise" space, to establish an "ecology" of being in which music, a music, figures as "a constant form of becoming of time, space, and everything that inhabits them" (Murphie 1996: 20). Music, a music, is not to be understood as being produced and received by already existing sovereign subjects; rather, the music — or, more specifically, *the refrain* — and the subjects involved with it, are considered part of a "machinic assemblage," productive of the ecology of the moment, productive, in turn, of (new) subjectivities.

Introducing a vital distinction, Deleuze and Guattari argue that the refrain, *la ritournelle*, is the "content of music" (1987: 300). In the bluntest sense, the refrain is repetition, or, literally, that which returns. The refrain is not simply the *rhythm,* either, or the beat, the *meter;* operating within an existing field of space-time; the refrain *territorializes.* It *makes* space/time, rather than operating within an already existing, Kantian spatio-temporal field.

"Rhythm," for Deleuze and Guattari, "is never on the same plane as that which has rhythm" (1987: 313). A dynamic space opens up, a potential, a throwing forward into being. Rhythm is never, they say, temporally exact: it is the *frisson,* the instability, the non-fit of the body and the meter that is generative, exciting: "[T]here is nothing less rhythmic than a military march" (313). The refrain, on Deleuze and Guattari's account, is the emergent totality of this *frisson.* This is the foundational moment of the ergonomics, as it were, of the refrain; in the language of jazz, as Keil notes, this is "swing": "the tension generated by a complex relationship between meter and rhythm" (Keil 1994: 59).

The refrain enjoys a complex relationship to "music," a term now reserved for a kind of domestication of this expansionary potential of the refrain. The refrain, however, is not simply the precursor to music. It is "a means of preventing music, warding it off, or forgoing it" (Deleuze and Guattari 1987: 313). Music is that which, Deleuze and Guattari continue, *de*territorializes the refrain, taking it up, laying hold of it, "forming a block" with the refrain in order to take it "somewhere else." That is, to an already existing somewhere else.

Here is a language for the way of being I have been describing on the dance floor, the surging over the dance floor of this being-ness (what Deleuze and Guattari call "becoming"); an analytic for this process, in which a vasty, oceanic tide of music/being reinvents space and reinvents being. Further, for Murphie, the refrain is that which facilitates a flight from self, that which "continually allows . . . escape from sovereignty" (1996: 29). There is a distinction being drawn here between the expansive, territorializing form of the refrain, in which affect displaces the sovereignty of the already-located subject, and the defining, de- and reterritorializing form of music, the moment in which the "outwardness" of the refrain is enclosed, or articulated to a narrative or discourse of "culture": the performative "becoming" is integrated into the pedagogic narrative of "being."

One part of the appeal of this Deleuze-Guattarian poetics lies in its concession to the irreducibility of the experience of the refrain. Placing aside the risks of what Žižek (1993) and Ferry (1992) have described in the Deleuze-Guattarian discourse as the Spinozist celebration of connectedness and the attendant withdrawal from a practical, communitarian ethics, I want to suggest that the appeal of this account for my purposes lies in its outward gaze. Behavior, performance, and being are understood as processes, unfolding, extending outward, as it were, rather than emanating from a given center.

And it is in this state of suspended time-space that I am going to leave this grooving crowd, while I turn my own unfortunately quite temporally constrained attention to another place, another time.

FLOW

Abrupt change of scene: Midwinter, well after midnight, a few months prior to "Rap City." I was at 2 SER, in the studio next door to the one in which J.U. and Mick E were to battle a few weeks later. A handful of rhymers had gathered to freestyle on air, an unprecedented, anything-goes opportunity.

There were perhaps half a dozen young men in the room, a few more outside in the foyer, and when somebody slipped in or out of the sound-proof door, snatches of laughter and the sweet/acrid smell of marijuana wafted in: there was a bit of a party going on. For the next couple of hours, the rhymers took it in turns to rap over instrumentals spun by a handful of DJs or "selectors." The contributions ranged from obviously prepared, rehearsed raps, through quasi–free verses, in which rehearsed, reliable rhyme schemas provided generative frameworks for more exploratory extemporizations, to fully improvised bursts of free-associative freestyles.

Style was at a premium. Not a shared, house, style, style defined as "the universe of discourses within which musical meanings arise" (Leonard Meyer in Feld 1994: 110), but *individual* style (although, as I will suggest below, a sense of shared style is constructed around the individual styles in the course of the proceedings). *Style* is what you "bring to the microphone," a distinctive deviation from the generic norm; marking a rhymer as different, a demonstration that you are *expressing yourself*. (The generic style became known, through the course of the evening, and on several subsequent nights, as "Sydney stylee.")

There was a range of styles here tonight. At one end of the scale was the Sleeping Monk's hilarious, smooth, loose-limbed, slump-shouldered, regular, sophisticatedly rhymed, metrically observant delivery. He raps:

> My style viscously flows, **goes up your nose**
> The dirty smelly funk supplied by the Monk
> Vindicator of the streets
> I attenuate my styles
> More confusing than a[n] episode of **"X-Files"**
> Secreting brain impulses like a roller coaster
> Don't fuck around
> Or you'll get pinned like a poster
> Wrecking shit up with the poets from the urban
> Lyrical lockjaws hug your head like a turban.
> Hard core connoisseur you're just a bunch of fairies
> Annihilating suckers from Bondi to St **Marys**
> I got my pla-toon like **Willem Dafoe**
> E I O E I O **I got the flow**
> . . . Disseminating metaphors too hard to explain
> I give you the lyrical Shao-Lin crane
> Giving eargasm
> Vain digs in the crates
> I don't wear Starter Caps 'cos I don't live in the States
> Combination of dexterity
> Here's a little sample
> Of the Monk . . .
> Dwelling in the temple

The bold-type words were punched by another rapper, suggesting that the lines were familiar and crafted or at least that certain couplets were standardized in the Monk's repertoire. The Monk prided himself on the sophistication of his verses, his elaborate intertextuality, the arcaneness of his metaphors. He was a devoted fan of the 1970s television series *Kung Fu*, the mediascape from which he borrowed his "monk" and "Shao-Lin" imagery.

On the other hand, J.U.'s roughshod, caterwauling syllables, poured
out in a rush, were associated less through semantic content than
through a feral homophonia: tumbling, headlong cascades of rhyming
words falling on top of each other, constructing strings of nonsense that
loop back to a suddenly recalled half-idea from two breaths beforehand,
creating fleeting moments of structural elegance, of narrative suture,
which abruptly dissolved with the exhaustion of his breath, a new idea
flooding into the flow with the next deep-chested intake. His arms chop-
ped the air in front of him, his body straining for the beat, lost in the urgent thrill of his delivery. Here J.U. introduced his rap, sidling up to the
microphone, speaking as his body started to feel out the beat:

> This is the live crazy freestyle stylees and this is how we wreck it in the
> east . . .

[and this is the moment of transition, the slide from a spoken discourse
into a rap]

> . . . because you know that

[J.U.'s body dipping and weaving, his voice hiccoughing into an iambic
marking of the pulse, soft *hard,* soft *hard*]

> At *twelve* to *one* the *fun* be*gun* with Sugar Ray

[but that is not going anywhere, and the formal device (soft *hard* soft
hard) yields to a more comprehensive, comfortable *flow,* his body rocking, swaying]

> But ah bullshit that's the hip hop that gets my \ shit
> My money yeah it's not funny
> My clothes not \ crummy like the cookie monster
> But I'll toast ya in the toaster
> I'll boast ya that I've got a flow
> That's sorta sorta \ oh slow and bring it back on the beat \
> One two I think I'd like it up in my earphones \
> But now it's red I get the bone \
> It's covered in the blue foam that's it Miguel \
> Now I can hear myself and that's the real shit \
> I pass it to Bullwinkle because you know he shines on the
> Microphone will kick your behind like the lazy arsed mule,\ *uh* . . .

J.U. tumbled in and out of the beat, drawing on his negotiation of the rhythm for the content of his rap ("oh slow it up and bring it back on the beat"), the rhyming of syllables ("toast ya / toaster / boast ya") driving his verses into uncharted semantic territory. The back slashes indicate pauses for breath, but the final two lines were delivered in a single lung-ful, his delivery accelerating as, already hyperventilating, he strained to end the semantic unit. Another taste:

> We get wild when you roll around the east \ uh! I kick it
> When I rock it I got it in my pocket
> I pull it out when I go into Club \
> X Yeah, I rock it I get vexed I flex then I \
> Knock the booty yeah that's my cutie
> Word up that's sleeper than a creep \
> For those that sleep on the microphone you stand alone \
> I hold mine when I doubt my confessions
> My lessons I'm bending my flow back in \
> I begin to ren with my friends yeah that's the Poets \
> I'll kick it to the Sabotage yeah 'cos they're large
> And Ben from Voodoo Flavor yeah \
> You'd better savour this, your saviour's in th'Australia no
> failures Up up and away-ay . . . *ye-ah* . . .

J.U.'s verses don't transcribe as well as the Monk's into a nice, orderly rhyme form. For J.U., the verses were broken by his breath, momentary pauses allowing him to redirect semantic energy, fueled by the generative possibilities of the "random" rhymes: "savour / saviour / Australia / no failure." More often than not, his contributions ended with an apos-trophic ejaculation: "uh!," or "ye-ah!"

And then there's Pewbic the Hunter, of the "freaky styles," his voice singing up into a falsetto register between gulped breaths, punctuating and apostrophizing his verses as he falls in and out of the strict rhythm of the beat. Here, the italics mark a syllable on which he allowed his voice to soar into an almost *falsetto vibrato,* arrhythmically punctuating his delivery:

> Stuck in the middle of a battle
> A huntsman I am
> Till the end
> No weapon but a mike

Strike at me I will defend
And
Send *a* message not to fear
I brought too many skills for me
They're coming out my ear
Like
      tears
           Which
Flow from out your eye
My peers *which* we look up at you and I
Ri-*sing*
We *bring*
Australia not a failure a Hip Hop don't you string a-
Long with culture too strong for the sell-out
Figs have an odour someone get that smell out of the ground
Yet under I wonder *crew*
Pursue more development many props are due to all of you *who*
Pay attention to our verses and our cur-*ses*
I need some to rehearse us
Merciless in the battle I'm a addict
Listen close and you can make a verdict

Pewbic's appeal to his colleagues lay both in his ability to effect logical connections between apparently randomly accessed material and the vulgarity of his verses. His rhymes were explicit, an armchair psychoanalyst's wet dream: first-person narratives of adolescent sexual derring-do, the affective intensity and graphic rendering of which surprised even Pewbic himself. His face would register the shock of his own raps, stifling his own guffaws as he protested innocence afterward: "I can't help it, man . . ."

Mr E., falling out of his flow, substituted nonsense syllables for words, straining, hoping to recover the momentum of his rhymes, slipping in and out of "Spanglish," the rapper's amalgam of English and Spanish:

Hence to commence the soliloquy
Bringin' a brief history
Mystery defender down [this drawn out]
Listen t'me [faster]
The negative \ relative to positive
Vertical superlative

Learn \ from the negative
Vibe antithesis sister and brother
Us and we and them . . .
. . . as individuals,
Playing a loop and along
Just going so-lo so low
That the only way to go is go up
From the playground
Get a renown found the
Rock in the sandpit
From the dark hit
spo-spo la hi-ho Silver away we go
Know the way that we play
Stay around and for ups
Locks up ama sa in the true meaning of the word
What up su-blitin subliminal
Minimal fus jus sus in te *hermanos*

Mr E. worked from a series of binary opposites, his body rocking from side to side as he started to flow. And when he got going, he was freed from words, from sense: "spo-spo la hi-ho" saved by "Silver away" — the end of the rhyme disintegrating into nonsense syllables, falling over into Spanish, his voice by now kicking up into a higher register, arms thrashing out . . . whoah! Try this one:

To the streets, originality keys to please the sound . . .
. . . and I'm down with reality checkin' it out talkin' about the
    totality of the spirit is so . . .
Unifying humanity the reasonable people of society is irrelevant
Blind by the smell of it the smell of [untranscribable]
Consider yourself bleh to earth
Incomprehensible reach \ speech unable to obtain but speaking
    out the words understands your heart looking
around at the problems easily pleased by the verio
scenario the stereo and video and tecking the blitin of the
original case yeow!

The verse structure yields to a foaming rush of sounds, and Pewbic, caught up in the thrill of it, thrilled: "That was motherfuckin' bent!!! Ah!!"

And Cec, the Chief, didn't freestyle, preferring to perform his word-perfect rhymes through a blunted haze:

It's The Chief, **back in the house with the keys**
Listen to the magical cuts **I release**
And these crazy metaphors from the east
1994 **here comes the beast**
Ripping up the microphone is not a crime
Here comes the rhyme, **dripping with slime**
What's the time? I think it's time to get ill
Listen to the wicked words from my grill
But still you can't defeat the **Latinos**
When you can't seem to fit your ass through the **keyhole**
Hold on now it's time to get it on
Fuck the love songs we're coming on strong
Doing no wrong we're just two **hip hoppers**
Listen to the twisted words from my *voca* **loca**
Do you hear what I'm saying
My words are spraying, and **I'm not playing around**
'Cos I grow underground
Here comes the West Side, check out the sound
Profound **knowledge** not like a **sausage**
I've got a lot flavour better than motherfucking **cottage**
Cheese, jeeze, what's that smell?
["Sausages are fat!" someone interjects]
I think it's the weed from the depths of hell

The Monk seemed to know this one as well, punching the marked syllables in a low, disaffected voice. The final line was received uproariously, although, in general, the Chief was the outsider in this gathering: he was not a freestyler, and his rhymes were, I was informed later, *wack*.

Finally, there was J.U.'s partner in rhyme, B.U. Together, they rapped as the Urban Poets, referred to in the Monk's rhyme. They shared an absolute devotion to freestyling. On a subsequent night a few months later, I watched J.U. and B.U., after two hours of more or less continuous improvising, having exhausted their own capacity for invention, solicit (alphabet) letters from the audience. They would then use the offered letter to construct completely alliterated rhymes. A kind of b-boy "Theatresports."[3] B.U. (an abbreviation for "Bullwinkle") based his freestyles on the elaboration of tropes, like this one:

Flying awa-ayy, through outer space yes I never dismay
because I catch the hootchy \ signal just in time my
radio functions came onto line I'm outta danger \ but
I'm coming down to Earth in my hootchy cap-sule \ so
all you MCs better run outta here \ because I'm the fat
lyrical ranger slappin' down sucker MCs I know those \
techno wizards on the microphone and on the decks \ it's
Bullwinkle here to snap necks \ Like E.P. and D. I'm soon
to cash large cheques \ I'll pass it on to some more MCs
to wreck shit . . .

On other occasions, he worked his way through a series of greengrocer
metaphors, characterizing himself and his fellow rhymers as various
fruits and vegetables available for sale in the rap supermarket.

THE RAPPING BODY

The thematic concerns of these raps are clear: a wonderful, heteroglossic, intertextual phantasmagoria, colorful and excessive. All the
Hip Hop discourses, the "Hip Hop Ideoscape" are to be found in these examples, as well as the textual and performative markers differentiating
the all-important self-expressive, personal *style* of the rhymers.

But I'm not only concerned with the question of style here, or with the
technicalities of rapping. Instead, I want to consider the affective, embodied dimension of rhyming, the rappers' accounts of their practice,
their account of how that practice relates to their understanding of their
Culture.

In the local, Sydney scene, to rap is to *flow*, "to flow" is to rap. The insider language directly correlates with Rose's critical musicology.
Rhymers talk of "flowing," of "getting on the flow," of losing themselves
to and in the flow ("I can't help it man . . ."). It is a feeling, a state of being. When a rapper is flowing, his friends cheer, hoot, groove along with
him.

And this flow is visible . . . a rhymer starts to rap by sidling up to the
beat, hand cupping a headphone to his ears, head bobbing up and down,
the movement growing, moving into the shoulders, a breath is drawn,
and the first lines start to come . . . A transmission shift, the transitional
moment between speaking and rapping . . . J.U.'s shoulders suddenly

hunch upward, his head is tucked down, in between them, and his hands move away from the side of his head, his forearms hesitatingly held in front of his chest, palms open, facing toward him. A second breath, and now he is closer to the beat, traveling alongside it, feeling it out. His hands start to move in front of him, gentle chopping motions, syncopated, one chop after the next marking the syllables he raps. The next breath and there! I can see it . . . now he is flowing, he is the beat. The words tumble out, his voice lifting two? three tones, his arms chop chopping the air, hands laying out rhyme after rhyme, and now his hips, his legs, his whole body rocking and swaying, his eyes closed. Another breath, and another, the words flying, popping, spitting, gushing out, exhausting his breath and there! again, you can see the moment, he slips out of the flow, and all I can think of is body-surfing, and the moment when the wave falls off below you, and you're left breathless, floating, floating, and it takes long seconds to come back to yourself, to turn yourself around and swim back out to the break.[4]

Each rapper had a preferred "beat": when a selector placed a particular track on the turntable, all the rappers present would feel it out, let it into their bodies: to me it always looked like someone trying on a new jacket, seeing if it fit, and if it did fit, whether they felt comfortable wearing it. "That's *my* beat, man," someone would say, moving to rhyme, nodding approval, starting to go . . . a rhymer drying up would be offered a new beat.

This idea of flow constituted the aesthetic discourse of this practice. The rhymers said, "I get on the flow," meaning that they went *with* it, wherever it was that it was going. The flow was primary: although they might say, "I flow . . . ," there was a certain discomfort with the subject-predicate grammar. The speaker might hesitate, and make a rolling, unfolding gesture with his (her) hands . . . "I . . . you know [gesture] . . . *flow.*" The flow, the rhymes, the rap, in these moments (you could see it, the kick, the lift, the release, the flight into and with the flow as their bodies softened, bent, moved without direction, undirected, at one with the flow) was understood as being beyond the rapper's agency; and this was, on their account, why they did it . . . they escaped their being, experienced an ecstasis, a flight buoyed by the refrain, and the stream of words became almost an impediment.

Sense is sacrificed to flow, to the imperative of staying on the flow, body-surfing the flow until, breathless, drawn, they (literally—you can see it) fall, fall, shrink back to life-size, all at once having to control arms, jaws, heads that have, for precious moments, been something else, been out of their control. The light seems to go out in their eyes, and somebody else steps to the mike.

■ J.U. looks like this, now, after his verse, eyes glazed, face drawn as he watches another rhymer go through the same thing: this struggle, negotiation with the beat, a fusion of self and beat that becomes not merely the self rapping with the beat, but a new be-ing, an emergent flowing of being. And this is the affective thrall of the freestyle: that dimension of the improvised rap that lies beneath the intoxicating (for the analyst) appeal of the lyrics themselves.

THE MYTHOLOGY OF IMPROVISATION

"But," another informant warns me, "you realise that none of them are really *improvising* . . ."

Allan Moore writes of improvisation that it "is surrounded by myths that treat it somehow as magical, in that it purports to bypass the mind's conscious mechanisms, providing a vehicle for performers to express themselves in a fashion unmediated by any other concerns" (1993: 73). Moore's purpose is to disavow this mythology: improvisation consists of a series of strategies, of formal guidelines, involving "the re-playing of formulae . . . representing the rules of shared by the community" (73). This isn't necessarily a terribly dramatic insight, and although I am puzzled by his use of the term "representing" here, it is not the mechanics of improvisation that I am primarily interested in. Suffice it to note that freestylers develop their techniques through (embodied) mimicry, rapping along to recorded commercial raps either at home or in social situations. I stress the active dimension of these rehearsals: the ability to freestyle is without exception articulated to a particular mode of embodiment. The process offers, additionally, one of the clearest possible examples of Bakhtin's principle of heteroglossia: it is possible to determine almost exactly a given freestyler's model freestyling texts through their performance, both in terms of rhyming and lyrical schemas and in terms of their physical involvement with the beat.

The romantic discourse of self-expression that Moore identifies here in writing about rock (see also Goodwin 1991) is one of the fundamental discourses circulating within and around Hip Hop. Self-expression is a key element in the political discourses of rap, and vast bodies of literature demonstrate, beyond question, the significance and centrality of oral practices in populations which are either preliterate (see Abrahams 1976, 1992; Ong 1982) or denied access to literacy (Gates 1988). I am not disputing the accuracy or relevance of such accounts when I choose to diminish their significance in the local, Sydney Hip Hop context. It is impossible to deny the (realized) potential of rap to give voice to politically circumscribed populations in the postindustrial wasteland of the inner cities of North America. And, as I have suggested, the discourse of "finding one's voice" has been significant in the locating of an authentic Hip Hop Community in the undeniably underresourced, demonized Western Suburbs of Sydney. To sit with a(n otherwise) barely articulate teenage boy as he flicks through a notebook packed with rhyming couplets, to see a page headed "similes" in that book, to overhear earnest discussions about "metaphor," and to listen to Def Wish Cast's rapped meditations on the nature of poetic composition ("Rappin' in Yer Sleep") is to understand the worth and, frankly, the power, of "rap."

The discourse of self-expression is, however, one that reaches its limit in the ecstatic freestyle: freestylers can more usefully be thought of as *exceeding* their self-ness, rather than simply expressing it. The discourse of self-expression can be thought of as being both a useful means of legitimizing various practices, as I have been arguing, and, more immediately, a means of explaining and accounting for an *intensely felt* experience. Derrida's critique of the metaphysics of the voice, of the spoken word, is here rendered in flesh. The freestylers, far from finding a self at the heart of their performance, find a void, or, more constructively, and in their terms, a *flow*. Even Ser Reck's non-freestyled verse in the abovementioned "Rappin' in Yer Sleep" reveals the anxiety at the heart of the discourse: the rapper concedes that his rhymes actually come from his dreams, from without his self. This potentially damaging admission is recovered by his reassertion of his writerly authority: "My skull as my barricade so you can't invade." Even though his raps come from somewhere other than his fully conscious "self," they do come from inside *his* head; thus Ser Reck successfully negotiates the potential *otherness* of what Barthes (1972) called the "middle voice": the speech that is neither your own nor the simple recital of someone else's speech, but that which speaks *through* you, leading you away from your self.

Of course, not every freestyle reaches this pitch of ecstatic intensity. Moments of flow are cherished, celebrated, mythologized, as Moore suggests. More often than not, rhymers fall short of ecstasis, instead finding themselves working as *themselves,* as it were; perhaps operating strategically, as Moore suggests is the case in rock improvisation, falling back on reliable, rehearsed grabs, familiar rhymes: the stock phrases that appear, like life preservers thrown from a passing boat, easing the rhymers through difficult territory, giving them time to think up something, to plan ahead. The rhyme, in such instances, is Bakhtin's principle of heteroglossia embodied: a collection of quoted speech/rap strung together, a dialogic textuality that resolves into monologism in order to conform to a discourse of self-expression through the interpolation of the discourse of individual "style."

But what of this interpolation: the *claiming* of a moment marked as, and experienced as, ecstatic? The *refrain* of the flow, its potential to move *beyond,* to the point at which it is impossible to say anything of it other than it is *flow,* is *territorialized* by narrative, is made *music.* The excess of being is articulated to a meaning: *this* is Hip Hop.

Recall J.U.: "You have to try to remember that the Hip Hop Community, it's a fucking sensitive thing man, because you're dealing with egos, that's what rappers are man, they're egos . . ." But that's in the context of a discussion about the "Hip Hop Community." And J.U. telling me that "it's the words, man, it's all about the words" is in the context of a discussion about "Hip Hop Culture." These are explanations, very respectable ones, for being *into,* for believing in something called Hip Hop. For, phenomenologically, it's not simply about the words at all. "It's" about these moments, this flow, this flight from ego, the feeling of being led away by the energy of the rhyme . . . Perhaps this is why rappers take new names: to paper over or to recover this flight, to claim it back: Pewbic is "really" Ben; J.U. "is" Ed; the Sleeping Monk is Raoul. The ecstatic, intense experience is a leaving behind of "Raoul" and being the Sleeping Monk for a few seconds, experiencing self as a flow. The words here are the devices for getting there, to that state.[5]

The moments of flow are framed by others present. Between these bursts of flight, the other rappers (it's always someone else, it seems) grab the microphone, ejaculating, "Sydney stylee!" or "Code of the street!" or "Word up. J.U. kicking the fat styles!" Again and again, the performances are book-ended (remember, this session is going live on the air as well: "This is the *live* crazy freestyle stylees!") within a range of discourses. The expression of individual style is celebrated: "Now it's time for the Monk, the Drunken Monk with his freeeee-style, the crazy high g galactic freeeestyle," announces another rhymer. A sense of collective style is constructed, a kind of house style circumscribing all the individual styles ("Sydney stylee!"). When Raoul busted a rhyme in Spanish, there was a general enthusiasm: the room broke into a round of "yeahs" and "alrights." Raoul described his contribution as "international flavour," and J.U. moved quickly to claim the moment: "That's the *Sydney* style, man." J.U. repeated himself for emphasis, tagging on an advertisement for his shop: "*Sydney* style . . . check it out at the Lounge Room!" Raoul responded in kind: "At the Lounge Room . . . remember the Lounge Room. It's the new shop for all you Hip Hop fiends. If you want your daily drug intake, see my man DJ Blaze at the Lounge Room." And both Raoul and Ed stepped back from their microphones. Ed stands directly in front of Raoul, and they exchange a handshake, gently slapping hands, as Ed nods his approval.

The shared style is not only framed geographically, locating the performances within the discourse of place ("Sydney," or, even more specifically, within the microgeographics of the Sydney scene: "Around the east!"), but located within a discourse of culture. Another rhymer, in a reflective mood, takes the microphone and thanks the audience: "*Big word up to everybody tuning in . . . thanks for supporting more freestyles.*" What is going on in here, he explains, is the "*real thing*": "You can leave the ballads to Rick Price, you can leave the ill shit to Peter André and if you want to chill with the real shit, you can get down to the Fonke Knowmaads, the Urban Poets, the Sabotage, the Mama's Funkstickles, the Finger Lickens, the Blaze . . ."

The link to a discourse about community is made explicit. The shout-outs to various crews support the thesis of community, fleshing out the next claim to be made, the claim that the handful of rappers here, in this room, *represented* that community: "We've got the whole Hip Hop scene here . . . we're still pretty small, but we're growing . . ."

This developmental theme was elaborated by the Monk, next on the microphone, who offered a grand vision, stressing the *realness* of this scene, its incontrovertible *live*-ness:

Well fuckin, what you're gonna see is all these new groups are comin' out and um, people out there instead of buying . . . yeah it's cool to buy Hip Hop from the States but you know, keep your skills Australia because basically we've got the flavours, and just give it a go and definitely you will be pleased 'cos we ain't no joke. We ain't going around prancing like we're the best and shit, you know, we just kick it live, doin' what we feel is true. So that's all I've got to say.

The fabric of a community, of a culture is built up around these performative moments. The *aporaic,* open, performative moment of becoming is sutured to a pedagogic narrative within which the immediacy of the experience is adduced as conclusive, unmediated evidence for the ontological precedence of the object of that narrative: Hip Hop Culture.

These moments are not always as solemn as they might appear. In the middle of this two-and-a-half-hour session, between the moments of flow, the framings, the earnest explanations and self-locations, there are also moments of parody. A rapper, exhausted, is unwilling to freestyle anymore. His friends chide him, hassle him, admonish him, and in mock anger he snaps back: "What else can I do, man? What else can I do? I'm standing up for my people, man, my people!" And the room dissolves in laughter.

Meanwhile . . .

Appropriately, I have left the dance floor at Rap City in a state of narrative suspension, echoing the suspension of time at the epicenter of the grooving crowd. Imagine that they're still grooving now, the seven minutes of Eric B and Rakhim's "Paid in Full" carnivalesque in intensity, joyous in a seeming self-sufficiency, an apparent completeness and *almost* (*pace* Derrida *et al.,* as I indulge my own moment of metaphysics of presence) timelessness.

And, as I move to reassert a chronology to the events in question, of course, the track fades away (Rakhim signs off: "Yo check this out . . . turn the bass down and let the beat keep on rockin', and we outta here . . . "), the bottom end drops out, the trebly skitter-scatter of the drum machine punctuated by an insistent, counterpointing record scratch, leaving, eventually, a sparse, skeletal cymbal crash, and a smoky voice asking, "Was it good enough for you?"

Afterward, on the dance floor, the energy drains away. The metaphorical postcoital detumescence implied at the end of the track is, at such moments, palpable: there is simply *less* of whatever this thing was that had got everyone going. And, of course, *this* is the moment, the return to being, in which a discourse of sexiness makes sense.

Now look at what happened next at Rap City . . .

The crowd had become restless. It was nearly 11:00 P.M., and still no performances: the techies swarmed around the mixing deck, plosively spitting the obligatory *check one check two*'s into microphones, to be met with the same ghastly electronic whine that had plagued the entire evening. The night was threatening to become a failure, a nonevent.

Until someone (I didn't see who) had a word to the DJ, and, abruptly, the music changed. In place of the muscular, fleshy beats of the Brand Nubians or Public Enemy or the loping West Coast gangsta rhythms of Dr. Dre, electronic, robotic, "old school" Casio beat-box and synth sounds started to pump from the speakers. The dance floor cleared (the girls left first), both in response to the *edginess* of these new beats (their clinical precision, perhaps, their synthesized clean-ness) and to the whisper passing through the room . . . A crowd formed around the edge of the dance floor; some of the boys were about to break . . .

The glory days of break-dancing in Sydney are well and truly in the past. Back in "tha dayz," breakers would gather on the forecourts of office blocks, in parks, in peoples' lounge rooms when their parents were out for the evening. A strip of linoleum would be rolled out, an "old school" track put on the turntable, or a compilation tape slipped into a ghetto blaster. The crews would gather to "battle," breakers going head to head in contests, the winner being whoever could produce the most astonishing move. These are the days mythologized in raps, hearkened back to in conversation. Def Wish raps:

A crew rides the last car to take part in another part of a culture
Where Puma tracksuits prevail from the closet, Jem R.O.C.K.
Enter the battlegrounds on the lino
Into the pocket the beanie and the padding for the cherry on my
    shoulder blade
Vame, slap over the cross fade
The crowd gathers round, two crews stand face to face
The first round — both sides on the all-out attack
Head rocks, flares, spinning on their head and back.
Swords clash as the clouds of dust rise
Sweat drips from the veterans on one side
The crowd thought it died chills going up their spine
Veterans seeking the crown (it's mine)
Getting chanted from both sides of the circle of hell
Many slipped up and fell
Round about the time to go another round and about
Gradually one by one another breaker gets taken out

One battle to go down in history
Known as the dance floor that turned into a slayer dome
Sooner or later one side must descend
An old soldier put his crew at risk to defend the crown
Sharpened his blade, step to the centre
Then silence flowed through the gathering (what do I do?)
Feel the vibes — pulled off a move never seen to man's eyes
The other side had a hearse awaiting them
Doors slam — off to the mausoleum
Roars heard all around
Encores for more wars
Perennial cross swords

Die C's contribution to this track:

. . . hard core combat in a perennial war
Wet paint and smell of rivalry
As pieces go up side by side . . .

. . . uses the same combative metaphors to describe graffiti battles, suggesting the kind of homologous relationship between the two practices that I want to call (after Feld) an "iconicity of style." Die C also explicitly develops the nostalgic tone of Def Wish's rhyme:

Breaking was just a dying craze to the majority
But a minority survive . . .

The implication is clear: this crew is part of that minority prepared to maintain the culture through a performative maintenance of the practices of Hip Hop Culture.

At Rap City, where circumstances and technology are conspiring to prevent such a performance (of rapping), Paul (Ser Reck) *steps,* marking out a space on the floor with a series of triangular square-dance-like moves. His legs cross each other with each jerky step, steps that seem to be charged with (at the risk of cliché) a certain electricity: each leg snaps into place at the completion of the step, the other leg ticked into motion seemingly at the knee, which leads into the next step, creating a strange, awkward, almost bobbing quality of movement informing an overall, speedy, precise, focused, but somehow shambling attitude. Forward, across, back again, eyes down, concentrating, concentrating on the beat, building, building, his breathing and (you can feel it) his heart reaching toward the moment of synthesis with the music. His arms scissor the air on either side of his body. His eyes are focused on the floor immediately in front of him, his body electric as he negotiates the beat, builds himself toward the first move. This preparatory moment is familiar: a curious blending of the extraordinarily tense, with a kind of strutting languidness. It is almost the break dancer's equivalent to the *capoiera ginga,* that series of movements with which the *capoierista* prepares himself for the sudden movement to come, establishing a kind of balance in imbalance (Lewis 1992).

And he throws himself forward, onto the floor. Balancing on his palms, the veins in his forearms in high relief, Ser Reck spins, his legs cartwheeling around each other as he steps from hand to hand, his pony tail flailing behind him; and then he flicks himself around, back to the floor, kicking his feet out in front of him in a sweaty burlesque of a Cossack dance. The few, fleeting seconds of frenzy over, Ser Reck leaps forward onto his feet, all jumping energy, and saunters to the side of the now empty dance floor, and another breaker steps forward.

The music to which these breakers move is not at all "funky," in the way that Eric B and Rakhim tap into a loose, smooth, sensuous, sex-sweat-slicked, somehow African-American-signifying *thing* . . . breakdancing is perhaps less about the sustained, the "flow" (see Rose 1994b: 38), the cumulative, intensional, repetitive, insistent, "plateau-nic" groove of the drums than ejaculatory bouts of fevered, tight-bodied, angular, striated,[6] *work-sweated* "ruptures in line" (38).

Watching this particular performance is like watching a demonstration of entropy in action. The breaker seems to be engaged in a struggle against the ground, against the gravity that threatens to slow and eventually halt his/her frenzy of motion. To break is to throw one's body and strength into a few hectic moments of improbable defiance, pushing physiological limits, defying propriety in taking care of one's body. Die C raps:

Roll out the lino
Break, break
Heads turn
Crack open our heads on the pavement
And burn backs
("Runnin' Amok," from *Knights of the Underground Table*)

233

A back is *burned* when the breaker spins off the unrolled lino onto carpet, concrete, or grass. (A great graffiti piece is called a *burner*). But at "Rap City," the dance floor is smooth and forgiving. The spinning, twisting, jerking, spasming bodies fight gravity, literally spending themselves, the dancer lifting himself up from his final pose, dusting himself off, picking up a discarded cap, grimacing and rubbing a burned knee or elbow, chest heaving, drawing gulping breaths as the rest of the crew clap him on the back and nod approval.

The breakers (there are about six of them here tonight) take it in turns on the floor. This, it is clear, is no competition: it's an exhibition. Breaking here is to the dance-floor groove as music is to the refrain. Def Wish is next. He has long since mastered the "freeze," abruptly coming to a halt, effecting a nonchalant calm belied by his sweat-slicked forehead, the throbbing, distended veins in his forearms and at his temples. Jean Baudrillard has described, in characteristically apocalyptic terms, just this moment, in his account of his travels across America:

> "Break-dancing" is a feat of acrobatic gymnastics. Only at the end do you realize it was actually dancing, when the dancer freezes into a lazy, languid pose (elbow on the ground, head nonchalantly resting in the palm of the hand, the pose you see in Etruscan tombs). The way they suddenly come to a halt like this is reminiscent of Chinese opera. But the Chinese warrior comes to a halt at the height of the action in a heroic gesture whereas the break dancer stops at the slack point of his movements and the gesture is derisive. You might say that in curling up and spiralling around on the ground like this they seem to be digging a hole for themselves within their own bodies, from which to stare out in the ironic, indolent pose of the dead. (Baudrillard 1988: 19)

But in Def Wish's execution of this same gesture there is little derision, little irony, little indolence. This breaking, here, in an inner-city club in Sydney in late 1994, is not the smug postmodern parody Baudrillard is so eager to diagnose, but an earnest celebration of what is understood as, is constructed as, a *tradition*. The "nonchalance" of the pose, its "languidness" is instead, in this context, a gesture of mastery, of *style* or *skills:* the ability to affect a sudden, unexpected (but expected) resolution of dervish-like activity into stillness (Baudrillard's reference to Etruscan coroplasty might not be so out of place: Def Wish is presenting his own performance here as an embodied cultural archaeology). And again the trope of the pause, or break, appears, emerging as a stylistic constant, fueling the watchers' desire for more, just as the break in the rap suspends the listeners, all the better to throw them into the next refrain, laying out the territory into which the music and voice will unfold.[7]

At Rap City, the exhibition is interrupted. A microphone check booms across the space, and it looks like the evening's program is about to start (at last). The last breaker picks himself up, reclaims his baseball cap, dusts off his tracksuit pants. Another claps him on the back, and he deferentially shrugs, as if to say, "Just doing my job," or "Well, someone's gotta do it." And I overhear someone else, another b-boy on the edge of the crowd who had been getting ready to take to the floor say to the person next to him, "Mate, I'm glad I didn't have to step . . . I haven't breaked for years."

THE GROOVE

But perhaps this celebratory account needs to be qualified. In the passage from Bakhtin that describes the exchange of bodies and loss of self in the carnival crowd, I added emphasis to the words "the pressing throng . . . *acquires a certain meaning.*" For events like this always take place within a context, a context that gives the throng its meaning, or rather, a context framing the event. Canetti, too, issues a cautionary caveat to his own account. The discharge, he warns, is based on an illusion: "[T]he people who suddenly feel equal have not really become equal; nor will they *feel* equal for ever" (2000: 18).

I have suggested that the affective density of these moments is recuperated or appropriated by interpretation. The (potentially? phenomenologically) transgressive moment is captured, its potential (for) becoming and (for) otherness colonized, subsumed to master discourses, located within the narratives of culture and community; a theory/practice binarism is invoked, whereby affect/experience is accounted for in terms of logics and discourses drawn from the contextualizing "ideoscape." For, of course, notwithstanding the idealism of Bakhtin's account, not everybody comes to such a moment identically: the "hard core b-boys," for example, are not so immediate in their (surrender?) response to the beats as the teenage women, for whom dancing is (meta)culturally sanctioned. The boys play it cool; the girls go for it. The power of the moment, of course, lies in the emergent communality of the experience that manages to overcome, for a short while at least, these resistances.

And this capturing may well be thought a *recapturing*: Bataille charted this territory, suggesting, in his famous formulation, that "the transgression does not deny the taboo but transcends it and completes it" ([1957] 1986: 63). Order, as it were, extends its domain through (permitted) transgression, a process through which the erotic impulse, that which drives the discontinuous individual to seek out a continuity of being with his/her fellows, is channeled, resolved.

This flow is that theorized by Csikszentmihalyi: "the experience of merging action and intention; the centering of attention on a limited field of stimulus" (the *beat*); a loss of ego — this provides "clear, unambiguous feedback"; is *autotelic*, seeming to need no goals outside itself (in V. Turner 1982: 56–58). Further, a "person 'in flow' finds himself 'in control of his actions and of the environment'" (Csikszentmihalyi in V. Turner 1982: 57). Although "he may not know it at the time of 'flow,'" Turner explains, "reflecting on it he may realize that his skills were matched to the demands made on him by ritual, art or sport" (V. Turner 1982: 57). The important word here is "reflecting": the autotelic, ego-less moment of flow itself is followed, Csikszentmihalyi is suggesting, by a capturing of that experience. Turner extends Csikszentmihalyi's thinking by suggesting that "flow" *may* function as a moment of "liquification" between existing structure and *communitas* (58): "It [flow] is one of the techniques whereby people seek the lost 'kingdom' or 'anti-kingdom' of direct, unmediated communion with one another" (58). Of course, this is not to say that "flow" *always* functions in such a manner. Indeed, such an account is perhaps a little too functional for my liking: there are other ways to approach these moments.

Feld's account of "the groove," for example — that "intuitive sense of style as process, a perception of a cycle in motion, a form or organising pattern being revealed" — understands "style" and "groove" as "distilled essences, crystallizations of collaborative expectancies" (1994b: 109), and this, free of Turner's nostalgic metaphysics of "lost empires" and of "unmediated communion," is perhaps a better way to approach the phenomena I am dealing with here. A groove, a feeling of groovy-ness, is, on Feld's account, "instantly perceived . . . [it] describes a feelingful participation, a positive physical and emotional attachment, a move from being 'hip to it' to 'getting down' and being 'into it'" (111). For Feld, "intuition" is an explanation that perhaps masks the effort of recognition and interpretation: "one's intuitive feelingful sense of a groove or beat is a recognition of style in motion" (112). Feld's argument is that the *feeling* of intuitiveness that constitutes "the groove" is learned, that the *fit* between any given experience and one's learned expectations of that experience is experienced, affectively, as primal, as unmediated, as "true to the music."

The trajectory of Feld's essay here leads him to the phenomenology of Robert Plant Armstrong. Armstrong, he writes, sought to understand "affecting qualities and works in terms of presentation, not representation; immediation, not mediation; and metaphor, not symbol" (Feld 1994: 144). This phenomenology recognizes an embodied knowing not reducible to semantics, to "meaning." Quoting Nelson Goodman by way of an illustration, Feld writes that "the *emotions function cognitively.* The work of art is comprehended through the feelings as well as through the senses" (145). "Getting into the groove feels so good because it frees us of a lot of abstractions, logics, 'culture,' 'knowledge' . . . etc" (Feld quoting Keil's correspondence to him, 146). Here is the dance-floor moment *as experienced.* The "freedom" (from self, from culture, knowledge, and so on) may be by no means a freedom at all. The moment is circumscribed, constructed framed by expectations; the groove, felt as an immediate, irreducible quality of affect, is, somewhat more prosaically, or perhaps less romantically, in Feld's definition, a "learnt recognition of style." Nonetheless, this experience of what Feld calls the "iconic," that is, the experience of "very direct, very feelingful resemblance relationships between things" (173), is a powerful form of *knowing,* a knowing so deeply *felt* and so inexplicable, so irreducible to words, that it is capable of sustaining an entire world of meaning, of interpretation and knowledge. "Put the needle on the record, and it'll take you there . . ." This order of (apparently) unmediated experience, a direct contact with the music, the beats, the flows, is, when accounted for in terms of *r*epresentation, the raw material of the construction of the idea of Hip Hop Culture.

As I have argued, for Bhabha (1994), nationalisms are created in this moment; the potential *aporia* opened up, minutely, in the moment of performance is immediately taken up, attached, or articulated to a pedagogic tradition. An explanation for being, and for all potential beings engendered in that moment, is enrolled to the national(ist) narrative. Sometimes, the pedagogical project is explicit; more often, the pedagogic project is enacted and performed implicitly: the openness of what Bhabha calls "the performative" is constantly overdetermined, defined and interpreted. Those interpretations and definitions are, in turn, "instituted" (Weber 1987) as, pure and simply, Knowledge. Pseudo-iconic semiotic relationships (that is, signs that are purported to be constituted by necessity) are instituted by authoritative voices, the claim to self-evidence supported affectively by the density and apparent irreducibility of the experienced moment.

The unfolding of events at Rap City saw the (energy? potential?) of this dance-floor *groove* claimed, directed, disciplined, performatively, publicly, into an explicit discourse of "representation." But I don't want to reduce this moment to a play of dialectics; the simple confrontation, perhaps, staged by Nietzsche between the individuating impulse of Apollo and the Dionysian mode of "intoxication and loss of self in primordial unity" (Carlson 1984: 261). Or one of the "gramscian" (Harris's 1992 gloss for the Hall/Hebdige/Birmingham subculture studies nexus) updates along the same lines: youth subcultural "rebellion," substituting for the (lost, disappointing, failed) working class as Agent of History: youth culture understood as a (series of?) futile, albeit, "genuine" liberatory gestures against hegemonic "powers that be" (*"Fight* the power . . . fight the *power,"* raps Chuck D), powers that be which only seem to allow such expressions, all the better to reclaim the energy of youth, to channel it back into acceptable forms.

Epilogue
The Real Thing

The Sleeping Monk performs a dumb show as he raps:

Input is the brain, output is the mouth
More smooth modulations are felt in the south . . .

. . . the final two words accompanied by a gesture toward his groin.

I have already suggested that, trying to write of the tidal pull of the beat, I find myself having recourse to metaphors of depth and, more disturbingly, to a kind of primitivist discourse. I want to describe the effect of the dance-floor epiphany as sexual, as primal, as hitting me in a place beyond (prior to) analysis, as somehow being capable of returning me to a simpler, more fundamental way of being. Yet the groove of the dance floor, the flow of the freestyle, does not hark back to a more immediate, immanent, unmediated, purer state of uncluttered being, but rather is demonstrative of the virtually unlimited potential of human beings to perform their being.

Pleasure, of course, is that dimension of affect that is all too easily omitted from analysis of youth culture, and certainly one of my intentions has been to stress the pleasurable dimensions of the freestyle, of the dance-floor groove. Žižek's Lacanian reading of nationalism recognizes the insufficiency of "discursive effect" in terms of compelling attraction to a (national) cause: following Lacan, Žižek in fact prioritizes a notion of *enjoyment* arguing that "[a] nation [and here I interpolate 'Hip Hop Culture/Community/Nation'] *exists* only as long as its specific *enjoyment* continues to be materialized in a set of social practices and transmitted through national myths that structure these practices" (Žižek 1993: 202).

This pleasure is not necessarily *sexual,* although this often is the explanation given: many accounts of enjoyment are couched in the (confessional) mode of sexual pleasure. The Monk's line above is one example; Mick E's (reflexive) candor in explaining to me the allure of the "sexy black man" in his explanation of the appeal of rap is even more illuminating in its conflation of ethnicity and sexuality. A female informant explained to me that boys rapped because they wanted to "get girls," offering this as a reason for there being so few girls interested in getting on the microphone. A writer tells me how irresistible his outlaw image is. Another rapper explains the joy of having younger girls at school acting "like groupies." Piecing a wall, another writer is clearly enjoying himself, grunting, half-singing to himself, putting on a bit of a show. "He's having an orgasm man!" jokes one of the watchers. "Well that's why you do it man," the other rejoins. "If it doesn't feel good, you don't do it."

The reduction of the pleasurable aspects of flowing, of grooving, to something basically sexual is more indicative of a generalized cultural incitement to a discourse of sexuality recognized long ago by Foucault (1979). This is not to deny the sexiness of rapping, the erotic appeal of the outlaw writer, the charisma of the spotlit rapper up on stage, microphone in hand with all the attendant phallic overtones (microphone-centered ribaldry is a commonplace). And raps (particularly freestyle, and particularly Pewbic the Hunter's freestyle) are often sexually explicit in nature. This has partly to do with adolescent boys, and here I will speak in Pewbic's defense, as it were: his rhymes often become extended, graphic accounts of sexual encounters, often with his girlfriend (I have watched her squirm with embarrassment as he rapped). Never have I heard him advocate the kinds of malicious mistreatment of women recounted in, for example, some of the controversial Miami-based crew 2 Live Crew's raps, or in those of Kool G Rap.[1]

But let's stick with Žižek's observations about nationalism. What is at stake, Žižek suggests, in claims to national belonging, and, I am arguing, by extension to the kinds of tropes for communality circulating in and informing the Hip Hop Scene in Sydney, is a question of enjoyment. The pleasure experienced in the freestyle and dance-floor flight from self constitutes a massive "semantic void" (Žižek 1993: 202): these moments are intense, immanent, unnameable. The exchange of ideas within the scene about these moments relies on an assumption of shared experience: a loosely defined interpretant, the groove, the flow, the "you know . . . [insert gesture] *feeling*," and heads nod . . . Remember Fibular writing in *Vapors:* "So how do you get there . . . Put the needle on the record and 'It'll take you there' . . . And if you still can't find it, then chances are, you never will." Here is the *"Thing"* placed by Žižek at the affective center of all modes of communality: "Members of a community . . . *believe in their Thing* . . . 'I believe in the (national [communal]) Thing' equals 'I believe that others (members of my community) believe in the Thing.' The tautological character of the Thing — its semantic void which limits what we

240

can say about the Thing to 'It is the real Thing' etc — is founded precisely in this paradoxical reflexive structure (1993: 202).

Feld has remarked on the apparent indeterminacy of speech about music, often mistaken for tongue-tied-ness, or inarticulacy: what is happening, he argues, is that "when people talk [about music] to each other, to themselves, to music analysts . . . they often draw upon [a] stock of interpretive moves . . ." (Feld 1994c: 92). "They are caught in a moment of interpretive time, trying to force awareness to words. They are telling us how much they assume that we understand *exactly* what they are experiencing" (92–93). These are quintessentially Peircian formulations. On Feld's account, the assumption of understanding constitutes the possibility of communication (as a transitive concept). Importantly, for Feld, this speech about music exceeds the "referential" or "lexically explicit semantic" function of speech: it is, instead metaphoric: "Metaphors involve the instantaneous recognition that things are simultaneously alike and unlike. And when most people talk about music, like and unlike is what they talk about" (92).

Recall the density of similes in Mick E and E.S.P.'s discourse about their own music. The experience of music is at once one's own, but is assumed to be the same as someone else's, although, as Feld suggests, this sameness can never be experienced as such (Feld 1994b: 162–65). This irreducible together-aloneness, is, for Žižek, the foundational moment of communal being. ("The national Thing exists as long as members of the community believe in it" (1993: 202). The inarticulable (since nonexistent) "essence" of the nation, of the community, of the culture, is determined in belief by a circularity of logic: the ecstatic moment, framed as being beyond mediation, as offering a direct experiential connection with . . . what? An otherness is constituted in discourse as proof of something, as, perhaps, because of its immediacy, its apparent incontrovertible *presence,* as "the *real* Thing."

There is, I have suggested, an affective dimension that engages bodies in this music, in moving to music. This is experienced as an immanence that is simultaneously a disappearance of self. The dance-floor groove, the flight of the freestyle rapper, and perhaps even the heady, chemically intoxicating, addictive flow of the graffitist: all these moments are experienced as movement away, as *flow.* In a subsequent moment, which is also a framing, and therefore an anterior moment, these states are marshaled, explained, and disciplined. I have used Deleuze and Guattari's

EPILOGUE

distinction between refrain and music to draw these moments apart; but, after all, all that Deleuze and Guattari are pointing toward is an ancient philosophical argument about being and becoming, about potential and realization. I have used this analysis to read the production of an idea about "culture," linking my observations of the field of Hip Hop in Sydney to Homi Bhabha's account of nationalisms: the processes by which becomings (experiences, practices, affects) are located within narratives, beings, ideologies.

The dance-floor groove becomes a break dance, performed as evidence, to represent a culture.

A flowing freestyle is recorded, its radical flight captured first of all within a discourse of *self*-expression, and then positioned, located within a narrative of cultural authenticity.

Refrain, that which opens up potential new being, becomes music: that which relocates agency; moves it not forward (outward? beyond?) to unanticipated otherness, but relates it to other places, and to other times, and in this creates a possibility of, and for, being together.

Glossary

The following is a selection of Hip Hop and related terms and slang used in the Sydney scene. Most are the same as those used in the United States; those that are particularly Australian usages are indicated. I have included some terms that were rarely heard in the Sydney context about which I was writing, although they are known, and sometimes referred to, rather than used per se. This is particularly the case with derogatory words for women. Note that many of the terms here operate both as verbs and nouns.

A-funk. Australian funk; Sydney stylee. A term that gained some small currency in 1994, sometimes jokingly.

battle. Contest between rappers or break dancers.

b-boy. Break-boy. Originally, someone who danced to the break. Sometimes "b-girl."

bhangra(-rap). Anglo-Hindi rap over a mixture of Hip Hop beats and Punjabi rhythms. Produced in northern England.

billy. A bong. From "billabong."

bitch. Girl. Generally derogatory.

bite, to. To copy or steal (a rhyme or style).

blunt. Marijuana joint. To be blunted means to be "stoned."

bomb, to. To completely cover in graffiti, usually in the form of tags or throw-ups.

bombing, going. An extended tagging session, either over an extended period or in a concentrated area. Thus writers might go "bombing," meaning that they will spend an afternoon riding trains, putting up their tags as often and as ubiquitously as possible.

bomber. One who bombs.

bong. A water pipe used for smoking marijuana. Also used as a verb: "to bong on."

booty. Sexually desirable woman, with specific reference to a woman's backside (see Rose 1990, 1991 and 1994b). Rarely heard in Sydney, but sometimes appeared in rhymes.

bpm. Beats per minute. In dance music (techno, house, trance), literally an indicator of the speed of the music, often referred to in reviews for the audiences of those genres. In Hip Hop, a technical term most usually used by producers and DJs programming drum machines. I have heard dance music enthusiasts referred to disparagingly as the "bpm crowd."

break. (v.) To break-dance. (n.) The "breakdown" in a track, where the vocal stops, and the rhythm track takes over.

breakbeat. A rhythmic figure or riff suitable for sampling.

buff, the. Physical and chemical process by which graffiti was removed from New York subway cars in the early 1980s (see Castleman 1982; Cooper and Chalfant 1984). By extension, any process used to remove graffiti.

burner. A superlative graffiti piece. Such a piece is said to "burn."

candy-rap. Pop music use of rap. Vanilla Ice, for example.

cap, to. To write graffiti over another writer's tag or piece. Also, "to go over."

character. A figure in a piece, generally taking the place of a letter.

chillin'. Relaxing, being cool.

chronic, the. Marijuana.

City, the. The inner city area of Sydney, enjoying a concentration of recreational resources.

coalies. Coal transport train carriages, common on the lines south of Sydney, from the coalfields north of Wollongong to the steel works at Port Kembla, and to the north, where coal from the Hunter Valley is transported to the works in Newcastle. Popular with writers, as they are often laid up for long periods and are flat-sided; cf. "ridgy."

colors. A colored piece of cloth worn to indicate allegiance to a particular gang. Not prevalent in Sydney.

cone. A conical metal container into which marijuana or hashish, sometimes "mulled" together with tobacco, is packed and then inserted into a bong.

crates, the. Containers for record collections. Often, fortuitously dimensioned milk crates are used for this purpose. To "dig in the crates" is to search through a collection either to find a particular record or to discover a new track.

crew. Group of writers, rappers, friends. Not to be confused with "gang." Also "posse": "West Side Posse."

C-Town. Campbelltown, an outer southwestern district of Greater Sydney.

cut. (n.) A track on a record; (v.) DJing technique involving sampling and overlaying tracks on side-by-side turntables.

DAT. Digital Audio Tape used to record backing tracks for playback during performance.

decks. Turntables. See "ones and twos."

def. Good.

diss, to. To disrespect, dismiss. By extension, to insult, slander, defame. Costello and Wallace suggest "dismissed" for "dis" (1990: 54).

DJ. Literally, "disc jockey," but, particularly, one who manipulates the records and cross-faders to contribute rhythmic and compositional accompaniment to a track. A "turntable instrumentalist," although this term would be considered a bit self-aggrandizing in Sydney.

dope. Very good. Dope is also, less frequently, a word for marijuana, as it is in common Australian usage. Vame's production company, "Dope Runner," puns on both these meanings.

down (with). Sympathetic to; aware of. "I ain't down with that."

drive-by. Shooting of a handgun from a moving vehicle. See Illegal Substance's rap "Drive-by."

drop, to. To deliver (a rap, a verse). "To drop science" is to rap knowledgably.

Eastside (Sydney). The coastal counterpart to the West Side, appearing in discourse throughout 1994 as a response to the increasing subcultural hegemony of the West Side.

fade in, to. To blend colors together in a piece. Highly skilled work.

fat. Literally "big," as in a "fat beat," "fat (shoe)laces," "fat lines" (in graffiti). By extension, good. Also "phat."

fat cap. An aerosol nozzle that yields a broad, thick spray. Favorite caps are collected and fitted to spray cans as required for particular effects: backgrounding, outlining, fading in. "Skinny cap" is the correlative term.

fill in, to. Literally adding color between the outlined letters in a piece. A task left to a less experienced writer when more than one writer is working.

fly. Attractive: "the fly girl."

flavour. Good quality: "I've got the flavour." Also spelled "flava."

flex. To rap ("flex skills") or sometimes to work the turntables. Shares a sense of both *flex*ible muscularity and the electric flexes linking microphone or turntable to amplifier.

flip skills, to. To rap; J.U.: "I flip skills with the crews around the east." To mess around; J.U.: "So wanna flip with me?" Also, "to flip *scripts.*"

flow, to. To rap, particularly freestyle, with great continuity and apparent ease. As a noun, the term refers to the result: "My flow . . ."

freestyle. Improvised (or mostly improvised) rhymes. Also "freestylee" (J.U.).

fresh. Good, up to date, of the highest quality. "The freshest clothes."

G. Familiar appelation: "What's up, G?" From "Gangsta" (gangster) (see Ro 1996).

gang. Graham Godbee uses the following definition: "A Street or Youth Gang is several people who regularly act together in an illegal or threatening manner. A gang has some sort of ongoing organisation" (Godbee 1994: 1). See "crew."

gangsta. Derived from "gangster." A street character associated with crime. Quasi-mythologized bad (black) dude. See "gat."

gangsta rap. Boasting rap over serious jeep beats, relating tales of crime and violence on the street. "Gangbanging" is what used to be called "rumbling," but with guns.

gat. Gun. Def Wish: "By golly 'G' I ain't no gangsta / Don't call me that / Not many people I know carry a gat" ("Runnin' Amok").

G-funk. Development of gangsta rap popularized by Los Angelino producer Dr. Dre, late of N.W.A.

Gibbo. An "Aussie": pejorative term for an everyday Australian, characterized as beer-drinking, rugby-following, pub-rock-loving. Def Wish Cast: "If a Gibbo stuffs our sound we make an abusive comment" ("Runnin' Amok").

go over, to. See "cap."

graff. Graffiti.

Graff Squad. See "transits."

hang out. A tag put on the outside of a (moving) train carriage by a writer literally "hanging out" of an open door or window. "To hang out" is to write in this manner. In May 1995, as I was writing this, local news reports were carrying a story about a fourteen-year-old boy killed while "hanging out" on his way to school.

hard core. Authentic; the *real* shit. "Always hard core, / 'Cos hard core means true to the music" (Def Wish Cast, "A.U.S.T.").

HardCore. Internet Hip Hop Bulletin Board.

homie. Someone from your neighborhood. From "homeboy."

ho(e). Derogatory. From "whore." I can't recall having heard this term used in Sydney in any context other than one of condemnation.

hood. Neighborhood.

hoodie. A hooded jacket.

hook up, to. To get together, generally in order to record.

hype. "An extremely good groove or situation" (K. M. Jones 1994: 120).

ill. Good, or bad, depending on both context of use and discretion of listener.

in (full) effect. Working very well; performing exceptionally; bombing a lot; going sick. "Fully" is used as a modifying adverb.

in the house. Present, in the room or venue.

jeep beats. Bass-heavy rhythms, designed for use in cars: "preferably [those] with customized stereo systems" (Rose 1994b: 197n). See Lipsitz, quoting Chuck D: "'Well, I got my speakers in my car and I'm turning my sound all the way up.' It's . . . a bass kind of thing" (1994a: 22).

kick, to. To offer a rap confidently, almost as a challenge (J.U. to Mick E: "I'll kick to you a rhyme . . ."); to pass along the "mic", literally or figuratively (Mick E to J.U.: "kick it to you"); to rap a verse; to perform well; to work/succeed ("kickin'").

kicks. Sports shoes, such as Nikes, Adidas, or Reebok: "Change your style; try a track suit and kicks once in a while" (Def Wish Cast, "Perennial Cross Swords").

king (of the line). A writer who has the most tags "up" on a rail line (or in a neighborhood). Kings often will add a small crown icon to their tags.

lay-up. A train yard.

legal, a. A commissioned piece.

lino. Piece of linoleum rolled out for break-dancing. Def Wish Cast: "Break out the lino / Break, break" ("Runnin' Amok").

Maccas. McDonald's family restaurant.

mad. Good.

MC. Rapper. Literally, "Master of Ceremonies" or "Microphone Chief."

metal beast. Popular term for a train: part of the mythologizing of piecing trains.

mic. The mike (from "microphone").

246

namecheck. Speaking someone's name over the air, during performance, or on a recording. Verb or noun. See "props" and "shout-out."

New Jack Swing. Music style closely related to R'n'B (rhythm and blues), incorporating rap: and, by extension, the club culture related to that music. "A dance style of R'n'B with rap music rhythms and drum beats" (Rose 1994b: 17).

N.S.O. "No Sell Out." Frequently appears in rhymes. Selling out is the opposite of "being true."

old school. Early Hip Hop music, dating from New York in the late 1970s and early 1980s, heavily influenced by European electronic music. To describe something as "old school stylee" is to approvingly endow it with authenticity.

ones and twos. Paired turntables as used by a DJ or selector.

outline. A plan for a piece, in pencil or pen, with color-code or color-pencil shading. Also, the sprayed outline of letters in for a piece or throw-up. Also used as a verb.

panel, full *or* half. A piece covering an entire (or half) section of carriage metal on a train.

Peace. Common salutation; generic form of "shout out": "Peace to my homies!"

phat. See "fat."

piece. A major graffiti work, from "masterpiece." Planned in advance in outline and executed over an extended period of time, generally on a wall (less often, on a train). Also a verb: "to piece," "piecing."

piecebook. A scrapbook of photographs of completed work, plus outline sketches, kept by a writer.

ping-pong, to. Mixing together individual tracks on a simple four-track mixer, a process involving reducing four tracks to one, and then repeating the process to layer up multiple tracks.

posse. Group of friends or associates. See "crew."

props. Recognition, acknowledgment of worth or contribution.

public style. Straightforward writing, easily read.

rack, to. To steal, particularly spray paint for graff.

ragga-rap. Rapping style derived from London Raggamuffin-rap. Def Wish's specialty.

rave. Dance party, involving techno or acid house music and hallucinogenic drugs: LSD and the LSD derivative Ecstasy ("Ecky" or "E"). Often conducted in clandestine conditions in warehouses. A "raver" is someone who attends such parties. See Redhead 1990 and Thornton 1996.

representing. Being seen, particularly to be seen contributing to "the culture."

rhymer. A rapper.

ridgy. A train carriage, the side panels of which are corrugated, making them difficult to piece on. Brisbane suburban trains are "ridgies."

rip, to. To perform exceedingly well: to "rip shit up"; "ripping up the microphone" (The Chief).

R'n'B. Music style involving singing over Hip Hop–type beats. See "New Jack Swing."

selector/selecta. Literally someone who selects tracks to play. "DJ" is reserved for someone who manipulates the turntables and records, scratching, cutting, and so on, in addition to selecting records.

Shao-Lin. The Eastern cult featured in the 1970s television series *Kung Fu*. This series enjoyed a popularity among a number of writers in Sydney in the early 1990s, and imagery borrowed from it features in particular in the rhymes of the Sleeping Monk. Thus, the Monk uses the expression "Shao-Lin funk" to describe his stylistic subgenre. See also Toop (1991: 128–29) on the appeal of Hong Kong martial arts films to New York b-boys in the late 1970s.

shit. With the definite article, "the real thing," as in this review: "Everybody I know who has heard it says this is the (as we say in Hip Hop) shit" (Miguel d'Souza, *3-D World,* May 15, 1995: 27). Without the definite article, "shit" means simply "stuff," without any pejorative intention.

shout-out. A spoken recognition, credit, or greeting. Used to describe any recognition; a record sleeve may include "shout-outs."

sick. Excessively good. Def Wish Cast: "Vame going [as] sick as a renegade."

skills. Technical proficiency as a rapper, DJ, writer, or breaker.

slamming. Adjective; see "kick."

Spanglish. A mixture of English and Spanish.

step, to. To challenge (another rhymer or breaker).

swingster. A New Jack Swing or R'n'B enthusiast. J.U.: "We ain't down with the swingsters."

tag. Graffiti "signature," often rendered in felt-tip pen or spray paint. Also as verb: "to tag."

technique. Skill. "Def technique."

techno. Electronic dance music.

3-D. Graffiti style involving creating a relief or a three-dimensional effect by shading in behind individual letters.

throw-up. A quickly executed minor piece, usually little more than an elaborated tag.

Tims. Timberland (U.S.) brand boots, initially marketed as hiking boots, but popular as street wear from 1992 to 1994.

tip. Refers to a style ("on the freestyle tip"); implies a "serious treatment of a subject" (K. M. Jones 1994: 120).

top 2 bottom. A piece covering the full height of a train carriage.

toy. A pretender, an amateur, a novice.

transits (Sydney). The Graffiti Taskforce of the New South Wales Police. Originally an internal unit of the State Rail Authority, hence "transit police." Also "graff squad."

wack. Variant of "whack."

waste, to. See "wreck," "bomb." A "wasted wall."

Westie. Pejorative term for someone living in Sydney's Western Suburbs. The valorization of the "West Side" is a successful inversion thereof. West Side (Sydney) refers to the Western Suburbs of Sydney, an area roughly definable as anywhere to the west of Parramatta. Originally derived from the West Side Posse, an early break-dancing and graffiti crew from which Sound Unlimited emerged.

whack. Very bad. Possibly derived from the word's use in cartoon sound-effect bubbles (as in *Superman, Batman,* etc.). "To whack" is to kill.

wild style. Writing style in which letter frames are distorted, interlocked, and extended, rendering the piece unreadable. See "public style."

word. Apostrophic exclamation, indicating that the speaker is to be taken in earnest. "Honestly!" See (Mowry 1992, *passim).*

word up. "Pay attention" or "now listen."

wreck, to. To bomb, or to perform excessively well: "to wreck the mic." A completely bombed train is "wrecked." "To wreck shop" is to rap exceedingly well.

write, to. To graffiti.

writer. A graffitist, generally of some ability.

Notes

Preface

1. As one reader of the manuscript on which this book is based put it.
2. My thanks to Michael Cohen, Paul Dwyer, and Laura Ginters at the Department of Performance Studies at the University of Sydney for this analysis.
3. A minor storm raged in the Australian media when, in May 2000, Steve Waugh, the captain of the national cricket team — it is a commonplace that this office is second in stature in Australia only to that of the prime minister — en route to England, took "his men" to the battlefield of Gallipoli. Recreating famous images of diggers (Australian soldiers) playing cricket on the sand as shrapnel exploded overhead, and crouching, slouch-hatted, in overgrown trenches, Waugh invoked the narrative of never-say-die mateship to motivate both his players and national sentiment for the upcoming "battle for the Ashes," the symbol of cricketing supremacy between Australia and the "Old Country." (Australia won the five-match series 4–1.)
4. In Australia, the Liberal Party generally takes up a center-right position, frequently in coalition with the more conservative, rural-based National Party. The Australian Labor Party has been broadly left-center, but through its history it has been riven by factionalism, ranging from conservative to progressive. Australian federal parliaments sit for a maximum of three years, although terms are not fixed, enabling a government, for reasons of political expediency, to call a general election early: hence the present Liberal-National Party government has been returned in three successive elections in less than six years.
5. In 1971 my own (Anglo-Celtic) parents traveled from the "Mother country" (the United Kingdom) as assisted immigrants, among the last of the "ten-pound tourists." My brother and I traveled free (see Appleyard et al. 1988).

Prologue

1. My convention will be to capitalize and separate, without a hyphen, "Hip" and "Hop."
2. Back slashes (\) indicate breaths within or at the end of lines of rap lyrics.

Part One: Introduction

1. 046's debut CD *L.I.F.E.* was the first major Dope Runner release, in 1995, although it was preceded by a number of cassette releases.

Chapter 1

1. See Maxwell and Bambrick 1994. I also recall dancing at a Sydney inner city nightspot, adumbratively named the Hip Hop Club, to Grandmaster Flash's "White Lines" in 1984, and memorizing the words to their earlier hit "The Message" and performing it at an undergraduate cabaret the year after.

2. I am particularly thinking of a revealing collection of essays, *Media, Culture and Society,* published in 1986, which reviewed the trajectory of British cultural and media studies through successive waves of Althusserian and Lacanian theory in the early years of that decade; theory that, in its determination to preserve increasingly fragile Marxian positions, could only account for lived experience in terms of discourses of false consciousness (see Collins et al. 1986).

3. Although as I type a rhyme by The Chief from a crew called The Ruffnecks swims around my head:

   Ripping up the microphone is not a crime
   Here comes the rhyme, dripping with slime
   What's the time? I think it's time to get ill
   Listen to the wicked words from my grill
   . . .

   Hold on now it's time to get it on
   Fuck the love songs we're coming on strong
   Doing no wrong we're just two hip hoppers
   Listen to the twisted words from my *voca loca*

4. See Curthoys and Docker (1996) for an argument addressed to what those writers understand as a similarly totalizing tendency in Foucault's foundational poststructuralist oeuvre.

5. As I write, I notice Wark quoted in a feature article about post-grunge youth culture in the *Sydney Morning Herald* (Alex Burke, "Make Mine a Martini," February 3, 1996, 7S). Wark offers a media-friendly sound-bite generalization: "[T]here is no memory in popular culture." By contrast, I want to suggest that the self-genealogizing, and thereby self-generating, project of the Sydney Hip Hop Community, is precisely illustrative of, at the very least, a desire for (collective) popular-cultural memory. Although, of course, perhaps Wark is right in the general case, and my example offers only the curiosity of a quirky aberration (a throwback?) amidst the schizophrenic (Jameson 1991) eternal present of the postmodern condition.

6. Blaze took his tag from a news story: "Big Blaze Destroys Building." "This thing wasted a building," he told a journalist: "I liked it" (Thwaite 1989: 72). To *destroy* or to *waste* a building or a train or a wall is to completely cover it with graffiti. And Blaze was one of the best graffitists ever to wield a spray can in Sydney.

Chapter 2

1. The Mothership Connection continued to go on air up to the time of writing. At the time, Miguel estimated his listenership (probably optimistically) as being in the vicinity of 10,000.

2. There is a certain lack of consistency in spelling within the Hip Hop Scene: a playful discretion is the norm, particularly if there is a possibility of punning on significant words. Thus the Fonke Knowmaads are also the Funky Nomads, and sometimes the Fönké Knomaads, or any combination thereof. The Knowmaads released an EP in 1993, "The Hills are Alive with the Sound of . . . ," reviewed in *Zest* (2, Spring 1993: 4–6), before disbanding when one of their rappers, Teop ("Poet" written backward) became a born-again Christian.

3. Abrahams's work on African-American orality (1970, 1976, and then 1992) has been developed perhaps most significantly into an ambitious Afro-American [*sic*] literary theory by Gates (1988), an account in which the oral cultures of the sub-Sahara survived the Middle Passage, to be inflected by, and to find strategic application in, the experience of slavery. With specific reference to rapping as it emerged in New York in the late 1970s, Toop (1991) offers a thorough analysis of the development of various African-American forms throughout the twentieth century in the context of post-slave urban populations (in Toop 1991). A subsequent wealth of literature has offered essentially the same narrative, variously inflectioned: the collection of essays collected and introduced by Spencer (1991) is particularly useful; Hager (1984) and Tate (1992) offered more accessible accounts; and a flurry of publications in 1994 ranged from Tricia Rose's academic treatment (1994b), through Fernando's generously readable offering to the rather poor popularization by K. M. Jones. Hebdige (1987) offers a thorough and entertaining account of the development of Jamaican toasting and boasting and the passage of these practices to New York in the early 1970s.

4. The italicized words are those used within the scene.

5. I will return to Def Wish Cast in chapters 3, 4, 5 and 6.

6. J.U. stands for "Junior." J.U.'s "real" name is Ed; he is also known as "Special Ed."

7. Awkward grammar. Try "I've heard the term 'elitist' has been flipped on me."

8. Harris, in his spirited critique of what he calls "the gramscians" of Birmingham subcultural theory, has a field day with what he understands as the tendentious romanticism of the entire project (1992: 3, 7–29 passim).

9. A writer *wrote* his or her name: a writer would ask a new acquaintance, "What do you write?," to which the second writer would respond with his or her *tag*: "I write Puma," for example. Ideally, this would be met with a recognition of that tag's ubiquity, and a discussion would ensue about *getting up*.

Chapter Three

1. Tricia Rose's *Black Noise* (1994), an efficient critical overview, will, no doubt, stand as the standard text in the area. Other useful sources include Nelson and Gonzales's encyclopedic *Bring the Noise* (1991) and Adler's photo-directory of prominent rap personalities (1991). Texts such as Nelson and Gonzales, Adler, Hager (1984), and Toop (1991), all very accessible, engagingly written, and liberally illustrated, were popular in the Sydney scene. Thompson's essay on break-dancing (1986) is salutary; Costello and Wallace's relentlessly reflexive post-modern "sampler" (1990), on the other hand, is mostly of value as a curiosity.

2. As a valuable adjunct to Gilroy's account of the flow of cultural material across the Northwestern Hemisphere, Richard Waterhouse has produced a fascinating history of processes of trans-Pacific cultural exchange in the latter half of the nineteenth century, when the North American vaudeville circuit included an Australian leg. Acts toured from America to Australia and from Australia to America. Many African-American artists took advantage of the apparently more sympathetic and tolerant cultural milieu to settle in Australia and continue their careers "down under" (see Waterhouse 1990 and 1995).

3. Spencer, summarizing such defenses of the "irruption of subjugated knowledges" into discourse, quotes Sartre's *Black Orpheus:* "What did you expect when you unbound the gag that had muted those black mouths?" (1991, 4). For a counterargument to these defenses, see Peterson-Lewis (1991; collected in the same volume as Spencer's essay).

4. The 1980 Talking Heads album *Remain in Light* also featured a rap in the song "Cross-Eyed and Painless." It is also interesting to note that in 1981 Talking Heads front man David Byrne, in collaboration with English producer Brian Eno, pioneered sampling methodologies in recording *My Life in the Bush of Ghosts*. The album used looped samples from such sources as proto–World Music recordings, radio call-in shows, broadcast sermons, and so forth, which were layered over synthesized and "live" drums, along with funky bass lines and guitars, creating very much a "hip hop–type" sound.

5. Hebdige has also charted out a comparable "alliance" between English punk and reggae (Hebdige 1979, 1987). It should be noted that the New York punk scene of the late 1970s was qualitatively very different to that of London. Arguably, where the London scene found its *initial* impetus among an underemployed, alienated youth underclass (Hebdige 1979), the New York scene enjoyed a somewhat bohemian art-crowd appeal from the start, dating from the Velvet Underground's involvement with Andy Warhol's Factory project (Heylin 1993). Marcus (1989) and Savage (1991) offer rereadings of the English punk scene, the former placing seminal punks the Sex Pistols within a narrative of somewhat highbrow counterculture movements, including dadaism and the Situationists, while the latter stresses the role of "actively interventionist journalism" (Hayward 1992a: 85) in firing up the

scene. Such interpretations point to the inadequacy of analyses of late-twentieth-century cultural movements premised largely on class correlates.

6. See chapter 4.

7. Quote taken from Miguel d'Souza's radio documentary "Sydney Hip Hop" broadcast on public broadcaster 2 SER-FM, July 1994 (Coolie Boy Productions).

8. Interview conducted with Sound Unlimited by Nikki Bambrick, July 1993 (see Maxwell and Bambrick 1994).

Chapter Four

1. Particularly through that paradigm of all colonialist sports, cricket, through which Australia maintains strong links with India, Pakistan, various West Indian nations, South Africa, New Zealand, and, more latterly, Sri Lanka and Zimbabwe. England, at present, offers substantially weaker competition in world cricket than all but Zimbabwe (and even then . . .). See Appadurai 1996.

2. In his introduction to a recent volume of essays collected from the Sydney-based *Perfect Beat: The Pacific Journal of Research into Contemporary Music and Popular Culture,* Philip Hayward notes that the cover design of the first issue of the *Journal of Popular Music Studies,* published by the *International* Association for the Study of Popular Music (my italics), featured a map "depicting the world as two spheres, overlapping around the mid-Atlantic," from which the "slice of the planet comprising the Islands of the Pacific, Australia, New Zealand and East and South-East Asia" had been "filleted" (Hayward 1998: 3).

3. There has been a welter of more recent publications, among which Hannerz 1996, Buell 1994, and Sklair 1995 are the pick. Appadurai 1996 offers a slightly revised version of the model I am using here, along with a number of case studies. Tony Mitchell's 1996 *Popular Music and Local Identity: Rock, Pop, and Rap in Europe and Oceania* is an excellent application of this body of thinking to music studies, as is Lipsitz 1994b and Taylor 1997.

4. I should note that of course this difference, and the specificity of each local incarnation of Hip Hop Culture, can be either emphasized or downplayed in given contexts, as agents locate themselves within tactically desirable positions.

5. By a fluke of geography, Melbourne's western suburbs stand to the "cosmopolitan" center of that city as Sydney's Western Suburbs stand to the "center" of Sydney, suffering from the same demonizations (see below).

6. At a freestyle session at the Lounge Room, in August 1994, Pewbic tha Hunta is struggling on the mic, looking around, trying to find (inspiration for) his verse. He spies Miguel, and breaks the room up with this great rhyme: "What's this in front of me? / I see a Pakistani."

7. Coolie Boy Productions (1994).

8. Paula and Goie were disappointed that Blaze did not attend one of their per-

formances after they had invited him; only months later, after Black Justice had attracted a bit of publicity, they told me, did Blaze make the attempt to contact them.

9. Author's interview with Graham Godbee of Pulse Consultants, Sydney, July 1994.

10. See Maxwell 1994b.

11. London Weekly Television, 1992.

12. Cable television didn't hit Australia until the mid-1990s; prior to that, a syndicated, locally produced and play-listed "MTV" screened twice weekly (Friday and Saturday, late) on a free-to-air channel. Rap was, at best, on low rotation.

13. See Maxwell and Bambrick 1994: 13–15 for my discussion of the various discursive strategies employed by Sound Unlimited to produce this kind of "reality."

14. Apocryphal anecdote shared with every prospective jazz player: to learn how to play saxophone, you have to learn to walk *black*. That is, to walk on the backbeat: one-*two*, one-*two*, rather than *one*-two, *one*-two . . .

15. Care was taken to ensure that the album was released on (scratchable) vinyl, as well as in CD format. See chapter 6, "Phat Beats," below for an extended analysis of the musical texts of both these albums, and for a consideration of the Hip Hop scene's response to them.

16. In both cases, I am quoting the raps as printed verbatim on the sleeve inserts.

17. For reasons (other than the requisite attention to scholarly verisimilituity) that will become apparent, in this and in all subsequent quotes from various Hip Hop sources, I have endeavored to retain the original typographic features and layout of the text (typefaces, paragraph breaks, etc.), as well as the various idiosyncratic (deliberate) misspellings and usages. I have also retained what may be involuntary misspellings and grammatical errors with-out using [*sic*], in order to retain the flavor of the original documents. My own elisions within such quotes are marked within square brackets thus: [. . .].

18. Rose cites, from conversations with the *Source* editor James Barnard, a pass-along rate for the magazine in the United States of "approximately 1 purchase for every 11–15 readers" (Rose 1994b: 8). The relatively high cost of the 'zine in Australia is offset by the higher disposable incomes of prospective buyers and the status with which possession of a latest issue endows the owner: I would suggest that the pass-along rate is perhaps a little lower in Australia. Rose also suggests that the *Source* enjoys "a prominently black teen readership" (8). This is an understanding (assumption?; Rose offers no data to support this assertion) operant in the Sydney milieu, constituting part of the magazine's appeal: it is *black* and therefore, at that point where the discourses of black and authenticity map onto each other, *real*.

19. A "Zines" review page in *Hype* 19 (page 21) includes rundowns and subscription addresses for *I.G.T.* (*International Get Hip Times*), *Underground Productions* ("from Sweden but all the text is in English"), *Over Kill* (from Germany, with "22 pages of mouth watering trains") and *Hardcore* from Sydney. "*Hardcore,*" we read, "has 16 pages all with a clear and easy to follow layout."

20. Other writers credited for articles here include WizDM and Mr E of the Brethren, Fibular, and Felicitè. Four others, including Blaze's girlfriend (later wife) Angela, receive "Special Thanx" along with "all others that hassled me in the streets," this being yet another evocation of "the street" as a locus of (therefore authentic) Hip Hop practice. Note also the inconsistency in the spelling of the magazine's name, oscillating between the Anglo and American conventions: "Vapours/Vapors." I have generally adopted the Americanized spelling, as it appears, as a "piece" outline, on the *Vapors* masthead.

21. I do not have the space to review the literature about rap and censorship. Gates 1990, Gore 1987, Morley 1992, Stanley 1992, and Peterson-Lewis 1991 offer various perspectives on this issue; all the standard Hip Hop references also offer extended commentaries on censorship and the right to freedom of expression: fascinatingly, K. M. Jones's rather weak celebration of the "Young Lions of America" in his 1994 *Say It Loud!: The Story of Rap,* written from an insider's perspective, coyly censors his transcription of the hard-hitting freestyles of the Oakland-based Souls of Mischief crew (1994: 10–12), either using a dash to mask offensive words ("sh — t" for "shit") or else completely omitting the offending items.

22. Public Enemy's "Brothers Gonna Work It Out" from 1989's *Fear of a Black Planet* contains a sample from James Brown's 1967 anthem to black power, "Get Up, Get into It, Get Involved" (1967).

23. Assuming an average cost of AU$25 per recording (imported CDs generally cost in excess of $30.00, while EPs on vinyl range down toward $15.00 — CDs generally retail around the $27.00–$28.00 mark), the reader was recommended, in the most direct terms, to invest $425.00 on these albums: if the reader was "cashed," the figure rises to $1,625.00.

24. Each issue of *Vapors* from issue no. 6 onward defiantly bore a "parental advisory: explicit lyrics" label, similar to those legally required on CDs and records.

25. Sometimes all three come together; a letter from Siamone, in Queens, New York reads: "I just want to say your mag is the best out . . . we're all brothers and sisters joined together by the love of Graff . . ." (*Hype*, no. 20: 28).

26. New York, of course, is the place of origin, the *source,* of (Hip Hop) graffiti, as I have been told dozens of times. The expression "home" recurs, as does the phrase "spiritual home," in discussions of New York: even now, when graffiti has all but disappeared from the New York subways, writers still

make hajj-like pilgrimages (this word, too, has been used to describe to me the import of such a trip) to the Big Apple to see where it all started. "There's a special feeling you get when you go to where something began," one writer told me of his visit to Manhattan.

27. I placed my name in *Hype* and received responses from Queensland, South Australia, Spain, and Canada, all in the same handwriting, the identifiable Hip Hop/graff script.

28. Educational books, widely understood as espousing "traditional" values directed at young children.

29. Another article, titled "Back to the Roots," apologized for the absence of any news about breaking in recent months: Unfortunately, this section has been vacant for a while but it's back to stay. This is the dance form of the Hip Hop culture, not half-stepping, so don't get confused by the real deal . . ." (*Hype* 2, no. 1, 1993: 21).

30. A credit hidden on page 2 qualifies this claim, noting that "this is not really printed on hemp paper, but it should be, as soon as hemp is made legal, we'll use it! One acre of hemp will produce as much paper as four acres of trees!!"

31. Arrested Development toured Australia in May 1994.

32. This kind of newspaper article seemed to surface every few months: see also Hutack and Borham 1994, Steyn 1994, and Petkovic, Kokokiris, and Kalinowska 1995, in addition to the other articles quoted.

33. The book itself was published "to coincide with the exhibition *Streetstyle* held at the Victoria and Albert Museum, London, 16 November 1994 to 19 February 1995" (Polhemus 1994: 4).

34. See also Derrida 1976.

Chapter Five

1. In Australian Rules Football, a hybrid of Gaelic football, football (soccer), and rugby, players are allowed to physically contact opponents, whether in possession of the ball or not, as long as the contact is made between the hip and shoulders, and the arms are not used to constrain or grab. The resulting mode of contact is fondly referred to as a "hip and shoulder (charge)," a charge often launched from several meters' distance, and is gruffly balletic in nature, as distinct from the explosive directness of the blocker's art in American football.

2. An analysis of the increasing reliance of venues on high-revenue-generating tribute and cover bands, and of the concomitant decline of the live-music scene in Sydney, is beyond the scope of this work.

3. DJing was included as the fourth key Hip Hop practice.

4. Gilroy, similarly, understands the construction of pan-Africanist nationalism in North America as a response to the African-American experience of dislocation; both a literal geographical dislocation ("the Middle Passage")

and the subsequent experience of marginalization and cultural invisibility through and after slavery. It is not a great stretch to predicate an analogous structure at the heart of the contemporary Australian experience: a profound sense of dislocation informs not merely a single demographic, or a fraction (no matter how large) of the population; a vast majority of the population has arrived on these shores within the space of 208 years. In such a context, Hip Hop Nationalism can be seen as a subgenre of a socially pervasive set of nationalist projects: "[T]he nation always figures as something yet to be achieved, or something that had been achieved in the past, was lost, but could be achieved again . . . If the nation is perceived as possible what is needed is something that explains the failure of this possibility to materialise, *so far*" (Hage 1993a: 99).

5. The "West Side" is an imaginary location whose geographical referent has actually shifted with successive generations of crews and other Hip Hop activists, in step with the gradual westward shift of Sydney's population. For the earlier generation — the West Side Posse, Sound Unlimited Posse — the Hip Hoppers of the mid-1980s, the West Side was the inner west: Burwood, Parramatta. When I was doing my research, in the early 1990s, the West Side had, following Sydney's demographic shift, crept closer to the Blue Mountains, out to Penrith and Mt. Druitt.

6. See Diane Powell on "slummer journalism" (1993: 18–35).

7. Recall Gertrude Stein's apocryphal assessment of Oakland, California: "There's no there, there."

8. Returned Servicemen's League Club.

9. Below, we will see how Hip Hop further marked its difference through the claiming not only of particular knowledges, but also through asserting Hip Hop as a *way* of knowing: Hip Hop as an epistemology.

10. And, on the other hand, to be a "transit" policeman [*sic:* they were all men in the "graff squad"] is also to be tough, to have a blast, to fight a guerilla action against a uniformed adversary, to enjoy the hunt and a beer afterward. And so the game goes on, night after night.

11. Of critical significance here is the implication of the investigator in the processes shaping "the community." Heeding the Bourdieuan advocacy of a reflexive sociology, I must note here the dialectical nature of this moment: the investigator has at least as much at stake in negotiating these questions of "community" as do the social agents constituting the object of the research. Particularly in the context of postgraduate research, in which a person who is, perhaps, an "apprentice" researcher, working in underresourced, insecure (in terms of income and employment), (virtual) isolation, there is necessarily a bias toward a kind of positivism, the product of a cathectic investment in the research object. There is a desire to find some "thing," to establish its significance in the eyes of fellow students and, of course, the academic staff within the institutional context, as well as in

broader academic contexts as the fledging scholar attempts to bring his or her work to notice. The pressure on doctoral candidates to market their work, to adopt an entrepreneurial pro-activity in regards to their projects, compounding this inevitable personal investment in research, is marked, and yet little remarked on.

Bachelard advocated the quasi-therapeutic divestment of one's philias (in addition to one's phobias) in the pursuit of "knowledge" (1987 [1964]: 6): I am making these remarks not (entirely) out of personal indulgence, but to point toward a set of biases informing much research, particularly in the fields with which I have had the most contact through this present research. The conflation of advocacy with analysis is particularly manifest in, for example, African-American studies (see Gates, for example), in areas of women's studies, in youth "subculture" studies, and in popular music studies.

12. And it is to these embodied dimensions of Hip Hop that I will return in the final chapters.

13. The quote is taken from Hegel's essay "The State," included in Kohn 1965: 110–12.

14. See Hage 1993b for an argument against the popular conflation of the discourses of republicanism and multiculturalism in Australia, and particularly the idea that Australian republicanism is inherently "multicultural." This conflation, Hage argues, masks what is in fact the inherently monocultural (specifically Anglocentric) nature of the dominant discourse of Australian republicanism.

15. Dick Hebdige's 1987 account of Rastafarianism is perhaps the most interesting attempt to contextualize nationalist ideologies within a broader historical account.

16. For Peirce, by contrast, all meaning and reference has always been determined by processes of open semiosis, in which "the real" is not that which can be retrieved through a process of representation, but that which is affected by, or affects, those processes. For such thinking, there is no terminal point guaranteeing "the real," but instead chains of interpretants layering up in networks of intertextuality and forming habits.

17. A term borrowed from Rastafarian discourse.

18. The ethnoscape of the Sydney Hip Hop Scene, as I have suggested, is probably more usefully thought of as being polychromatic, rather than simply "white." My point here, however, is to foreground the problems confronted by "nonblacks" in attempting to negotiate a "national" identity predicated on "blackness."

19. See Hage's critique of tolerance (1994a).

20. See Maxwell and Bambrick 1994 for an account of the discursive strategies of Sound Unlimited as it attempted to authenticate its signing with a major record label. Light 1991, Swedenburg 1992, Wark 1992, and Blair 1993 offer perspectives on Hip Hop notions of "selling out."

21. Phillips wrote that "above our [Australia's] writers — and other artists — looms the intimidating mass of Anglo-Saxon culture. Such a situation almost inevitably produces the characteristic Australian Cultural Cringe" (Phillips 1958: 89).

22. Among a plethora of publications — in Australian literary and public affairs/political journals such as *Meanjin* and *Quadrant,* popular press, and current affairs media — the Research Centre for Intercommunal Studies publication *Communal/Plural* stands out in its sustained treatment of the issues circulating around Australian nationalism and cultural identity during this period. See particularly Hage and Johnson 1993: *Communal/Plural,* no. 2, subtitled *Republicanism/Citizenship/Community,* which includes important reflections on both the question of national identity (cf. Burchell 1993) and the nature of popular debate about the issue (M. Morris 1993b). *Communal/Plural,* no. 4 (1995: *An Inquiry into the State of Anglo-Saxonness within the Nation,* ed. Hage, Lloyd, and Johnson), develops postcolonialist perspectives on multiculturalism (Hage 1994b, Perera and Pugliese 1994, Jayamanne 1994).

Chapter Six

1. Compare/contrast Madonna's "Justify My Love" with PE's "Security of the First World" from 1989's *It Takes a Nation of Millions.*

2. A number of collections review this volatile period in the nascent discipline of "cultural studies.' See, for example, Hall et al. (1980), *Culture, Media and Language,* a collection of working papers from the BCCCS dating from 1972 to 1979, which includes an important overview by Stuart Hall himself (1980a) as well as his "critical note" evaluating the impact of "theories of language as ideology" (1980b). Another retrospective collection published in 1986, titled *Media, Culture and Society* (Collins et al. 1986), includes essays by Nicholas Garnham and Raymond Williams introducing Bourdieu's work to the English academic field (Garnham and Williams 1986) as well as a translation of one of Bourdieu's introductory essays (Bourdieu 1986 [1979]).

   The Birmingham melting pot of the leftist "culturalist" positions of Hoggart, Williams, and Thompson, ethnography, Western Marxism (particularly the work of Gramsci and the Lacanian-structuralist Althusser), and the later (at least in terms of their impact on the English scene) waves of Barthesian, Kristevan, Foucauldian, Bourdieuan, and Baudrillian thought has been somewhat ruthlessly critiqued by Harris (1992).

3. Adler (1991) estimated that a rap track usually contains four to five times the number of words of a song of comparable length.

4. Fascinatingly, Brian Cross's review of the Los Angeles rap scene (1993) includes several pages of photographs of rappers' bedrooms. Sarah Thornton's recent analysis of club and rave "culture" in England describes the construction within domestic spaces of sonic barriers ("walls of sound")

through teenagers' use of stereo systems in their bedrooms, and the extension and portability of those discrete sonic spaces through the use of Walkman cassette players (Thornton 1996: 19–20).

5. Although the acclaim was not universal within the scene: one crew took great delight in showing me a clipping from the British magazine *Hip Hop Connection,* in which a correspondent had taken issue with a favorable review of the Def Wish Cast album. My informant seemed to enjoy reading the letter out to me as I recorded: "Who do those Australian shitheads Def Wish Cast think they are? Their album's wack and how can they say they haven't heard 'Patriot Games' I heard two tracks off your album and thought Damn! They're imitating Gunshot. The quality is crap. I'm sure that Gunshot didn't have a million dollar recording studio either. But my recording sounds ten times as good. Also, you say it's hardcore. Bullshit. It's hardcore as Hammer. Ain't no b-boys been listening to that shit. I think the great Barry Sugarman [who reviewed the album] is generous giving you two stars so mutherfuckers you *are* wack and do not forget it."

6. From this position, Rose develops just the kind of homologic "reading" of the cultural meaning of rap music critiqued above.

Chapter Seven

1. I frame, or perhaps qualify, all my attempts to describe music with reference to Barthes's expression of despair: "Alas . . ." he writes, "music . . . is that which at once receives an adjective, the poorest of linguistic categories" (1990 [1977]: 293).

2. I share Costello and Wallace's (1990) enthusiasm for this particular track, reproduced in notated musical transcript form as an appendix to their book, one of the highlights of that particular text.

3. "Theatresports" is "improvised theatre entertainment played as a spectator sport" (Pierse 1993: 3). I include this reference because of the somewhat discordant nature of the rapper boyz' benign enthusiasm for rhyming: far from the hard core posturing expected of a rhymer, here was a moment more akin to the polite, actorly indulgence of the theatresports crowd.

4. Reminding me of a range of modes of self-induced narcosis: the giddying rapture of a whirling dervish who, accelerating himself into a state of breathless physical extremis, seeks "the annihilation of self in the unity of the One . . . [the] state of ecstasy known as *fenafillah*" (Adelaide Festival Programme, 1996: 5). Or the hyperventilating shaman preparing himself for mystical flight; the Nepali *jhankri,* for example, "a being who goes into a trance, at which time voices speak through his body" (Shrestha and Lediard c1980: 29).

5. The drug of choice in the scene in question is, as I have noted, marijuana. Marijuana smoothes out selves — one gets "blunted," the edge is taken away. The use of cannabis is understood to facilitate the flow, to help with listening, as one rapper told me. Another explained that all the American Hip

Hop producers are blunted while making recordings, so it was appropriate, even necessary, to be in a similar state when listening to the tracks in question. I note here A. F. Moore's warning against reading homologies between subcultural drug preference and musicological features (1993: 156–58).

Not every rhymer used cannabis; none to my knowledge used anything harder. Heroin and cocaine were never seen, and were identified with other "cultures," often marked as somewhat degenerate: heroin was understood to be part of the reviled pub rock scene; coke was a yuppie drug. Crack was not generally available in Sydney, although it must be said that there is a kind of romanticized discourse about it. It was identified very strongly with the imaginary of ghetto life, an identification encouraged by films, television shows, raps, press reports, and so on.

6. The reference is to the distinction that Deleuze and Guattari (1987) draw between "smooth" and "striated" space.

7. And, although I have been assured that it *does* (or perhaps *did,* back in "tha dayz") happen, I have never seen a girl break.

Epilogue

1. The question of obscene rap lyrics is keenly debated in the media, in academic circles, and within the local scene, frequently bound up in discourses of the "right" to free speech, to expressing one's self. The right to self-expression is mobilized frequently as a defense; it is this discourse which circulates most often in the local scene (see, for example, Stanley 1992 and Morley 1992). More sophisticated arguments in defense of rap obscenity are mounted by Gates, who suggests that no one should be surprised that such anger, misogyny, and violence should be expressed by a brutalized people. On the other side of the debate, Tipper Gore's 1987 *Raising PG Kids in an X-Rated Society* stands as the model text. An excellent rebuttal of Gate's defense of obscene lyrics can be found in Peterson-Lewis (1991).

There is a subtle racism in many of the discourses about rap and sexuality, a racism that is sometimes celebratory in tone (witness Ice T's braggadocio in performance, boasting of his black man's prowess, the length of his penis, his *rhythm*), and, more frequently, demonizing: the "rap equals rape" equation. The relationship of sexuality to rhythm, to the beats, is one to which I will return below when considering the musicological semiotics of rap.

Sources and References

Miguel d'Souza's work has been generously quoted throughout the text.
Miguel wrote a weekly column and occasional features for *3-D World,* a free
newspaper distributed weekly through record shops, bookshops, clubs, cafés,
universities, and newsagents throughout the Sydney Metropolitan area.
Its circulation ranged toward 30,000 a week, and the paper is predominantly
concerned with "club" or "dance culture," offering listings, reviews, and
photographs of the latest parties and nights. Miguel's column was something
of a regular anomaly in the midst of full-page advertisements for raves and
acid house nights. Rather than list each cited issue of *3-D World* in this bibli-
ography, I have included the relevant information in the text.

The Hip Hop Press

A number of magazines published by people active within the Australian
Hip Hop Scene have been referred to in the text. These magazines are of
limited availability, for a number of reasons, and are generally available
through specialist record shops, or by subscription. Some, for varying
periods, were distributed through news agencies (newsstands) where
finances and legality allowed. Circulation is hard to establish, with nobody
really willing to offer hard figures, although it would be unlikely that sales
exceed 1,000 for any of them. 'Pass-on' rates accounts for most of the
readership. The major local publications are *Vapors* and *Slingshot!* (Sydney),
Hype (Brisbane, Queensland), *Raptanite* (Cessnock, a town some 170 kilometers north of Sydney in the middle of the Hunter-Newcastle urban area), and
Zest! (The Gold Coast, Queensland). Other small, often photocopied,
word-processed publications surface and disappear from time to time, of
ten circulating from a particular high school. An example is *Those Damn
Kids!,* published occasionally in photocopy form from the upper North Shore
of Sydney. All of the above would be available on a semireliable basis from
specialist record shops, such as Central Station, in Central Sydney's Oxford
Street, and, of course, the Lounge Room. References to pieces in these magazines are given in full in the text.

I have tried not to quote directly from international Hip Hop magazines,
such as the *Source* (New York) and *Hip Hop Connection* (London), although
I note that these do circulate throughout the Hip Hop Scene in Australia,
passed from hand to hand at shows, stacked in piles, borrowed, and so on.

Other Source Material

I have referred, where necessary, to my own records of interviews with numerous people. Some of this material was audio-recorded, some video-recorded, and much simply gleaned through conversations and 'hanging out.'

I note again that some sources requested not to be quoted for various reasons, ranging from a fear of police harassment to a concern not to ruffle feathers. I have respected anonymity where necessary.

I have also taken some quotes from a radio documentary produced by Miguel d'Souza and broadcast for 2 SER-FM (Sydney) in August 1994, "Hip Hop Culture in Sydney" (Coolie Boy Productions, 1994), as well as some material from his weekly program on that same public broadcast station, *The Mothership Connection*, broadcast on Tuesday afternoons throughout the period of my research. Miguel's help and interest in my project has been enormously valuable.

Recordings

There are a limited number of Australian Hip Hop releases generally available, although, of course, poor-quality cassettes occasionally circulate. The following are the major CD releases:

Sound Unlimited. *A Postcard from the Edge of the Underside*. Columbia 1992.
Def Wish Cast. *Knights of the Underground Table*. Random Records 1993.
Illegal Substance. *Off da Back of a Truck*. 1994.
046. *L.I.F.E.* Dope Runner Productions 1995.

Sound Unlimited's involvement with a "major" recording and distribution company was little less than disastrous. Inexperience with big-company contracts and the associated obligations and loss of control of artistic direction resulted in the failure of the album to find a market, particularly in the face of the local Hip Hop Community's rejection of the work as a "sell-out," led to massive debt (six figures, the rumor in the scene has it) and the subsequent dissolution of the group in 1994 (see Mitchell 1992; Maxwell and Bambrick 1994: 6–15).

The failure of Sound Unlimited to deliver a market to their recording company no doubt confirmed the nonviability of Australian Hip Hop as a commercial possibility in the eyes of such companies. Of course, from the Hip Hop side of the fence, all this merely confirms the unwillingness of "the industry" to deal with "reality."

Subsequent local Hip Hop releases have been "underground," and therefore limited, with occasional vinyl records made at the single vinyl pressing plant still in operation in Australia. Groups sell copies of low-quality cassettes, for example, out of carry bags at performances.

By the mid-1990s, CDs could be printed at a fairly low unit cost (around AU$3–AU$4), and Def Wish Cast's CD sold rapidly at up to 1,000 copies before they, too, ran into distribution hassles with a major (Australian) company. The members of Illegal Substance recorded, printed, and distributed their disc by themselves, investing around AU$5,000 of their own cash. They literally drove copies of the disc around to record shops themselves. They also spoke with me about the potential for being "ripped off" by would-be producers and distributors, having had some bad experiences.

The opening of the Lounge Room in mid-1994 provided a key distribution point for local product. Another record shop specializing in Hip Hop, Phat Wax, in Sydney's Oxford Street, had closed a few months earlier. A handful of other record shops could be relied on to stock Hip Hop: Central Station Records, for example, also in Oxford Street, was particularly popular and useful. Very few of the major stockists were interested in accepting local Hip Hop product.

In 1995, Sean Duggan, aka DJ Vame, late of Def Wish Cast (he left in late 1994), using his own equipment and reputation, set up Dope Runner Productions, with the intention of allowing as many up-and-coming rappers, particularly from Sydney's West Side, the opportunity to record and circulate their material, offering his own producing skills. His stable of crews were thriving at the time of this writing, as he set about the dual project of circumventing traditional distribution mechanisms and offering experience and skills to the acts in question, preparing them for the recognition he thinks at least some of them will receive from "the industry" proper. When that time comes, he wants to make sure that they do not naively stumble into the same seductive trap that felled Sound Unlimited. 046's album is the first CD release to come from Dope Runner.

This "underground" model of releasing Hip Hop material takes as its precedent the success of Def Jam records, an independent Hip Hop label taken over by, or under the wing of, major label CBS in 1985 (see Hirschberg 1992: 118), retaining its A&R ("artists and repertoire") autonomy while gaining access to global promotion and distribution.

Other local releases included the Fonke Knowmaad's 1994 12" "The Hills Are Alive with the Sound of . . . ," the Brethren's self-titled 4-track cassette, also in 1994, and the EasyBass Posse cassette in 1995. A dance music compilation released in 1994 also included some work by the Urban Poets and the Fonke Knowmaads.

Once again, I have chosen not to focus on rap records coming from America, and, increasingly, from the U.K. and Europe, except to note that, of course, any major release from America constitutes valuable cultural capital and is leapt upon by aficionados and circulated, played, memorized, and (figuratively and literally) cataloged. I have referred to only a handful of African-American albums:

Eric B and Rakhim. *Paid in Full* Island 1986.
Public Enemy. *Yo! Bum Rush the Show*. Def Jam 1987.
———. *It Takes a Nation of Millions to Hold Us Back*. Def Jam/Columbia 1988.

————. *Fear of a Black Planet*. Def Jam/Columbia 1990.

————. *Apocalypse '91: The Empire Strikes Black*. Columbia 1991.

Roxanne Shanté. *The Complete Story of Roxanne . . . The Album*. Compleat 1984.

Souls of Mischief. *93 'til Infinity*. Vibe 1993.

Books and Articles

Abrahams, Roger D. 1970. *Deep Down in the Jungle: Negro Narrative Folklore from the Streets of Philadelphia*. Chicago: Aldine.

————. 1976. *Talking Black*. Rowley, Mass.: Newbury House.

————. 1992. *Singing the Master: The Emergence of African-American Culture in the Plantation South*. New York: Pantheon.

Abrahams, Roger D., and John Szwed. 1983. *After Africa*. New Haven, Conn.: Yale University Press.

Adler, Bill. 1991. *Rap: Portraits and Lyrics of a Generation of Black Rockers*. New York: St. Martin's.

Adorno, Theodor W. [1938] 1993. "On the Fetish Character in Music and the Regression of Listening." Pp. 270–99 in *The Essential Frankfurt School Reader*, ed. Andrew Arato and Eike Gebhardt. New York: Continuum.

Agamben, Giorgio. 1993. *The Coming Community*. Minneapolis: University of Minnesota Press.

Anderson, Benedict. 1991. *Imagined Communities: Reflections on the Spread of Nationalism*. London: Verso.

Appadurai, Arjun. 1990. "Disjuncture and Difference in the Global Cultural Economy." *Public Culture* 2, no. 2:1–24.

————. 1996. *Modernity at Large: Cultural Dimensions of Globalization*. Minneapolis: University of Minnesota Press.

Appleyard, Reg, with Alison Ray and Allan Segal. 1988. *The Ten Pound Immigrants*. London: Boxtree.

Arato, Andrew, and Eike Gebhardt, eds. 1993. *The Essential Frankfurt School Reader*. New York: Continuum.

Attali, Jacques. 1985. *Noise: The Political Economy of Music*. Manchester: Manchester University Press.

Bachelard, Gaston. [1964] 1987. *The Psychoanalysis of Fire*, trans. Alan C. M. Ross. London: Quartet.

Bakhtin, Mikhail. [1965] 1984. *Rabelais and His World*, trans. Hélène Iswolsky. Bloomington: Indiana University Press.

Barthes, Roland. 1972. "To Write: An Intransitive Verb?" Pp. 157–65 in *The Structuralists from Marx to Lévi-Strauss*, ed. Richard DeGeorge and Fernande DeGeorge. New York: Doubleday.

————. [1977] 1990. "The Grain of the Voice." Pp. 293–300 in *On Record: Rock, Pop and the Written Word*, ed. Simon Frith and Andrew Goodwin. London: Routledge.

Basso, Keith H. 1996. "Wisdom Sits in Places: Notes on a Western Apache

Landscape." Pp. 53–90 in *Senses of Place,* ed. Steven Feld and Keith H. Basso. Seattle: School of American Research Press.

Bataille, Georges. [1957] 1986. *Erotism: Death and Sensuality,* trans. Mary Dalwood. San Francisco: City Lights.

Baudrillard, Jean. 1983. *Simulations.* New York: Semiotext(e).

———. 1988. *America.* London: Verso.

Best, Paul. 1991. "Graffiti Artists' Work Recognised." *The Australian* (18 October), 19.

Bhabha, Homi K. 1994. "Dissemination: Time, Narrative and the Margins of the Modern Nation." Pp. 139–70 in Bhabha, *The Location of Culture.* London: Routledge.

Biggs, Charles L., and Richard Bauman. 1992. "Genre, Intertextuality and Social Power." *Journal of Linguistic Anthropology* 2, no. 2:131–72.

Blair, M. Elizabeth. 1993. "Commercialization of the Rap Music Youth Subculture." *Journal of Popular Culture* 27, no. 3:21–34.

Bourdieu, Pierre. 1977. *Outline of a Theory of Practice,* trans. Richard Nice. Cambridge: Cambridge University Press.

———. 1984. *Distinction: A Social Critique of the Judgement of Taste,* trans. Richard Nice. Cambridge, Mass.: Harvard University Press.

———. [1979] 1986. "The Aristocracy of Culture." Pp. 164–93 in *Media, Culture and Society: A Critical Reader,* ed. Richard Collins et al. London: Sage.

———. 1991. *Language and Symbolic Power,* ed. with introduction by John B. Thompson and trans. Ginao Raymond and Matthew Adamson. Cambridge: Polity.

Bourdieu, Pierre, and Loïc J. D. Wacquant. 1992. *An Invitation to Reflexive Sociology.* Chicago: University of Chicago Press.

Brewer, Devon D. 1992. "Hip Hop Graffiti Writers' Evaluations of Strategies to Control Illegal Graffiti." *Human Organization* 51, no. 2:188–96.

Brewer, Devon D., and Marc L. Miller. 1990. "Bombing and Burning: The Social Organization and Values of Hip Hop Graffiti Writers and Implications for Policy." *Deviant Behaviour* 11:345–69.

Browne, Rachel. 1992. "Koori Rap — With Talent on Tap." *Daily Telegraph Mirror* [Sydney] (6 October), 13.

Budd, Jeff. 1989. "Graffiti: Vandalism Masquerades as Art." *Australian Police Journal* (April/June), 76–81.

Buell, Frederick. 1994. *National Culture and the New Global System.* Baltimore, Md.: Johns Hopkins University Press.

Burchell, David. 1993. "The Virtuous Citizen and the Commercial Spirit: The Unhappy Prehistory of Citizenship and Modernity." *Communal/Plural* 2 [ed. Ghassan Hage and Lesley Johnson]: 17–46.

Butler, Judith. 1988. "Performative Acts and Gender Constitution: An Essay in Phenomenology and Feminist Theory." *Theatre Journal* 20, no. 3:519–31.

Button, James, and Kimina Lyall. 1993. "Northern Exposure." *Time* [Australia] (27 September 27), 52–53.

Cameron, Deborah. 1993. "Methylated Spirits Is the Answer." *Sydney Morning Herald* (25 January), 13.

Cameron, Michael, and Brad Crouch. 1990. "Graffiti Boys 'Threat to Life.'" *Daily Telegraph Mirror* [Sydney] (9 October), 5.

Canetti, Elias. [1960] 2000. *Crowds and Power*, trans. Carol Stewart. London: Phoenix.

Carlson, Marvin. 1984. *Theories of Theatre: A Historical and Critical Survey, from the Greeks to the Present*. Ithaca, N.Y.: Cornell University Press.

Carlyon, Les. 2001. *Gallipoli*. Sydney: Pan Macmillan.

Carrington, Kerry. 1989. "Girls and Graffiti." *Cultural Studies* 3, no. 1:89–100.

Carthaigh, Sean. 1992. "Graffiti Grates on Paris Rail Chief." *The Australian* (14 January), 6.

Casimir, Jon. 1992. "Rap: Public Enemy and Ice T." *Sydney Morning Herald* (19 August), 14.

———. 1993a. "The Piece Keeper." *Sydney Morning Herald* (27 August), metro supplement, 1–2S.

———. 1993b. "Bonding by Abuse." *Sydney Morning Herald* (31 August), 22.

———. 1994. "For the Jordan Generation, Footy Doesn't Make the Grade." *Sydney Morning Herald* (17 January), 3.

Castleman, Craig. 1982. *Getting Up: Subway Graffiti in New York*. Cambridge, Mass.: MIT Press.

Castles, Stephen. 1993. "Ethnicity, Community and the Postmodern City." *Communal/Plural* 1 [*Identity/Community/Change*, ed. Ghassan Hage and Lesley Johnson]: 47–60.

Chalfant, Henry, and James Prigoff. 1987. *Spraycan Art*. New York: Thames and Hudson.

Chambers, Iain. 1990. "A Miniature History of the Walkman." *New Formations* 11:1–4.

Chester, Andrew. 1970. "Second Thoughts on a Rock Aesthetic: The Band." *New Left Review* 62:75–82.

Chester, Andrew, and Richard Merton. 1970. "For a Rock Aesthetic." *New Left Review* 59:83–87.

Christensen, Dieter, ed. 1988. *Yearbook for Traditional Music*. New York: International Council for Traditional Music.

Christie, Tiffany. 1994. "Tagging Along." *Sydney Morning Herald* (18 March), metro supplement, 1–2S.

Clarke, John, Stuart Hall, Tony Jefferson, and Brian Rogers. 1976. "Subcultures, Cultures and Class: A Theoretical Review." Pp. 9–74 in *Resistance through Rituals: Youth Subcultures in Post-War Britain*, ed. Stuart Hall and Tony Jefferson. London: Hutchinson.

Clegg, Stewart. 1989. *Frameworks of Power*. London: Sage.

Cloonan, Martin. 1995. "Not Taking the Rap: NWA Get Stranded on an Island of Realism." Pp. 55–60 in *Popular Music, Style and Identity: International As-*

sociation for the Study of Popular Music Seventh International Conference on Popular Music Studies, ed. Will Straw, Stacey Johnson, Rebecca Sullivan, and Paul Friedlander. Montreal: Centre for Research on Canadian Cultural Industries and Institutions.

Cochrane, Peter. 1991. "Rap, Graffiti and Street-rods — The Stuff of Which Political Art Is Made." *Sydney Morning Herald* (28 August), 6.

Cohen, Sara. 1991. *Rock Culture in Liverpool: Popular Music in the Making.* Oxford: Clarendon.

———. 1994. "Identity, Place and the 'Liverpool Sound.'" Pp. 117–34 in *Ethnicity, Identity and Music: The Musical Construction of Place,* ed. Martin Stokes. Oxford: Berg.

Cohen, Stanley. [1972] 1980. *Folk Devils and Moral Panics.* London: McGibbon and Keen.

Collins, Richard, James Curran, Nicholas Garnham, Paddy Scannell, Philip Schlesinger, and Colin Sparks, eds. 1986. *Media, Culture and Society: A Critical Reader.* London: Sage.

Commonwealth of Australia (Cultural Policy Advisory Panel). 1994. *Creative Nation: Commonwealth Cultural Policy October 1994.* Canberra: National Capital Printing.

Conley, Verena Andermatt, ed. 1993. *Rethinking Technologies.* Minneapolis: University of Minnesota Press.

Cooper, Martha, and Henry Chalfant. 1984. *Subway Art.* London: Thames and Hudson.

Costello, Mark, and David Foster Wallace. 1990. *Signifying Rappers: Rap and Race in the Urban Present.* New York: Ecco.

Coupland, Douglas. 1991. *Generation X.* London: Harper Collins.

Cross, Brian. 1993. *It's Not about a Salary: Rap, Race + Resistance in Los Angeles.* With additional texts by Reagan Kelly and T-Love. London: Verso.

Curthoys, Ann, and John Docker. 1996. "Is History Fiction?" *UTS Review* 2, no. 1 (May): 12–37.

Danielson, Shane. 1991. "Spray Guns." *Sydney Morning Herald* (15 March), metro supplement, 3S.

———. 1992. "A Real Rage." *Sydney Morning Herald* (14 August), metro supplement, 1–2S.

Davis, Mike. 1990. *City of Quartz: Excavating the Future in Los Angeles.* London: Vintage.

———. 1992. *Los Angeles Was Just the Beginning: Urban Revolt in the United States: A Thousand Points of Light.* Westfield, N.J.: Open Magazine Pamphlet Series.

Decker, Jeffrey Louis. 1993. "The State of Rap: Time and Place in Hip Hop Nationalism." *Social Text* 34:53–84.

DeGeorge, Richard, and Fernande DeGeorge, eds. 1972. *The Structuralists from Marx to Lévi-Strauss.* New York: Doubleday.

Deleuze, Gilles, and Félix Guattari. 1987. *A Thousand Plateaus: Capitalism and Schizophrenia,* trans. Brian Massumi. Minneapolis: University of Minnesota Press.

Derrida, Jacques. 1976. *Of Grammatology,* trans. Gayatri Chakravorty Spivak. Baltimore, Md.: Johns Hopkins University Press.

Derriman, Philip. 1994. "Changing Trends Show That Cricket Is Not Hot with the Kids." *Sydney Morning Herald* (11 February), 35.

de Vine, Brett. 1991. "Graffiti Is All Above Board." *Daily Telegraph Mirror* [Sydney] (12 November), 15.

Dryza, Tess. 1994a. *Legal Walls.* Exhibition catalog. Liverpool, Australia: City Council.

———. 1994b. "Workshops for Graffiti and Stage." *ARTSWEST* (July), 13.

During, Simon, ed. 1993. *The Cultural Studies Reader.* London: Routledge.

Dyson, Michael Eric. 1991. "Performance, Protest and Prophecy in the Culture of Hip Hop." Pp. 12–24 in *The Emergency of Black and the Emergence of Rap,* ed. Jon Michael Spencer. Durham, N.C.: Duke University Press.

Eco, Umberto. 1977. *A Theory of Semiotics.* London: Macmillan.

———. 1979. *The Role of the Reader: Explorations in the Semiotics of Texts.* London: Hutchinson.

Erlmann, Veit. 1996. "The Aesthetics of the Global Imagination: Reflections on World Music in the 1990s." *Public Culture* 8, no. 3:467–87.

Ethnic Affairs Commission. 1994. *The People of New South Wales: Statistics from the 1991 Census.* Ethnic Affairs Commission of New South Wales.

Featherstone, Mike. 1991. *Consumer Culture and Postmodernism.* London: Sage.

Feld, Stephen. 1994a. "From Schizophonia to Schismogenesis: On the Discourses and Commodification Practices of 'World Music' and 'World Beat.'" Pp. 257–89 in *Music Grooves: Essays and Dialogues,* ed. Charles Keil and Steven Feld. Chicago: University of Chicago Press.

———. 1994b. "Aesthetics as Iconicity of Style (uptown title), or, (downtown title) 'Lift-Up-Over Sounding': Getting into the Kaluli Groove." Pp. 109–50 in *Music Grooves: Essays and Dialogues,* ed. Charles Keil and Steven Feld. Chicago: University of Chicago Press.

———. 1994c. "Communication, Music, and Speech about Music." Pp. 77–95 in *Music Grooves: Essays and Dialogues,* ed. Charles Keil and Steven Feld. Chicago: University of Chicago Press.

Feld, Steven, and Keith H. Basso, eds. 1996. *Senses of Place.* Seattle: School of American Research Press.

Fenster, Mark. 1995. "Two Stories: Where Exactly Is the Local?" Pp. 83–88 in *Popular Music, Style and Identity: International Association for the Study of Popular Music Seventh International Conference on Popular Music Studies,* ed. Will Straw, Stacey Johnson, Rebecca Sullivan, and Paul Friedlander. Montreal: Centre for Research on Canadian Cultural Industries and Institutions.

Fernando, S. H., Jr. 1994. *The New Beats: Exploring the Music, Culture, and Attitudes of Hip-Hop.* New York: Anchor.

Ferry, Luc. 1992. *The New Ecological Order*, trans. Carol Volk. Chicago: University of Chicago Press.

Fine, Elizabeth. 1991. "Stepping, Saluting, Cracking and Freaking: The Cultural Politics of Afro-American Step Shows." *Drama Review* 35, no. 2:39–59.

Fitzgerald, Jon. 1996. "*Down into the Fire:* A Case Study of a Recording Session." *Perfect Beat: The Pacific Journal of Research into Contemporary Music and Popular Culture* 2, no. 2:63–77.

Fitzgerald, Shirley. 1994. "The City." Pp. 79–83 in *Community in Australia*, ed. Patrick O'Farrell and Louelle McCarthy. Sydney: University of New South Wales Community History Programme.

Flores, Juan. 1987. "Rappin', Writin', and Breakin'," *Dissent* 34, no. 4:580–84.

———. 1994. "Puerto Rican and Proud, Boyee! Rap Roots and Amnesia." Pp. 89–98 in *Microphone Fiends: Youth Music and Youth Culture,* ed. Andrew Ross and Tricia Rose. New York: Routledge.

Folb, Edith. 1980. *Runnin' Down Some Lines.* Cambridge, Mass.: Harvard University Press.

Fornäs, Johan. 1994. "Listen to Your Voice! Authenticity and Reflexivity in Rock, Rap and Techno Music." *New Formations* 24:155–73.

Foucault, Michel. 1979. *The History of Sexuality,* trans. Robert Hurley. London: Allen Lane.

Frith, Simon. 1983. *Sound Effects: Youth, Leisure and the Politics of Rock'n'Roll.* London: Constable.

———. 1987. "Towards an Aesthetics of Popular Music." Pp. 133–49 in *Music and Society: The Politics of Composition, Performance, and Reception,* ed. Richard Leppert and Susan McClary. Cambridge: Cambridge University Press.

Frith, Simon, and Andrew Goodwin, eds. 1990. *On Record: Rock, Pop and the Written Word.* London: Routledge.

Game, Ann. 1990. "Nation and Identity: Bondi." *New Formations* 11:105–21.

Garnham, Nicholas, and Raymond Williams. 1986. "Pierre Bourdieu and the Sociology of Culture: An Introduction." Pp. 116–30 in *Media, Culture and Society: A Critical Reader,* ed. Richard Collins et al. London: Sage.

Gates, Henry Louis, Jr. 1988. *The Signifying Monkey: A Theory of Afro-American Literary Criticism.* New York: Oxford University Press.

———. 1990. "2 Live Crew, Decoded." *New York Times* (19 June), sect. A, 23.

George, Nelson. 1988. *Death of Rhythm and Blues.* New York: Plume.

———. 1990. *Stop the Violence: Overcoming Self-Destruction.* New York: Pantheon.

———. 1994. *Buppies, B-Boys, Baps and Bohos: Notes on Post-Soul Black Culture.* New York: Harper Perennial.

Gilroy, Paul. 1987. *There Ain't No Black in the Union Jack.* London: Hutchinson.

———. 1993. *The Black Atlantic: Modernity and Double Consciousness.* London: Verso.

Godbee, Graham. 1994. *Street Gangs: Study for the NSW Police Service.* Beecroft, NSW: Pulse Consultants.

SOURCES AND REFERENCES
Goffman, Erving. [1956] 1973. *The Presentation of Self in Everyday Life*. New York: Overlook.

Gonzales, Michael A. 1994. "Bomb's Away." *Rolling Stone* [U.S. edition] (August), 46–50, 98–101.

Goodwin, Andrew. 1990. "Sample and Hold: Pop Music in the Digital Age of Reproduction." Pp. 258–74 in *On Record: Rock, Pop and the Written Word*, ed. Simon Frith and Andrew Goodwin. London: Routledge.

———. 1991. "Popular Music and Post-Modern Theory." *Cultural Studies* 5, no. 2:174–203.

Gore, Mary Elizabeth (Tipper). 1987. *Raising PG Kids in an X-Rated Society*. Nashville, Tenn.: Abingdon.

Grace, Helen, Ghassan Hage, Lesley Johnson, Julie Langsworth, and Michael Symons. 1997. *Home/World: Space, Community and Marginality in Sydney's West*. Sydney: Pluto.

Graffiti Task Force, New South Wales Police. c. 1991. "Vandalism Frameworks." Resource Paper.

Gripper, Ali, and Andrew Hornery. 1996. "Wicked! The Teenage Tribes." *Sydney Morning Herald* (26 August), 10–11.

Grosz, Elizabeth. 1990. *Jacques Lacan: A Feminist Introduction*. Sydney: Allen and Unwin.

Guilliatt, Richard. 1994. "U.S.Eh? Why Young Australia Is Smitten with American Culture." *Sydney Morning Herald* (25 June), Spectrum Weekend Supplement, 1A, 4A.

Hage, Ghassan. 1993a. "Nation-Building Dwelling-Being." *Communal/Plural* 1 [ed. Ghassan Hage and Lesley Johnson]: 73–103.

———. 1993b. "Republicanism, Multiculturalism, Zoology." *Communal/Plural* 2 [ed. Ghassan Hage and Lesley Johnson]: 113–38.

———. 1994a. "Locating Multiculturalism's Other: A Critique of Practical Tolerance." *New Formations* 24:19–34.

———. 1994b. "Anglo-Celtics Today: Cosmo-Multiculturalism and the Phase of the Fading Phallus." *Communal/Plural* 4 [ed. Ghassan Hage, Justine Lloyd, and Lesley Johnson]: 41–78.

———. 1995. "The Limits of 'Anti-Racist Sociology.'" *UTS Review* 1, no. 1:59–82.

———. 1997. "At Home in the Entrails of the West: Multiculturalism, 'Ethnic Food' and Migrant Home-Building." Pp. 99–153 in *Home/World: Space, Community and Marginality in Sydney's West*, ed. Helen Grace, Ghassan Hage, Lesley Johnson, Julie Langsworth, and Michael Symons. Sydney: Pluto.

———. 1998. *White Nation: Fantasies of White Supremacy in a Multicultural Society*. Sydney: Pluto.

Hage, Ghassan, and Lesley Johnson, eds. 1993a. *Communal/Plural* 1 [*Identity/Community/Change*]: v–vii [introduction].

———. 1993b. *Communal/Plural* 2 [*Republicanism/Citizenship/Community*].

Hage, Ghassan, Justine Lloyd, and Lesley Johnson, eds. 1994. *Communal/ Plural 4 [An Inquiry into the State of Anglo-Saxonness within the Nation]*.

Hager, Steven. 1984. *Hip Hop: An Illustrated History of Breakdancing, Rap Music and Graffiti*. New York: St. Martin's.

Hall, Stuart. 1980a. "Cultural Studies and the Centre: Some Problematics and Problems." Pp. 15–47 in *Culture, Media, Language: Working Papers in Cultural Studies 1972–1979*, ed. Stuart Hall, Dorothy Hobson, Andrew Lowe, and Paul Willis. London: Hutchinson.

———. 1980b. "Recent Developments in Theories of Language as Ideology: A Critical Note." Pp. 157–62 in *Culture, Media, Language: Working Papers in Cultural Studies 1972–1979*, ed. Stuart Hall, Dorothy Hobson, Andrew Lowe, and Paul Willis. London: Hutchinson.

Hall, Stuart, Charles Critcher, Tony Jefferson, John Clarke, and Robert Brian, eds. 1978. *Policing the Crisis: Mugging, the State, and Law and Order*. London: Hutchison.

Hall, Stuart, Dorothy Hobson, Andrew Lowe, and Paul Willis, eds. 1980. *Culture, Media, Language: Working Papers in Cultural Studies, 1972–1979*. London: Hutchinson.

Hall, Stuart, and Tony Jefferson. 1976. *Resistance through Rituals: Youth Subcultures in Post-War Britain*. London: Hutchinson.

Hamilton, Annette. 1990. "Fear and Desire: Aborigines, Asians and the National Imaginary." *Australian Cultural History* 9:14–35.

Hannerz, Ulf. 1996. *Transnational Connections: Culture, People*. New York: Routledge.

Haraway, Donna. 1989. *Primate Visions: Gender, Race, and Nature in the World of Modern Science*. New York: Routledge.

Harris, David. 1992. *From Class Struggle to the Politics of Pleasure: The Effects of Gramscianism on Cultural Studies*. London: Routledge.

Harvey, Sandra. 1990. "New Church Smeared by Graffiti." *Sydney Morning Herald* (9 July), 3.

Hayward, Philip. 1992a. "Cash, Chords, Chaos and Hype." *Perfect Beat: The Pacific Journal of Research into Contemporary Music and Popular Culture* 1, no. 1:84–89.

———. 1998. *Music at the Borders: Not Drowning, Waving and Their Engagement with Papua New Guinean Culture (1986–96)*. Sydney: John Libbey.

———, ed. 1992b. *From Pop to Punk to Postmodernism: Popular Music and Australian Culture from the 1960s to the 1990s*. Sydney: Allen and Unwin.

Hebdige, Dick. 1976. "The Meaning of Mod." Pp. 87–96 in *Resistance through Rituals: Youth Subcultures in Post-War Britain*, ed. Stuart Hall and Tony Jefferson. London: Hutchinson.

———. 1979. *Subculture: The Meaning of Style*. London: Methuen.

———. 1987. *Cut'n'Mix: Culture, Identity and Caribbean Music*. New York: Methuen.

———. 1988. *Hiding in the Light: On Images and Things*. London: Routledge.

Hennion, Antoine. 1983. "The Production of Success: An Anti-musicology of the Pop Song." *Popular Music* 3:159–93.

Hesmondhalgh, David, and Keith Negus, eds. 2002. *Popular Music Studies: International Perspectives.* London: Arnold.

Heylin, Clinton. 1993. *From the Velvets to the Voidoids: A Pre-Punk History for a Post-Punk World.* Harmondsworth, U.K.: Penguin.

Hirschberg, Lynn. 1992. "King Rap." *Vanity Fair* (July), 92–121.

Hobsbawm, Eric, and Terence Ranger. 1983. *The Invention of Tradition.* Cambridge: Cambridge University Press.

Holloway, Peter, ed. 1987. *Contemporary Australian Drama.* Sydney: Currency.

Holston, James. 1989. *The Modernist City: An Anthropological Critique of Brasília.* Chicago: University of Chicago Press.

Horvath, Ronald J., Graeme E. Harrison, and Robyn M. Dowling. 1989. *Sydney: A Social Atlas.* Sydney: Sydney University Press in association with Oxford University Press.

Hutack, Michael, and Susan Borham. 1994. "Generation Who?" *Sydney Morning Herald* (7 February), 11.

Hymes, Dell. 1972. *Directions in Sociolinguistics.* New York: Blackwell.

Ingram, Terry. 1992. "Graffiti Comes into Its Own as an Artform." *Australian Financial Review* (28 May), 27.

Iyer, Pico. 1988. *Video Night in Kathmandu.* New York: Knopf.

Jackson, Michael. 1996. *Things as They Are: New Directions in Phenomenological Anthropology.* Bloomington: Indiana University Press.

Jameson, Frederic. 1991. *Postmodernism, or the Cultural Logic of Late Capitalism.* London: Verso.

Jayamanne, Laleen. 1994. "'Post-Ethnicity': Hung up on the Telephone, Not on Ethnicity: Notes on Three Short Films by Paulin Chan." *Communal/Plural* 4 [ed. Ghassan Hage, Justine Lloyd, and Lesley Johnson]: 115–30.

Johnson, Bruce. 1995. "The Pursuit of Excellence?" *Arena* 19 (October–November), 9–10.

———. 1996. "Directions in Popular Music Studies." *Perfect Beat: The Pacific Journal of Research into Contemporary Music and Popular Culture* 2, no. 4:98–105.

Jones, K. Maurice. 1994. *Say It Loud! The Story of Rap Music.* Brookfield, Conn.: Millbrook.

Jones, Simon. 1988. *Black Culture, White Youth: The Reggae Tradition from JA to UK.* Basingstoke, U.K.: Macmillan Education.

Keil, Charles. 1994. "On Civilization, Cultural Studies and Copyright." Pp. 227–37 in *Music Grooves: Essays and Dialogues,* ed. Charles Keil and Steven Feld. Chicago: University of Chicago Press.

Keil, Charles, and Steven Feld. 1994. "Grooving on Participation." Pp. 151–80 in *Music Grooves: Essays and Dialogues,* ed. Charles Keil and Steven Feld. Chicago: University of Chicago Press.

Kelly, Regan. 1993. "Hip Hop Chicano: A Separate but Parallel Story." Pp. 65–78 in Brian Cross, *It's Not about a Salary: Rap, Race + Resistance in Los Angeles.* London: Verso.

Kohn, Hans, ed. 1965. *Nationalism: Its Meaning and History.* Malabar, Fla.: Krieger.

Lachmann, Richard. 1988. "Graffiti as Career and Ideology." *American Journal of Sociology* 94:229–50.

Laclau, Ernesto, and Chantal Mouffe. 1985. *Hegemony and Socialist Strategy: Towards a Radical Democratic Politics.* New York: Verso.

Leary, Philippa. 1990. "The Rhetoric of the Man-of-Words: Continuity and Change in the African-American Folk Oral Tradition." B.A. honors thesis, Department of History, University of Sydney.

Leppert, Richard, and Susan McClary, eds. 1987. *Music and Society: The Politics of Composition, Performance, and Reception.* Cambridge: Cambridge University Press.

Lette, Cathy, and Gabrielle Carey. 1981. *Puberty Blues.* Melbourne: Gribble McPhee.

Lewis, J. Lowell. 1992. *Ring of Liberation: Deceptive Discourse in Brazilian Capoiera.* Chicago: University of Chicago Press.

———. 1995 "Genre and Embodiment: From Brazilian *Capoiera* to the Ethnology of Human Movement." *Cultural Anthropology* 10, no. 2 (May): 221–43.

Light, Alan. 1991. "About a Salary or Reality: Rap's Recurrent Conflict." *South Atlantic Quarterly* 90, no. 4:855–70.

Lipsitz, George. 1994a. "We Know What Time It Is: Race, Class and Youth Culture in the Nineties." Pp. 17–28 in *Microphone Fiends: Youth Music and Youth Culture,* ed. Andrew Ross and Tricia Rose. New York: Routledge.

———. 1994b. *Dangerous Crossroads: Popular Music, Postmodernism, and the Poetics of Place.* London: Verso.

Lott, Eric. 1993. *Love and Theft: Blackface Minstrelsy and the American Working Class.* New York: Oxford University Press.

Lyotard, Jean-François. 1986. *The Postmodern Condition: A Report on Knowledge,* trans. Brian Massumi and Geoff Bennington. Manchester: Manchester University Press.

Marcus, Greil. 1989. *Lipstick Traces: A Secret History of the Twentieth Century.* Cambridge, Mass.: Harvard University Press.

Mattson, Kevin. 1990. "The Dialectic of Powerlessness: Black Identity, Culture and Affirmative Action." *Telos* 84:177–84.

Maxwell, Ian. 1994a. "Busting Rhymes." *RealTime* 3 (October–November): 4–5.

———. 1994b. "True to the Music: Authenticity, Articulation and Authorship in Sydney Hip Hop Culture." *Social Semiotics* 4, nos. 1–2:117–37.

———. 1997a. "Hip Hop Aesthetics and the Will to Culture." *Australian Journal of Anthropology* 8, no. 1:50–70.

———. 1997b. "On the Flow—Dancefloor Grooves, Rapping 'Freestylee' and the Real Thing." *Perfect Beat: The Pacific Journal of Research into Contemporary Music and Popular Culture* 3, no. 3:15–27.

———. 2001. "Sydney Stylee: Hip Hop Down Under Comin' Up." Pp. 259–79 in

Rapping the Globe: The Universal Language of Hip Hop, ed. Tony Mitchell. Hanover, N.H.: Wesleyan University Press.

———. 2002. "The Curse of Fandom." Pp. 103–16 in *Popular Music Studies: International Perspectives,* ed. David Hesmondhalgh and Keith Negus. London: Arnold.

Maxwell, Ian, and Nikki Bambrick. 1994. "Discourses of Culture and Nationalism in Sydney Hip Hop." *Perfect Beat: The Pacific Journal of Research into Contemporary Music and Popular Culture* 2, no. 1:1–19.

McClary, Susan. 1985. "Afterword." Pp. 149–60 in Jacques Attali, *Noise: The Political Economy of Music.* Manchester: Manchester University Press.

———. 1987. "The Blasphemy of Talking Politics in Bach Year." Pp. 13–62 in *Music and Society: The Politics of Composition, Performance, and Reception,* ed. Richard Leppert and Susan McClary. Cambridge: Cambridge University Press.

———. 1994. "Same as It Ever Was: Youth Culture and Music." Pp. 29–40 in *Microphone Fiends: Youth Music and Youth Culture,* ed. Andrew Ross and Tricia Rose. New York: Routledge.

McClary, Susan, and Robert Walser. 1990. "Start Making Sense! Musicology Wrestles with Rock." Pp. 277–92 in *On Record: Rock, Pop and the Written Word,* ed. Simon Frith and Andrew Goodwin. London: Routledge.

McDonnell, Judith. 1992. "Rap Music: Its Role as an Agent of Cultural Change." *Popular Music and Society* 16, no. 3:89–108.

McDougall, Bruce. 1994a. "City Street Gangs Crisis: Gangland Special Investigation." *Daily Telegraph Mirror* [Sydney] (21 November), 1, 4–5.

———. 1994b. "Street Gangs — What Makes Them Run." *Daily Telegraph Mirror* [Sydney] (21 November), 11.

McEvoy, Marc. 1990. "Terror of the Colour Gangs: Special Investigation." *Sunday Telegraph* [Sydney] (15 July), 15.

McRobbie, Angela. 1980. "Settling Accounts with Subcultures: A Feminist Critique." *Screen Education* 34:37–49.

———, ed. 1988. *Zoot Suits and Second-Hand Dresses: An Anthology of Fashion and Music.* Boston: Unwin Hyman.

———. 1991. "New Times in Cultural Studies." *New Formations* 13:1–18.

———. 1993. "Shut up and Dance: Youth Culture and Changing Modes of Femininity." *Cultural Studies* 7, no. 3:406–42.

McRobbie, Angela, and Mica Nava, eds. 1984. *Gender and Generation.* London: Macmillan.

Melly, Roger. 1970. *Revolt into Style.* Harmondsworth, U.K.: Penguin.

Middleton, Richard. 1985. "Articulating Musical Meaning/Re-Constructing Musical History/Locating the Popular." *Popular Music* 5:5–43.

———. 1990. *Studying Popular Music.* Milton Keynes, U.K.: Open University Press.

Mitchell, Tony. 1992. "World Music, Indigenous Music and Music Television in

Australia." *Perfect Beat: The Pacific Journal of Research into Contemporary Music and Popular Culture* 1, no. 1:1–16.

———. 1996. *Popular Music and Local Identity: Rock, Pop and Rap in Europe and Oceania.* London: Leicester University Press.

———. 1999. "Another Root: Australian Hip Hop as a 'Global' Subculture." *UTS Review* 5, no. 1 (May): 126–41.

———, ed. 2001. *Rapping the Globe: The Universal Language of Hip Hop.* Hanover, N.H.: Wesleyan University Press.

Monaghan, David. 1988. "Vandals Learn Art on Govt Grant." *Sydney Morning Herald* (1 February), 3.

Moore, Allan F. 1993. *Rock: The Primary Text.* Buckingham, U.K.: Open University Press.

Moore, Sally Falk. 1989. "The Production of Cultural Pluralism as Process." *Public Culture* 1, no. 2:26–48.

Morley, Jefferson. 1992. "Rap Music as American History." Pp. xv–xxxi in *Rap: The Lyrics. The Words to Rap's Greatest Hits,* ed. Lawrence A. Stanley. London: Penguin.

Morris, Linda. 1994. "ALP Street Gang Strategy Forces Carr into a Fight." *Sydney Morning Herald* (15 June), 6.

Morris, Meaghan. 1993a. "Things to Do with Shopping Centers." Pp. 295–319 in *The Cultural Studies Reader,* ed. Simon During. London: Routledge.

———. 1993b. "The Very Idea of a Popular Debate (or, Not Lunching with Thomas Keneally)." *Communal/Plural* [ed. Ghassan Hage and Lesley Johnson]: 153–67.

Mostyn, Suzanne. 1991. "Now, Having an Art Attack Is Not So Bad." *Sydney Morning Herald* (29 August), 3.

Mowry, Jess. 1992. *Way Past Cool.* London: Chatto and Windus.

Murphie, Andrew. 1996. "Sound at the End of the World as We Know it: Nick Cave, Wim Wenders' Wings of Desire and a Deleuze-Guattarian Ecology of Popular Music." *Perfect Beat: The Pacific Journal of Research into Contemporary Music and Popular Culture* 2, no. 4:18–42.

Nelson, Angela Spence. 1991. "Theology in the Hip Hop of Public Enemy and Kool Moe Dee." Pp. 51–59 in *The Emergency of Black and the Emergence of Rap,* ed. Jon Michael Spencer. Durham, N.C.: Duke University Press.

Nelson, Havelock, and Michael A. Gonzales. 1991. *Bring the Noise.* New York: Harmony.

Neuenfeldt, Karl. 1994. "The Cultural Production and Use of the Didjeridu in World Music." *Perfect Beat: The Pacific Journal of Research into Contemporary Music and Popular Culture* 2, no. 1:88–104.

O'Farrell, Patrick, and Louelle McCarthy, eds. 1994. *Community in Australia.* Sydney: University of New South Wales Community History Programme.

Olsen, Sandra. 1992. "Graffiti Rail Blackout." *Daily Telegraph Mirror* [Sydney] (19 October), 9.

Ong, Walter J. 1982. *Orality and Literacy: The Technologizing of the Word.* London: Routledge.

Papadopolous, Nick. 1992. "Love of Graffiti Claimed Jason's Life." *Sydney Morning Herald* (7 August), 2.

Pearce, Wade. 1993. "Street Artists Push for Legal Centre." *Adelaide Advertiser* (25 January), 5.

Peirce, Charles Saunders. [1905] 1960. "What Pragmatism Is." Pp 272–92 in *Collected Papers of Charles Sanders Peirce,* vol. 5, ed. Charles Hartshorne and Paul Weiss. Cambridge: Harvard University Press.

Perera, Suvendi, and Jospeh Pugliese. 1994. "The Limits of Multicultural Representation." *Communal/Plural* 4 [ed. Ghassan Hage, Justine Lloyd, and Lesley Johnson]: 91–114.

Perkins, William Eric. 1991. "Nation of Islam Ideology in the Rap of Public Enemy." Pp. 41–50 in *The Emergency of Black and the Emergence of Rap,* ed. Jon Michael Spencer. Durham, N.C.: Duke University Press.

Peterson-Lewis, Sonja. 1991. "A Feminist Analysis of the Defences of Obscene Rap Lyrics." Pp. 68–79 in *The Emergency of Black and the Emergence of Rap,* ed. Jon Michael Spencer. Durham, N.C.: Duke University Press.

Petkovic, Daniella, Maria Kokokiris, and Monica Kalinowska. 1995. "The Legions of the Lost." *Sun-Herald* [Sydney] (30 April), 132.

Phillips, A. A. 1958. "The Cultural Cringe." Pp. 89–95 in Phillips, *The Australian Tradition.* Melbourne: Cheshire.

Pierse, Lyn. 1993. *Theatresports Down Under: A Guide for Coaches and Players.* Sydney: Improcorp.

Polhemus, Ted. 1994. *Streetstyle: From Sidewalk to Catwalk.* London: Thames and Hudson.

Powell, Diane. 1993. *Out West.* Sydney: Allen and Unwin.

Redhead, Steve. 1990. *The End-of-the-Century Party: Youth and Pop towards 2000.* Manchester: Manchester University Press.

Ro, Ronin. 1996. *Gangsta: Merchandising the Rhymes of Violence.* New York: St. Martin's.

Robbins, Bruce. 1993. "Introduction: The Public as Phantom." Pp. vii–xxvi in *The Phantom Public Sphere,* ed. Bruce Robbins. Minneapolis: University of Minnesota Press.

Roberts, Greg. 1992. "A Brush with the Law in Brisbane Reduces Graffiti Crime." *Sydney Morning Herald* (14 July), 6.

Rose, Tricia. 1990. "Never Trust a Big Butt and a Smile." *Camera Obscura* 23:109–30.

———. 1991. "'Fear of a Black Planet': Rap Music and Black Cultural Politics in the 1990s." *Journal of Negro Education* 60, no. 3:276–90.

———. 1994a. "Introduction." Pp. 1–16 in *Microphone Fiends: Youth Music and Youth Culture,* ed. Andrew Ross and Tricia Rose. New York: Routledge.

———. 1994b. *Black Noise: Rap Music and Black Culture in Contemporary America.* Hanover, N.H.: Wesleyan University Press.

———. 1994c. "A Style Nobody Can Deal With: Politics, Style and the Post-industrial City in Hip Hop." Pp. 71–88 in *Microphone Fiends: Youth Music and Youth Culture,* ed. Andrew Ross and Tricia Rose. New York: Routledge.

Ross, Andrew, and Tricia Rose, eds. 1994. *Microphone Fiends: Youth Music and Youth Culture.* New York: Routledge.

Royster, Philip M. 1991. "The Rapper as Shaman for a Band of Dancers of the Spirit: 'U Can't Touch This.'" Pp. 60–67 in *The Emergency of Black and the Emergence of Rap,* ed. Jon Michael Spencer. Durham, N.C.: Duke University Press.

Savage, Jon. 1991. *England's Dreaming: Sex Pistols and Punk Rock.* London: Faber and Faber.

Shepherd, John. 1982. "A Theoretical Model for the Sociomusicological Analysis of Popular Musics." *Popular Music* 2:145–77.

———. 1987. "Music and Male Hegemony." Pp. 151–72 in *Music and Society: The Politics of Composition, Performance, and Reception,* ed. Richard Leppert and Susan McClary. Cambridge: Cambridge University Press.

———. 1991. *Music as Social Text.* Cambridge: Polity.

Shepherd, John, Paul Virden, George Vulliamy, and Trevor Wishart. 1977. *Whose Music? A Sociology of Musical Languages.* London: Latimer New Dimensions.

Shrestha, Ramesh M., with Mark Lediard. c. 1980. *Faith Healers: A Force for Change.* Kathmandu: United Nations Population Fund.

Shusterman, Richard. 1991. "The Fine Art of Rap." *New Literacy History* 22, no. 3:613–32.

Simone, Timothy Maliqualim. 1989. *About Face: Race in Postmodern America.* New York: Autonomedia.

Skelsey, Mark. 1992. "Rail Graffiti Blitz after Vandal Dies." *Daily Telegraph Mirror* [Sydney] (7 August), 19.

Sklair, Leslie. 1995. *Sociology of the Global System.* London: Prentice Hall/ Harvester Wheatsheaf.

Skrbis, Zlatko. 1994. "A Neglected Issue: Ethnic Group as Community." In *Progress . . . Went West: Papers from the Postgraduate "Work in Progress" Conference, July 1993,* ed. Jonathan Wooding, Helen Smith, and Liz Gardiner. Kingswood, Australia: University of Western Sydney Postgraduate Association.

Spearritt, Peter, and Christina DeMarco. 1988. *Planning Sydney's Future.* Sydney: Allen and Unwin (in conjunction with the Department of Planning, New South Wales).

Speicher, Barbara L. 1992. "Some African-American Perspectives on Black English Vernacular." *Language in Society* 21:383–407.

Spencer, Jon Michael, ed. 1991. *The Emergency of Black and the Emergence of Rap.* Durham, N.C.: Duke University Press.

Spivak, Gayatri. 1976. "Translator's Introduction." Pp. ix–lxxxvii in Jacques Derrida, *Of Grammatology,* trans. Gayatri Chakravorty Spivak. Baltimore, Md.: Johns Hopkins University Press.

Stanley, Lawrence A., ed. 1992. *Rap: The Lyrics. The Words to Rap's Greatest Hits.* London: Penguin.

Stephens, Gregory. 1991. "Rap Music's Double-Voiced Discourse: A Crossroads for Communication." *Journal of Communication Inquiry* 15, no. 2:70–91.

————. 1992. "Interracial Dialogue in Rap Music: Call-and-Response in a Multicultural Style." *New Formations* 16:62–79.

Stephens, Ronald Jemal. 1991. "The Three Waves of Contemporary Rap Music." Pp. 25–40 in *The Emergency of Black and the Emergence of Rap,* ed. Jon Michael Spencer. Durham, N.C.: Duke University Press.

Steyn, Mark. 1994. "The Death of Pop." *Sydney Morning Herald* (12 March), Spectrum Supplement, 7A.

Stokes, Martin, ed. 1994. *Ethnicity, Identity and Music: The Musical Construction of Place.* Oxford: Berg.

Straw, Will. 1991. "Systems of Articulation, Logics of Change: Communities and Scenes in Popular Music." *Cultural Studies* 5, no. 3:368–88.

Straw, Will, Stacey Johnson, Rebecca Sullivan, and Paul Friedlander, eds. 1995. *Popular Music, Style and Identity: International Association for the Study of Popular Music Seventh International Conference on Popular Music Studies.* Montreal: Centre for Research on Canadian Cultural Industries and Institutions.

Swedenburg, Ted. 1992. "Homies in the 'Hood': Rap's Commodification of Insubordination." *New Formations* 18:53–66.

Sydney Morning Herald. 1994. Editorial. "Cricket: Just Another Sport?" (1 January), 12.

Symonds, Michael. 1993. "Imagined Colonies: On the Social Construction of Sydney's Western Suburbs." *Communal/Plural* 1 [*Identity/Community/ Change,* ed. Ghassan Hage and Lesley Johnson]: 63–72.

Tagg, Phillip. 1982. "Analysing Popular Music: Theory, Method and Practice." *Popular Music* 2:37–67.

Taksa, Lucy. 1994. "Definitions and Disjunctions." Pp. 22–25 in *Community in Australia,* ed. Patrick O'Farrell and Louelle McCarthy. Sydney: University of New South Wales Community History Programme.

Tate, Greg. 1992. *Flyboy in the Buttermilk: Essays on Contemporary America.* New York: Simon and Schuster.

Taylor, Timothy Dean. 1997. *Global Pop: World Music, World Markets.* New York: Routledge.

Thompson, Robert Farris. 1986. "Hip Hop 101." *Rolling Stone* [Australia] (April), 37–43.

Thornton, Sarah. 1996. *Club Cultures: Music, Media and Subcultural Capital.* Hanover, N.H.: Wesleyan University Press.

Thwaite, Rhonda. 1989. "How Vandalism Became Art." *The Bulletin* (5 December), 70–73.

Toop, David. 1991. *Rap Attack 2: African Rap to Global Hip Hop.* London: Serpent's Tail.

Turner, Graeme. 1992. "Australian Popular Music and Its Contexts." Pp. 11–24 in *From Pop to Punk to Postmodernism: Popular Music and Australian Culture from the 1960s to the 1990s,* ed. Philip Hayward. Sydney: Allen and Unwin.

———. 1994. *Making It National: Nationalism and Australian Popular Culture.* St. Leonards, Australia: Allen and Unwin.

Turner, Victor. 1982. "Liminal to Liminoid, in Play, Flow and Ritual: An Essay in Comparative Symbology." Pp. 20–60 in Turner, *From Ritual to Theatre: The Seriousness of Human Play.* New York: Performing Arts Journal Publications.

Uncredited. 1990. "Clean Machine." *Sydney Morning Herald* (23 June), Good Weekend Magazine, 9.

———. 1991a. "Graffiti Gang Stop Train." *Daily Telegraph Mirror* [Sydney] (23 March), 11.

———. 1991b. "Waging War on Graffiti Gangs." *Daily Telegraph Mirror* [Sydney] (25 March), 62.

———. 1992a. "Arrest over Graffiti on Police Cars." *Daily Telegraph Mirror* [Sydney] (28 April).

———. 1992b. "Jail for Graffiti." *Daily Telegraph Mirror* [Sydney] (5 June), 18.

———. 1992c. "20 Students in Brawl." *Sydney Morning Herald* (6 August), 4.

———. 1992d. "LA Lore." *Sun-Herald* [Sydney] (6 September), 9.

———. 1992e. "'Graffiti' Boy Hit on Train Track." *Daily Telegraph Mirror* [Sydney] (25 November), 5.

———. 1992f. "Police to Hit Summer Train Crime." *Daily Telegraph Mirror* [Sydney] (10 December), 17.

———. 1993. "The Dice-Man Is Caught Red-Handed." *Daily Telegraph Mirror* [Sydney] (23 March), 3.

Venkatesh, Sudhir Alladi. 1994. "Learnin' the Trade: Conversation with a Gangsta'." *Public Culture* 6:319–41.

Visontay, Michael. 1991. "Graffiti Art Carries the Can." *Sydney Morning Herald* Eastern Herald supplement (2 May), 16.

Wacquant, Loïc J. D. 1992. "Toward a Social Praxeology: The Structure and Logic of Bourdieu's Sociology." Pp. 1–59 in Pierre Bourdieu and Loïc J. D. Wacquant, *An Invitation to Reflexive Sociology.* Chicago: University of Chicago Press.

Walser, Robert. 1993. *Running with the Devil: Power, Gender and Madness in Heavy Metal Music.* Hanover, N.H.: University Press of New England.

———. 1995. "Clamor and Community: Rhythm, Rhyme, and Rhetoric in the Music of Public Enemy." Pp. 292–308 in *Popular Music, Style and Identity: International Association for the Study of Popular Music Seventh International Conference on Popular Music Studies,* ed. Will Straw, Stacey Johnson, Rebecca Sullivan, and Paul Friedlander. Montreal: Centre for Research on Canadian Cultural Industries and Institutions.

Wark, MacKenzie. 1992. "Ornament and Crime: The Hip Hop Avant-Garde of the Late 80s." *Perfect Beat: The Pacific Journal of Research into Contemporary Music and Popular Culture* 1, no. 1:48–62.

SOURCES AND REFERENCES

———. 1994. *Virtual Geography: Living with Global Media Events.* Bloomington: Indiana University Press.

Waterhouse, Richard. 1990. *From Minstrel Show to Vaudeville: The Australian Popular Stage 1788–1914.* Sydney: NSW University Press.

———. 1995. *Private Pleasures, Public Leisure: A History of Australian Popular Culture since 1788.* Melbourne: Longman Australia.

Watson, Ian. 1983. *Song and Democratic Culture in Britain: An Approach to Popular Culture in Social Movements.* London: Croom Helm.

Weber, Samuel. 1987. "Texts/Contexts." Pp. 3–17 in Weber, *Institution and Interpretation.* Minneapolis: University of Minnesota Press.

Willis, Paul. 1978. *Profane Cultures.* London: Routledge and Kegan Paul.

Windschuttle, Keith. 1994. *The Killing of History: How a Discipline Is Being Murdered by Literary Critics and Social Theorists.* Paddington, NSW: Macleay.

Wingett, Fiona. 1992. "Not as Bad as He's Painted." *Daily Telegraph Mirror* [Sydney] (9 March), 13.

Xiberras, Carolyn.1994. *Def Wish Cast.* Press Release. Kingswood, NSW: Cazz Management.

Žižek, Slavoj. 1993. *Tarrying with the Negative: Kant, Hegel, and the Critique of Ideology.* Durham, N.C.: Duke University Press.

Index

aboriginal Australians, xi, 142; "Dreamtime" of, xi; arrival in Australia, xii; dispossessed, xiii, 61; land rights of, xv; aboriginal words in Def Wish Cast raps, 67; and Hip Hop, 67–68

Abrahams, Roger D., 82, 190, 227

Adelaide, 9, 86, 108, 144, 168

Adorno, Theodor W., 189–90

aesthetics, Hip Hop, 98–101, 225. *See also* phatness; dope(ness)

African American: Hip Hop as origin, 12, 45, 50, 54, 189; oral practices, 23, 41–42, 90, 204; and public/private space, 190

Afrocentric rap, 43, 153, 155–57

"Ain't That a Bitch," 22

Americanization of Australian culture, 71–73

Anderson, Benedict, 61

Aotearoa/New Zealand, 80; Treaty of Waitangi, xvi

Appadurai, Arjun, 16, 59–60; on ideoscape, 15, 121–22, 164; on global cultural flows, 62–63; on ethnoscape, 64; on mediascape, 69

appropriation, ix, x

Armstrong, Robert Plant, 237

Arranta Desert Posse, 67

Arrested Development, 81, 87, 112

Attali, Jacques, 148

"A.U.S.T. (Down Under Comin' Upper)," 39; namechecking West Side, 134–35; as anthem, 166–68; analyzed, 199–204; and "hard core," 206

Australia: race and, ix–xvi; colonization of, xi; immigration to, xii; transportation of convicts to, xii; Australian accent, 26, 203; white colonization as invasion of, 68; globalization and, 61–62

Australian Broadcasting Corporation (ABC), 39; 2 JJJ-FM (National Youth Radio), 52, 81, 114; television, 120

Australian Labor Party, xiv, 61, 167

Australian Rules Football, 127

authenticity, 15; opposed to "Imitation," ix; discourses of in Hip Hop, 12, 15, 26, 42–43; in youth culture, 33; Australian Hip Hop claims to, 44–47; bestowed by "representing," "skill," and "respect," 65; Die C and authentic b-boy wear, 84; as motif in Miguel's writing, 113; and blackness, 161–62, 209; and sampling, 193, 194; and voice, 203, 227; sound as, 204–5; hard core as, 205–6

Bakhtin, Mikhail, 215, 235; heteroglossia, 226, 228

Bambaataa, Afrika, 42, 86, 156, 214

Bambrick, Nikki, 48, 80, 83, 120, 136, 197

Barthes, Roland, 181, 227

Basso, Keith H., x

Bataille, Georges, 236

"Battlegrounds of Sydney," 77, 135, 231–32

battles, battling: J.U. and Mick E's battle recounted, 1–7; J.U. and

ABOUT THE AUTHOR

Ian Maxwell is Chair of the Department of Performance Studies at the

University of Sydney, where he teaches courses in critical theory and acting.

A graduate of the Victorian College of the Arts School of Drama, Maxwell

completed his Ph.D. at the University of Sydney. He writes on a range of

subjects, from Australian Rules football to courtroom performance.

MUSIC/CULTURE
A series from Wesleyan University Press
Edited by George Lipsitz, Susan McClary, and Robert Walser

Library of Congress Cataloging-in-Publication Data

Maxwell, Ian, 1964–
    Phat beats, dope rhymes : hip hop down under
    comin' upper / Ian Maxwell.
        p. cm. – (Music/culture)
    Includes bibliographical references (p.) and index.

ISBN 0-8195-6637-3 (cloth : alk. paper)
ISBN 0-8195-6638-1 (pbk. : alk. paper)
1. Rap (Music)–Social aspects–Australia. 2. Hip-hop.
I. Title. II. Series.

ML3918.R37M39 2003
782.421649'0994–dc21

                                    2003053452